Michael Cooper's Buyer's Guide to New Zealand Wines

Michael Cooper is New Zealand's most acclaimed wine writer, with 13 books, hundreds of magazine articles, and four prestigious literary awards to his credit.

He is the wine columnist for *North and South*, *Liquor Link* and *Wine Star* magazines, and New Zealand editor of the Australian *Winestate* magazine. He is writing a series of historical studies of influential winemakers for the major government publication *The Dictionary of New Zealand Biography*. A consultant to The Wine Society in Australia, he frequently judges wine on magazine and competition panels, and is a senior judge at the Liquorland Royal Easter Wine Show.

In 1977 he obtained a Master of Arts degree from the University of Auckland with a thesis entitled 'The Wine Lobby: Pressure Group Politics and the New Zealand Wine Industry.' He was marketing manager for Babich Wines from 1980 to 1990, and is now a full-time wine writer, lecturer and consultant. The fifth edition of his classic book, *The Wines and Vineyards of New Zealand*, was published in 1996 and in 1997 won the Leisure and Lifestyle category at the Montana Book Awards.

GW00703216

1998
MICHAEL COOPER'S

BUYER'S GUIDE
TO
NEW ZEALAND
WINES

Hodder Moa Beckett

ISBN 1-86958-570-4

Published in 1997 by Hodder Moa Beckett Publishers Limited
[a member of the Hodder Headline Group]
4 Whetu Place, Mairangi Bay, Auckland

Designed and produced by Hodder Moa Beckett
Typeset by TTS Jazz, Sandringham, Auckland.
Printed by GP Print, Wellington.

Contents

The Winemaking Regions of New Zealand

Area in producing vines 1998 (percentage of national producing vineyard area)

WAIKATO/BAY OF PLENTY
126 ha (1.8%)
Cabernet Sauvignon,
Chardonnay, Sauvignon
Blanc

AUCKLAND/NORTHLAND
215 ha (3.0%)
Chardonnay, Cabernet
Sauvignon, Merlot

GISBORNE
1188 ha (16.6%)
Chardonnay,
Müller-Thurgau
Muscat

WAIRARAPA
236 ha (3.3%)
Pinot Noir,
Chardonnay,
Sauvignon Blanc

HAWKE'S BAY
2036 ha (28.4%)
Chardonnay,
Cabernet Sauvignon
Sauvignon Blanc

NELSON
162 ha (2.3%)
Chardonnay,
Sauvignon Blanc,
Pinot Noir

MARLBOROUGH
2758 ha (38.5%)
Sauvignon Blanc,
Chardonnay, Pinot Noir

CANTERBURY
239 ha (3.3%)
Chardonnay,
Pinot Noir, Riesling

OTAGO
205 ha (2.8%)
Pinot Noir, Chardonnay,
Sauvignon Blanc

These figures are extracted from the 1996 New Zealand Vineyard Survey.
Between 1996 and 1999, total plantings of producing vines are expected to expand from
6015 to 7571 hectares – a rise of 26 per cent.

Preface

Do you dream of owning a small vineyard and winery? For many who took the plunge, the dream is turning into a glut-induced nightmare.

What exactly is a small winery? According to the Wine Institute, a small winery has an annual output of below 200,000 litres (22,222 cases). Over 90 per cent of New Zealand's 250-odd wine companies fall into this category and, in the past three years, 72 new small wineries have joined the battle for market share. Faced with a heavy flow of wine imports, expanding vineyard areas, and the plentiful supply from the 1995 and 1996 vintages, many are struggling in the marketplace.

For a new producer with decent, but not brilliant, wines, it is now extremely difficult to win shelf space in the major retail chains. "Out of every 100 new wines, we normally take three or four," says one influential buyer. Independent fine-wine stores may not be the small producers' salvation either. "Lots of winemakers approach us," says a Ponsonby retailer. "Every week, we're asked to stock a new label I've never heard of. But unless they've won a gold medal or a five-star award, we don't buy it. Our customers don't want a 'no-name' wine."

Montana, by contrast, is short of stocks. After the small 1997 grape harvest – at 60,000 tonnes, 20 per cent less than anticipated – the country's wine giant offered to buy surplus wine from smaller producers. "Our local and export sales of bottled wine are expanding to the point where we were never going to get as much [grapes] as we needed," says managing director Peter Hubscher. "We could sell double what we have taken in this season."

Montana is even importing French red wines (from Bordeaux, the Rhône and Languedoc) and promoting them to New Zealand consumers. "The French reds are not in competition with our own," insists Hubscher. "The truth is, New Zealand is not a good country for producing *vin ordinaire* red, because in our cool climate you can't get a sufficient tonnage per hectare of fully ripe grapes."

How good are the 1997 wines likely to be? High rainfall and humidity caused mid-season problems in Gisborne and Hawke's Bay, but an Indian Summer raised hopes for the late-ripening varieties, especially the Cabernet-based reds. Other regions had their problems too – an exceptionally wet summer in Waipara; April frosts in the Kawarau Gorge near Queenstown. Of all the regions, the most uniformly enthusiastic reports flowed from Marlborough. Although the North Island Chardonnays from '97 will be of variable quality, Marlborough's Sauvignon Blancs, Chardonnays and Rieslings should be excellent, sometimes outstanding.

What to drink in 1998? The 1997 Marlborough Sauvignon Blancs, the 1996 Chardonnays from any of the regions, which will be starting to develop bottle-aged complexity, and the notably robust and richly flavoured 1995 Cabernet-based reds from Hawke's Bay.

The vast collection of tasting notes (about 4000 this year) on which each year's guide is based are jotted down during my visits to wineries; daily tastings at home; participation as a senior judge in the Liquorland Royal Easter Wine Show and Top 100 Liquorland International Wine Competition; and regular comprehensive tastings for *Wine Star* (a *Liquor Link* publication) and the Australian magazine, *Winestate*. If, for the price of a decent bottle of Chardonnay, this book steers you away from ordinary and overpriced wines to some great bottles and bargains, it will have served its purpose well.

Michael Cooper

Cooper's Classics

It's early days yet, but from the crowd of New Zealand wines now on the shelves, a number of classics are starting to emerge. From one vintage to the next, and in their respective categories, these are the wines that in quality terms consistently rank in the very forefront.

The status of wines like Cloudy Bay Sauvignon Blanc, Kumeu River Chardonnay and Te Mata Estate Coleraine Cabernet/Merlot is widely agreed; what follows is my personal choice of New Zealand's wine aristocrats. For every wine listed, another two or three pushed hard for inclusion (Pegasus Bay Chardonnay and Wither Hills Chardonnay look likely to join the list in the near future.) To qualify for selection, each label must have achieved an outstanding level of quality for at least three vintages; there are no flashes in the pan here.

Wines elevated to classic status for the first time this year are highlighted by an asterisk.

Chardonnay

Ata Rangi Craighall
Babich Irongate
Brookfields Reserve
Church Road Reserve
Clearview Estate Reserve
Cloudy Bay
Collards Rothesay Vineyard
Corbans Cottage Block Gisborne
Corbans Private Bin Gisborne
Corbans Private Bin Marlborough
Delegat's Proprietors Reserve
Dry River
* Esk Valley Reserve
Hunter's
Kumeu River Kumeu
* Kumeu River Mate's Vineyard
Martinborough Vineyard
Matua Ararimu
Mills Reef Elspeth
Morton Estate Black Label
Neudorf Moutere

Palliser Estate
Revington Vineyard
Te Mata Elston
Vavasour Single Vineyard (previously Reserve)
Vidal Reserve
Villa Maria Reserve Barrique Fermented

Chenin Blanc
Collards
The Millton Vineyard Dry

Gewürztraminer
Dry River

Pinot Gris
Dry River

Riesling
Collards Queen Charlotte (previously Marlborough)
Coopers Creek Hawke's Bay
Corbans Private Bin Amberley (previously Robard & Butler Amberley)
Dry River Craighall Estate
Grove Mill
Neudorf Moutere
Palliser Estate
Stoneleigh Vineyard
The Millton Vineyard Opou Vineyard

Sauvignon Blanc
Cloudy Bay
Delegat's Proprietors Reserve Oak Aged
* Grove Mill Marlborough
Hunter's
Hunter's Oak Aged
Jackson Estate
Kumeu River Sauvignon/Sémillon
Matua Valley Reserve
Nautilus Marlborough
Nga Waka
Palliser Estate
Selaks Sauvignon Blanc/Sémillon
Te Mata Estate Cape Crest
Vavasour Single Vineyard (previously Reserve)
Villa Maria Reserve Wairau Valley
Wairau River

Sweet Whites
Corbans Cottage Block Noble Riesling
Dry River Botrytis Bunch Selection Gewürztraminer and Riesling
Giesen Botrytised Riesling
Ngatarawa Glazebrook Noble Harvest
Rongopai Reserve Botrytised Riesling
Te Whare Ra Riesling Botrytis Bunch/Berry Selection
Villa Maria Reserve Noble Riesling

Bottle-fermented Sparklings
Daniel Le Brun Blanc de Blancs
Daniel Le Brun Vintage
Deutz Marlborough Cuvée
Domaine Chandon Marlborough Brut
Pelorus

Cabernet Sauvignon-predominant Reds
Babich Irongate Cabernet/Merlot
Brookfields Cabernet/Merlot
Coopers Creek Reserve Huapai Cabernet/Merlot
* **Fenton**
Goldwater Estate Cabernet/Merlot/Franc
St Nesbit
Stonyridge Larose Cabernets
Te Mata Estate Awatea Cabernet/Merlot
Te Mata Estate Coleraine Cabernet/Merlot
Vidal Reserve Cabernet Sauvignon
Vidal Reserve Cabernet Sauvignon/Merlot
Villa Maria Reserve Cabernet Sauvignon
Villa Maria Reserve Cabernet Sauvignon/Merlot

Merlot
Esk Valley Reserve Merlot/Cabernet/Franc (blend varies)
Esk Valley The Terraces

Pinot Noir
Ata Rangi
Dry River
Martinborough Vineyard
Rippon Vineyard Selection

Syrah
Stonecroft

Best Buy of the Year

Saints Gisborne Chardonnay 1996

With about 300 different New Zealand labels clamouring for your attention, there's a bewildering array of Chardonnays on the shelves. For consistency, availability and value, Montana sets the pace, producing rich-flavoured wines under its Saints, Church Road and Montana Reserve labels at prices up to $10 less than Chardonnays of a similar standard from many small wineries. A shining example is this year's winner of the Best Buy of the Year award – Saints Gisborne Chardonnay 1996.

Full of upfront appeal, this is a mouthfilling, deliciously well-rounded wine with strong, lush tropical fruit flavours wrapped in toasty, buttery oak. It's the sort of Chardonnay that doesn't cost a fortune, yet draws you back for a second glass, and a third . . .

"It's a New World Chardonnay – a real fruit-driven style," says Steve Voysey, winemaker at Montana Gisborne Winery. For consumers, Saints Gisborne Chardonnay is designed to be the next step up from Montana Gisborne Chardonnay, with better fruit and more wood. "Basically we use reductive processing [which protects the wine from air to avoid oxidation] to preserve the fruit," says Voysey, "and make it highly approachable with good American oak."

The grapes are grown principally in Montana's Patutahi Vineyard on the western edge of the Gisborne plains, where Voysey finds the soil and local climate yield "big, open, fruit-flavoured styles of Chardonnay". An inland site, it is not cooled by easterly breezes from the Pacific, and is sheltered from cold southerlies. Although the soils are heavy clay, the vineyard is well above sea level, with good natural drainage.

Soon after the 1996 vintage, and despite heavy rainfall in February and late March, Montana claimed to have harvested some fine quality Chardonnay. For the Saints label, ripe fruit – mainly of the Mendoza clone – was picked in early April at an average of 22.5 brix. "The fruit quality was excellent," recalls Voysey. "The grapes would have been good enough to include in our [flagship] Ormond Estate Chardonnay, if they'd been needed."

At the winery, a range of vinification techniques were used to enhance the wine's complexity, without subduing its rich, vibrant fruitiness. Once crushed, the grapes were given extended skin contact to boost the juice's flavour, and after draining and pressing only the free-run juice was retained. Fermentation was entirely in barriques (40 per cent new), of which 60 per cent were American oak and 40 per cent were French oak. To add richness and creaminess, the wine was matured on its yeast lees in the casks for five months, with regular stirring of the lees to boost flavour absorption; 30 per cent of the final blend also underwent a secondary, softening malolactic fermentation. The result: a bold, punchy Chardonnay with a range of complexities that is still, essentially, a celebration of Gisborne's smashing fruit flavours.

Saints Gisborne Chardonnay 1996 is a wine to savour this summer, while its fragrance and fresh, buoyant fruit flavours are in full flower. There's plenty of it – 20,000 cases were produced. That's expected to be enough to keep the local market supplied for the next few months, although it's also being sold in the UK exclusively to Marks & Spencer.

1997 Vintage Report

A Small Harvest of Variable Quality

"Winemakers are excited about the quality of grapes harvested in 1997," the Wine Institute declared in late June. In fact, the 1997 vintage had its fair share of problems and, as in all seasons, the wines will be a mixed bag. Of one thing we can be certain – 1997 was a low-yielding vintage.

A total of 60,000 tonnes of grapes were harvested, making the 1997 crop 20 per cent smaller than the 1996 vintage. The fall occurred despite a 10 per cent increase in the total area of bearing vineyards. The average yield this year was only 8.2 tonnes of grapes per hectare, compared with the 1989 to 1996 average of 11.2 tonnes per hectare. The reduced crop can be ascribed to a reduced number of berry clusters on the vines and lower individual berry weights.

An important aspect of the vintage is that production of the key export varieties, Chardonnay (down 8.6 per cent on 1996) and Sauvignon Blanc (down 6.8 per cent) held up relatively well, with the harvest of these varieties being the second largest on record. However, the crop of bulk white wine grapes was far below 1996. Müller-Thurgau dropped by 30 per cent from 13,838 tonnes to 9739 tonnes, and Muscat varieties by 25 per cent from 5028 tonnes to 3753 tonnes.

The crop of red wine grapes also fell heavily. The Cabernet Sauvignon harvest declined by 32 per cent, from 4169 tonnes to 2824 tonnes; the Pinot Noir crop dropped by 25 per cent, from 4617 tonnes to 3427 tonnes; and the Merlot crop fell by 29 per cent from 2857 tonnes to 2036 tonnes.

Apart from Nelson, which recorded a crop 10 per cent larger than in 1996, production was down in all regions, with yields down by 19 per cent in Gisborne and Marlborough, and by 22 per cent in Hawke's Bay.

An Indian Summer in most regions following earlier problems of high rainfall and humidity has raised hopes of high quality wines from 1997. In March, Gisborne and Hawke's Bay experienced particularly wet weather, caused by frequent depressions and cyclones of tropical origin tracking over the North Island. Later in the season, things looked up. More anticyclones slipped across the Tasman, bringing drier weather from late March to May and boosting the quality of the later-ripening varieties.

Despite the positive aspects of the vintage, it is clear that the quality of the 1997 wines will be variable, with the North Island Chardonnays a mixed bag, the Cabernet-based reds of Hawke's Bay looking promising, and everyone pleased with Marlborough Sauvignon Blanc.

Auckland

After a cold spring affected the vines' flowering, leading to a poor fruit "set", Auckland had a very low-cropping vintage – 30 per cent smaller than in 1996.

"With three cyclones, it was a pretty poor summer," recalls Michael Brajkovich of Kumeu River. January was the coolest for 14 years, although sunshine hours were slightly above average, and March proved wetter than usual. April, however, was the sunniest since sunshine records began in 1909. "It looked touch and go after the last cyclone," says Brajkovich. "Autumn saved the day, with long warm days and cool nights, but the 1997 vintage wasn't as good as '96."

Waiheke Island winemaker, Kim Goldwater, views 1997 as "a very atypical vintage. Summer was overcast and cooler than usual, but from Easter onwards the weather was beautiful." Goldwater admits it was a "battle" to ripen his fruit. Due to a lack of warmth to dry out the soil, the vines kept growing vigorously late in the season, even forcing Goldwater and his staff to trim the vines after the bird nets had been installed. In the end, he reports, the Merlot was "variable" but the Cabernet Sauvignon and Cabernet Franc were "exceptional".

Gisborne

James Millton, of The Millton Vineyard, reports 1997 was a "warm, humid" season in Gisborne. After a good bud initiation, spring continued favourably and the flowering took place in warm, still conditions. Early summer was characterised by 10-day cycles of overcast weather, with cool easterlies and tropical depressions, followed by fine, clear days with hot, dry nor'-westers.

In January, however, the Longbush winery reported that the Gisborne region was "certainly down in terms of sunshine hours, has been affected by one cyclone, and has had three bouts of hail, with crop losses of up to 20 per cent in some vineyards."

After Cyclone Gavin struck in early March, the Wine Institute issued a press release claiming the vineyards had "escaped any significant problems". A week later, Jeff Clarke, chief winemaker of Montana, declared the giant company was harvesting most of its

Chardonnay in response to disease pressure, a move which would reduce the volume of premium quality Chardonnay from the region; Montana's top Ormond Estate Chardonnay is not expected to appear from the 1997 vintage. Nobilo winemaker, Greg Foster, described the Chardonnay grapes his company received from Gisborne as "reasonably clean but a bit diluted in flavour".

Later in the season, things looked up. Steve Voysey, winemaker at Montana Gisborne Winery, reported "good, fully ripe Gewürztraminer; some was late-picked at 28 brix". Denis Irwin, of Matawhero, harvested "very clean white-wine grapes with adequate sugars and very good flavours, and the reds are about the best since 1989." James Millton characterised the vintage as giving fruit with lower brix (sugar) levels than usual, but well balanced acidity, low pH levels and an "exciting" degree of varietal flavour enhanced by the cool February/March period.

Hawke's Bay

Alwyn Corban, of Ngatarawa, sees 1997 as an abnormal vintage in the Bay: "Spring was reasonably early; bud-burst and flowering were ahead of schedule. It was really dry around December. Summer was wet, although the heat summation figures were good. February was very hot and humid, which created early *Botrytis* infections. There was a lot of crop removal in the vineyards – more to relieve disease pressure than advance ripening."

From Easter onwards, however, the weather was largely fine and dry, with low humidity, cool nights and day temperatures above 20°C. This allowed much of the *Botrytis* to dry – a critical quality factor.

"Some Sauvignon Blanc was hard hit by *Botrytis*," says Grant Edmonds, of Alpha Domus and Redmetal Vineyard, and his own Chardonnay was "variable, with average Mendoza and good clone 15". Tim Turvey, of Clearview Estate, believes "a lot of people panicked and harvested early". Alwyn Corban, however, reports harvesting Sauvignon Blanc and Chardonnay with "excellent" flavours: "The Sauvignon Blanc was riper and perhaps more concentrated than in '96; so was the Chardonnay."

The reds look promising. "You could hang the grapes out forever," says Dr Alan Limmer, of Stonecroft. "They're our ripest yet in sugar terms, but flavour-wise, we'll have to wait and see, because we didn't get the desirable peaks of temperature in summer." Winemaker Michelle Richardson reports that Villa Maria doesn't have a large volume of reserve reds – much less than from '95 – but has good commercial reds.

"Overall, it was a better vintage for reds than whites," says Jeff Clarke, Montana's chief winemaker. Montana won't be producing a Church Road Reserve Chardonnay from 1997. "The reds did relatively well because the grapes were greener during the cyclonic weather, and so less affected," says Clarke. "Our red-wine crops were small, with reasonably concentrated flavours, so we're quietly confident."

Wairarapa

"Very light, but very good," is how Larry McKenna, of Martinborough Vineyard, sums up the 1997 vintage.

Strong, cold winds during flowering severely reduced the crop – down 27 per cent on 1996. "During summer there were lots of cold days," says Chris Lintz of Lintz Estate, "but it stayed pretty dry until mid March." The late summer rains created some disease pressure, but McKenna reports that "most of the *Botrytis* dried out, with the result that the fruit became very ripe, very fast".

For Martinborough Vineyard, "Pinot Noir is the pick of the wines, benefitting from the small crop – this is showing in colour and structure. We let the Pinot Noir hang and it ripened beautifully, reaching 25 brix."

Whereas 1996 was slightly warmer than average, the 1997 vintage was slightly cooler. Neil McCallum of Dry River expects "slightly stronger varietal statement and elegance for '97 wines and a little more richness and concentration for the '96s."

Nelson

"I think that Nelson had a very good vintage, but I wouldn't say it was great," says Phil Jones of Spencer Hill Estate. "It was as good as 1996 or 1994, but I wouldn't call it the vintage of the decade." However, for Tim Finn of Neudorf Vineyard, the summer of 1997 was "the best since 1991 or 1989".

The total Nelson crop exceeded that of 1996, reflecting recent heavy plantings, but yields were down: Seifried Estate crushed 700 tonnes in 1996, but only 500 tonnes in 1997. "It was a cool summer," says Hermann Seifried, "but we didn't have any major rain problems. Autumn was great – we were able to ripen our Riesling and Cabernet Sauvignon fruit on the vines until mid May." Seifried reports harvesting "very clean fruit with lower than usual acids and excellent sugar accumulation". Some parcels of Gewürztraminer, Riesling and Sauvignon Blanc are the winery's "best ever".

Marlborough

Jeff Clarke, chief winemaker of Montana, sees the 1997 vintage in Marlborough as "an absolute cracker. It was a cool vintage, with not a lot of rain and crops down 20 per cent, so ripeness was no concern. The Sauvignon Blanc crop is an excellent backup to the [fine quality] '96s, but the problem is there's not a lot of it."

In summer, December and January were both cooler than usual, with above average rainfall in January "hitting some anxiety buttons", according to Cloudy Bay. February was overcast and variable, and March was also cooler and less sunny than normal.

April continued slightly cooler than usual, but rainfall was also below average. Steady breezes kept the bunches dry, reducing the spread of disease.

"Late April was an all time classic," says Cloudy Bay. "Cold nights with UV-laden days and gentle breezes – ideal conditions that allowed an almost leisurely harvest." Fine weather during the first half of May allowed the vintage to be completed in warmth and sunshine.

Winepress, the newsletter of the Marlborough Grapegrowers' Association, quoted Cloudy Bay winemaker James Healy as rating 1997 as a $7^{1}/_{2}$ out of 10 vintage, compared to $8^{1}/_{2}$ out of 10 for 1991. *Winepress* also quoted other winemakers as rating 1997 as an 'above average' and "good but not great" vintage.

However, for Warwick Stichbury of Jackson Estate, it was a "brilliant vintage – you'd be hard pushed to make a bad one this year. You could leave the fruit out as long as you wanted. The long ripening period was ideal for optimum flavour development."

Canterbury

Canterbury had an extremely light harvest, with 1997 yielding only 512 tonnes – less than half the 1059 tonnes picked in 1996. "Look for cooler-vintage flavours in the wines," says Pegasus Bay winemaker, Matthew Donaldson.

Between January and March, six times the average rainfall descended on the Waipara region in North Canterbury. In early autumn the hills were still green, instead of their customary brown. Because the vines had flowered early, ripening was well advanced, which assisted the spread of *Botrytis*. "Those with good vineyard management removed the infected fruit,' says Donaldson, 'but that made '97 an even lower-cropping year."

In April and May, the weather improved with a procession of warm, dry days. Overall it was still a cool season in Waipara; warmer than 1992 and 1993, but cooler than 1995 and 1996. "We're rapt with our Sauvignon Blanc and Riesling," says Donaldson, "and the Pinot Noir is pretty good. All the varieties developed good sugar levels and flavour depth, but overall it wasn't quite as good a vintage as '96."

Further south, around Christchurch, summer was unusually cool, slowing the grapes' development. Warm, dry autumn weather then assisted ripening and Petter Evans, until recently winemaker at St Helena, reported harvesting "good" Riesling, Pinot Blanc and Pinot Noir. However, Evans also noted that other varieties had failed to ripen fully, even though their crops were small, and that high acidities were common.

Otago

A cool spring got the season off to a slow start, but Central Otago basked in hot, sunny weather during January and February. In April the vineyards along the Kawarau Gorge were struck by frost, at a time when all grape varieties (especially Sauvignon Blanc) could have used at least a couple of weeks' more ripening. The early frosts brought the growing season in the Kawarau to an abrupt end, and the grapes missed out on the sizzling temperatures (6°C above average) of early May.

Black Ridge at Alexandra reported a lot of "hen and chicken" (bunches with large and small berries), intensely flavoured grapes and "some wonderful wines in the making". Bannockburn escaped the frosts, "so with the low crops [across the region, 40 per cent less than 1996], the grapes ripened well," says Grant Taylor, winemaker at Gibbston Valley. Taylor reported drawing "quite good" Chardonnay and Riesling from Bannockburn and "some of the best Otago Pinot Noir I've ever seen, with excellent concentration of flavour and colour."

Variety Focus

Pinot Gris, Future Star of New Zealand Whites?

There's a new star on the horizon. New Zealand's producing area of Pinot Gris, one of the great grapes of Alsace, is tripling between 1996 and 1999. This grey-blue, or sometimes brownish pink, permutation of Pinot Noir produces dull Pinot Grigio wines in northern Italy yet excitingly weighty, spicy, rich-flavoured whites in Alsace.

Why the mounting interest here in Pinot Gris? 'People are getting tired of drinking Chardonnay all the time,' says Dr Neil McCallum of Dry River, producer of New Zealand's first outstanding Pinot Gris. "And it's a superb food wine."

In Alsace, where it has been known traditionally as Tokay d'Alsace – a practice the EC bureaucrats are determined to stamp out – Pinot Gris produces the region's most robust but least perfumed dry wines, and is also prized for its *vendange tardive* (late harvest) wines. Pinot Gris is the wine Alsatians recommend most fervently with the local cuisine, especially pâté de foie gras.

Pinot Gris is widely planted across central Europe. In Germany, where it is called Rulander, the grape produces full-bodied, soft dry whites. From north-east Italy, especially Friuli, flows a torrent of nondescript Pinot Grigio, some of which even finds a market in New Zealand. In Fruili, Pinot Gris is typically harvested early to prevent the grape's characteristic rapid loss of acidity at full ripeness – but before the fruit has accumulated any flavour richness.

In the New World, so far Pinot Gris has made little impact. In New Zealand, government viticulturist Romeo Bragato praised the grape in 1906 ("in the far north [it] bears heavily and produces an excellent white wine"), but it later lost favour with most growers because of a tendency to crop erratically. Now, with 149 tonnes harvested in 1997 (enough to make about 11,000 cases of wine) Pinot Gris is on the comeback trail. Over a third of all plantings are in Marlborough, with further significant pockets in Otago, Hawke's Bay, Canterbury and the Wairarapa.

So what does Pinot Gris taste like? Imagine a wine that couples the satisfying body and subtlety of aroma and flavour of Chardonnay with some of the rich spiciness of Gewürztraminer. In Neil McCallum's view, its flavours "tend to a peachy character with a certain spiciness – Muscat with an almost earthy undertone".

Pinot Gris is not a difficult variety to cultivate, according to David Jackson and Danny Schuster, Canterbury-based co-authors of *The Production of Grapes and Wines in Cool Climates*. A moderately vigorous vine, it adapts well to most types of well-drained soils. The grapes possess good resistance to bunch rot, and ripen with fairly low acidity to high sugar levels.

McCallum, who sourced his vines from Mission Vineyards, believes them to be an old Alsace clone, imported into New Zealand in 1886, that belongs to the low-yielding clonal class called Tokay à petit grain (small berry Pinot Gris). "We follow the Alsace tradition, which places so much emphasis on ripeness and quality of fruit. The vines mustn't be cropped too heavily; the people in Alsace go on about the necessity of having the small berry clone."

Pinot Gris ripens fairly early; McCallum harvests around the end of April (when he's picking the last of his Pinot Noir). "For the success of the wine, it is critical to achieve physiological ripeness [mature skin colour, berry texture, flavour, phenolic changes, etc], not just the right brix level. If you don't get that right, the first thing you lose is weight and richness. Acid loss isn't a problem, because Pinot Gris has such good weight and alcohol." Sometimes McCallum leaves fruit on the vines until early May to produce Dry River Selection Pinot Gris, a bold, sweet, late harvest style equivalent to an Alsace *vendange tardive*.

In the winery, McCallum finds Pinot Gris easy to work with. "The wine's made at the time you pick the grapes. We favour a reductive [non-oxidative] approach, although we are able to handle it less reductively than our other whites, because it's so robust. It's got awkward phenolics [Pinot Gris wine often shows a slight tannic hardness], so we whole-bunch press. We don't mature it in oak, but if you do, you need to be cautious; it doesn't take wood easily." In Alsace, the best Pinot Gris are matured in large casks, but the wood is old, so as not to interfere with the grape's subtle flavour.

If you like substantial, refined dry whites that enhance food and can flourish long-term in the cellar, Pinot Gris is worth getting to know. For Neil McCallum, the key attraction of Pinot Gris is its "ability to age and show the interest and subtleties which justify the description 'fine wine'." Dry River Pinot Gris drinks splendidly at five years old; the Germans recommend drinking the wine when it (not the drinker) has "grey hairs".

Cellar Sense

Who doesn't relish the idea of a personal wine cellar, packed with vintage wines maturing slowly to their peak? Yet most of the wine consumed in this country is bought shortly before its consumption. So much for cellaring – we love contemplating it, but few of us actually do it.

It is worth the effort. To enjoy wine at the height of its powers, when its flavour is at its most complex, harmonious and downright enjoyable, you need to lay it down for a few years. Keeping a stock of wine in the house is also economical – you can buy by the case at lower prices and it's the cheapest way to obtain mature vintages – and convenient.

Which wines most repay cellaring? First, forget the idea that all wines improve with age. Much New Zealand wine is best drunk young, especially light, mild-flavoured white wine like Müller-Thurgau, which after a year or two loses the floral, fresh fruitiness that is the essence of its charm. Only the wine of a few classic grape varieties blossoms in the bottle for several years.

New Zealand Chardonnay, Riesling and Cabernet-based reds should be the mainstays of your cellar. Chardonnay from top vintages has the weight and flavour richness to flourish for up to five years; resist broaching the best labels for at least three years. Top Riesling improves even longer – Montana's Marlborough Rieslings and Corbans' Stoneleigh Vineyard Rieslings from the mid-1980s are currently spellbinding. Top vintages of the best Cabernet-based reds from Hawke's Bay and Waiheke Island need at least five years.

A sprinkling of other New Zealand varietal wines will add interest and diversity to your cellar: good Chenin Blanc, Gewürztraminer, Pinot Gris, barrel-aged Sauvignon Blanc and Sémillon, and Pinot Noir and Merlot will age well for three years and often longer.

Build your cellar in the coolest, darkest place you can find in (or under) the house. Start by buying full or half cases of your favourite wines, lay the bottles in beer crates turned on their sides, and for a few years try to forget they're there!

Cellaring Guidelines

Grape variety	*Best age to open*
WHITE	
Müller-Thurgau	6 months – 1.5 years
Sauvignon Blanc	
(non-wooded)	6 months – 2 years
(wooded)	1 – 3 years
Gewürztraminer	2 – 4 years
Chenin Blanc	2 – 4 years
Sémillon	2 – 4 years
Pinot Gris	2 – 5 years
Chardonnay	3 – 5 years
Riesling	3 – 10 years
RED	
Pinotage	2 – 4 years
Cabernet Franc	2 – 4 years
Pinot Noir	3 – 5 years
Syrah	3 – 5 years
Cabernet Sauvignon	3 – 7+ years
Cabernet/Merlot	3 – 7+ years
OTHER	
Bottle-fermented sparklings	3 – 5 years
Vintage port	5 – 10 years

Vintage Charts

1987 – 1997

7 = Outstanding 6 = Excellent 5 = Above average
4 = Average 3 = Below average 2 = Poor 1 = Bad

WHITES

	AUCKLAND	GISBORNE	HAWKE'S BAY	WAIRARAPA	NELSON	MARLBOROUGH	CANTERBURY	OTAGO
1997	6	3 – 5	4 – 6	6 – 7	6 – 7	6	5 – 6	4 – 5
1996	5	4 – 6	4 – 6	6 – 7	5	6	3 – 6	4 – 5
1995	4	4 – 6	3 – 7	5 – 6	2 – 4	2 – 3	6 – 7	5
1994	6	6	6 – 7	6	5 – 6	5 – 6	4	4
1993	7	4	3 – 4	4	4	3 – 4	3 – 4	5
1992	5	6	6	4	5	4 – 5	3	3
1991	6	5	6 – 7	6 – 7	6	6 – 7	4	4
1990	4	3 – 5	3 – 6	4	4 – 6	5	5	5
1989	5 – 6	6	7	5 – 7	6 – 7	6 – 7	7	4
1988	3	2 – 4	2 – 4	6 – 7	6	6	4	–
1987	5 – 6	4 – 6	4 – 6	3 – 6	5	4 – 6	5	–

REDS

	AUCKLAND	GISBORNE	HAWKE'S BAY	WAIRARAPA	NELSON	MARLBOROUGH	CANTERBURY	OTAGO
1997	5 – 6	4	4 – 7	7	6 – 7	5	5 – 6	5 – 6
1996	4 – 5	3 – 4	4	7	5 – 6	4	4 – 6	5
1995	4 – 5	2 – 4	5 – 7	6	2 – 4	2 – 3	6 – 7	6
1994	6	6	5 – 6	6	5	5	4	5
1993	7	3	2	4 – 5	3 – 4	3 – 4	3 – 4	5
1992	5	4	4	4	4	3 – 4	3	3
1991	6	4	7	5	5 – 6	5	4	4
1990	5	4	6	4 – 5	4 – 6	5 – 6	6	6
1989	7	7	7	6 – 7	6	6	7	4
1988	4	1 – 2	2 – 4	5 – 7	5 – 6	5	4	–
1987	6	4 – 5	6 – 7	3 – 4	4 – 5	5	5	–

How to Use this Book

It is essential to read this brief section to understand how the book works. Feel free to skip any of the other preliminary pages – but not these.

The majority of wines have been listed in the book according to their principal grape variety. Esk Valley Chardonnay, for instance, can be located simply by turning to the Chardonnay section. Non-varietal wines (with names that do not boldly refer to a grape variety or blend of grapes), such as Collards Private Bin Dry White or Cross Roads The Talisman, can be found in the Generic and Branded sections for white and red wines.

Most entries are firstly identified by their producer's names. Wines not usually called by their producer's name, such as Shingle Peak Sauvignon Blanc (from Matua) or Oyster Bay Chardonnay (from Delegat's), are listed under their most common name.

The star ratings for quality reflect my own opinions, formed where possible by tasting a wine over several vintages, and often a particular vintage several times. *The star ratings on the right-hand side of the page are therefore a guide to each wine's overall standard in recent vintages*, rather than simply the quality of the latest release. However, for the first time this year, in the body of the text I have added a *quality rating for the latest vintage of each wine*.

I hope the star ratings give interesting food for thought and succeed in introducing you to a galaxy of little-known but worthwhile wines. It pays to remember, however, that wine tasting is a business fraught with subjectivity. You should always treat the views expressed in these pages for what they are – one person's opinion.

The quality ratings are:

☆☆☆☆☆	Outstanding quality (gold medal standard)
☆☆☆☆½	Excellent quality, verging on outstanding
☆☆☆☆	Excellent quality (silver medal standard)
☆☆☆½	Very good quality
☆☆☆	Good quality (bronze medal standard)
☆☆½	Average
☆☆	Plain
☆	Poor
No star	To be avoided

These quality ratings are based on comparative assessments of New Zealand wines against one another. A five-star Cabernet Sauvignon/

Merlot, for instance, is an outstanding-quality red judged by the standards of other Cabernet Sauvignon/Merlot blends made in New Zealand. It is not judged by the standards of overseas reds of a similar style (for instance Bordeaux); such international comparisons always lead into a minefield of controversy.

Where brackets enclose the star rating on the right-hand side of the page, for example (☆☆☆), this indicates the assessment is only tentative, because I have tasted very few vintages of the wine. A hyphen is used in the relatively few cases where a wine's quality has oscillated over and above normal vintage variations (for example ☆ – ☆☆☆).

Classic wines (see p. 8) are shown in the text by the following symbol:

Each wine has also been given a dryness-sweetness, price and value-for-money rating. The precise levels of sweetness indicated by the four ratings are:

DRY	Less than 5 grams/litre of sugar
MED/DRY	5 – 14 grams/litre of sugar
MED	15 – 49 grams/litre of sugar
SWEET	50 and over grams/litre of sugar

Less than 5 grams of sugar per litre is virtually imperceptible to most palates – the wine tastes bone-dry. With between 5 and 14 grams, a wine has a distinct hint of sweetness. Where a wine harbours over 15 grams (most Müller-Thurgaus are around 20), the sweetness is clearly in evidence. At above 50 grams per litre, a wine is unabashedly sweet.

Prices indicated are based on the average price in a retail wine outlet, except where most of the wine is sold directly to the public, either over the vineyard counter or by mail order.

The art of wine buying involves more than just discovering top quality wines. The greater challenge – and the greatest satisfaction – lies in identifying wines at varying quality levels that deliver outstanding value for money. The symbols I have used are self-explanatory:

-V	= Below average value
AV	= Average value
V+	= Above average value

The ratings discussed thus far are all my own. Many of the wine producers themselves, however, have also contributed individual vintage ratings of their own wines back to the 1990 vintage and the "When to drink" recommendations. (The symbol WR indicates Winemaker's Rating, and the symbol NM alongside a vintage means the wine was not produced that year.) Only the producers have such detailed knowledge of the relative quality of all their recent vintages (in a few cases they have revised the ratings supplied for the last edition). *The key point you must note is that each producer has rated each vintage of each wine against his or her highest quality aspirations for that particular label, not against any absolute standard.* Thus, a 7 out of 7 score merely indicates that the producer considers that particular vintage to be an outstanding example of that particular wine; not that it is the best quality wine he or she makes.

The "When to drink" recommendations (which I find myself referring to constantly) are largely self-explanatory. The P symbol for PEAKED means that a particular vintage is already at, or has passed its peak; no further benefits are expected from aging.

Here is an example of how the ratings work:

SEIFRIED	VINTAGE	96	95	94	93	92	91	90		**DRY $16 AV**
NELSON	WR	5	4	6	5	6	6	6		
CHARDONNAY	DRINK	97-02	98-9	98-02	97-8	P	P	P		☆ ☆ ☆

The quality of this wine has risen sharply in recent years. The '95 is less ripe and rich than the strapping '94, but fresh-scented, with appley, nutty, steely flavours. The 1996 vintage (***1/2) is fine value. Thirty per cent of the blend was barrel-fermented and lees-aged for nine months; another 30 per cent was barrel-aged for five months. A mouthfilling, characterful wine with a toasty bouquet, strong grapefruit/oak flavours and a slightly buttery, moderately crisp finish, it offers very good drinking from now onwards.

The symbols indicate that Seifried Nelson Chardonnay is generally a wine of good quality (very good quality in the case of the '96). It is dry in style, and at its price of around $16 delivers average value for money. The winemaker's own ratings (W R) indicate that the 1996 vintage is of above average quality, and suggest when each vintage will be drinking at its peak.

White Wines

Auxerrois

When cropped lightly, this exceptionally rare (in New Zealand) variety can yield richly flavoured soft wines, but in Alsace it is commonly blended away into wines labelled Pinot Blanc. Auxerrois (pronounced Ox-er-wa) is also established in Luxembourg, where it is valued for its typical low acidity.

LINTZ ESTATE AUXERROIS

DRY $18 AV

☆ ☆ ☆ ⚹

Martinborough winemaker Chris Lintz made only 55 cases of his debut 1996 Auxerrois (***1/2), but the variety looks promising. It's a full-bodied dry white with a non-aromatic bouquet and rather Chardonnay-like palate – fleshy, savoury, slightly earthy and rounded. A satisfying and subtle wine that would sit well at the dinner table.

Breidecker

A nondescript crossing of Müller-Thurgau (for which it is easily mistaken in a blind tasting) and the white hybrid Seibel 7053, Breidecker is lightly planted in New Zealand, with only 12 hectares of bearing vines in 1998 (0.2 per cent of the country's total). Breidecker yields light, fresh quaffing wines, best drunk young.

HUNTER'S BREIDECKER

MED $13 AV

☆ ☆ ☆

Much more characterful than most Breideckers I've tasted, the 1996 vintage (***) of this Marlborough wine is pale lemon-green, light and distinctly sweetish, with attractive fruit flavours – lemony, limey, delicate, fresh and crisp – in a rather Riesling-like style.

LANGDALE BREIDECKER DRY

DRY $15 -V

☆ ☆

The 1996 vintage (**1/2) of this pale, light Canterbury wine was estate-grown at West Melton and made by Dayne Sherwood. It's a nondescript wine with a neutral bouquet, but a bit more oomph on the palate than past vintages. Medium-bodied, with clean, mild, lemony, slightly limey flavours and a dryish, crisp finish, it's very much a drink-young style.

LANGDALE BREIDECKER MEDIUM

MED $15 -V

☆ ☆

Estate-grown at West Melton in Canterbury and made by Dayne Sherwood, this is typically a pale, slender, slightly sweet wine with a very restrained flavour. The 1996 vintage (**¹/₂) has a shy bouquet, medium body and mild flavour: clean, lemony and rather short.

MED $12 AV

LARCOMB
BREIDECKER

☆☆⯪

Grown at Rolleston, south-west of Christchurch, the 1995 vintage (**¹/₂) is a very typical Breidecker – pleasant enough, but pale, light and plain. The fresh, lemony, appley scents lead into a soft, mildly fruity palate with reasonable flavour depth and a slightly sweet finish.

MED $12 AV

SANDIHURST
BREIDECKER

☆☆⯪

Displaying a bit more character than many Breideckers, the 1995 vintage (**¹/₂) of this West Melton, Canterbury wine is a light (10.5 per cent alcohol), slightly sweet, distinctly cool-climate style with tense acidity and lively, lemony, limey flavours.

Chardonnay

Is oak an essential ingredient in the recipe of a decent Chardonnay? Not always. Recently there's been a surge of "unoaked" and "unwooded" Chardonnays onto the shelves. Relying for their appeal on deliciously fresh, vibrant, delicate fruit flavours, uncluttered by oak, these wines offer highly enjoyable summer sipping.

There's a dazzling range of New Zealand Chardonnays to choose from. Almost every winery in the country makes at least one; many produce several and giant wineries like Corbans make a dozen. The hallmark of New Zealand Chardonnays is their delicious varietal intensity. The leading labels display such concentrated aromas and flavours, underpinned by appetising acidity, that they have rapidly emerged on the world stage.

Top Chardonnays are flowing from several countries, including France, Italy, the United States, Australia and New Zealand. Great white Burgundy is still in a class of its own, but New Zealand can compete well with the leading Chardonnays from other New World countries. At the 1997 International Wine and Spirit Competition in London, the trophy for the best Chardonnay of the show was awarded to Tasman Bay Chardonnay 1996.

The price of New Zealand Chardonnay ranges from $10 to over $30 per bottle. The quality differences are equally wide. The low-priced wines are typically fermented in stainless steel tanks and bottled young with minimal barrel aging; these wines rely on fresh, lemony, uncluttered fruit flavours for their appeal. The major example is Montana Gisborne Chardonnay, New Zealand's most popular Chardonnay.

The mid-price wines (like Matua Eastern Bays Chardonnay and Babich East Coast Chardonnay) are typically tank-fermented and then matured in oak casks, which adds to their complexity and richness. The top labels are invariably at least partially fermented, as well as matured, in oak barrels; there may also be extended aging on (and regular stirring of) yeast lees and varying proportions of a secondary, softening malolactic fermentation (sometimes referred to in the tasting notes as "malo".) The best of these display the arresting depth and subtlety of flavour for which Chardonnay is so highly prized.

Chardonnay plantings have recently outstripped those of every other variety in New Zealand, and in 1998 constitute 26.5 per cent of the bearing vineyard. The vines are spread throughout the major wine regions, particularly Marlborough (where more than a third of the vines are concentrated), Hawke's Bay (where it is now the number one grape) and Gisborne.

Chardonnays of exciting quality are flowing from all of New Zealand's key wine regions, from Auckland to Otago. Of the three dominant regions, Gisborne is renowned for its deep-scented and soft Chardonnays, which offer very seductive drinking in their youth; Hawke's Bay yields impressively robust, peachy, ripe wines with power and longevity; and Marlborough's Chardonnays are leaner but stylish and mouth-wateringly crisp.

Chardonnay has often been dubbed "the red-wine drinker's white wine". Chardonnays are almost invariably bone dry, as are all reds with any aspirations to quality. Chardonnay's typically mouthfilling body and absorbing, multi-faceted flavours are also characteristic of top reds. The variety's ability to flourish long-term in the bottle is another obvious red-wine parallel.

Broaching a top-flight New Zealand Chardonnay at less than two years old is infanticide; the best of the 1992s are now at their peak. If you must drink Chardonnay when it is only a year old, it pays to buy one of the cheaper, less complex wines specifically designed to be enjoyable in their youth.

AKARANGI CHARDONNAY

DRY $15 -V

☆ ⚊

Most vintages I have tasted of Morton Osborne's Hawke's Bay Chardonnay, grown on the banks of the Tukituki River near Havelock North, have been sound wines, but lacked weight and flavour richness. The pale 1995 vintage (**) was one-third barrel-fermented. Again, it's short of flavour and a bit tart, with a restrained wood influence and light, crisp, green-apple characters.

ALLAN SCOTT MARLBOROUGH CHARDONNAY

VINTAGE	96	95
WR	6	5
DRINK	97-01	97-8

DRY $20 AV

☆ ☆ ☆ ⚊

"I want Chardonnay with a bit of weight but not too much oak," says Allan Scott. The '95 is full of drink-young charm, with plenty of fresh, uncomplicated, citrus and melon-evoking flavour, crisp and lively. The French oak-aged '96 (****) is a stylish wine, aging well. A mouthfilling style with ripe fruit aromas, it is still very fresh and crisp, with good mouthfeel and depth of citrusy, subtlely oaked flavour.

ALPHA DOMUS AD CHARDONNAY

VINTAGE	97	96
WR	6	5
DRINK	99-04	98-02

DRY $32 AV

(☆☆☆☆☆)

With Grant Edmonds, formerly chief winemaker for Villa Maria, at the production helm, it's no surprise this fledgling Hawke's Bay winery has immediately produced a striking Chardonnay. The debut 1996 vintage (*****) of the flagship AD label was estate-grown at Maraekakaho, barrel fermented and oak matured for 10 months. An immaculate wine with a very fragrant, richly oaked, mealy bouquet, it is big and broad on the palate, with a lovely balance of intense, ripe melon/peach flavours, nutty oak and a crisp, slightly buttery, long finish. This is a powerful, very refined and complex wine for drinking 1998 onwards.

ATA RANGI CRAIGHALL CHARDONNAY

VINTAGE	96	95	94	93	92	91	90
WR	7	7	7	6	NM	7	6
DRINK	99-04	98-03	97-00	97-8	NM	97-8	P

DRY $29 AV

☆☆☆☆☆

An extremely impressive Martinborough wine, with the 1994 to 1996 vintages achieving great heights. The 1994 is exceptionally concentrated and the '95 is very, very rich, with an explosion of flavour. The '96 (*****) is again memorable, in a very succulent and complex style. Bright yellow, it is a bold, robust wine (13 per cent alcohol), with a seamless array of very ripe, mealy, butterscotch-like, well-spined flavours, notably intense and long. It's approachable already, but full of cellaring potential. Arguably the region's greatest Chardonnay.

ATA RANGI DALNAGAIRN CHARDONNAY

VINTAGE	96	95	94	93	92
WR	6	6	7	NM	7
DRINK	97-01	97-8	97-00	NM	P

DRY $22 AV

(☆☆☆☆)

Grown in the Dalnagairn Vineyard in Hawke's Bay, this is typically a delightful wine in its youth. The '95 is less lush and concentrated than the '94, with fresh, appley, oaky aromas and flavours, good weight, a touch of complexity and a moderately soft finish. The 1996 vintage (****) is delightful already, with a rich, ripe fragrance, strong grapefruit-like flavours, nutty, buttery characters and a lush, well-rounded, long finish.

	VINTAGE	97	96		
AZURE BAY	WR	6	5		**MED/DRY $10 V+**
CHARDONNAY/	DRINK	99-4	98-2		(☆☆☆⚬)
CHENIN BLANC					

The 1996 vintage of Montana's low priced wine is a medium-dry blend of Hawke's Bay Chardonnay and Gisborne Chenin Blanc. Fruity, with a gentle splash of sweetness, it's a smooth, very undemanding, ripe-tasting wine, citrusy and peachy, with crisp underlying acidity. A decent all-purpose dryish white. The '97 vintage (**½), a blend of New Zealand and Australian wine, is a straight Chardonnay with good body and smooth, ripe flavour.

	VINTAGE	96	95	94	93	92	91	90	
BABICH EAST	WR	6	7	7	7	7	7	6	**DRY $14 V+**
COAST	DRINK	97-01	97-00	97-00	97-8	P	P	P	☆☆☆
CHARDONNAY									

A good standard Chardonnay, grown in the east coast regions of Gisborne, Hawke's Bay and Marlborough. Drinking well now and offering excellent quality for its modest price, the 1995 vintage is an elegant, finely balanced wine with subtle oak, good depth of ripe, delicate, citrusy flavours and a rounded finish. The '96 (***) is still very fresh and youthful, with good weight and depth of citrusy fruit, oak complexity and balanced acidity; open 1998 onwards.

	VINTAGE	96	95	94	93	92	91	90	
BABICH	WR	7	7	7	6	7	6	6	**DRY $26 V+**
IRONGATE	DRINK	99-05	97-00	97-01	97-9	97-9	97-9	P	☆☆☆☆☆
CHARDONNAY									

A stylish, taut and steely wine, leaner and less voluptuous than many other top Chardonnays, but a strong performer in the cellar. It is based on intensely flavoured fruit from the shingly Irongate vineyard west of Hastings, barrel fermented and lees matured for up to nine months. The 1995, more expressive in its youth than some past vintages and one of the finest Irongates yet, is richly flavoured, finely balanced and maturing superbly. Pale lemon-green, it is a beautifully poised wine, crisp and tight, with an impressive concentration of appley, lemony, mealy flavour and a long finish. The '96 (*****) is also relatively full, rich and approachable in its youth. A mouthfilling, intense, complex and well-spined wine in the classic Irongate mould, it's all there for superb drinking in 1999.

	VINTAGE	96	95	94	93	92	
BABICH MARA	WR	7	6	7	6	6	**DRY $17 V+**
ESTATE	DRINK	97-02	97-00	97-9	97-8	97-8	(☆☆☆☆⚬)
CHARDONNAY							

Mara Estate has typically rested its case on ripe, citrusy fruit, subtly oaked, with strong drink-young appeal. The pale, delicate 1995 vintage is crisp, appley and lemony; a fairly lean style, still developing. The 1996 vintage (****) is the finest yet. Grown at Fernhill in Hawke's Bay and fermented and lees-aged for eight months in French oak barriques (25 per cent new), in its youth it's a tighter, more complex wine than its predecessors – very elegant, fresh, savoury and crisp, and needing to rest until mid 1998.

BABICH THE	VINTAGE 96	**DRY $30 AV**
PATRIARCH	WR 7	
CHARDONNAY	DRINK 99-05	(☆☆☆☆☆)

Dedicated to company founder Josip Babich, The Patriarch is Babich's super-premium label. The debut 1995 vintage was grown in Gimblett Road, Hawke's Bay and fermented and lees aged for nine months in French oak barriques (50 per cent new). It's a highly fragrant, subtle, finely structured wine with fresh acidity, lovely, ripe, delicate fruit, a biscuity, mealy richness and deftly judged oak. Drink now to 1999. The 1996 vintage (*****) is even more arresting. Described by chief winemaker Neill Culley as "the first wine I've really put my own thumbprint on", it was hand-picked, whole bunch-pressed, fermented with natural yeasts, and handled in a higher percentage of new oak than is used for Irongate Chardonnay. The bouquet is notably rich; the palate very powerful, with a strong surge of nutty, savoury, mealy flavour and a well-spined but rounded finish. Looks great for 1999.

BABICH	**DRY $12 V+**
UNWOODED	
CHARDONNAY	(☆☆☆)

The Babich trademark of freshness, delicacy and finely tuned acidity is clearly on display in the debut 1996 vintage (***) of this attractive Gisborne wine. Pale lemon-green, it is very clean, lively and tangy, with quite good depth of apple/lemon flavours. Drink now to 1998.

BLACK	**DRY $10 V+**
GECKO	
CHARDONNAY	(☆☆)

Montana's cheap Chardonnay is a decent, gutsy quaffer, full and fresh, citrusy and rounded, with a slightly hard finish. No taste delights but a solid, reasonably flavoursome wine.

BLACK	**DRY $18 AV**
RIDGE	
CHARDONNAY	☆☆☆

The 1996 vintage (***) of this Alexandra wine wasn't handled in oak, but it's a weighty style with good depth of appley, slightly nutty flavour. Underpinned by firm acidity, it's still very fresh and youthful, and should reward keeping to mid 1998 onwards.

BLACK RIDGE	**DRY $23 -V**
SELECT	
CHARDONNAY	(☆☆☆☆)

This is the Alexandra winery's top Chardonnay. The weighty and complex '95 is an appley, oaky, savoury wine, slightly creamy, with a cool-climate vigour and steeliness and obvious aging potential. The 1996 vintage (****1/2) is very similar. Matured for eight months in new French oak casks, it is a mouthfilling, richly flavoured wine with an oaky bouquet, toasty, mealy, complex flavours and good acid spine. It needs time; open 1998-99.

	VINTAGE	95	94	93	92	91
BLUE						
ROCK	WR	6	5	6	5	6
CHARDONNAY	DRINK	97+	P	P	P	P

DRY $25 -V

(☆–☆☆☆☆)

The 1995 vintage (***1/2) of this fully barrel-fermented Martinborough Chardonnay is powerful, strongly flavoured and likely to be long-lived. Not so the 1994; my two samples were both very oxidised. The 1995, however, is a good wine in a cool-climate style – strapping (14 per cent alcohol) and tautly structured, with vigorous acidity and strong, steely, appley flavours, overlaid with nutty oak.

**BRADSHAW
EST. NON-WOODED
CHARDONNAY**

DRY $15 AV

(☆☆☆)

To produce a wine "you can drink at lunch without falling asleep", Hawke's Bay winemaker Hans Peet gives it "no oak, no malolactic fermentation, no nothing". The ripely fruity 1995 vintage (***), blended from 80 per cent Hawke's Bay and 20 per cent Gisborne grapes (which "fattens it out a bit", says Peet), offers strong, crisp, lemon/apple flavours, opening out well with age.

**BRADSHAW
ESTATE RESERVE
CHARDONNAY**

DRY $23 -V

(☆☆☆)

The first 1995 vintage (***) of this Hawke's Bay wine was 80 per cent fermented and matured for 10 months in new French oak barriques; the rest was handled in tanks. Light yellow hued, it's a citrusy, oaky wine, savoury and crisp, with quite good flavour depth. Drink now to 1998.

**BRAJKOVICH
KUMEU
CHARDONNAY**

DRY $18 AV

☆☆☆

Since the phasing out of the Auckland Chardonnay label (last vintage 1995), this is the only Chardonnay under the Brajkovich brand from Kumeu River. The 1996 vintage (***1/2) was grown at Kumeu, fermented with natural yeasts in stainless steel tanks and given a full, softening malolactic fermentation. It's an instantly likeable wine, fragrant, with good weight and depth of well-rounded, grapefruit and butterscotch-like flavour. Wine from a top year at Kumeu, it's drinking attractively now, and likely to develop well through 1998.

	VINTAGE	96	95
BROOKFIELDS			
ESTATE	WR	7	6
CHARDONNAY	DRINK	97-8	97+

DRY $17 AV

☆☆☆

This is proprietor Peter Robertson's "house wine". The 1995 vintage has an advanced, light yellow colour, a "malo"-induced softness of texture and lots of flavour and character. The '96 (***), grown at Fernhill in Hawke's Bay, was fermented and matured for four months in French and American oak casks. It's a full, rounded wine (softened by 50 per cent malolactic fermentation) with some richness and complexity, and deliciously approachable for 1997-98.

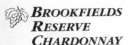

BROOKFIELDS	VINTAGE	96	95	94	93	92	91	90	DRY $34 -V
RESERVE	WR	7	7	7	7	7	6	7	
CHARDONNAY	DRINK	99	98+	00	98	P	P	P	☆☆☆☆☆

A powerful Hawke's Bay wine of outstanding quality, robust and flavour-packed. Quite Burgundian in style, the '94 is a weighty, mealy wine, peachy, soft and buttery. The '95 vintage is also reminiscent of a fine Burgundy and superior to the '94. The 1996 (*****) was grown at Fernhill and fermented and matured for eight months in all-new French Alliers oak barriques. It carries the new wood effortlessly. Worth cellaring for several years, this is a substantial, fat, very rich wine with sweet, concentrated, lush, figgy flavours, complexity and a lovely, creamy mouthfeel.

BULLRUSH CHARDONNAY

DRY $15 AV

(☆☆⚡)

The Bullrush label is owned by Matua Valley winemaker, Mark Robertson, and his wife, wine merchant Jane Osborne. The 1995 vintage is an easy-drinking Hawke's Bay wine, with soft, peachy, slightly buttery flavours. The 1996 (**¹/₂) was grown in the Willimott vineyard at Gisborne and handled in stainless steel tanks rather than wood. It's a forward style, full-bodied, with straightforward, ripe citrusy flavours and a rounded finish.

BULLRUSH RESERVE CHARDONNAY

DRY $17 AV

(☆☆☆)

Fully barrique-fermented, the 1996 vintage (***) was grown in the Willimott vineyard at Gisborne. Pale straw, it is full-bodied, citrusy, slightly nutty, ripe and rounded, offering attractive although not memorable drinking through 1997 and 1998.

CAIRNBRAE MARLBOROUGH CHARDONNAY

DRY $17 -V

(☆☆⚡)

Murray and Daphne Brown's wines, grown in the prestigious Jacksons Road area, are consistently enjoyable in a straightforward, drink-young style. The '95 is a vigorous, delicately flavoured wine with passionfruit and lemon-like aromas and a tangy, well-balanced palate. The 1996 vintage (**¹/₂) was matured for four months in American oak casks. It's a fruity, thoroughly pleasant but simple wine with fresh, citrusy, lightly wooded flavours.

CAIRNBRAE	VINTAGE	96	DRY $23 -V
RESERVE	WR	7	
CHARDONNAY	DRINK	98	(☆☆☆⚡)

Fresh, flavourful but fairly straightforward, the first 1996 vintage (****¹/₂) of this Marlborough wine was estate-grown and fermented and matured for five months in new American oak casks. Well-ripened, passionfruit and melon-evoking flavours hold sway, with restrained wood and a crisp, tight finish. Attractive drinking from now onwards.

VINTAGE	96	95	94
WR	5	5	6
DRINK	98-00	98-00	98-00

CANADORO CHARDONNAY

DRY $23 -V

(☆☆☆⯪)

The 1995 vintage of this little known but characterful Martinborough wine is full and soft, with appley, buttery, slightly toffee-like flavours, a creamy texture and good length. The '96 (***) was fermented and lees-aged for ten months in new and one year-old French oak barriques, and given a full, softening malolactic fermentation. Straw-coloured, it's a bold, soft, very forward wine with ripe, peachy fruit flavours rather dominated by toasty, cheesey, oak and "malo" characters. Still, that's a style many like, and it's full of flavour.

CHARD FARM CLOSEBURN CHARDONNAY

DRY $22 -V

(☆☆☆⯪)

The Central Otago winery's second-tier Chardonnay. The 1995 vintage, a blend of estate-grown and Bannockburn grapes, is a crisp, elegant, citrusy wine, savoury and tight-structured, with plenty of aging potential. The '96 (***¹/₂) was 80 per cent fermented in a mix of new to four year-old casks; the rest was handled in tanks. It's an elegant style, emphasising fresh, crisp, citrusy fruit flavours and appetising acidity, with toasty oak adding richness. A full-flavoured, slightly buttery wine, for now to 1998.

CHARD FARM JUDGE AND JURY CHARDONNAY

DRY $29 -V

☆☆☆⯪

A vertical tasting of the 1991 to 1995 vintages proved this high-priced Central Otago wine ages well. Since the 1994 vintage, it has been a blend of estate-grown and Bannockburn fruit. The '95 reveals a richly wooded bouquet and crisp, peachy fruit flavours wrapped in toasty oak. The '96 (****), a big, richly flavoured wine, was fermented in French oak barriques, 80 per cent new. It carries the strong new oak well. A more refined, better balanced wine than some past vintages, it possesses intense citrusy fruit, a creamy, mealy richness and a long, firm, mouth-wateringly crisp finish. Open 1998–99.

CHIFNEY CHARDONNAY

DRY $20 AV

☆☆☆⯪

The quality of Chifney's Martinborough Chardonnays has risen sharply in recent vintages. The '95 vintage has delicate, pure, lemon and apple-like flavours, not concentrated, but with lots of early-drinking appeal. The 1996 (***¹/₂) was estate-grown and lees-aged in oak for eight months. It's a more powerful wine than the '95, harbouring 14 per cent alcohol, with strong, grapefruit-like, nutty, crisp flavours in a moderately complex style. Well worth keeping to mid 1998 onwards.

CHURCH ROAD CHARDONNAY	VINTAGE	96	95	94	93	92	91	90	DRY $20 AV
	WR	6	7	7	4	5	6	4	
	DRINK	98-00+	97-00+	97-00+	97-8	97-8	97-8	P	☆☆☆☆

This consistently robust and rich-flavoured Chardonnay is produced by Montana at The McDonald Winery in Hawke's Bay. The '95 is a richly fragrant and weighty wine with an intense array of peachy, nutty, mealy, complex flavours, very elegant, crisp and sustained. The 1996 vintage (****) was barrel-fermented, mainly in French oak (one-third new) and matured on its yeast lees for eight months. It's a classic Hawke's Bay style, fragrant, full and lush, with rich, ripe grapefruit-like flavours and a buttery, toasty, mealy complexity. Crafted for early appeal, it offers delicious drinking anytime from now onwards, but will also reward cellaring.

CHURCH ROAD RESERVE CHARDONNAY	VINTAGE	96	95	94	93	92	91	DRY $29 AV
	WR	7	6	7	5	6	7	
	DRINK	98-00+	97-00+	97-00+	97-00+	97-9+	97-9+	☆☆☆☆☆

A super-stylish wine based on the "pick" of Montana's Hawke's Bay Chardonnay crop (always the shy-bearing Mendoza clone, but not always grown in the same vineyard). A very full and rich style, yet retaining elegance, the 1995 vintage offers a delicious marriage of peachy, very ripe fruit with quality oak, building across the palate to a savoury, complex, powerful finish. This is a classically proportioned wine for the long haul. The '96 (*****) was grown in the Korokipo and Phoenix vineyards, fermented in French oak barriques (two-thirds new) and matured on its yeast lees in oak for eight months. A celebration of rich, concentrated Hawke's Bay fruit flavours, it is a bright, light yellow-green wine with intense grapefruit-like characters, tight and deep, integrated wood and finely balanced acidity. A wine of great finesse, it should age splendidly. (There will probably not be a 1997 vintage.)

C.J. PASK CHARDONNAY	VINTAGE	96	95	94	93	92	91	90	DRY $18 AV
	WR	7	7	6	6	6	6	6	
	DRINK	98-00	98	98	P	P	P	P	☆☆☆☆

For her sub-$20 wine, winemaker Kate Radburnd emphasises Hawke's Bay's citrusy fruit characters ("the fruit should shine through") fleshed out with restrained wood. The 1995 vintage is a full, buoyantly fruity wine with persistent, lemony, slightly limey flavours, light oak and a fresh, crisp finish. The 1996 vintage (****1/2) is a skilfully balanced, still youthful wine, grown in the Gimblett Road shingle country. Very lightly oaked, it's a full-bodied style (13.5 per cent alcohol) with pleasing depth of delicate, slightly limey flavour, very fresh and crisp.

C.J. PASK RESERVE CHARDONNAY	VINTAGE	95	94	93	92	DRY $25 AV
	WR	7	7	6	6	
	DRINK	00	00	98	P	☆☆☆☆

Grown in Gimblett Road, Hawke's Bay, this wine has shown great form from the 1994 and 1995 vintages. Splendid drinking now, seductively scented and soft, the '94 is a mouthfilling, intensely citrusy, rich-flavoured, mealy wine with loads of character. The '95 (*****) fermented and matured for 10 months in new French oak barriques, is very elegant, savoury, biscuity and concentrated; lower in alcohol than its non-Reserve stablemate but richer and much more complex. Already very appealing, it confirms the quality lift seen in the 1993 and (especially) 1994 vintages.

CLEARVIEW EST.	VINTAGE	96
BEACH-HEAD	WR	6
CHARDONNAY	DRINK	97-9

DRY $20 AV

☆☆☆☆

This tiny Hawkes' Bay winery, on the coast at Te Awanga, has a reputation for bold Chardonnays – and the 1996 vintage (****¹/₂) of its second-tier label is no exception. Grown in the neighbouring vineyard of Lionel and Pat Wilkins, it was 60 per cent fermented in predominantly American oak casks. The bouquet is rich, with strong oak and buttery "malo" aromas; the palate is fat (14 per cent alcohol), soft and awash with flavour. With its rich, very expressive fruit enhanced by complex oak, malo and lees-aging characters, this is a delicious mouthful.

CLEARVIEW EST.	VINTAGE	96	95	94	93	92	91
RESERVE	WR	6	6	6	6	6	5
CHARDONNAY	DRINK	98-01	99-01	98-00	97-9	97-8	P

DRY $29 AV

☆☆☆☆☆

For his premium Chardonnay label, Te Awanga winemaker Tim Turvey aims for a "big, grunty, upfront" style – and hits the target with ease. The '95 vintage is memorable, with a voluminous, complex bouquet, grand scale (a whopping 14.5 per cent alcohol) and richly concentrated, peachy-ripe flavours. Exciting stuff! The 1996 (*****), fully barrel-fermented and oak-aged for almost a year, is a hedonist's delight – even bigger than its Beach-Head stablemate (above) from '96. Still in its infancy, it is an arrestingly bold, intense, savoury, mealy, complex wine with layers of flavour and a tautness and freshness that promise great things in the cellar. A shame to broach it before mid-late 1998.

CLOUDY	VINTAGE	95	94	93	92	91	90
BAY	WR	5	6	5	6	6	6
CHARDONNAY	DRINK	99	99	98	98	P	P

DRY $32 AV

☆☆☆☆☆

A mouthfilling, muscular Marlborough wine with an arresting concentration of savoury, citric, mealy flavours, bold oak and alcohol, and a proven ability to mature well over the long haul. The 1994 vintage is a more overtly fruity style than usual, with rich, deliciously ripe, grapefruit-like flavours overlaid with oak and lees-aging complexity. The '95 (****) is a typically weighty style (13.5 per cent alcohol), with concentrated citrusy fruit and strong oak and mealy barrel-ferment characters adding richness and complexity. However, it lacks the authority of a top vintage, with flintier acidity than usual and slightly less ripe (apple/citrus) fruit flavours.

COLLARDS	VINTAGE	97	96	95
BLAKES MILL	WR	7	6	6
CHARDONNAY	DRINK	97-9	97-8	P

DRY $13 V+

(☆☆☆⯪)

A good drink-young style, Collards' "minimally" oaked Chardonnay is named after the old Blakes Mill settlement, now the site of the company's Rothesay Vineyard in West Auckland. The debut 1995 vintage exhibits a fresh, basket-of-fruit bouquet and crisp, very pure and appealing palate. The '96 (***¹/₂) is a fresh, crisp, vibrantly fruity wine, partly based on Auckland fruit. Ripe and bouyant, it's not complex but shows good flavour depth. It should develop with age, but why bother? It's already delicious.

COLLARDS HAWKE'S BAY CHARDONNAY

VINTAGE	97	96	95	94	93	92	91	90
WR	7	7	6	6	7	7	6	6
DRINK	98-00	97-9	97-8	P	P	P	P	P

DRY $18 AV

☆☆☆☆⟡

In past years positioned at the top end of Collards' range, but now in the middle, this is still a good wine (the word "Reserve" identifies the best vintages). The 1995 is more complex than its Marlborough stablemate of the same year, with fullness of body, quite good depth of peachy, lemony flavour, toasty oak and a rounded finish. Offering good drinking for 1998, the '96 vintage (***¹/₂) was predominantly barrique-fermented and lees-aged and 100 per cent oak-matured. It's a ripe, easy-drinking wine, gently wooded, with a touch of complexity and crisp, delicate, lively citrus/melon flavours of good depth.

COLLARDS MARLBOROUGH CHARDONNAY

VINTAGE	97	96	95	94	93	92	91	90
WR	7	6	5	7	6	6	7	6
DRINK	98-00	97-9	97-8	97-8	P	P	P	P

DRY $18 AV

☆☆☆☆⟡

This elegant, fruit-driven wine displays subtle barrel-fermentation and lees-aging characters and mouth-watering acidity. The word "Reserve" is added in top vintages. The relatively light-bodied '95 (11.5 per cent alcohol) is highly scented, with delicate apple/lemon flavours, very fresh and forward. The '96 (***¹/₂), labelled Reserve, is still a bit shy, but stylish, with good depth of ripe, citrusy, gently oaked, well-rounded flavour.

COLLARDS ROTHESAY VINEYARD CHARD

VINTAGE	97	96	95	94	93	92	91	90
WR	7	7	6	7	7	7	7	6
DRINK	98-01	97-9	97-8	97-8	P	P	P	P

DRY $28 AV

☆☆☆☆☆

A consistently top-flight wine grown in Bruce and Geoffrey Collard's Rothesay Vineyard at Waimauku, West Auckland. The 1995 vintage is a celebration of ripe fruit. It was barrel-fermented and lees-aged, but seems less oak-influenced than past vintages (as was the '94), with rich peach and melon-like fruit flavours shining through. Light yellow, it's a full-bodied style with a crisp, long finish, but lacks the power of a top vintage. The '96 (*****) brings a return to top form. Mouthfilling and fleshy, with ripe, vibrant fruit overlaid with mealy barrel-ferment characters, it displays lovely depth, balance and harmony. It's approachable now, but will richly reward keeping to mid 1998 onwards.

CONDERS BEND CHARDONNAY

DRY $19 AV

☆☆☆⟡

Craig Gass produced several vintages of soft, richly flavoured Marlborough wines in a very forward style, but lately sold his Conders Bend brand and stocks of maturing wine to Delegat's. The fully barrel-fermented '95 (***) has incisive, citrusy flavours mingled with nuances of riper, passionfruit-like characters, fleshed out with restrained oak, leading to a fresh, crisp finish.

COOKS WINEMAK.	VINTAGE	95	94	93	92	91	90	DRY $23 AV
RESERVE	WR	7	7	NM	7	7	7	
CHARDONNAY	DRINK	98-05	97-04	NM	97-00	97-00	97-9	☆☆☆☆

The 1995 vintage (***¹/₂) of Corbans' yellow-hued Hawke's Bay wine spent 10 months aging on its yeast lees in new American and French oak barriques – and it tastes like it. The bouquet is powerfully wooded; the palate bold, with soft, ripe, tropical fruit and grapefruit-like flavours slightly dominated by oak. Still fresh and lively, it's worth holding to mid 1998.

COOPERS CREEK	VINTAGE	97	96	95	94	93	92	91	90	DRY $16 V+
GISBORNE	WR		5	6	5	6	4	7	4	4	
CHARDONNAY	DRINK		97-8	97-00	97-8	97-8	P	P	P	P	☆☆☆⯪

If anyone knows how to make Chardonnay taste great at a year old, it's Kim Crawford, winemaker at Coopers Creek. The '96, oak-aged for three months, is very typical of the label – full and fresh, with good depth of ripe, citrusy flavour fleshed out with perfumed, sweet American oak. The '97 (***¹/₂) offers fresh, vibrant, citrusy, toasty flavours and a smooth not quite bone-dry finish.

COOPERS CREEK	VINTAGE	96	95	94	93	92	91	90	DRY $19 AV
HAWKE'S BAY	WR		6	5	6	6	7	5	6	
CHARDONNAY	DRINK		97-9	97-9	97-8	P	P	P	P	☆☆☆☆

Winemaker Kim Crawford says he prefers a "fruit-driven" style for his middle-tier Chardonnay label, which is planned to drink well at 18 months to two years old, but oak is always clearly in evidence. The 1996 vintage was matured in American oak casks, almost all new. Mouthfilling (13.5 per cent alcohol), with a very lifted, toasty bouquet, it's a delicious mouthful in its youth, fresh and vibrant, with strong, ripe citrus/melon flavours wrapped in biscuity oak. A high impact style, best in 1998. The '97 (****) is typically immaculate, with satisfyingly full body and excellent depth of fresh, crisp, deftly oaked, citrusy flavour.

COOPERS CREEK	VINTAGE	96	95	94	93	92	91	90	DRY $25 AV
SWAMP RESERVE	WR		6	6	6	NM	7	NM	5	
CHARDONNAY	DRINK		98-00	97-8	97-00	NM	97-8	NM	P	☆☆☆☆⯪

Based on the cream of the winery's Hawke's Bay Chardonnay crop, this wine is fermented and lees-aged in new and one-year-old French and American oak barriques. The light yellow '95 exhibits a lovely fragrance of ripe fruit and biscuity oak. Delicious in its youth, yet worth cellaring for at least a couple of years, it is very full on the palate, with rich, ripe, soft grapefruit/melon flavours and a slightly buttery finish. The 1996 vintage (****¹/₂) was grown in the Havelock North vineyard of Andrew and Cyndy Hendry. Oak-matured for a year, as the winery's top label it could use a tad more complexity, but still offers a seductive harmony of rich, citrusy fruit and balanced oak. A New World style, emphasising fresh, concentrated fruit.

CORBANS COTTAGE BLOCK GISBORNE CHARDONNAY

VINTAGE	95	94	93
WR		7	7	7
DRINK		97-02	97-00	97-9

DRY $29 AV

(☆☆☆☆☆)

This label shot to fame when the 1994 vintage swept all before it at the 1995 Air New Zealand Wine Awards. The debut 1993 vintage is notably rich and complex for a '93; the '94 has a voluptuous bouquet, with a powerful, firm, very stylish, complex and long palate. By any standards, the 1995 vintage (*****) is an exciting mouthful. Hand-picked then whole bunch-pressed, fermented with natural yeasts and matured for 10 months with weekly lees-stirring in new French oak puncheons, it's a striking wine with a ravishingly fragrant, rich and complex bouquet. The palate is robust, mealy and deep, with great concentration of sweet, ripe, grapefruit/lemon flavours, quality oak and a beautifully balanced, slightly buttery finish.

CORBANS COTTAGE BLOCK HB CHARDONNAY

VINTAGE	94	93
WR		7	6
DRINK		97-04	97-00

DRY $29 -V

(☆☆☆☆)

The label claims "exciting aging potential", but the debut 1993 vintage is starting to tire and is certainly ready now. More forward than its Marlborough stablemate of the same year, it is golden, with a honeyish, toasty bouquet, nutty, honied flavour with some mealy richness and a soft finish. The '94 (****½) is clearly superior. Yellow-hued, with a very toasty/buttery bouquet, it is robust and high-flavoured, with ripe peachy/figgy fruit, strong oak influence and good acid spine. A very powerful and savoury wine, with a lovely flavour spread. Great drinking from 1997 on.

CORBANS COTTAGE BLOCK MARL. CHARDONNAY

VINTAGE	94	93
WR		7	6
DRINK		97-03	97-00

DRY $29 -V

(☆☆☆☆)

A generous wine approaching its peak, the debut 1993 vintage was fully barrel-fermented and matured on its yeast lees for a year. Light yellow, it is full-bodied and rich-flavoured, toasty, limey and savoury, with good length and a crisp, flinty finish. The '94 (****½) is a classic cool-climate, rather Chablis-like wine. Pale lemon-green, with a very classy, lemony, appley, nutty fragrance, it is intense and still youthful, with incisive fruit flavours, subtle, creamy, mealy characters adding richness and complexity, and a lively, long finish. A classy wine, still ascending.

CORBANS EST. GISBORNE CHARDONNAY

DRY $12 V+

(☆☆☆)

Balanced for early-drinking appeal, the 1996 vintage (***) of this fruity wine was partly barrel-fermented, with six months aging in French and American oak. It's a fresh, ripe and buoyant wine with tropical/citrus flavours and a very smooth finish.

CORBANS PRIV.	VINTAGE	95	94	93	92
BIN GISBORNE	WR	7	7	7	7
CHARDONNAY	DRINK	97-00	97-00	97-8	P

DRY $22 V+

☆☆☆☆☆

One of Gisborne's greatest wines. The 1994 vintage is a richly fragrant, lush, flavour-packed beauty. The '95 (****) is less memorable than the '94, but still a delicious, vibrantly fruity wine of excellent depth. Fully barrel-fermented and matured for eight months in new and one year-old French oak, with 80 per cent "malo" influence, it is fragrant and full, with good fruit/oak balance and an abundance of fresh, ripe, grapefruit and melon-like flavour.

CORBANS PRIV.	VINTAGE	96	95	94	93	92	91	90
BIN MARL.	WR	7	6	7	NM	7	7	6
CHARDONNAY	DRINK	98-03	97-02	97-02	NM	97-00	97-9	P

DRY $23 V+

☆☆☆☆☆

At its best, a top-flight wine. Intensely flavoured and impressively complex, it also displays the steely, authoritative finish of Marlborough's top Chardonnays. Still very fresh and lively, the 1994 vintage spent 18 months in new and seasoned French oak barriques. Pale and robust, creamy, appley and mealy, it is a vigorous, cool-climate style with a long, taut flavour. The '95 (***1/2) a rather Chablis-like wine, is much less memorable than the '94, with appley, milky, strongly "malo"-influenced aromas, good depth of mealy, citrusy, slightly green-edged flavour and a freshly acidic finish.

CORBANS WHITE LABEL SELECTION CHARDONNAY/ CHENIN BLANC

DRY $9 V+

(☆☆)

The first 1995 vintage of Corbans' low-priced Chardonnay is a decent, no-fuss dry white with full body and straightforward, lemony, appley flavours, crisp and fresh. The '96 (**) is a pale blend of Gisborne and Hawke's Bay fruit, lees-aged in tanks and then oak-matured for three months. It's a plain quaffer – light, simple, green-edged and crisp.

COVELL	VINTAGE	92
ESTATE	WR	6
CHARDONNAY	DRINK	97-02

DRY $20 -V

(☆☆☆)

From Galatea in the eastern Bay of Plenty flows this rare Chardonnay. Still available, the 1992 vintage (***) was fermented and lees-aged for 2 1/2 years in new Nevers oak barriques. It's a slightly austere, but clean and flavoursome wine, still fresh, with a light yellow hue, buttery and citrusy bouquet, and lots of lemony, appley, leesy flavour, underpinned by spine-tingling acidity. Ready; no rush.

CROSS	VINTAGE	96	95	94	93	92	91	90
ROADS	WR	6	5	7	7	6	6	5
CHARDONNAY	DRINK	97-9	97-8	97-8	P	P	P	P

DRY $16 AV

☆☆☆

The 1994 vintage is a powerful wine: ripe, full-bodied and complex with creamy, citrusy flavours. The '95 (* – ***1/2) was grown in the Yates and Belvine vineyards, fully barrel-fermented and oak-aged for nine months. At an early tasting, I thought the wine to be complex and harmonious with fairly intense, citrusy, mealy flavours and a beguiling roundness. However, when tasted again early in 1997, I found it to be lacking freshness, and slightly dull on the nose and palate.

CROSS ROADS RESERVE HB CHARDONNAY

VINTAGE	95	94	93	92	91
WR	6	7	NM	6	6
DRINK	97-9	97-9	NM	P	P

DRY $25 -V

(☆☆☆⅓)

The 1994 vintage, the pick of Cross Roads' trio of '94 Chardonnays, is a stylish, slightly creamy wine with very good concentration of citrusy, figgy fruit flavours and a touch of mealy complexity. The '95 (***¹/₂) is on a distinctly lower plane. Grown in Dr David Yates' vineyard at Clive and fermented and lees-aged in new French oak barriques, it is a straw-hued, perfectly drinkable wine, full-bodied, crisp and slightly honied, with some complexity, but also (like the non-reserve wine from 1995) rather flat, lacking freshness and vigour.

DANIEL SCHUSTER BARREL FERM. MAR. CHARDONNAY

DRY $18 -V

(☆☆⅓)

With age, there are distinct *Botrytis*-derived honey characters emerging in the 1995 vintage (***¹/₂). It's a crisp, lemony wine with a touch of savoury, buttery complexity, but the fruit is slightly flat and tired; drink up. The 1995 is the last of this label.

DASHWOOD MARLBOROUGH CHARDONNAY

VINTAGE	96	95	94	93	92	91
WR	6	5	6	NM	4	6
DRINK	97-9	97-8	97-8	P	P	P

DRY $18 AV

☆☆☆⅓

Vavasour's second-tier Chardonnay is a drink-young style with fresh, vigorous fruit flavours and refreshing acidity. The 1996 vintage (***¹/₂) grown in the Awatere and Wairau valleys, was 30 per cent fermented in new French oak barriques, with malolactic fermentation; the rest was tank-fermented. It's a full-flavoured, well-spined wine, elegant and steely, with a fresh, citrusy, slightly mealy bouquet, incisive lemon/melon flavours with some complexity, and mouth-watering acidity.

DELEGAT'S HAWKE'S BAY CHARDONNAY

VINTAGE	96	95	94	93	92	91	90
WR	6	5	6	5	6	5	7
DRINK	97-9	97-8	P	P	P	P	P

DRY $15 V+

☆☆☆

This is Delegat's "commercial" Chardonnay. Here, winemaker Brent Marris wants "the fruit to do the talking", with wood relegated to an underlying role. The '95 is a lesser vintage – forward, with a touch of *Botrytis*-derived honey characters. However, 1996 (***¹/₂) sees the label in top form. Tank-fermented then oak-matured, with no "malo" influence, it is a softly flavoursome and weighty wine, ripe, citrusy, peachy and slightly buttery, offering very enjoyable, well-priced drinking from now onwards.

DELEGAT'S PROP. RESERVE CHARDONNAY

VINTAGE	96	95	94	93	92	91	90
WR	7	5	7	6	7	7	6
DRINK	97-00	97-9	97-9	P	P	P	P

DRY $25 V+

☆☆☆☆☆

Delegat's multiple gold medal-winning Chardonnay is a marriage of lush Hawke's Bay tropical-fruit flavours and barrel-ferment complexity. Half tank, half barrel-fermented, then oak matured on its yeast lees for nine months, the 1994 is a mouth-filling wine with exceptionally rich, ripe grapefruit-like flavours, quality oak handling and a long, creamy finish. (Served in early 1997 at Delegat's 50th birthday party, it looked slightly oak-dominated.) The light yellow '95 (****¹/₂) is less powerful and more forward than the '94, yet offers some of the lush, creamy richness typical of the label. A representative barrel sample of the 1996 suggested this will be a very stylish and concentrated vintage, robust, rich and savoury.

DE REDCLIFFE DEDICATION SERIES CHARD.			
VINTAGE	96	95	
WR	7	6	
DRINK	98	P	

DRY $29 -V

(☆☆☆☆)

The first 1995 vintage of De Redcliffe's top-tier, fully barrel-fermented Hawke's Bay Chardonnay is a lovely wine with good weight (13.5 per cent alcohol) and excellent concentration of very ripe passionfruit/melon flavours wrapped in strong, biscuity oak. The '96 (****) was matured for eight months on light yeast lees in fresh oak barriques (70 per cent new). Light yellow, it is a robust wine with a lightly fragrant, citrusy, mealy bouquet and rich, complex, long flavour.

DE REDCLIFFE LYONS ROAD CHARDONNAY			
VINTAGE	97	96	95
WR		6	NM 5
DRINK		97-8 NM	P

DRY $14 AV

(☆☆☆⟩)

The 1995 vintage (**¹/₂)is the first release of this wine, grown in De Redcliffe's estate vineyard at the end of Lyons Road, Mangatawhiri. It is a drink-young, simple style with light yellow colour and a slightly honied nose and palate. Rounded and ready.

DE REDCLIFFE MANGATAWHIRI CHARDONNAY		
VINTAGE	96	95
WR	7	6
DRINK	97-8	P

DRY $16 V+

☆☆☆⟩

Estate-grown in the Mangatawhiri Valley, at its best this sharply priced wine displays strong, lively grapefruit and buttery oak flavours, a touch of complexity and a long, tight finish. The delicious 1994 vintage is fragrant and mouthfilling, with rich fruit flavours, oak/lees complexity and impressive length. French oak-fermented and wood-matured for six months, the '95 (***) is less intense than its predecessor, with medium-full body and lemony, leesy, buttery flavour in a forward, easy-drinking style.

DRY RIVER CHARDONNAY							
VINTAGE	96	95	94	93	92	91	90
WR	7	7	7	6	7	6	7
DRINK	20-05	98-04	98-02	97-01	97-00	97-9	P

DRY $28 AV

☆☆☆☆☆

A robust Martinborough wine with bold alcohol, penetrating grapefruit-like fruit flavours, savoury oak and taut acidity. The 1995 vintage is a strapping wine (14 per cent alcohol) with fresh citrus/oak aromas and intense, mealy flavours, tight and controlled. The '96 (*****) was 100 per cent barrel-fermented in French oak, and matured on its lees with regular stirring (*batonnage*) for 10 months. An aristocratic wine in its youth, with impressive concentration, harmony and vigour, it's already highly drinkable but was not made with drink-young appeal in mind! Light yellow, with a deep, ripely citrusy, mealy, complex fragrance, it is a very intense, appetisingly crisp, tight and powerful wine, sure to deliver splendid drinking around 1999.

ESKDALE CHARDONNAY

DRY $25 -V
☆☆☆☆

Kim Salonius, Eskdale's Canadian-born winemaker, aims "to make wine a little differently". In the case of his Chardonnay, this involves maturing the wine for a full two years in wood. Fortunately, his Esk Valley, Hawke's Bay fruit has the richness to handle this extraordinarily long (by New Zealand standards) exposure to oak. The 1992 vintage (****) was released in early 1997 (and there is no '93). Light gold, with a mature, rather oxidative bouquet from its long sojourn in new French oak casks, the '92 is a fat, full-flavoured wine, lush, peachy, and now probably at the height of its powers.

ESK VALLEY HAWKE'S BAY CHARDONNAY

VINTAGE	97	96	95	94	93	92	91	90
WR	6	6	6	7	5	6	5	5
DRINK	97-00	97-00	97-8	97-9	97-8	P	P	P

DRY $16 V+
☆☆☆½

This is a typical, well-made Hawke's Bay Chardonnay. The 1995 vintage is full, with a fresh, buttery fragrance, appealingly creamy texture, a touch of complexity and good depth of well-ripened grapefruit and melon-like flavours. Satisfying drinking now, the '96 (****½) was 50 per cent barrel-fermented and 100 per cent barrel-aged. Pale lemon-green in hue, it is mouthfilling (13.5 per cent alcohol) and lively, with good depth of citrusy, slightly nutty flavours and a fresh, crisp, finely tuned finish.

ESK VALLEY RESERVE CHARDONNAY

VINTAGE	96	95	94	93	92	91	90
WR	7	7	7	NM	6	7	5
DRINK	98-00	97-02	97-02	NM	P	97-8	P

DRY $29 AV
☆☆☆☆☆

The most recent vintages of this Hawke's Bay label are the greatest. Grown at Meeanee and in Gimblett Road, the 1995 vintage is a notably weighty wine, crammed with flavour. Bright, light lemon-green in hue, it offers striking depth of ripe, citrus and tropical fruit flavours, very skilfully integrated wood and positive acidity. The '96 (*****) is a beauty! Grown in three Hawke's Bay vineyards, and fermented and matured for 10 months in oak (60 per cent new), with 35 per cent "malo" influence, it is a superbly fragrant wine, mingling nutty oak with ripe, peachy fruit aromas. The fresh, elegant palate is deliciously poised and persistent, with mouthfilling body, great delicacy and richness. Highly expressive already.

FAIRHALL DOWNS CHARDONNAY

VINTAGE	97	96
WR	6	4
DRINK	98-02	97-9

DRY $19 AV
(☆☆☆½)

The Fairhall Downs label belongs to Brancott Valley grapegrowers Ken and Jill Small, in partnership with their daughter, Julie, and son-in-law, Stuart Smith. The 1996 Chardonnay (***½), produced by Marlborough winemaker John Forrest, is a full, fresh, ripe-tasting wine with good depth of citrusy, slightly nutty flavour and a touch of mealy richness. A well-balanced wine with some class, for drinking now onwards.

FORREST	VINTAGE	96	95	94
ESTATE	WR		6	4	5
CHARDONNAY	DRINK	98+	P	P

DRY $19 AV

☆☆☆⯨

John Forrest favours a faintly oaked style of Chardonnay to keep the focus on pure, vibrant fruit flavours, but looks to very ripe Marlborough fruit and extended lees-aging to give his wine character. The 1995 vintage is full, fruity and fresh, with an abundance of vibrant, melon-like flavour offering highly enjoyable, although not complex, drinking. Hard to resist already, the '96 (****) is a vibrant, fruit-driven wine, with just a small proportion given a secondary malolactic fermentation in oak barrels. It's very juicy and appley, with a hint of "malo"-derived butterscotch characters, fullness of body and a delicate, balanced, lingering finish.

FOXES	VINTAGE	96	95	94	93	92
ISLAND	WR		7	NM	6	4	5
CHARDONNAY	DRINK	99-00+	NM	98-00	P	97-8

DRY $30 -V

☆☆☆☆⯨

This fleshy, rich-flavoured Marlborough Chardonnay is produced by John Belsham, part-owner and manager of Rapaura Vintners. The 1994 vintage was grown in three vineyards and 60 per cent barrel-fermented, with 40 per cent of the wine undergoing a softening malolactic fermentation. Approaching full maturity, this is a golden wine with a richly toasty bouquet. Soft, peachy and biscuity, it's a robust, high-flavoured, generous wine for drinking now. The '96 (*****) is a superb wine that should easily outperform the '94 in the cellar. Bright, light lemon-green in hue, it is a very youthful, richly fragrant wine in a bold (13.5 per cent alcohol), broad style with intense citrus/apple characters, a savoury, mealy complexity, a touch of butterscotch and a tight, complex, very long and powerful finish.

GIBBSTON VALLEY	VINTAGE	96	95
CENTRAL OTAGO	WR	6	6
CHARDONNAY	DRINK	97-00	97-00

DRY $25 -V

(☆☆☆☆)

The 1995 vintage, Gibbston Valley's first locally grown Chardonnay, is a very full-bodied (13.5 per cent alcohol) wine, peachy, ripe, complex and rounded in a rich-flavoured and forward style. The '96 (****) is very similar. Grown in two Central Otago vineyards and fermented and matured for a year in new French oak barriques, it is light yellow, with toasty oak aromas. It's a high-flavoured style with ripe grapefruit-like, slightly limey flavours, rich and complex, and a firm, crisp finish.

GIBBSTON VALLEY
GREENSTONE
CHARDONNAY

DRY $15 AV

(☆☆☆)

The debut 1996 vintage (***) of this Central Otago wine was made from "lesser fruit", says proprietor Alan Brady, and handled entirely in stainless steel tanks. It's still an enjoyable wine – fleshy, with a pleasing depth of peachy-ripe fruit flavour and fresh, well-balanced acidity. A good drink-young style.

GIESEN CANTERBURY CHARDONNAY

DRY $18 AV

(☆☆☆⯪)

With his standard Chardonnay, winemaker Marcel Giesen says he's "aiming for elegance rather than power". The 1996 vintage (***¹/₂) a blend of three vineyard sites and 60 per cent barrel-fermented, is an astutely balanced, quite full bodied Canterbury wine with a light straw hue, pleasing depth of citrusy fruit flavour wrapped in toasty oak and good acid spine. Fresh, savoury and flinty, with a cool-climate vigour, it is enjoyable now but should also mature well.

GIESEN RESERVE BURNHAM SCHOOL ROAD CHARDONNAY

DRY $30 -V

(☆☆☆☆)

Giesen deliberately hold back their top Chardonnays for a couple of years before release. Built for the long haul, the 1995 vintage (****) of this Canterbury wine is muscular (13.5 per cent alcohol), with a toasty, mealy bouquet. Yellow-hued, it offers strong, firm, peachy, citrusy flavours with wood/lees-aging richness and an invigoratingly crisp, lingering finish. Open 1998–99.

GIESEN RESERVE MARLBOROUGH CHARDONNAY

VINTAGE	94	93
WR	6	5
DRINK	97-00	97-9

DRY $30 -V

☆☆☆☆⯪

Drinking at its best right now, the 1993 vintage is a strapping, flavour-packed wine. Golden, with a richly toasty, slightly honied bouquet, it offers a delicious depth of citrusy, toasty, nutty flavour, complex, firm, lively and sustained. The '94 (*****) is a high impact wine that offers truly exciting drinking. Grown in the Isabel vineyard and fully barrel-fermented, it is light yellow hued, with a toasty, buttery fragrance, mouthfilling body and a powerful surge of mealy, nutty, peachy-ripe flavour, very rich, creamy and long.

GILLAN MARLBOROUGH CHARDONNAY

VINTAGE	96	95	94
WR	6	5	6
DRINK	97-00 P	97-8	

DRY $19 AV

(☆☆☆⯪)

The '95, grown in the Eastfields vineyard and 30 per cent oak-aged, was one of the more successful wines of the vintage. Currently drinking well, it is pale gold, with good weight and depth of ripe, citrusy, slightly honied, toasty flavour and a crisp, balanced finish. The 1996 vintage (***¹/₂) is full-bodied, with ripe tropical fruit flavours, integrated oak and fresh acidity in a moderately complex style with good depth. This is a very enjoyable, skilfully balanced wine for current enjoyment.

GLADSTONE CHARDONNAY

VINTAGE	96	95
WR	6	4
DRINK	97-8 P	

DRY $23 -V

(☆☆-☆☆☆☆☆)

This small Wairarapa winery's debut 1994 Chardonnay, grown in Jim Scotland's vineyard near Clive in Hawke's Bay, was reserved in its youth, with strong, savoury oak and restrained lemony, appley fruit flavours. The '95 vintage, grown in the same vineyard and matured for 11 months in half-new Burgundy oak barriques, is disappointing: dull on the nose, plain on the palate, with earthy flavours, crisp and short. The 1996 vintage (****) is the last of the line – and by far the best. A full, savoury wine, light yellow-hued, with strong, toasty oak aromas, it is rich and satisfying, peachy and mealy on the palate, with prominent oak and good acid backbone. A well-structured wine for 1998–99.

GLENMARK WEKA PLAINS CHARDONNAY

DRY $27 -V

☆☆☆

A North Canterbury Chardonnay, grown by John McCaskey and made by Kym Rayner, that is a distinctive, consistently satisfying wine, with subtle, lingering flavours. The 1994 vintage, based on hand-picked Weka Plains fruit, fermented and lees-aged in French oak, is light yellow, with a fragrant, citrusy, toasty bouquet. The palate is characterful, with harmonious, delicate fruit flavours, oak/lees complexity and a crisp, long finish. The '95 (***) was based on two rows of vines and handled in two barriques. Similar in style to the '94, it is a medium-bodied, mealy wine with ripe, slightly honied, peachy/citrusy fruit and sustained flavour.

GLOVER'S NELSON CHARDONNAY

DRY $15 AV

(☆☆☆)

The first 1996 vintage (***1/2) is a blend of fruit grown at Upper Moutere and on the Waimea Plains. It's designed as a drink-young style, and not matured in oak. The bouquet is shy; the palate slightly austere, with appley, lemony flavours, dry and flinty.

GOLDWATER ROSELAND MARL CHARDONNAY

DRY $24 -V

(☆☆☆☆)

Opened in 1997, the 1994 vintage (not labelled as Roseland) was bright yellow, with very powerful toasty oak on the nose and palate, bold alcohol (14 per cent) and lush, ripe fruit flavours. The '96 (***1/2) was grown in the Wairau Valley, French oak-fermented and lees-aged for 10 months. Still very fresh and youthful, it's a big wine (13.5 per cent alcohol) with ripe citrus/melon flavours and toasty oak, needing time to integrate; open 1998–99.

GROVE MILL ESTATE CHARDONNAY

DRY $15 AV

(☆☆☆)

The 1995 vintage of this "lightly oaked" Marlborough wine is a drink-young style, very soft and forward, with pleasant, appley, citrusy flavours, fresh and rounded.

GROVE MILL LANSDOWNE CHARDONNAY

VINTAGE	96	95	94	93	92	91	90
WR	6	NM	7	5	6	5	4
DRINK	98+	NM	98+	97-00	97+	97-9	P

DRY $29 -V

☆☆☆☆

This is typically a fatter, richer wine than its lower-priced "Marlborough" stablemate. The slightly austere '94 was partly barrel-fermented and then all wood-aged for almost two years. Light in colour, it's restrained on the nose, but offers good body and depth of tight, lemony, crisp flavour in a distinctly cool-climate style. The '96 (*****1/2) is much more attractive. A blend of the best vineyards and clones, and fermented and matured in French oak barriques for 14 months, it is a deep-scented wine with a bright, light lemon-green hue. The palate is weighty and sophisticated, with toasty oak fleshing out rich grapefruit characters, balanced acidity and a long finish. The most stylish Lansdowne Chardonnay yet.

GROVE MILL MARLBOROUGH CHARDONNAY	VINTAGE	96	95	94	93	92	91	90	DRY $19 AV
	WR		6	5	6	5	7	4	3	☆☆☆☆½
	DRINK	97-00 P	P	P	P	P	P		

Typically a lemony, skilfully balanced and flavourful wine with well-integrated oak, a hint of malolactic-derived butteriness and fresh, lively acidity. The 1995 vintage, a blend of Marlborough and Gisborne fruit, labelled New Zealand Chardonnay, is a rather charmless wine, clearly reflecting the poor year, with crisp, citrusy, slightly honied and hard flavours. The '96 (***1/2) is clearly superior. Partly fermented in French and American oak barriques, it is still unfolding, with delicate wood influence and good depth of fresh, ripe citrus/lime flavours in a crisp, elegant style.

GUNN ESTATE CHARDONNAY	VINTAGE	96	95	94	DRY $16 AV
	WR	5	5	4	(☆☆☆☆)
	DRINK	97-00	97-9	97-98	

The 1994 Chardonnay from Denis and Alan Gunn's vineyard in Ohiti Road, across the Ngaruroro River from Gimblett Road, was an exciting debut: a robust style with rich, well-rounded fig/melon flavours, delicious in its youth. The '95, oak-matured for five months, is on a lower plane: appley and crisp, but lacking the ripeness and richness of the '94. The '96 (***) was 50 per cent tank-fermented, with the rest fermented and matured for four months in one and two-year-old casks. It's a mouthfilling wine (13.5 per cent alcohol), not highly complex but offering good depth of crisp, ripe citrus/peach flavours.

GUNN ESTATE RESERVE CHARDONNAY	VINTAGE	96	95	94	DRY $25 AV
	WR	6	6	6	(☆☆☆☆☆½)
	DRINK	97-00	97-00	97-00	

The debut 1994 vintage of this Hawke's Bay wine is a mouthfilling style with a delicious array of fig/melon/oak flavours. The 1995 vintage (*****), picked at a very ripe 23.8° brix, and fermented and matured for 10 months in oak casks (half new), is far superior to its lower-tier stablemate from '95 (above). This richly expressive wine looked exciting a year ago, and it's maturing superbly. Grown in the Windburn vineyard in Ohiti Road, it is light gold and robust, with a lovely concentration of ripe tropical fruit and toasty oak flavours – rich, mealy, complex and downright delicious.

HAWKESBRIDGE SOPHIE'S VINEYARD CHARDONNAY			DRY $18 AV
			(☆☆☆☆½)

Grown at Mike and Judy Veal's Marlborough vineyard near Renwick, and made for them at a Nelson winery, the 1995 vintage (not labelled Sophie's Vineyard) is a robust (13.5 per cent alcohol) wine with light yellow colour, plenty of ripe, citrusy, peachy, buttery flavour and a fractionally coarse finish that no doubt reflects the difficult vintage. The much more attractive '96 (****) is a celebration of fresh, ripe fruit flavours, with "minimal" oak contact. Highly scented, with tropical fruit aromas in abundance, it displays excellent body and depth of lush, pure, pineapple and passionfruit-evoking flavours, with a crisp, finely balanced finish. Drink 1997–98.

HERON'S FLIGHT	VINTAGE	96	DRY $29 -V
BARRIQUE FERM.	WR	6	
CHARDONNAY	DRINK	97-9	(☆☆☆)

The 1996 vintage (****) of this Matakana Chardonnay is easily the finest white wine yet from Heron's Flight. Partly barrel-fermented, the '95 is a fresh, appley, moderately flavoursome wine with a touch of complexity. The '96 was fermented in new oak barriques, given a full malolactic fermentation and extended lees contact. It's a classy wine with good weight, strong, ripe, almost sweet-tasting citrus/melon fruit characters wrapped in toasty oak, firm acidity and a slightly buttery, rich, lingering finish.

HERON'S	VINTAGE	96	DRY $16 AV
FLIGHT	WR	5	
LA VOLÉE	DRINK	97-8	(☆☆☆)

With its clear bottle and see-through label, this is a smartly packaged wine, and the contents are good too. Launched from the 1996 vintage (***), it is a Matakana Chardonnay, tank-fermented and handled entirely without oak. Bright, light lemon-green in hue, with a clean, light bouquet, it is full-bodied, crisp and fresh, with vibrant grapefruit/apple flavours, a well-rounded finish and lots of drink-young appeal.

HIGHFIELD			DRY $26 AV
ELSTREE			
CHARDONNAY			(☆☆☆☆⯪)

Layers of sweet, ripe fruit and oak/lees-aging flavours characterise the voluptuous 1994 vintage, Highfield's first "reserve" Marlborough Chardonnay. Rich, citrusy and nutty, it reveals good weight, a lovely, soft, creamy texture and very impressive depth. The '96 (*****) is even more finely balanced and classy, its rich, mealy, grapefruit-like flavours very intense and tight.

HIGHFIELD	VINTAGE	96	95	94	93	92	91	90	DRY $20 AV
ESTATE	WR	6	5	6	5	5	5	5	
CHARDONNAY	DRINK	97-00+	97-00	97-00+	97-00+	97-00	P	P	☆☆☆⯪

The quality of this Marlborough wine has forged ahead in recent vintages. The barrel-fermented 1995 looked rich, savoury and complex in its youth, with a buttery, mealy bouquet, mouthfilling body, strong, vibrant melon/grapefruit flavours wrapped in nutty oak, and a long, well-rounded finish. The '96 (****) is still very youthful, with an attractive, buttery, mealy fragrance and strong, fresh grapefruit/oak flavours.

HUNTAWAY	VINTAGE	96	95	DRY $20 V+
RESERVE GISB.	WR	7	7	
CHARDONNAY	DRINK	97-02	97-00	(☆☆☆☆⯪)

Very seductive in its youth, the 1996 vintage (*****½) of Corbans' wine was fermented and lees-aged for 10 months in French and American oak casks, with 60 per cent of the final blend also undergoing a softening malolactic fermentation. Richly fragrant, with an outpouring of instantly appealing, ripe fruit and oak aromas, it is a weighty, lush wine crammed with deliciously ripe fruit wrapped in oak, leading to a long, rounded finish. Drink now to 1998.

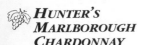

HUNTER'S	VINTAGE	95	94	93	92	91	90		DRY $24 V+
MARLBOROUGH	WR		4	5	5	4	6	5	☆☆☆☆☆
CHARDONNAY	DRINK		98	98	P	P	P	P	

"Obvious fruit" is what Jane Hunter and her winemaker, Gary Duke, pursue as the key ingredient in Hunter's Chardonnays. Finesse is the key attribute of this consistently immaculate wine, which places its accent on fresh, vibrant, searching, citrusy flavours, overlaid with subtle, mealy barrel-ferment characters. The wine is always a strong performer in the cellar. From a hard vintage in 1995 (****), Hunter's came up with a very stylish wine. Fermented and matured for eight months in French oak barriques (40 per cent new), it's pale lemon-green, with very fresh and pure, appley fruit flavours, subtle mealy characters and classic cool-climate delicacy and style.

JACKMAN	VINTAGE	96	95	94	MED/DRY $10 V+
RIDGE	WR	6	6	6	(☆☆)
CHARDONNAY	DRINK	97-8 P	P		

Montana's low-priced wine is a fresh, light, easy-drinking style that is typically medium-bodied, with restrained wood influence and moderate depth of crisp, citrusy flavours. Enjoy while young and frisky. The 1997 vintage is a slightly off-dry (6 grams/litre of sugar) blend of Hawke's Bay and Australian juice, with some exposure to American oak.

JACKSON	VINTAGE	96	DRY $19 AV
ESTATE	WR	5	☆☆☆☆⸾
CHARDONNAY	DRINK	97-9	

This Marlborough producer's Chardonnay can be excellent, although in the past it has been overshadowed by the breathtaking qualities of the renowned Sauvignon Blanc. Lovely already, the fully French oak-fermented 1996 vintage (****) is a very full-bodied (13.5 per cent alcohol) wine with a rich bouquet packed with the aromas of ripe fruit. The palate is creamy and soft, with a hint of "malo" influence and pure, cascading fruit flavours, deliciously ripe and long.

JACKSON EST.	VINTAGE	96	DRY $29 AV
CHARDONNAY	WR	6	(☆☆☆☆☆)
RESERVE	DRINK	99-02	

The debut 1994 vintage was based on the pick of the crop, fermented in oak barriques (70 per cent new) and given a total malolactic fermentation. Rich and ripe on the nose, it is very powerful, fat and savoury on the palate, with intense grapefruit, mealy, nutty flavours and a long, well-spined finish. The '96 (*****) was harvested in Marlborough at 23.5° brix, fully fermented in French oak barriques (70 per cent new) and given a full, softening malolactic fermentation. Still a baby, but very classy, it's very full-bodied, tight and savoury, with well-ripened passionfruit/lemon flavours, a hint of butterscotch and quality oak. Immaculate, complex, refined wine for cellaring.

JOHANNESHOF CELLARS CHARDONNAY	VINTAGE	96	95	94		DRY $21 -V
	WR	5	NM	4		
	DRINK		97-05	NM	97-02	(☆☆✫)

Lean, and likely to prove long-lived, the 1994 vintage (**½) of this Marlborough wine was fermented and matured for 16 months (a notably long period) in French oak casks. Pale, with fresh, limey, appley aromas and flavours, it is a slightly austere and steely style with a distinctly cool-climate feel.

KANUKA FOREST CHARDONNAY	VINTAGE	94	93		DRY $19 -V
	WR	7	6		
	DRINK	97-00	97-9		(☆☆)

Grown on the coast at Thornton, 15 km west of Whakatane, this is an exceedingly rare Bay of Plenty wine. Those vintages I have tasted (the debut 1993 and 1994) have been reasonably full-bodied and lemony, with some complexity, but also a pungent woodiness from fermentation and maturation for two years in new French oak casks, which can leave the wine out of balance and hard to enjoy.

KAWARAU ESTATE CHARDONNAY		DRY $15 AV
		(☆☆✫)

Designed as a lightly oaked "summer Chardonnay", the solid 1996 vintage (**½) from this fledgling Otago producer is based on Marlborough fruit. It's a very easy-drinking, medium-bodied wine, pale, with appley, lemony flavours, fresh and smooth.

KEMBLEFIELD CHARDONNAY	VINTAGE	95	94		DRY $19 AV
	WR	5	6		
	DRINK	97-8	97-8		(☆☆☆✫)

Opening out well with age, the 1994 vintage of this barrel-fermented, lees-aged Hawke's Bay wine is stylish and tight-structured, its strong, ripe, lemony fruit overlaid with nutty oak. The '95 (***½) fermented in French oak casks and aged "sur lie" for nine months, is also a rewarding wine in a crisp, elegant, fairly complex and flavoursome style.

KERR FARM KUMEU CHARDONNAY	VINTAGE	96	95		DRY $17 AV
	WR	6	5		
	DRINK	97-9	97-8		(☆☆☆)

Wendy and Jaison Kerr's vineyard is near the old Abel & Co winery in Kumeu. Their debut '95 Chardonnay, made on their behalf at a Henderson winery, is crisp and moderately ripe, with restrained wood influence and reasonable depth of lemony, slightly limey flavour. The 1996 (***½), of which 70 per cent of the final blend was fermented and matured for nine months in French and American oak casks, is more rewarding. Straw-coloured, it is a weighty wine with plenty of savoury, leesy, slightly creamy flavour in a forward, rounded style that offers characterful drinking from now onwards.

KIM CRAWFORD	VINTAGE	97	96	**DRY $25 AV**
TIETJEN GISB.	WR	6	6	
CHARDONNAY	DRINK	98-9	97-8	(☆ ☆☆☆☆)

The debut 1996 vintage (*****) from Coopers Creek winemaker, Kim Crawford, is Gisborne Chardonnay at its finest. It's a pale gold beauty with a classy, very rich, citrusy, buttery fragrance. The palate is intense and vibrant, with a beguiling depth of ripe citrus/melon flavours, overlaid with oak/lees characters. Notably weighty and rich, with layers of flavour, it offers truly delicious drinking now to 1998.

KIM CRAWFORD	VINTAGE	97	96	**DRY $17 V+**
UNOAKED MARL.	WR	7	6	
CHARDONNAY	DRINK	97-8 P		(☆ ☆☆☆)

The debut 1996 vintage (****) from Kim Crawford, winemaker at Coopers Creek, shows just how satisfying unwooded Chardonnay can be. Grown in the Omaka Valley, it's a big wine (13.5 per cent alcohol) with strong, fresh, appley, citrusy aromas. Mouthfilling and tangy, it's a crisp and lively wine with intense lemon/apple flavours and a slightly flinty finish. Drink now.

KINDALE	**MED/DRY $16 -V**
WILLOWBROOK	
CHARDONNAY	(☆ ☆☆)

Grown in the Omaka Valley, Marlborough, and matured for three months in French oak casks, the 1995 vintage (**¹/₂) is a pleasantly fruity but simple wine, its touch of sweetness balanced by fresh, lively acidity. There is no '96.

KUMEU RIVER	VINTAGE	96	95	94	93	92	91	90	**DRY $32 AV**
KUMEU	WR	7	5	7	7	6	7	4	
CHARDONNAY	DRINK	00-01	97-8	97-00	97-9	P	P	P	☆☆☆☆☆

One of the most celebrated Chardonnays in the land, this is typically a superbly constructed, power-packed West Auckland wine with a bold, nutty, taut palate of compelling length. The '95 is lighter, less ripe and lush than usual – true to style, savoury and oatmealy, but lacking its customary concentration, likely to peak early and clearly overshadowed by its Mate's Vineyard stablemate. The 1996 vintage (*****) was made from the Mendoza clone grown at five vineyard sites around Kumeu, and fermented and matured for 11 months in French oak barriques (25 per cent new). It's a tighter, finer wine in its youth than past vintages, with a less obvious "malo" influence, yet slightly more forward than the '96 Mate's Vineyard. Richly fragrant, savoury and complex, with good acidity, quality oak and long, delicate, grapefruit-like flavours, it's still a baby, well worth keeping to at least 1999.

KUMEU RIVER	VINTAGE	96	95	94	93	**DRY $38 -V**
MATE'S VINEYARD	WR	7	6	7	7	
KUMEU CHARD.	DRINK	00-02	97-9	97-00	P	☆ ☆☆☆☆

This extremely classy single-vineyard wine is Kumeu River's flagship – as the high price indicates. It is made entirely from vines planted in 1990 on the site of the original Kumeu River vineyard purchased by Mate Brajkovich in 1944. The '95, tasted side-by-side with its

Kumeu stablemate (above) is clearly superior, with richer, sweeter-tasting, more intense fruit. The 1996 vintage (*****), given more new oak than the Kumeu label, is again a superb wine, noticeably bigger in the mouth than its '96 Kumeu stablemate. The bouquet is lush, with rich, ripe fruit aromas; the palate very delicate, with sweet, concentrated grapefruit flavours and biscuity wood, still very youthful. Open 1999 onwards.

LANGDALE ESTATE CHARDONNAY

`DRY $22 -V`

(☆ ☆☆)

The 1995 vintage is fresh, very crisp and lightly oaked, with appealing lemon/apple flavours to the fore and a sliver of sweetness. The '96 (***½) was estate-grown at West Melton in Canterbury and fermented and matured in American and French oak barriques. Fully dry, it is a reasonably flavoursome wine but lacks any real fruit character, with crisp acidity and strong, cheesey, "malo"-influenced aromas and flavours.

LAWSON'S DRY HILLS MARL CHARDONNAY

VINTAGE	96	95	94
WR	6	6	6
DRINK	97-04	97-04	97-04

`DRY $22 V+`

☆ ☆☆☆ ☆

Typically an impressively ripe, robust, richly flavoured wine. The '95 is mouthfilling, with strong grapefruit/peach flavours, toasty oak and taut acidity. By 1998, the 1996 vintage (*****) should be stunning! A powerful, very ripe-flavoured wine (harvested at 24° brix), it was 70 per cent fermented and matured for nine months in French oak casks. The bouquet is enticing, with deep tropical fruit and oak aromas; the palate is mouthfilling, rich, complex, toasty, firmly structured and very persistent. Already immensely drinkable, it will richly repay cellaring.

LINCOLN GISBORNE CHARDONNAY

VINTAGE	96
WR	4
DRINK	97-00

`DRY $13 AV`

(☆☆)

This budget-priced label was launched from the 1993 vintage, superseding the East Coast Chardonnay. The pale '95, a fruit-driven style matured briefly in seasoned American and French oak casks, is citrusy, nutty and crisp, but relatively unripe-tasting and plain, and now past its best. The 1996 vintage (**) was matured for a couple of months in two to three-year-old casks. It's a pale wine, solid but unexciting, with quite high acidity, moderate flavour depth and a short finish.

LINCOLN PARKLANDS CHARDONNAY

VINTAGE	96
WR	5
DRINK	97-03

`DRY $18 AV`

☆ ☆☆

Soft creaminess of texture is a feature of this easy-drinking wine, grown at Chris Parker's Gisborne vineyard. The 1994 vintage was deliciously fruity in a very full-flavoured, nutty, forward style. Maturing solidly, the 1995 vintage is not highly fragrant, but offers plenty of flavour. American oak-aged for three months, it's full, crisp, citrusy and tight, with a touch of complexity. The '96 (***½) is again less lush and enticing in its youth than some of the earlier vintages, but still very solid, with plenty of body and soft, peachy, toasty flavour.

LINCOLN VINTAGE	VINTAGE	95				DRY $22 -V
SELECTION	WR	6				
CHARDONNAY	DRINK	97-05				☆ ☆–☆ ☆ ☆ ☆

The first 1992 vintage of this flagship wine remains Lincoln's finest Chardonnay to date – intense, delicate, buttery, long. The '93 was a worthy follow-up, but the '94 is slightly dull, lacking freshness and vigour, and very disappointing at its high price. The 1995 vintage (***¹/₂) lacks the upfront, delicious appeal of the '92, but is very clean, savoury and tight; a mealy, complex wine with definite cellaring potential.

LINDEN ESTATE	VINTAGE	96	95	94	93	92	DRY $18 AV
HAWKE'S BAY	WR	5	5	6	5	6	
CHARDONNAY	DRINK	97-9	97-8	97-8	P	P	(☆ ☆☆)

The big, full-flavoured 1996 vintage (***¹/₂) was grown in the Esk Valley and 70 per cent matured for eight months in American oak casks. Light yellow in hue, it's a strongly wooded style with an abundance of ripe, citrusy, crisp, slightly buttery flavour, capable of maturing well.

LINDEN ESTATE	VINTAGE	95	DRY $26 -V
RESERVE	WR	6	
CHARDONNAY	DRINK	97-00	(☆ ☆☆☆)

The first 1995 vintage (****) of this Esk Valley, Hawke's Bay wine was given full barrel and malolactic fermentation. The fragrant, nutty aromas lead into a fleshy, complex palate with peachy-ripe, soft, sustained flavours. An impressively robust and characterful wine on the rise, well worth cellaring.

LINTZ	VINTAGE	96	95	94	93	92	DRY $25 -V
ESTATE	WR	7	6	6	5	4	
CHARDONNAY	DRINK	99-01	98-00	97-8	P	P	(☆ ☆☆☆)

The 1996 vintage (*****¹/₂) of this Martinborough Chardonnay is the most impressive yet. Light yellow, with a savoury bouquet, it's a big, robust wine with generous peach/melon flavours, complex, mealy and rounded.

LINTZ ESTATE	DRY $15 AV
CHARDONNAY	
ESTATE CUVEÉ	(☆ ☆☆)

Chris Lintz's junior Martinborough Chardonnay was launched from the 1996 vintage (***). It's a full, rounded, slightly savoury wine with fresh wood evident on the nose and palate and quite good flavour depth. Decent drinking for 1997–98, and fairly priced.

	DRY $15 AV
LOMBARDI	
CHARDONNAY	(☆ ☆☆)

The 1996 vintage (***) of this Hawke's Bay wine was French and American oak-aged for 10 months. It's an enjoyable drink-young or cellaring proposition, fresh, crisp and lively, with good depth of citrusy, slightly buttery flavour, clean, well balanced and lightly seasoned with wood.

LONGBUSH GISBORNE CHARDONNAY

DRY $18 AV

☆ ☆☆

The 1994 vintage was dull, but the '95 is a characterful Gisborne wine, full-bodied, with plenty of ripe, citrusy, oaky, slightly buttery flavour and a softening finish. The '96 vintage (***) was 50 per cent handled in tanks, with the rest fermented and matured in French oak casks (one-half new). It's a very easy-drinking although not complex wine, with an attractive fullness of body and ripe, rounded flavour.

LONGBUSH WOODLANDS RESERVE CHARDONNAY

DRY $24 AV

(☆ ☆☆ ☆)

The flagship Chardonnay from the Longbush winery in Gisborne. The 1995 vintage is a mouthfilling, citrusy, slightly nutty wine with a touch of complexity and a crisp, slightly buttery finish. The '96 (****¹/₂) is the winery's finest Chardonnay yet. Light gold in hue, with a rich, buttery, oaky bouquet, it was fermented in half-new French oak barriques. It rolls effortlessly across the palate, with impressive weight, a soft, creamy texture and delicious depth of ripe, peachy, toasty flavour. Ready, but no rush.

LONGRIDGE OF HAWKE'S BAY CHARDONNAY

VINTAGE	96	95	94	93	92	91	90
WR	7	7	7	6	6	5	5
DRINK	98-02	97-00	97-00	97-00	97-8	97-8	97-8

DRY $16 V+

☆☆☆☆ ⌐

A sound Hawke's Bay wine with a touch of quality, priced right. Produced by Corbans, the wine features fresh citrus-lemon fruit characters and a delicate oak underlay. The rich, citrusy, slightly nutty fragrance of the '95 is inviting; so is the flavoursome palate. This is a smartly made wine, with fresh, ripe fruit, sweet oak, impressive delicacy of flavour and a moderately crisp finish. The 1996 vintage (***¹/₂) is instantly likeable. Fermented and matured for 10 months in French and American oak barrels, it is a finely balanced wine with good body, vibrant fruit, fresh oak and pleasing depth of ripe, crisp citrus/melon flavours. It should perform well in the cellar, but why bother? It's already delicious.

LONGVIEW CHARDONNAY

DRY $16 AV

(☆☆☆)

The 1994 vintage of this Northland wine, grown just south of Whangarei, showed good depth of citrusy/oaky flavour but a slightly hard finish. The '93, a more elegant, impressively fragrant, delicate and rich-flavoured wine, proved what can be done. The 1996 (**¹/₂) lacks fragrance and is currently fairly closed, with fullness of body and reasonable depth of peachy, lemony flavour. A solid but so far rather ungiving wine that may unfold with age; open 1998.

MANUKA HILL CHARDONNAY

DRY $11 AV

(☆☆)

Produced by Lincoln Vineyards for supermarkets, the 1995 vintage (**) is a briefly oak-aged Gisborne wine. It's a simple, fruit-driven style, lacking any real varietal character, with lemony, slightly hard flavours. OK as a dry white quaffer, but no match for similarly priced wines like Montana Gisborne Chardonnay.

MARGRAIN VIN. MARTINBOR. CHARDONNAY

VINTAGE	95
WR	6
DRINK	97-00

DRY $26 AV

(☆☆☆☆⭒)

The debut 1995 vintage (****½) shows very sophisticated winemaking. Fermented and matured in oak for 16 months, it is a deftly balanced, richly flavoured wine. Light yellow, with impressive body (13.5 per cent alcohol), it reveals a lovely depth of ripe, citrusy, nutty, mealy flavour, a slightly creamy texture and a long, firm finish. A top-flight debut, for drinking now onwards.

MARK RATTRAY VINEYARDS WAIPARA CHARD.

VINTAGE	96	95	94	93
WR	6	5	5	6
DRINK	99-01	98-00	97-9	97-9

DRY $20 AV

(☆☆☆⭒)

The beautiful, Burgundian-style label is very enticing. The '95 is a cool-climate style of Chardonnay, medium-bodied, with appley, flinty flavours. It lacks great richness, but should reward cellaring for a couple of years. The 1996 vintage (***½), oak-aged for nine months, is an elegant wine, not highly concentrated, but full-bodied (13.5 per cent alcohol) and offering quite good depth of appley, citrusy, mealy flavour.

MARTINBOROUGH VINEYARD CHARDONNAY

VINTAGE	96	95	94	93	92	91	90
WR	7	6	7	6	5	7	5
DRINK	00	98+	98+	97+	P	P	P

DRY $26 AV

☆☆☆☆☆

Typically a mouthfilling, peachy/oaky Martinborough wine with concentrated fruit flavours, bold alcohol, and a long, savoury finish. The '95 is very classy, with a long, controlled, finely balanced palate revealing intense, ripe, grapefruit-like flavours, mealy, soft, subtle and very sustained. The '96 (*****) is a very elegant wine boasting sweet, ripe fruit flavours, good acid spine and well-integrated oak. It is a finely structured wine, built to last, open 1999+.

MATAWHERO CHARDONNAY

DRY $27 -V

☆–☆☆☆☆

The quality of this Gisborne label has inconsistently matched its high price. At its best, the wine is rewardingly robust, complex and rich-flavoured, but some vintages have looked tired and dull. Denis Irwin's fermentation with natural yeasts and full use of malolactic fermentation gives a softer, less fragrant style than is the norm with Gisborne Chardonnay. The 1990 vintage (****) is the best of recent releases – full, fresh, weighty and savoury. The '91 has a rather oxidative, non-aromatic bouquet, but is robust, with plenty of figgy, mealy flavour. The '93 (***½) is better – full, fresh, figgy, savoury and soft. The Matawhero style is distinctive, but it's not for the Roseworthy College-trained winemaking purists.

MATAWHERO ESTATE CHARDONNAY

DRY $17 AV

(☆☆☆)

This Gisborne winery's "house" Chardonnay is made in a soft, ripe, mouthfilling style that offers enjoyable, smooth drinking. The 1994 vintage (***), fermented with natural yeasts and given a softening malolactic fermentation, is light gold and gutsy, with ripe, peachy flavour, rounded and ready.

MATUA ARARIMU CHARDONNAY

VINTAGE	94	93	92	91
WR	6	7	6	7
DRINK	00+	00+	97-8	97-8

DRY $25 AV

☆☆☆☆☆

If you like fleshy, bold-flavoured, upfront Chardonnays, you'll adore this wine. Grown in the Judd vineyard at Gisborne, barrique-fermented and aged for 10 months, the 1994 vintage (****¹/₂) was a taste sensation in its youth – a fat, very mouthfilling style with a delicious depth of flavour showcasing intense, citrusy fruit, deftly overlaid with oak/lees characters. At over three years old, it generates less excitement, but is still highly enjoyable, with plenty of flavour and a softening finish. The 1996 vintage was estate-grown at Waimauku (like the '93) and given a full, softening malolactic fermentation. Tasted as a barrel sample, it was a relatively refined and restrained Ararimu; an elegant, citrusy, savoury, tight, full-flavoured wine, full of promise.

MATUA EASTERN BAYS CHARDONNAY

VINTAGE	96
WR	7
DRINK	97-00+

DRY $14 V+

(☆☆☆)

Looking for a modestly priced Chardonnay with a real touch of class? Here it is! A blend of Gisborne and Hawke's Bay fruit, matured for six to eight months in seasoned oak barrels, the 1996 vintage (****) is a full, generous wine with rich, concentrated tropical fruit flavours, deft wood handling and an overall depth and refinement that makes it a "steal" at $14.

MATUA JUDD ESTATE CHARDONNAY

VINTAGE	96	95	94	93	92	91	90
WR	6	5	7	6	7	6	6
DRINK	98-00+	97-8	97-00+	P	P	P	P

DRY $20 AV

☆☆☆☆

Based on fruit grown in the Gisborne vineyard owned by Maurice Judd and Matua, this is typically a full-bodied wine, deliciously fruity and soft, with a touch of complexity. The 1994 vintage, the best yet, is a very elegant wine, soft and seductive; the '95 slightly lacks the richness of the '94, but is still an attractive and full-flavoured wine. The '96 (****) was fermented and lees-aged for eight months in new and seasoned oak casks. A harmony of soft, citrusy fruit and nutty wood flavours, it is slightly less fragrant, ripe-tasting and lush than the '94, but a complex wine, already quite developed.

MATUA UNWOODED CHARDONNAY

VINTAGE	96
WR	6
DRINK	97-00+

DRY $14 V+

(☆☆☆⯪)

One of the best unoaked Chardonnays around, the seductive 1996 vintage (***¹/₂) is a 50/50 blend of Auckland and Hawke's Bay grapes. It's fresh, fruity and ripe, with very delicate melon/citrus flavours in a buoyant, moderately crisp style that offers enjoyable drinking right now.

MELNESS CHARDONNAY

DRY $18 AV

(☆ ☆☆)

The 1995 Chardonnay (**¹/₂) from this small Canterbury winery is light gold, with a slightly honied nose and palate. Based entirely on Canterbury fruit and barrel-fermented, it is weighty and full-flavoured, but clearly overshadowed by the 1996 vintage (****), blended from Canterbury and Marlborough grapes. The '96 is a big, rather Burgundian wine, pale straw, with a very inviting, mealy, nutty fragrance. It's a complex, broad, subtle wine, with excellent flavour depth and good acid spine, best opened 1998–99.

MILL ROAD CHARDONNAY

VINTAGE	96	95
WR	6	5
DRINK	97-8	P

DRY $14 AV

(☆ ☆☆)

The 1995 vintage of Morton Estate's bottom-tier, non-wooded Hawke's Bay Chardonnay is fresh and lively, with ripe, lemony fruit in an uncomplicated style with reasonable flavour depth. The '96 (**¹/₂) is very similar – pale yellow, with plenty of body and ripe, citrusy flavour in a no-fuss style.

MILLS REEF ELSPETH CHARDONNAY

VINTAGE	96	95	94	93	92	91
WR	7	7	7	NM	7	7
DRINK	98-02	97-00	97-9	NM	97-8	97-00

DRY $29 AV

☆☆☆☆☆

Mills Reef's flagship Chardonnay, named in honour of proprietor and winemaker Paddy Preston's mother, is consistently outstanding. The 1994 vintage is strikingly rich and succulent, and still maturing. The very elegant and concentrated '95 was grown in Hawke's Bay and fermented in new French oak barriques. Light straw in colour, with fragrant, toasty oak on the nose, it's a powerful wine, mouthfilling, with searching, ripe, citrusy flavours, quality oak and a creamy-soft, persistent finish. The '96 (*****) is an opulent wine, dangerously drinkable now, but too good not to keep. Light lemon/green, it is richly fragrant, full-bodied and very refined, with ripe, intense, sweet-tasting fruit, savoury oak and a lovely overall balance. A top vintage.

MILLS REEF MOFFAT ROAD SEL. CHARD.

VINTAGE	96	95	94
WR	6	6	5
DRINK	97-9	97-8	P

DRY $13 V+

(☆ ☆☆)

Mills Reef's bottom-tier Chardonnay (formerly called Mere Road). The 1995 vintage is a bargain: a powerful, flavour-packed Hawke's Bay wine, fleshy, with a "malo"-induced softness, strong, figgy, appley fruit flavours and depth right through the palate. The '96 (***) was 60 per cent oak-aged, and 20 per cent of the final blend was given a softening malolactic fermentation. It's a fragrant, soft, peachy, buttery wine, immediately appealing, with a touch of complexity, offering good flavour depth and character for its low price.

MILLS REEF RESERVE CHARDONNAY

VINTAGE	96	95	94
WR	7	7	7
DRINK	97-01	97-00	97-9

DRY $20 AV

(☆☆☆☆)

Mills Reef's middle-tier Chardonnay. A pleasure to drink now, the 1995 vintage of this Hawke's Bay wine is light yellow, with toasty oak aromas, fullness of body and good depth of ripe, lemony, buttery flavour, harmonious and well-rounded. The '96 (****) also looks great in its youth. Pale yellow, with a lifted, complex bouquet, it possesses loads of fresh, ripe, citrusy, nutty flavour, complexity and a crisp, persistent finish. Already delicious.

MILLTON VINE., THE, CHARD. BARREL FERM.

VINTAGE	96	95	94	93	92	91	90
WR	6	5	7	6	7	5	6
DRINK	97-00	97-8	97-00	97-8	97-8	P	P

DRY $27 -V

☆☆☆☆½

This is Millton's best-known Gisborne Chardonnay, typically a fat, full-flavoured wine, hand-picked and French oak-fermented, with good depth and a buttery-soft, lingering finish. The '95 is oatmealy and complex, a less lushly fruity style than usual, with a malolactic fermentation-derived roundness and butteriness. The 1996 vintage (****½) is one of the best yet. Fermented in oak barrels (15 per cent new), it has a rather Burgundian richness, mealiness and roundness, with very impressive flavour depth. Light gold, with a peachy, toasty fragance, it is a fat, savoury, complex wine with a tight finish, offering deeply satisfying drinking from now onwards.

MILLTON VINE., THE, ESTATE CHARDONNAY

DRY $16 AV

(☆☆☆)

This lightly oaked Gisborne wine is a very easy-drinking, drink-young style with its accent squarely on ripe, citrusy fruit flavours. Organically grown, with about 20 per cent of the final blend handled in American oak barrels, it is typically a fresh, ripely fruity wine with lemony flavours and well-balanced acidity: a generous, full-flavoured wine in a straightforward style.

MISSION HAWKE'S BAY CHARDONNAY

VINTAGE	96	95	94	93	92	91	90
WR	5	5	5	4	5	6	5
DRINK	97-9	P	97-8	P	P	P	P

DRY $13 V+

☆☆☆

Mission's lower-priced Chardonnay offers typical Hawke's Bay citric-fruit flavours and light wood handling. Solid, sometimes plain in the past, it has shown distinct signs of improvement in recent vintages. The '95 is deliciously well-balanced, its ripe, melon-like fruit characters, slightly creamy mouthfeel and zesty acidity all in harmony, with a persistent finish. The '96 (***) was 40 per cent barrel-fermented and oak-aged for six months, with 60 per cent of the final blend handled in tanks. It's a full-flavoured, forward wine with a citrusy, slightly toasty bouquet and flavour, ripe fruit characters, a touch of complexity and a buttery, rounded finish. Fine value.

MISSION JEWELSTONE CHARDONNAY	VINTAGE	95	94	93	92
	WR	6	7	NM	6
	DRINK	97-00	97-00	NM	P

DRY $26 AV

(☆ ☆☆☆☆⅓)

Mission's top-tier label has recently emerged as one of Hawke's Bay's top Chardonnays. The 1994 is an exceptional, very stylish and mouthfilling wine with a delicious, creamy texture. The '95, grown in the Chanel vineyard adjacent to the winery, was matured for eight months in oak (35 per cent new), with regular lees-stirring, and 75 per cent of the wine also underwent a softening malolactic fermentation. Pale, with appley, buttery aromas, it is slightly more restrained, less lush than previous vintages, but maturing well, offering nutty, complex flavours, creamy oak influence and a firm, well-structured, steely finish. The '96 (****¹/₂) was fermented in French oak casks (50 per cent new) and wood-matured for seven months. A tight, elegant wine, full-bodied, with elegant, savoury, citrusy, oaky flavours and a lingering finish, it should age extremely well.

MONTANA GISBORNE CHARDONNAY	VINTAGE	97	96	95	94	93	92	91	90
	WR	5	7	7	7	6	5	6	6
	DRINK	97-9	97-9	97-8	97-8	P	P	P	P

DRY $12 V+

☆ ☆☆

New Zealand's biggest-selling Chardonnay. If you haven't tried this long-popular wine lately, don't miss the '96 – it's an unexpectedly good wine for its highly affordable price. Vibrantly fruity, it's a full, ripe-tasting wine with good weight and flavour depth, with a touch of oak (5 per cent was matured in new American and French barrels) adding richness and a well-rounded finish. The '97 (***) is already delicious, with good weight and light oak adding interest to its fresh, crisp tropical flavours.

MONTANA MARLBOROUGH CHARDONNAY	VINTAGE	96	95	94	93	92	91	90
	WR	6	5	7	5	6	7	6
	DRINK	98-00	97-9	97-9	P	P	P	P

DRY $15 V+

☆ ☆☆☆⅓

Displaying much more assertive oak character than Montana's huge-selling Gisborne Chardonnay (above), this is a beguilingly easy-to-drink wine. The 1995 vintage is a nutty, mealy wine, slightly less powerful than the highly acclaimed (but over-oaked) '94, but offering attractive, figgy, grapefruit-like flavours, complex and buttery-soft. The '96 (***¹/₂) is a vigorous cool-climate style, French and American oak-aged. The bouquet is oaky; the palate full and fresh, with good depth of ripe fruit flavours, pronounced toffee-like "malo" characters and firm underlying acidity. It's very much a style wine, strongly influenced by sweet oak and malolactic fermentation, and probably at its best in its youth.

MONTANA ORMOND EST. CHARDONNAY	VINTAGE	95	94	93	92	91	90
	WR	6	7	6	7	NM	7
	DRINK	97-00	97-00	P	P	NM	P

DRY $27 -V

☆ ☆☆☆☆⅓

Montana's flagship Gisborne Chardonnay. Recommended for cellaring "up to ten years", the '94 is a classy wine. Fresh, exotic fruit aromas light up the bouquet of this very ripe-tasting, toasty and complex wine. Fleshy and savoury, with soft, tropical-fruit characters shining through and a long, silky finish, it offers highly seductive drinking from now onwards. The bright yellow 1995 vintage (*****¹/₂), fermented in French oak barriques (60 per cent new), is a big, fat, creamy-rich marriage of strong, well-ripened, citrusy fruit flavours and toasty oak, with a long, soft finish.

MONTANA RENWICK EST. CHARDONNAY	VINTAGE	95	94	93	92	91	90	DRY $26 -V
	WR	5	6	6	NM	6	6	☆☆☆☆
	DRINK	97-00	97-9	P	NM	P	P	

The 1994 vintage of Montana's premier South Island Chardonnay is a stylish wine, weighty, complex and aging well, with creamy, mealy, malolactic and barrel fermentation characters fleshing out fresh, rich fruit. The '95 (***1/2), a pale, rather Chablis-like wine, was fermented in French oak casks (60 per cent new). Fresh, crisp and appley, with yeast/oak characters filling out the palate, it's a moderately complex wine, nutty and flinty, quite flavoursome but not highly concentrated.

MONTANA RES. BARRIQUE FERM. CHARDONNAY	VINTAGE	96	DRY $18 AV
	WR	7	(☆☆☆☆)
	DRINK	97-02	

The debut 1996 vintage (****) was made "from the best of our new Marlborough vineyards, with small crops of ripe fruit," says chief winemaker Jeff Clarke. French and American oak-aged, it's a more stylish, intensely fruity wine than its Montana Marlborough Chardonnay stablemate of the same vintage. A pale, elegant wine with rich citrusy fruit characters and a creamy mouthfeel, it's still very fresh and youthful, but potentially quite complex.

MORTON EST. BLACK LABEL CHARDONNAY	VINTAGE	96	95	94	93	92	91	90	DRY $33 AV
	WR	6	6	6	5	5	7	5	☆☆☆☆☆
	DRINK	97-02	97-00	97-8	P	P	97-8	P	

Grown at the company's cool, slightly elevated Riverview Vineyard in Hawke's Bay, this is an increasingly refined and classy Chardonnay. I can't think of a '95 New Zealand Chardonnay I'd rather drink than this beauty. Fermented and matured for 14 months in new French oak barriques, it's a bright yellow-green, richly fragrant wine – vibrant, complex and very long on the palate. With its mouthfilling body, searching, ripe tropical/citrus flavours and slightly creamy texture, this is an extremely classy wine for drinking over the next couple of years. The '96 (*****) was French oak-fermented, with 20 per cent malolactic fermentation. Light yellow, it has a deep, rich bouquet and mouthfilling, intensely fruity palate, with rich citrus fruit characters, savoury oak and good acid spine. The '96 has yet to unfold, but everything looks in place for another classic.

MORTON EST. WHITE LABEL H.B. CHARD.	VINTAGE	96	95	94	93	92	91	90	DRY $17 V+
	WR	6	6	7	4	5	6	5	☆☆☆☆
	DRINK	97-00	97-00	97-00	P	P	P	P	

Based on Riverview Vineyard, Hawke's Bay fruit, this is typically a rich wine with strong, ripe fruit and biscuity wood flavours. Although less fragrant and deep-flavoured than the remarkable '94, the '95 is still an enjoyable wine with good weight, delicate, citrusy, nutty flavours and a crisp, slightly creamy finish. The 1996 vintage (***1/2) doesn't match the '94, but is clearly superior to the '95. French oak-fermented and wood-matured for nine months, it's a light yellow wine with a clean, light fragrance. The palate is smooth (65 per cent malolactic fermentation), with good depth of ripe, lemony flavour, restrained wood influence and balanced acidity; a drink-young style with character.

MORTON EST. WHITE LABEL MARL. CHARDONNAY

DRY $19 AV

(☆ ☆☆☆)

The first 1996 vintage (****) is a creamy, rich, beautifully balanced wine. Grown in the company's Stone Creek vineyard, French oak-fermented and lees-aged in the barrels for eight months, it is forward in its appeal, with impressive weight and depth of savoury, mealy, peachy, well-rounded flavour. Drink now to 1999.

MOUNT LINTON MARLBOROUGH CHARDONNAY

VINTAGE	95
WR	7
DRINK	97-8

DRY $18 V+

(☆ ☆☆☆)

A very rewarding '95 (****). In its youth full, fresh, scented and ripe, with persistent, strongly citrusy flavours and subtle oak influence (from six months barrel-aging), it is now at its peak, having offered delicious drinking during the past year. A low-output label worth discovering.

MOUNT RILEY MARLBOROUGH CHARDONNAY

DRY $14 AV

(☆ ☆☆)

Mount Riley is the second label of Allan Scott. There's no sign of oak in the light, elegant 1996 vintage (***), but the wine is very fresh and bouyant, its lively apple/lemon flavours threaded with mouth-watering acidity.

MOUTERE HILLS NELSON CHARDONNAY

DRY $19 -V

(☆ ☆☆)

A bit clumsy in its youth, the mouthfilling, French oak-fermented 1996 vintage (***½) is oaky on the nose, with assertive, toasty wood dominating its very crisp, citrusy fruit flavours. Cellaring to 1998–99 may achieve a more attractively balanced wine.

NAUTILUS EST. RESERVE CHARDONNAY

VINTAGE	96	95	94
WR	6	NM	5
DRINK	98-00	NM	97-8

DRY $30 AV

(☆ ☆☆☆☆

Gorgeous flavour intensity is a feature of the striking 1994 vintage of this Marlborough Chardonnay, grown in Nautilus's own vineyard. Eighty per cent of the wine was fermented and lees-aged in French oak barriques (60 per cent new). With its lifted, mealy fragrance, bottomless depth of grapefruit, fig and oak flavour and rich, rounded, complex, very persistent finish, it's maturing splendidly. The '96 (****½) is still very fresh and tight, with strong grapefruit and nutty oak flavours, sure to unfold well during 1998.

NAUTILUS MARLBOROUGH CHARDONNAY

VINTAGE	97	96	95	94	93	92
WR	5	5	4	6	4	4
DRINK	98-00	97-9	97-8	P	P	P

DRY $20 AV

☆ ☆☆☆

Typically a mouthfilling wine with a fresh, citric-and-oak flavoured palate and great elegance. The '95 is one of the better Marlborough Chardonnays, although it slightly lacks intensity; a cool-climate style, fresh and immaculate, with appley, lemony, slightly creamy flavours and good acid spine. The excellent '96 (****) was two-thirds fermented and matured in French oak barriques (30 per cent new); the balance was tank-fermented. It's an attractive wine with very satisfying depth of vibrant, ripe fruit flavours, well-integrated oak adding richness, fresh, lively acidity and impressive weight.

NEUDORF	VINTAGE	96	95	94	93	92	91	90	
MOUTERE	WR	6	5	6	6	6	6	5	
CHARDONNAY	DRINK	98-06	97-9	97-00+	97-00+	97-9	97-00	P	

DRY $35 AV

☆☆☆☆☆

Tim and Judy Finn's arresting Upper Moutere wine is one of New Zealand's most acclaimed Chardonnays. Fermented in French oak barriques (typically 50 per cent new), and given extended lees contact, it is very powerful, lush and mealy. Only three barrels were produced from the poor 1995 vintage, and although it's not a great classic of this label, it's still an impressive wine. Light gold, it offers very good depth of flavour, rich, citrusy, toasty and slightly buttery, with balanced acidity in a relatively forward style; drink now to 1999. The '96 (****1/2) is still shy and tight, but stylish, mouthfilling and richly flavoured, although again not quite as concentrated as top vintages like 1994. Light yellow, it offers strong, fresh, grapefruit-like flavours with a lush, sweet-fruit appeal, biscuity, mealy complexities and good weight. Cellar to mid 1998; ideally well beyond.

NEUDORF
VILLAGE
CHARDONNAY

DRY $19 -V

(☆☆☆)

From the poor 1995 vintage (***), Neudorf produced a characterful second-tier Nelson Chardonnay, barrel-fermented. Golden, and tasting fuller than its slender 10.5 per cent alcohol, it has *Botrytis*-derived honey characters on the nose and palate, but offers plenty of lemony, crisp flavour. I'd drink it now.

NGA WAKA	VINTAGE	96	95	94
MARTINBOROUGH	WR	6	6	6
CHARDONNAY	DRINK	98+	97+	97+

DRY $29 -V

(☆☆☆☆½)

Roger Parkinson's wine is an ideal candidate for the cellar, making few concessions to early-drinking appeal. The '95, barrel-fermented (35 per cent new oak), with 11 months lees-aging and 30 per cent malolactic fermentation, reveals a fresh, piercing bouquet and very tight, intensely flavoured palate, crisp, complex and mealy. A powerful, classically proportioned wine, it is still developing. The '96 (****1/2) bears the Nga Waka stamp of scentedness and intense, ripe fruit. A strapping wine (14 per cent alcohol), it has fresh, almost sweet-tasting tropical fruit flavours to the fore, coupled with mealiness and quality oak. Fermented in French oak barriques (one-third new) and lees-aged for almost a year, it is a delicious wine, more forward than its predecessor; open 1998 onwards.

NGATARAWA
CLASSIC
CHARDONNAY

DRY $13 V+

(☆☆☆½)

Delicious now, the debut 1996 vintage (***1/2) is a strongly "malo"-influenced Hawke's Bay wine with buttery/cheesy aromas and a full, soft palate. Weighty, with good depth of peachy, buttery flavour and a creamy texture, it offers very smooth, undemanding, satisfying drinking from now onwards.

	VINTAGE	95	94	93	92	91	90	DRY $26 AV
NGATARAWA	WR	6	7	6	6	6	6	☆☆☆☆⟨
GLAZEBROOK	DRINK	97-00	97-00	97-9	97-8	P	P	
RES. CHARD.								

This top Chardonnay label from Hawke's Bay winemaker Alwyn Corban is typically a rich, mouthfilling wine with intense flavour. Sweet fruit and obvious, quality oak give the '95 (*****½) a real stamp of class. Estate-grown at Bridge Pa, it was fermented in French oak barriques (80 per cent new) and then oak-matured on its yeast lees for almost a year. The bouquet is rich and nutty; the palate robust, fresh and balanced, with soft, ripe fruit, creamy barrel-stir characters and delicate, lingering flavours. Tasted as a barrel sample, the '96 looked full of promise, with good weight and rich, ripe citrusy fruit wrapped in strong French oak.

	VINTAGE	96	95	94	93	92	91	90	DRY $16 AV
NGATARAWA	WR	6	6	6	6	6	6	6	☆☆☆
STABLES	DRINK	97-9	97-8	P	P	P	P	P	
CHARDONNAY									

Ngatarawa's middle-tier Chardonnay label is a robust, easy-drinking Hawke's Bay wine with some complexity. Pale, with strong, milky/cheesy aromas and flavours, the '95 is appley, rounded and forward, with quite good body and flavour depth. The pale 1996 vintage (***) was half barrel-fermented (20 per cent new oak) and 80 per cent oak-matured. The fresh, appley, citrusy aromas and flavours are woven with "malo"-derived butterscotch characters, creating a pleasant, easy-drinking and characterful wine for drinking now onwards.

		MED/DRY $14 V+
NICKS		(☆☆☆)
HEAD		
CHARDONNAY		

The Longbush winery's lower-tier Gisborne Chardonnay is a non-wooded, fractionally sweet style designed for early consumption. Delicious already, the '96 (***) is pale straw, with good body, pleasing depth of ripe, tropical fruit flavours and an off-dry, seductively soft finish. Rates highly on the drinkability scale.

	VINTAGE	96	MED/DRY $12 V+
NOBILO FALL	WR	7	(☆☆☆)
HARVEST	DRINK	97-98	
UNOAKED CHARD.			

The first 1996 vintage (***) of this gentle, soft Gisborne wine is a drink-young style with moderate acidity, ripe, delicate fruit characters and good depth of fresh, rounded, citrus/pineapple flavours.

	VINTAGE	95	94	93	92	91	90	DRY $13 AV
NOBILO	WR	6	7	NM	6	NM	6	☆☆⟨
GISBORNE	DRINK	P	97-8	NM	P	NM	P	
CHARDONNAY								

A fruit-driven style designed for early drinking, this wine is fermented in stainless steel tanks and briefly matured in oak casks. The yellow-hued 1995 vintage (***½), oak-aged for five months, is slightly lacking in fragrance and delicacy, but full-bodied, with plenty of citrusy, honeyish flavour. Ready. The 1995 vintage is the last; since 1996 this label has been replaced by the Fall Harvest Chardonnay.

NOBILO GRAND RESERVE CHARDONNAY

DRY $29 -V

(☆☆☆☆⚝)

Still a baby, Nobilo's new flagship Chardonnay was launched from the 1996 vintage (****¹/₂). Half Marlborough, half Gisborne in origin, 85 per cent of the final blend was fermented and lees-aged for nine months in all-new oak barriques (70 per cent French, 30 per cent American); the wood-aged portion also had a softening malolactic fermentation. It's a big, rich-flavoured wine, powerfully wooded, with an impressive depth of mealy, citrusy flavour, needing until at least mid 1998 to open out.

NOBILO ICON CHARDONNAY

DRY $20 AV

(☆☆☆☆)

Nobilo's new middle-upper tier Chardonnay is a blend of Marlborough and Gisborne fruit, with the softening influence of 70 per cent malolactic fermentation. A portion of the final blend was handled in tanks, but most was fermented in oak barrels (20 per cent new). It's a refined wine, quite tight in its youth, with excellent depth of savoury, citrusy, buttery flavour and good acid spine. Drink 1998 onwards.

NOBILO POVERTY BAY CHARDONNAY

VINTAGE	96	95	94	93	92	91	90
WR	7	6	7	6	6	5	5
DRINK	97-8 P	P	P	P	P	P	P

DRY $12 V+

☆☆⚝

A no-fuss, low-priced wine succinctly described by the winery as "Cold fermented in stainless-steel. Bottled early. Best drunk young." The 1995 vintage (***¹/₂) is an excellent example of unoaked Chardonnay. Grown in Gisborne, it is a surprisingly satisfying wine, full-bodied, with light yellow colour, good depth of fresh, citrusy flavour and a finely balanced, long finish. Great value.

NOB. RES. DIXON VINEYARD HAND PICKED CHARD.

VINTAGE	94	93	92
WR	7	NM	7
DRINK	96-9	NM	P

DRY $28 AV

(☆☆☆☆☆)

The 1992 vintage of this Gisborne wine matured into a real stunner, and the '94 (****¹/₂) isn't far behind. Whole bunch-pressed, it was fermented in half-new French oak barriques and wood-aged on its gross lees for eight months. It's a voluptuous wine, light gold, with a voluminous, oaky fragrance and soft, rich palate – lush, fruity, nutty, complex and very full-flavoured. However, the 1994 vintage will be the last Dixon Chardonnay from Nobilo; this flagship wine has been replaced by the new Grand Reserve label from 1996.

	VINTAGE	94	93	92	91	90	DRY $20 AV
NOBILO RES.	WR	7	5	7	7	7	
MARLBOROUGH							☆☆☆☆
CHARDONNAY	DRINK	97-8 P	P	P	P		

This label has typically displayed crisper, more authoritative acidity and greater subtlety than most of its stablemates. The lively, moderately complex 1994 vintage was fermented and matured for six months in new French oak barriques. The crisp, citrusy flavours with nuances of tropical, passionfruit-like characters are fleshed out with toasty oak, leading to a fresh, lingering finish, just starting to soften. The '95 (***), barrel-fermented (30 per cent new oak) with a much higher degree of malolactic fermentation than usual, is less powerful, ripe and intense than the '94, but still offers plenty of citrusy, buttery, crisp flavour.

	VINTAGE	95	94	93	92	91	90	DRY $18 AV
NOBILO RES.	WR	5	7	NM	6	6	NM	
TIETJEN VINE.								☆☆☆⸮
CHARDONNAY	DRINK	97-8	97-8	NM	P	P	NM	

This single-vineyard Gisborne wine is typically lush, toasty and ripe-tasting – a buxom style. Still lively, the '94 was fermented in new French oak and wood-aged for eight months. Full yellow, with a restrained bouquet, it is lemony and crisp, savoury and tight, with some complexity. The 1995 (***1/2) is a forward, slightly savoury and well-rounded wine with quite good depth of ripe melon/citrus flavours. The '95 vintage is the last of this label.

	VINTAGE	96	95	94	DRY $17 AV
	WR	6	6	5	
ODYSSEY					(☆☆☆)
CHARDONNAY	DRINK	97-9	97-8	P	

Odyssey is the personal label of Rebecca Salmond, winemaker at Pleasant Valley. Grown in Hawke's Bay, the 1995 vintage is a fruit-uppermost style, with strong, ripe citrusy fruit flavours and a well-integrated touch of oak adding depth. Appealing now, the '96 (***) is a partly barrel-fermented (French and American oak) Gisborne wine, full-bodied and buoyant, with strong, ripe, delicate, slightly honied, lemony flavours.

	VINTAGE	96	95	94	93	92	DRY $20 -V
OKAHU EST.	WR	5	6	4	6	4	
CLIFTON							☆-☆☆☆⸮
CHARDONNAY	DRINK	98-02	97-01	97-8	97-8	P	

This wine is produced from Te Hana (near Wellsford, north of Auckland) fruit, which is barrel-fermented and lees-aged in French oak barriques. Past vintages have been of variable quality, but the 1995 (***1/2) is very well made. Robust and complex, with a rich, oaky fragrance, it offers good depth of fresh, citrusy, nutty, leesy flavour and a well-rounded finish. A characterful wine, it is enjoyable now but also maturing well.

	VINTAGE	96	95	94	93	DRY $13 V+
OLD COACH	WR	5	4	6	5	
ROAD						(☆☆☆)
CHARDONNAY	DRINK	97-01	97-8	P	P	

For its humble price tag, Seifried's bottom-tier Nelson Chardonnay is consistently good. The '95 is a tangy wine with quite good depth of straightforward, lemony, slightly limey flavours. The 1996 vintage (***) is a fruit-driven style – 70 per cent of the final blend was handled entirely in stainless steel tanks, and 30 per cent was matured for six months in one year-old French oak barriques. The fresh, direct fruit aromas lead into a full-bodied, crisp and lively wine with good depth of peachy, citrusy, slightly limey flavours and a smooth, fractionally off-dry finish.

OMAKA SPRINGS CHARDONNAY

DRY $11 V+

(☆☆⯨)

Tasting the '95 vintage of this Marlborough wine is like biting into a crisp, green apple. A lightly wooded style, it's a simple wine with a sliver of sweetness adding to its drink-young appeal. The '96 (**¹/₂) is very similar. Pale, with a quiet bouquet and restrained oak influence (20 per cent was French oak-fermented), it's a fresh, light wine with crisp, green-edged, appley flavours, clean and lively. There's no excitement here, but it's a bargain at its widely reduced price of $11 (the '97 will retail at $14). Drink it young, while it's appetisingly fresh and flinty.

OYSTER BAY CHARDONNAY

VINTAGE	96	95	94	93	92	91	90
WR	6	5	7	5	7	6	7
DRINK	97-9	97-8	P	P	P	P	P

DRY $20 V+

☆☆☆☆⯨

This wine is consistently classy, with Marlborough's pure, incisive fruit flavours beautifully showcased. The 1995 vintage is seductively well-balanced, with ripe citrus/passionfruit flavours, a touch of mealy richness and great elegance. Hard to resist right now, the '96 (*****) was 30 per cent tank-fermented, with the rest barrel-fermented and lees-stirred. It's a mouthfilling, creamy, richly flavoured wine with toasty oak on the nose and palate, lovely freshness and vigour and a tight, well-spined, long finish. Great value.

PALLISER BAY MARTINBOROUGH CHARDONNAY

DRY $18 AV

(☆☆☆)

Good drinking now, Palliser Estate's second-tier wine from 1995 (***) was partly aged sur lie in tanks and partly fermented and matured in French and American oak. It's a pale, fresh, distinctly cool-climate style with good fruit/wood balance and tight, citrusy, appley, nutty flavours.

PALLISER EST. MARTINBOROUGH CHARDONNAY

 DRY $30 AV

☆☆☆☆☆

Winemaker Allan Johnson produces an extremely classy Martinborough Chardonnay. In a retrospective tasting of the 1989 to 1995 vintages, held in March 1997, the bright yellow, rich, integrated and complex '89 stood up remarkably well, and the '91, '92 (especially) and '94 were all impressive, with rich, citrusy flavours. The '95 (***¹/₂) was fermented in French oak casks and lees-aged for nine months, with one-third of the wine undergoing a softening malolactic fermentation. Reflecting the wet vintage, it's crisper and clearly less lush and concentrated than usual, but with good vigour and depth of lemony, appley, yeasty flavour; open 1998.

PEGASUS BAY CHARDONNAY

VINTAGE	95	94	93
WR	6	6	5
DRINK	97-00	97-06	97-00

DRY $26 V+

(☆☆☆☆☆)

An emerging Waipara classic. The strapping (14 per cent alcohol) 1994 vintage is a very classy wine indeed with a delicious surge of citrusy, savoury, slightly buttery flavour, good acid spine, and cool-climate delicacy and intensity. The '95 (*****), from a "perfect" season, confirm's the label's status. Fermented in French oak barriques (30 per cent new), oak-aged for a year, and then matured on its lees for a further eight months in stainless steel tanks prior to bottling, it is a bold wine (14 per cent alcohol) with pale straw colour and a voluptuous, ravishingly intense fragrance. It's an exciting mouthful too, with a seamless array of citrusy, biscuity, oaky flavours, superbly complex, concentrated and sustained.

PELORUS CHARDONNAY

VINTAGE	95	94	93	92
WR		4	5	4	3
DRINK	P	97-9	P	P

DRY $20 AV

☆☆☆☆

This tiny Nelson winery's 1994 Chardonnay is a stylish, bold, still youthful wine with savoury, searching flavours. The '95, blended from Nelson and Gisborne fruit, is a less distinguished, more early-maturing style with a full, soft palate. The '96 (***) is a well-crafted wine, estate-grown at Hope, near Richmond. Half tank, half French oak-fermented, and given a full malolactic fermentation, it offers ripe although not intense citrus and peach-like flavours lightly coated with toasty oak in a lively, well balanced style, worth cellaring to 1998.

PHOENIX HAWKE'S BAY CHARDONNAY

VINTAGE	94
WR	4
DRINK	97-8

DRY $15 AV

☆☆☆

Pacific's top wines are labelled "Phoenix". The 1994 vintage (***) was two-thirds fermented in French and American oak barriques, with extended lees contact. Still drinking well, it offers a fragrant, buttery, mealy bouquet and pleasing depth of flavour, with a crisp, firm finish.

PLEASANT VAL. GISBORNE CHARDONNAY

VINTAGE	96
WR	6
DRINK	97-9

DRY $15 AV

☆☆☆

This very lightly oaked wine rests its case on drink-young charm. The 1996 vintage (***) was briefly aged on its yeast lees in tanks and 35 per cent of the final blend was given a softening malolactic fermentation. Delicious by June, within three months of the harvest, it is a light yellow wine, fresh-scented and vibrantly fruity, with ripe citrusy flavours and a smooth, fractionally off-dry, buttery finish. Very easy-drinking indeed.

PLEASANT VAL. SIGNATURE SEL. CHARDONNAY

VINTAGE	95	94
WR	5	6
DRINK	97-8	97-8

DRY $19 AV

(☆☆☆☆)

Pleasant Valley's top Chardonnay. The '95, a barrel-fermented Hawke's Bay wine, is fresh and taut, with some flavour intensity, oak richness and a slightly creamy, crisp finish. The enjoyably fresh and lively '96 (***¹/₂) was grown in Gisborne and fermented and lees-aged in French oak barriques. It offers good body and depth of flavour, with ripe citrusy characters enriched with a touch of nutty oak, leading to an appetisingly crisp finish. A beautifully balanced wine, it is less wood-influenced than the '95, and already delicious.

PONDER	VINTAGE	96	95		DRY $19 -V
ESTATE	WR	6	5		
CHARDONNAY	DRINK	97-9 P			(☆ ☆☆)

The 1995 vintage of this small Marlborough producer's Chardonnay is a soft, full, French and American oak-aged wine with fresh, appley flavours and a touch of complexity. The '96 (**) is disappointing. Estate-grown, given "light" oak treatment and a full malolactic fermentation, it is a straw-coloured wine with soft, cheesy, "malo"-derived characters, but it lacks freshness, flavour intensity and fruit character. Over-priced.

QUAIL FARM	VINTAGE	95	DRY $13 AV
GISBORNE	WR	5	
CHARDONNAY	DRINK	97-98	(☆☆)

Pale, light, vigorous and appley, Pacific's lightly oaked 1995 wine (**) is slightly austere, with green-edged flavours and a crisp acid finish. The '95 is the first and last vintage of this label.

REVINGTON	VINTAGE	96	95	94	93	92	91	90	DRY $25 AV
VINEYARD	WR	6	NM	6	5	5	4	3	
CHARDONNAY	DRINK	97-03	NM	97-04	97-9	97-9	97-8	P	☆ ☆☆☆☆

Ross Revington and his wife, Mary Jane, own a four-hectare vineyard (but no winery) in the Ormond Valley, near Gisborne city. The Revington Vineyard yields complex, savoury, citrusy wines, elegant rather than huge, with a distinguished record in show judgings. The typically immaculate 1994 vintage is mouthfilling, with intense lemon and melon-evoking flavours, a touch of savoury mealiness and good acid spine. There is no '95. The '96 (*****) was fermented and matured in all-new French oak barriques. It's quite forward, with a seamless array of lush, peachy, buttery, complex flavours in a deliciously soft, rich and powerful style.

RICHMOND	VINTAGE	95	DRY $20 -V
PLAINS	WR	4	
CHARDONNAY	DRINK	97-8	(☆ ☆☆)

Grown in the Holmes brothers' Nelson vineyard, which has full Bio-Gro status, and made by Jane Cooper, formerly winemaker at Seifried Estate, the '95 vintage (**¹/₂) was 25 per cent fermented and aged in oak barriques. It's an austere, high acid style with an appley, Chablis-like bouquet. It lacks real ripeness and richness, but has a certain cutting, cool-climate vigour and impact.

RIPPON VINEYARD CHARDONNAY

DRY $24 -V

☆☆☆☆

Grown on the shores of Lake Wanaka, this is typically a very lively wine with fresh, lingering, citrusy, appley flavours and a steely undertow of acid. The 1995 vintage is a pale, elegant and penetrating wine, very well-balanced, with a Chablis-like vigour and sharpness. The '96 (****) is very impressive. Bold (13.5 per cent alcohol), very savoury and flinty, it has intense, complex flavours enlivened by fresh acidity and real depth through the palate. Drink 1998–99.

RIVERSIDE CHARDONNAY

DRY $14 AV

(☆☆☆)

The 1996 vintage (***¹/₂) of this Dartmoor Valley winery's lower-tier Chardonnay was made before the arrival of Nigel Davies, the new qualified winemaker. French oak-matured for four months, it lacks fragrance, but is full, fresh, clean, lemony and crisp on the palate, with quite reasonable flavour depth in a straightforward, easy-drinking style.

RIVERSIDE RESERVE CHARDONNAY

VINTAGE	96
WR	5
DRINK	98-02

DRY $20 -V

☆☆☆

This small Dartmoor Valley's 1995 Reserve Chardonnay has a shy bouquet but quite good depth of lemony, nutty, slightly mealy flavour. The '96 (***¹/₂) is clearly superior. Fermented and matured for eight months in French oak barriques (30 per cent new), it's not highly concentrated but still very attractive, with a toasty fragrance, good weight, ripe grapefruit/lemon flavours with some mealy, buttery complexity and a crisp, well-balanced finish. Riverside's best Chardonnay yet.

ROBARD & BUT. GISBORNE MEN. CHARDONNAY

VINTAGE	96	95
WR	6	7
DRINK	98-00	97-9

DRY $11 V+

(☆☆☆☆)

The 1995 was simply the best low-priced Chardonnay of the vintage – an unwooded but lovely wine with a soft, creamy, ripe, citrusy palate, weighty and full-flavoured. The '96 (***) lacks the magic of the '95, but still offers great value. Fermented and lees-aged in stainless steel tanks, 80 per cent of the final blend was given a softening malolactic fermentation. Bright, light lemon-green, it's an enjoyable, vibrantly fruity wine in its youth with a fresh, ripe, citrusy, slightly buttery fragrance and flavour, good depth and a crisp finish.

ROBARD & BUT. HAWKE'S BAY CHARDONNAY

VINTAGE	96	95
WR	7	7
DRINK	98-02	97-00

DRY $12 V+

(☆☆☆☆)

Here's a bargain! Drinking well now, the 1995 vintage of Corbans' wine was matured and partly fermented in one and two-year-old French and American oak casks. Bright, light yellow, it's a fragrant, well structured wine with good depth of ripe, grapefruit-like flavour and subtle oak in a firm, elegant style. The '96 (***) is also well-crafted, with smooth, fresh, citrusy, slightly buttery flavours in a very easy-drinking style.

ROCKWOOD RESERVE SEL. CHARDONNAY

DRY $21 AV

(☆☆☆☆)

The Rockwood Cellars winery in Hastings is owned by the Mason brothers of Sacred Hill, winemaker Tony Bish and other shareholders. They've gone all out with the 1995 vintage (****) – hand-picking, whole bunch-pressing, 100 per cent fermentation in half new, half one-year-old French oak barriques. A muscular wine, harbouring 14 per cent alcohol, it is very crisp and tangy, with vigorous, appley, lemony fruit flavours, rich, mealy, creamy characters, and good length.

RONGOPAI TE KAUWHATA CHARDONNAY

DRY $18 AV

(☆☆☆)

The 1995 vintage, a 3:1 blend of Te Kauwhata and Hawke's Bay fruit, is a full-bodied wine with a touch of oatmealy complexity, but only moderately ripe. The '96 (***) was grown in four Te Kauwhata vineyards and the majority of the blend was fermented and matured for six months on its yeast lees in oak casks. Light yellow in hue, it's a moderately complex wine with good weight, fresh, ripe, citrusy fruit flavours and a slightly mealy, crisp finish. Drink 1997–98.

RONGOPAI RES. TE KAUWHATA CHARDONNAY

DRY $26 -V

☆☆☆☆

The 1996 (***1/2) is a very solid wine, but not a memorable vintage of this label. Based on "selected" grapes given "extended" wood maturation, it's not very fragrant, and lacks the fatness and lush fruit characters of such past successes as the '94. That said, it's still a weighty, ripely flavoured wine with some figgy, mealy richness, but it just doesn't "sing", at least not yet. Open 1998.

ROSEBANK CANTERBURY CHARDONNAY

VINTAGE	95
WR	7
DRINK	97-05

DRY $20 AV

(☆☆☆☆⦣)

Rosebank's first 1995 vintage Canterbury Chardonnay (***1/2) is a delicious wine, with lots of character and depth. Based on grapes grown at French Farm, on Banks Peninsula, and 70 per cent oak-fermented, it is pale lemon-green, with a fresh-scented bouquet. Maturing well, it is a mouthfilling wine with strong, appley, nutty flavours, a slightly creamy mid-palate and crisp, lively finish.

ROSEBANK CANTERBURY RES. CHARD.

VINTAGE	95
WR	7
DRINK	97-05

DRY $25 -V

(☆☆☆☆)

Rosebank's first wine to earn "reserve" status is a 1995 Chardonnay (****) harvested on 15 May at French Farm, on Banks Peninsula, fermented in small French oak casks, and lees-aged for six months. Still very youthful, with a light yellow/green hue, it is a robust wine with rich, citrusy, slightly limey flavours, still fresh and crisp, wrapped in quality oak. This is a powerful, complex, rich wine that should handsomely reward cellaring.

ROSEBANK	VINTAGE	95	94		**DRY $19 -V**
MARLBOROUGH	WR	7	7		
CHARDONNAY	DRINK	97-05	97-05		(☆☆☆)

The Marlborough Chardonnays from this Canterbury winery are of consistent quality. The '94 is a stylish, tight-structured wine with good body, fresh citrusy fruit, savoury oak and a crisp, lively finish. The '95 (***) is on a slightly lower plane: a solid wine with fullness of body, restrained oak influence and a lively, lemony, appetisingly crisp flavour.

ROSSENDALE		**DRY $23 AV**
BARREL SEL.		
CHARDONNAY		(☆☆☆☆)

This small Canterbury winery's premium Chardonnay is consistently classy. The 1994 vintage, grown in Marlborough, is a voluptuous wine with impressive depth of mealy, toasty flavour, rich and rounded. The '95 (****1/2) is even finer. Estate-grown at Halswell, on the outskirts of Christchurch, it is a very stylish, fragrant, robust, rather Burgundian wine with savoury, buttery flavours, cool-climate delicacy and excellent depth, complexity and persistence.

| *ROSSENDALE* | | **DRY $14 V+** |
| *CHARDONNAY* | | (☆☆☆⚬) |

This small Canterbury winery produces consistently rewarding wines. Designed for drinking with "light, salad-type meals or by itself", the bargain-priced '96 (***1/2) is a blend of Canterbury and Marlborough fruit, given "very little" exposure to oak. It's a delicious wine with fragrant lemon/apple aromas and very good depth of flavour – fresh, immaculate, crisp and lively. Open 1997–98.

RUBY	VINTAGE	95	94		**DRY $20 AV**
BAY	WR	6	5		
CHARDONNAY	DRINK	P	P		(☆☆☆⚬)

This tiny Nelson winery adopts a low profile, but the Chardonnay is consistently robust, peachy-ripe and toasty, with a seductive creaminess of texture. The barrique-fermented 1995 vintage (***1/2) is fleshy, mealy and complex – full of character.

SAINT CLAIR	VINTAGE	96	95	94	**DRY $17 AV**
MARLBOROUGH	WR	6	6	6	
CHARDONNAY	DRINK	97-9	P	P	(☆☆☆)

Neal Ibbotson produces a "fruit-driven" style of Chardonnay, lightly oaked but fresh and vibrantly fruity. The 1996 vintage (***) was handled predominantly in tanks, but 30 per cent of the final blend was fermented and matured in new American oak casks. The fresh, appley, lemony aromas lead into a full, crisp and flavoursome palate with a twist of sweet oak, lots of fruity appeal in its youth, and enough depth and spine to age well.

	VINTAGE	96		
ST HELENA	WR	5		**DRY $15 V+**
CHARDONNAY	DRINK	97-9		☆ ☆☆

At its best this is a weighty Canterbury wine with strong lemon/apple flavours and a crisp, steely finish. The '95 is lemony and crisp, with reasonable flavour depth, but lacks the richness of a top vintage. The 1996 (****¹/₂) is from a year in which St Helena elected not to produce a Reserve Chardonnay, but it is still clearly superior to the '95. Oak-aged for 10 months, it is a pale yellow, full-bodied wine, savoury, lemony and flinty, with a Chablis-like structure. A slightly austere, flavoursome wine, already drinking well, it will appeal to those who enjoy their Chardonnay firm and flinty.

	VINTAGE	95		
ST HELENA	WR	6		**DRY $22 AV**
RES. CANTER.	DRINK	97-9		(☆ ☆☆☆☆)
CHARDONNAY				

St Helena's first reserve Chardonnay, produced from the 1995 vintage (****), was worth the wait. It's a slightly austere style with lively, very crisp Canterbury acidity, very good depth of lemony, slightly buttery flavour and nutty, well-integrated oak. This is an elegant wine, impressively concentrated and lingering. There is no '96.

	VINTAGE	95	94	93	92		
ST JEROME	WR	7	7	NM	6		**DRY $21 -V**
HAWKE'S BAY	DRINK	97-8 P		NM	P		☆☆ ☆☆
CHARDONNAY							

The 1994 vintage slightly lacked freshness and vigour, but the '95 (***¹/₂) is a big step forward. Barrel-fermented, with 50 per cent of the blend given a softening malolactic fermentation, it is a yellow-hued wine with a richly oaky fragrance. Drinking well now, it is a weighty, savoury wine with good depth of ripe, citrusy flavours fleshed out with buttery oak.

	VINTAGE	96		
SACRED HILL	WR	7		**DRY $20 V+**
RES. BARREL	DRINK	97-9		(☆ ☆☆☆☆⯨)
FERM. CHARD.				

The 1994 vintage of this Hawke's Bay wine is a mouthfilling style, fragrant, with excellent depth of citrusy, appley, mealy flavour. The '96 (****¹/₂) is even more impressive. A blend of fruit grown in the Ohiti Valley and the company's Whitecliff vineyard in the Dartmoor Valley, it was whole bunch-pressed and fermented in new French oak casks. Full of character, it is a mouthfilling and complex wine with intense, ripe, tropical/citrus fruit flavours fleshed out with mealy, lees-stirred characters and toasty oak. This is a powerful wine, still coming together, but already delicious.

	VINTAGE	95		
SACRED HILL	WR	7		**DRY $30 AV**
RIFLEMANS	DRINK	97-00		(☆ ☆☆☆☆)
CHARDONNAY				

Is the debut 1995 vintage (*****) Sacred Hill's finest wine yet? Huge in body and flavour, it was grown in Hawke's Bay and fermented and lees-aged in French oak. The rich, savoury, citrusy aromas lead into a powerful, creamy palate with lovely, ripe, very intense grapefruit and fig-like flavours, nutty oak and firm acidity. A strapping wine (14 per cent alcohol), it's still developing.

SACRED HILL WHITECLIFF
HAWKES BAY
CHARDONNAY

DRY $15 AV

☆ ☆☆

Less complex and more forward than its stablemates (above), this is a medium-bodied wine designed for early drinking. The 1995 vintage, 25 per cent barrel-fermented, is aging well, with pleasant, citrusy, slightly buttery flavours and a touch of wood, finishing very clean and crisp. The '96 (***) is a non-wooded style, but again very enjoyable. Full, lively and crisp, with fresh, ripe fruit aromas, it offers good depth of clean, delicate lemon/lime flavours and a lasting, very well balanced finish.

SAINTS
GISBORNE
CHARDONNAY

VINTAGE	96	95	94
WR	7	6	7
DRINK	97-00	97-8	97-9

DRY $16 V+

(☆ ☆☆☆)

The debut 1994 vintage of Montana's mid-priced wine was seductively mouthfilling and soft, with the character and flavour richness that many wineries ask over $20 for. The '95 is less fragrant and delicious than the '94, but still a very decent wine and fine value. Full of upfront appeal, the '96 (*****¹/₂) is the irresistible winner of the Best Buy of the Year award. Grown mainly in Gisborne's Patutahi district, it was fermented and lees-aged for five months in American and French oak casks (40 per cent new). Richly fragrant and fleshy, and bursting with deep, lush tropical fruit flavours and buttery oak, this is a luscious wine for drinking over the next couple of years, and bargain priced.

SANDIHURST
CANTERBURY
CHARDONNAY

VINTAGE	95
WR	4
DRINK	97-8

DRY $16 AV

(☆ ☆☆)

The pale, rather Chablis-like 1995 vintage (***) of this wine was estate-grown at West Melton and matured on its yeast lees in French oak casks (15 per cent new) for 10 months. Full-bodied, it offers delicate, appley, slightly buttery flavours and a touch of complexity in a crisp, flinty style that should age well.

SANDIHURST
CHARDONNAY

DRY $15 AV

(☆ ☆☆)

Piercingly crisp and lively, the 1995 vintage (**¹/₂) of this "very lightly oaked" blend of Marlborough and Canterbury grapes is a slightly austere, cool-climate style with citrusy, steely flavours.

SCHNAPPER ROCK
MARLBOROUGH
CHARDONNAY

DRY $? AV

(☆ ☆☆)

Produced by Corbans exclusively for sale in restaurants (at around $28), the first 1995 vintage (***) was fermented and matured in new and seasoned French oak barrels. It's a full-bodied, savoury wine in a distinctly cool-climate style, with citrusy, appley flavours, slightly lacking full ripeness, a creamy texture and rounded finish. Drink now to 1998.

SEIBEL BARREL FERM. MARLBOROUGH CHARDONNAY

DRY $16 AV

(☆ ☆☆)

The 1995 vintage (***) is a fruit-driven style, not highly complex but clean, fresh and lively, with quite good depth of reasonably ripe, slightly toasty flavour and a crisp finish. Drink 1997–98.

SEIBEL LIMITED ED. MARLBOROUGH CHARDONNAY

DRY $19 AV

(☆ ☆☆⚘)

Pale straw, with excellent flavour depth, the fleshy 1996 vintage (****) was 100 per cent barrel-fermented and 80 per cent of the final blend also went through a softening malolactic fermentation. The rich, ripe peach/lemon flavours are fresh, crisp and slightly buttery, creating a reasonably complex, savoury, harmonious wine for drinking now and over the next couple of years.

SEIFRIED BAR.-FERM. CHARDONNAY

VINTAGE	95	94	93	92	91
WR	4	5	5	6	5
DRINK	98-9	97-04	97-8	97-8	P

DRY $22 -V

(☆ ☆☆)

The first, 1991 vintage of this label was Seifried's first attempt at a Rolls-Royce Nelson Chardonnay. The 1992 vintage is a golden, powerful, strongly wooded wine with rich citrusy fruit and toasty bottle-aged characters, maturing well. However, the deep-gold '93 (**1/2), a big, peachy wine, is soft, tiring and clearly past its best.

SEIFRIED NELSON CHARDONNAY

VINTAGE	96	95	94	93	92	91	90
WR	5	4	6	5	6	6	6
DRINK	97-02	98-9	98-00	97-8	P	P	P

DRY $16 AV

☆ ☆☆

The quality of this wine has risen sharply in recent years. The '95 is less ripe and rich than the strapping '94, but fresh-scented, with appley, nutty, steely flavours. The 1996 vintage (***1/2) is fine value. Thirty per cent of the blend was barrel-fermented and lees-aged for nine months; another 30 per cent was barrel-aged for five months. A mouthfilling, characterful wine with a toasty bouquet, strong grapefruit/oak flavours and a slightly buttery, moderately crisp finish, it offers very good drinking from now onwards.

SELAKS DRYLANDS CHARDONNAY

DRY $20 AV

(☆ ☆☆☆)

Launched from the 1996 vintage (****), this middle-tier Chardonnay was grown in Marlborough, fermented in French and American oak casks and given a higher proportion of new oak than its Marlborough Chardonnay stablemate (below). It's a stylish wine with delicate, nutty, complex flavours and a slightly creamy texture, well worth cellaring to 1998–99.

SELAKS	VINTAGE	96	95	94	93	92	91	90	DRY $17 V+
MARLBOROUGH	WR	6	6	7	6	7	6	6	
CHARDONNAY	DRINK	97-9	97-8	97-8	P	P	P	P	☆☆☆⟟

The "standard" Chardonnay from Selaks has often shown a touch of class. Worth keeping to 1998, the stylishly constructed 1996 vintage (***1/2) was fermented and matured for seven months in new and one-year-old French and American oak casks. Light lemon-green in hue and still youthful, it's very fresh and crisp, its delicate lemon/apple flavours lightly seasoned with oak. A finely balanced cool-climate style.

SELAKS FOUN.	VINTAGE	96	95	94	93	92	91	90	DRY $22 V+
RESERVE	WR	7	6	7	7	7	7	6	
CHARDONNAY	DRINK	98-00	97-9	97-8	97-8	P	P	P	☆☆☆☆⟟

When it was based on Gisborne grapes, Selaks' top Founders Chardonnay was a fat, soft style. Now sourced from Marlborough, it is crisper and more refined. The '95 is a full, rich, lively wine, light yellow-hued, with a biscuity, mealy fragrance and impressive depth of citrusy, complex, slightly oaky flavour. The 1996 vintage (****1/2) was fermented and lees-aged for a year in all-new French oak barriques. Not quite as powerful as the memorable '94, but very elegant, it's a lovely wine with fresh, deep grapefruit-like flavours, quality oak and a savoury, buttery finish. Open mid 1998 onwards.

SELWYN RIV.	DRY $15 AV
MARLBOROUGH	
CHARDONNAY	(☆☆⟟)

Produced by Giesen, the 1996 vintage (**1/2) is a rather Chablis-like wine with fresh, taut, steely flavours in a distinctly cool-climate style. Lemony and appley, with no sign of oak and high acidity, it offers sound drinking 1997–98.

SERESIN	VINTAGE	96	DRY $20 AV
ESTATE	WR	5	
CHARDONNAY	DRINK	97-01	(☆☆☆☆)

The very stylish debut 1996 vintage (****) was estate-grown near Renwick. Fermented in a new French oak vat (60 per cent) and new French oak barriques (40 per cent), it was lees-aged for 10 months, with regular stirring, and 70 per cent of the wine passed through malolactic fermentation. Fragrant and full-bodied, it's an immaculately fresh and crisp wine, still a baby but brimful of promise. Tight and vibrantly fruity, with ripe fruit flavours and biscuity oak, it's a poised and persistent wine, revealing very sophisticated winemaking.

SERESIN EST.	VINTAGE	96	DRY $26 AV
RESERVE	WR	6	
CHARDONNAY	DRINK	97-01	(☆☆☆☆☆)

Finesse is the keynote quality of the brilliant debut 1996 vintage (*****). Hand-picked from "prime terraces" in the estate vineyard near Renwick, it was fermented in all-new French oak barriques and matured on its yeast lees for 11 months. To soften the wine and add complexity, 100 per cent went through malolactic fermentation. The result is a memorable wine, intensely fragrant and robust (13.5 per cent alcohol), with an exciting concentration of vibrant, nutty, mealy flavour and firm acid spine. This is a classically proportioned, exceptionally well-structured wine – a top candidate for the cellar.

SETTLER CHARDONNAY

> DRY $19 AV

(☆☆☆⛧)

The 1995 vintage is a characterful wine with a mealy, leesy bouquet, fullness of body and good depth of well-rounded flavour. The '96 (***½) was grown at Fernhill and 75 per cent barrel-fermented. Still fresh, it is a stylish, full-bodied wine with lemony, sweet-fruit flavours and leesy, buttery complexities. Everything is in balance, but the wine just needs another year or so to fatten up; open mid 1998 onwards.

SHALIMAR ESTATE CHARDONNAY

> DRY $15 AV

(☆☆⛧)

Past vintages of this Gisborne winery's Reserve Chardonnay have been of variable quality. However, the '96 non-reserve Chardonnay (***) is attractive. A lightly oaked wine with a light yellow hue, it offers good body and depth of citrusy, buttery, well-rounded flavour. Open 1997–98.

SHERWOOD EST. RES. CHARDONNAY

VINTAGE	96	95	94	93	92	91
WR	7	6	5	5	6	4
DRINK	98-9	97-8	97-8	P	P	P

> DRY $24 -V

(☆☆☆☆⛧)

The 1994 and 1995 vintages were both enjoyable, but the '96 (****) is the best yet. Estate-grown at West Melton and fermented in new French oak barriques, this is a full-flavoured, complex Canterbury wine, already very forthcoming. Light yellow, with a fragrant, mealy, toasty bouquet, it is mouthfilling, with strong citrusy fruit flavours, good acid spine, a slightly creamy texture and long, rich finish.

SHERWOOD ESTATE UNOAKED CHARDONNAY

> DRY $15 AV

(☆☆☆)

Designed as a drink-young style, the first 1996 vintage (***) was estate-grown at West Melton. The fresh fruit aromas lead into an attractively full and vibrantly fruity palate, appley and lemony, with a fractionally off-dry (4 grams/litre of sugar), appetisingly crisp finish.

SHINGLE PEAK MARLBOROUGH CHARDONNAY

VINTAGE	96	95	94	93	92
WR	6	6	7	5	6
DRINK	97-00	97-8	97-8	P	P

> DRY $17 V+

☆☆☆☆⛧

Matua Valley's wine is released very young but matures well. The 1995 vintage shows plenty of depth and character, with unusually rich and persistent flavour for the vintage. The flavoursome but not highly complex '96 (***) was one-half handled in tanks; the rest was fermented and matured for eight months in new and seasoned oak casks. Already drinking well, it's a full, ripe style with quite good depth of citrus and melon-like flavours, a touch of oak and fresh acidity.

	VINTAGE	95	94	93
SILVERSTREAM **CHARDONNAY**	WR	6	5	6
	DRINK	97-00	97-8	97-8

DRY $16 V+

(☆☆☆☆⯪)

The 1995 vintage from this small Canterbury winery is a distinctly cool-climate style, very much in the mould of Chablis. Pale straw in colour, it is a weighty wine with oak complexity and fresh, vigorous, appley, nutty aromas and flavours.

	VINTAGE	96	95	94
SOLJANS BAR. **RESERVE H.B.** **CHARDONNAY**	WR	6	6	6
	DRINK	97-02	97-00	97-8

DRY $18 AV

(☆☆☆)

The 1995 vintage was attractively peachy, toasty, ripe-tasting and rounded in its youth, but peaked early and is now past its best. The yellow-hued '96 (***) was 50 per cent fermented and lees-aged for six months in new and seasoned French oak barrels; the rest was handled in tanks. It's a forward style, fat, lush and soft, with plenty of weight and flavour, but likely to be at its best during 1997–98.

	VINTAGE	96	95
SOLJANS **HAWKE'S BAY** **CHARDONNAY**	WR	6	5
	DRINK	97-00	P

DRY $14 AV

(☆☆⯪)

The 1995 vintage of this very lightly wooded Hawke's Bay wine shows moderate depth of flavour in a solid but plain style. The '96 (**½) was 10 per cent barrel-fermented. It's not highly fragrant, but a big (13.5 per cent alcohol), ripe-tasting, rounded wine, best drunk young.

SPENCER **HILL** **CHARDONNAY**

DRY $24 AV

(☆☆☆☆☆⯪)

Launched from the 1995 vintage (*****½), this is the top label from the Spencer Hill winery in Upper Moutere, best known for its Tasman Bay Chardonnay. Grown at the Brentwood vineyard in Marlborough, barrel-fermented with natural yeasts and matured for 11 months in French and American oak barriques, the '95 is a beautifully crafted wine, forward in its appeal, with impressive weight and depth of citrusy, nutty flavours in a heavily "malo"-influenced style with strong butterscotch-like characters. Complex, harmonious, persistent and extremely drinkable.

	VINTAGE	95	94
STONE CREEK **MARLBOROUGH** **CHARDONNAY**	WR	4	5
	DRINK	97-8	P

DRY $18 AV

(☆☆☆)

A fruit-driven style, the 1995 vintage (***) of Morton Estate's Chardonnay is fresh and crisp, with a hint of honey amid its vigorous, lemony, limey flavours. It's not complex, but enjoyable. This label has recently been phased out and replaced from the 1996 vintage by Morton Estate's White Label Marlborough Chardonnay.

	VINTAGE	96	95	94	93	92	91	90	DRY $26 AV
STONECROFT	WR		6	6	6	6	5	5	5	
CHARDONNAY	DRINK		98-9	97-8	97-8	P	P	P	P	☆☆☆☆✦

Hawke's Bay winemaker Alan Limmer aims for a "restrained style of Chardonnay which ages well". The '95 is a full-bodied wine with a rich, oaky bouquet and impressive depth of ripe, mealy, slightly woody flavour. The more finely balanced 1996 vintage (*****) was fermented in French oak barriques and matured on its yeast lees for 10 months. Already delicious, it's a notably mouthfilling, rich and savoury wine with very ripe fruit shining through its concentrated, lush, citrusy, nutty flavours, finishing long and soft.

	VINTAGE	96	95	94	93	92	91	90	DRY $19 AV
STONELEIGH *VINEYARD MARL.*	WR	7	6	7	6	6	6	6	
CHARDONNAY	DRINK	98-01	97-00	97-00	97-8	97-8	97-8	P	☆☆☆✦

The Chardonnays from Corbans' Stoneleigh Vineyard typically display fresh, cool-climate appley aromas, good weight, vibrant lemon/apple fruit flavours and a subtle oak and lees-aging influence. Maturing well, the full-bodied, flavoursome 1995 vintage (***1/2) was fermented and matured on its yeast lees for six months in new and seasoned French oak casks, with a full softening malolactic fermentation. Still fresh, it's a savoury, nutty, mealy, creamy-soft wine with some toffee-like "malo" characters and good length.

TASMAN
BAY
CHARDONNAY

DRY $20 V+

(☆☆☆☆✦)

American Philip Jones, of the Spencer Hill winery in Nelson, made a big splash with his first 1994 Tasman Bay Chardonnay, a deliciously rich-flavoured and forward wine. The '95 is good, although slightly less striking. The exceptional 1996 vintage (*****) is a mix of Marlborough (predominantly), Gisborne and Nelson grapes, oak-aged for seven months and given a full, softening malolactic fermentation. It's a substantial, hugely attractive wine, astutely blended and balanced, with a lovely, seamless integration of ripe, citrusy fruit, buttery "malo" characters and quality oak, leading to a fresh, deliciously rounded, persistent finish. Few others in New Zealand can make Chardonnay taste this good, this young.

	VINTAGE	95	DRY $28 -V
TE AWA FARM *BOUNDARY*	WR	6	
CHARDONNAY	DRINK	98-01	(☆☆☆✦)

Aging gracefully, the first '95 vintage (***1/2) of this Hawke's Bay company's top-tier Chardonnay was fermented and matured for a year in French oak barriques. Light yellow-green, it is elegant and tight, steely and slowly evolving, with good body, crisp grapefruit-like flavours and subtle, nutty oak.

	VINTAGE	96	95	94	DRY $18 AV
TE AWA FARM *LONGLANDS*	WR	7	6	5	
CHARDONNAY	DRINK	97-00	97-9	P	(☆☆☆)

The 1995 vintage of this subtle Hawke's Bay wine is a lean, flinty style with very elegant flavours emerging. Balanced for early consumption but capable of aging, the well-made '96

(****1/2) was estate-grown in the Gimblett Road/Roy's Hill district and 70 per cent fermented and matured for six months in French and American oak barriques. Made by Tony Bish and Jenny Dobson, it's a smooth-flowing wine with ripe fruit aromas, good depth of delicate, slightly buttery and nutty flavours and a well-rounded finish.

TE AWANGA VINEYARDS HAWKES BAY CHARDONNAY

DRY $19 -V

(☆☆☆)

The debut 1995 vintage is an attempt at a complex style, but lacks fragrance, freshness and delicacy. Grown on the banks of the Tukituki River, whole bunch-pressed, and fermented and matured for 10 months in new and seasoned French oak barriques, it's slightly musty on the nose, with a full-bodied palate that offers some nutty complexity, but again a lack of delicacy and finesse. The '96 (****1/2) is a big improvement. It is a full-bodied, crisp wine with a nutty, buttery fragrance, good weight and plenty of fresh, lemony, biscuity flavour.

TE KAIRANGA CHARDONNAY

VINTAGE	96	95	94	93	92	91	90
WR	7	6	7	5	5	6	NM
DRINK	98-01	97-8	97-9	97-8	P	P	NM

DRY $22 AV

☆☆☆☆

At its best, this Martinborough wine is a bold, distinctly cool-climate style with deep flavour and taut acid spine. The 1994 vintage is delectably rich and clearly superior to the sturdy, but slightly green-edged and austere '95. The '96 (****) is another impressive release. Harvested very ripe (at 23 to 25° brix) and fermented and matured for nine months in French and American oak casks, it is a pale, fragrant and sturdy (14 per cent alcohol) wine, strongly "malo"-influenced, with rich, creamy, appley, nutty flavours. Open 1998 onwards.

TE KAIRANGA RESERVE CHARDONNAY

VINTAGE	96	95	94
WR	7	7	7
DRINK	99-01	97-00	97-00

DRY $30 -V

☆☆☆☆½

The 1994 vintage is this Martinborough winery's best white wine yet, with searching flavours and authoritative acidity. The '95 is not as concentrated as the '94, but displays the same lovely harmony of strong, citrusy flavours, quality oak and lively acidity. The '96 (*****1/2) is another distinguished wine. Picked at high sugar levels (24 to 25° brix), it was fermented and matured for 10 months in new and seasoned barrels. It's a huge wine (14 per cent alcohol) and still a baby, with tight, intense grapefruit-like, mealy flavours, quality oak and invigorating acidity. It makes no concessions to drink-young appeal, but should flourish in the cellar.

TE MANIA NELSON CHARDONNAY

VINTAGE	96
WR	5
DRINK	97-00

DRY $18 V+

(☆☆☆☆)

Jon and Cheryl Harrey, grapegrowers on the Waimea Plains, had the excellent 1996 vintage (****) produced on their behalf at a local winery. Matured in new French and American oak casks, with some barrel fermentation, it's a light straw wine with an enticingly rich, buttery, mealy fragrance. It's a delicious wine, robust and bursting with flavour – ripe, creamy, savoury, complex and persistent. Great drinking now to 1998, and sharply priced.

TE MATA
CHARDONNAY

DRY $22 AV

(☆☆☆☆⯪)

The new junior partner for Te Mata's illustrious Elston Chardonnay was launched from the 1996 vintage (****). Whole bunch-pressed, half the wine was fermented in oak and given a malolactic fermentation; the rest was kept in tanks without going through "malo". Very forward in its appeal, it reveals rich, ripe fruit aromas and ripe, peachy, slightly buttery flavours, with plenty of muscle.

TE MATA
ELSTON
CHARDONNAY

VINTAGE	97	96	95	94	93	92	91	90
WR	7	7	7	7	7	7	7	6
DRINK	97-8	99-04	98-02	99-04	97-00	P	P	P

DRY $33 AV

☆☆☆☆☆

Consistently one of New Zealand's most distinguished Chardonnays, this wine is grown in the Elston vineyard and an adjacent vineyard at Havelock North. It is a robust, grapefruit-flavoured, mealy wine of great concentration that blossoms in the cellar for at least five years. The '95, fully barrel-fermented (40 per cent new oak), is the equal of the '94 – very robust and fragrant, with great depth of flavour, still youthful and tight. The outstanding 1996 vintage (*****) is the first given a 100 per cent softening malolactic fermentation – and it does affect the style. Hand-harvested, whole bunch-pressed, and fermented and matured for 10 months in new and older oak casks, it is a light yellow wine with a superbly rich, rather Burgundian bouquet. The palate is bold and very concentrated, with intense citrusy, nutty, mealy flavours, a definite touch of butterscotch and a rounded, very rich finish. This is a top-flight Elston, offering memorable drinking from now onwards.

TERRACE
ROAD
CHARDONNAY

VINTAGE	96
WR	5
DRINK	97-8

DRY $17 V+

(☆ ☆☆☆⯪)

This is the pick of Cellier Le Brun's trio of still (non-sparkling) wines under its Terrace Road label. The first 1996 vintage (***¹/₂) was grown in Marlborough and 60 per cent of the final blend was fermented and matured in one, two and three-year-old barrels. It's an enjoyable wine in a very forward style, with a fragrant, buttery bouquet and broad, soft palate with lots of flavour.

TERRACE
VIEW
CHARDONNAY

VINTAGE	95
WR	5
DRINK	P

DRY $15 AV

(☆☆☆)

The Kemblefield winery's lower-tier, drink-young label. Grown in Hawke's Bay and fermented and matured for six months in oak, the 1995 vintage (***) is a strongly "malo"-influenced style with a buttery bouquet, ample body and soft, grapefruit and toffee-like flavours. Ready.

TE WHARE RA
BOOTS 'N ALL
CHARDONNAY

DRY $22 AV

(☆☆☆☆)

Named in memory of Allen and Joyce Hogan's faithful old dog, Boots, who died in 1994, the

'94 vintage (****) was estate-grown at Renwick, oak-aged, and matured for a year on its gross lees. The powerful, mealy, slightly buttery bouquet leads into a muscular palate, chock full of body and flavour. An impressively complex wine, savoury and toasty, it is tautly structured, crisp and long, offering very good drinking from 1997 onwards.

TE WHARE RA
DUKE OF
MARLBOROUGH CHARDONNAY

DRY $20 AV

☆ ☆☆☆

Winemaker Allen Hogan produces distinctive, muscular, richly alcoholic Chardonnays, peachy-ripe and chewy. The 1994 vintage (fermented both in tanks and barrels, then oak-matured for varying periods, with some lees-aging) is a typically opulent, ripe, robust style, peachy and savoury. The '95 (***1/2), made from bought-in grapes, is lighter than the '94, but a very good effort from a wet vintage. Light yellow, with lifted, citrusy, oaky aromas, it is a weighty wine with good acid spine and plenty of citrusy, slightly buttery and nutty flavour. Drink 1997–98.

TIMARA
CHARDONNAY/
SEMILLON

MED/DRY $9 V+

☆ ☆☆

This non-wooded, slightly sweet quaffer from Montana packs plenty of flavour into the glass. The '95 (***1/2) is full and smooth, its marriage of peachy Chardonnay and tangy Semillon yielding a sound, tasty white, ready now. (The 1997 vintage is a blend of Marlborough, Hawke's Bay and Australian wine.)

TORLESSE
WAIPARA RES.
CHARDONNAY

VINTAGE	95
WR	6
DRINK	00-02

DRY $25 -V

(☆ ☆☆☆)

Torlesse's first North Canterbury Chardonnay, made in the 1995 vintage (***1/2), is a stylish debut. Grown in winemaker Kim Rayner's Waipara vineyard, barrel-fermented and given eight months lees contact, with 70 per cent of the wine also undergoing a softening malolactic fermentation, it's a light yellow wine with peachy, citrusy flavours, toasty oak, mealiness and a rounded, very buttery finish. Full-flavoured and well-balanced, it is already drinking well.

TRINITY HILL
SHEPHERD'S
CROFT CHARD.

VINTAGE	97	96
WR	6	5
DRINK	98-01	98-00

DRY $23 AV

(☆ ☆☆☆)

The words "by John Hancock" emblazoned across the label leave you in no doubt this wine was made by the high profile winemaker who built his reputation at Morton Estate. Grown in the Shepherd's Croft vineyard at Ngatarawa and 75 per cent barrel-fermented, the debut 1996 vintage (****) is a classic Hawke's Bay style, full-bodied (13.5 per cent alcohol), tight, elegant and youthful, with crisp grapefruit/lemon flavours, rich mealy characters and a long, immaculate finish.

TWIN ISLANDS	VINTAGE	97	96	95	94	93		DRY $14 AV
UNWOODED	WR		6	5	4	6	4	
CHARDONNAY	DRINK		97-8 P	P	P	P		☆☆☆

Produced by the wine distributor, Negociants, from 1996 this Marlborough wine has replaced the former Twin Islands Marlborough Chardonnay, which was a lightly oaked style. A good drink-young proposition, the thoroughly enjoyable '96 (***) is fresh and lively, with balanced acidity and pleasing depth of apple/lemon flavours – a decent, no-fuss wine for now to 1998. (Note: the pre-1996 vintage ratings apply to the Marlborough Chardonnay.)

VAVASOUR	VINTAGE	96	DRY $22 AV
AWATERE VAL.	WR	7	
CHARDONNAY	DRINK	98-00	(☆☆☆☆☆)

Launched from the 1996 vintage (****¹/₂), this is Vavasour's middle-tier Chardonnay. Grown in two Awatere Valley vineyards, and fermented in new (20 per cent) and seasoned French oak casks, it's a light lemon-green, muscular (14 per cent alcohol) wine, vibrantly fruity, with an excellent spread of citrusy, biscuity, complex flavour, very refined and tight. A prime candidate for cellaring.

VAVASOUR SIN.	VINTAGE	96	95	94	93	92	91	90		DRY $30 AV
VINEYARD	WR	7	NM	7	6	6	7	6	
CHARDONNAY	DRINK	98-00	NM	97-9	P		P	97-98	P	☆☆☆☆☆

Launched from the 1996 vintage (*****), this wine replaces the Reserve label as the Awatere Valley winery's premier Chardonnay. The Reserve Chardonnay was a regional classic – concentrated, savoury, taut and steely – and the '96 Single Vineyard Chardonnay preserves, even lifts, the established standard. Grown in the Awatere Valley, and fermented and matured on its yeast lees for nine months in French oak barrels (20 per cent new), it's a strapping wine (harbouring 14 per cent alcohol) with sweet, ripe fruit, a lovely intensity of savoury, mealy flavour, a touch of butterscotch and a well-rounded, trailing finish. Superb power, richness and length. (Note: vintage ratings for 1990 to 1994 apply to Vavasour Reserve Chardonnay.)

VIDAL EAST	VINTAGE	96	95	94	93	92	91	90		DRY $13 V+
COAST	WR	6	6	6	6	5	6	6	
CHARDONNAY	DRINK	99	98	P	P	P	P	P	☆☆☆

Vidal's lower-tier wine is sharply priced and consistently enjoyable. The '95 was a great buy – a full, flavoursome wine with fresh, ripe fruit against a backdrop of toasty oak. Balanced for current consumption, the 1996 vintage (***) is a blend of Gisborne and Hawke's Bay grapes, oak-aged for four months. It's very fresh and crisp, with good depth of apple/lemon flavours and a touch of wood. In a blind tasting, it comes across as almost identical to its Hawke's Bay stablemate (below).

VIDAL	VINTAGE	96	DRY $13 V+
HAWKE'S BAY	WR	6	
CHARDONNAY	DRINK	97-9	(☆☆☆)

The 1996 vintage (***) is a ripe, enjoyable wine for early consumption. Oak-matured for three months, it reveals fresh fruit aromas of apples and lemons, leading into a crisp, buoyant palate with a very restrained wood influence, in a very easy-drinking style.

VINTAGE	96	95	94	93	92	91	90
WR	6	6	6	5	5	6	6
DRINK	98-01	98-00	99	98	P	P	P

**VIDAL
RESERVE
CHARDONNAY**

DRY $25 AV

☆☆☆☆☆

Clearly one of Hawke's Bay's great Chardonnays. It is evolving, as winemaker Elise Montgomery puts it, towards a "more elegant, still big, but less oaky" style. The 1994 is a classically proportioned wine, crisp, savoury and long, with lovely depth of ripe, grapefruit, passionfruit and fig-like fruit flavours, still developing. Still youthful and fairly restrained, the '95 (****) was grown in the Simcox vineyard and fermented and lees-aged for nine months in French oak. Maturing gracefully, it's a poised, crisp wine with fullness of body and quality oak in an elegant, reasonably intense style that needs more time; open mid 1998 onwards.

**VIDAL
THE BAYS
CHARDONNAY**

DRY $20 AV

(☆ ☆☆☆)

Broad, well-integrated and complex, Vidal's recently launched middle-tier wine from the 1995 vintage (****) was grown in Hawke's Bay, barrel-fermented and French oak-matured for nine months. Pale straw, it's a weighty style with a hint of "malo"-derived softness, generous depth of ripe tropical fruit and citrus flavours, a mealy, biscuity richness and lasting finish. Open now onwards.

VINTAGE	96	95	94	93	92	91
WR	6	6	6	5	5	6
DRINK	97-00+	97-00+	97-00	97-9	97-8	P

**VILLA MARIA
CELLAR SEL.
CHARDONNAY**

DRY $18 V+

☆☆☆↲

This mid-priced label places its accent on fresh, citrusy, incisive fruit flavours. The highly scented 1995 is a delicate, ripe style with crisp, fresh, passionfruit and lemon characters, a touch of wood and good persistence and vigour. A drink-young or cellaring proposition, the stylish '96 (****) is a blend of Gisborne and Marlborough fruit, of which 30 per cent was fermented in new French barriques and oak-matured for six months on light yeast lees. It's a full-bodied wine (13.5 per cent alcohol), delightfully fresh, aromatic and crisp, with intense, ripe, apple/lemon flavours, a touch of complexity and a persistent, quite rich finish.

VINTAGE	97	96	95	94	93	92	91	90
WR	6	7	5	6	5	6	5	4
DRINK	97-9	97-8	P	P	P	P	P	P

**VILLA MARIA
PRIVATE BIN
CHARDONNAY**

DRY $13 V+

☆☆☆

The latest releases of this popular, predominantly Gisborne-grown wine are the best yet. The 1995 vintage, a blend of far-flung regions – 80 per cent Gisborne, 15 per cent Marlborough and 5 per cent Mangere fruit – is a good commercial style with plenty of body, fresh, uncluttered lemon and melon-evoking flavours, very restrained wood and a crisp, tangy finish. The '96 (****), grown in Gisborne, is the finest wine yet under this highly affordable label. There's some French and American oak influence adding richness (15 per cent of the final blend was matured briefly in seasoned oak casks), but the wine is basically about fruit. The bouquet offers fresh, ripe, scented fruit aromas; the palate is full and flavoursome, with excellent depth of ripe, extremely delicate fruit flavour, supported by finely balanced acidity. A very elegant fruit-driven style, offering lovely drinking now to 1998.

VILLA MARIA	VINTAGE	96	95	94	93	92	91	90
RES. BARRIQUE	WR		7	6	6	7	6	7	5
FERM. CHARD.	DRINK		98-00	97-00+	97-00+	97-00	97-8	97-8	P

DRY $29 AV

☆☆☆☆☆

One of the country's most acclaimed wines, with a host of gold medals to its credit. In the past, it was usually based wholly on Gisborne grapes, but the 1993 vintage is an Auckland wine, and since 1994 the Hawke's Bay and Marlborough regions have come to the fore. Each year the pick of the winery's fruit, barrel fermentation, partial malolactic fermentation, and oak maturation, yields a strikingly rich and savoury wine. The '95 is stylish and full, with toasty oak aromas, rich, ripe, citrusy fruit and deep, firm flavour. The lush, exciting, strapping 1996 (*****) is a French oak-fermented and matured blend of Hawke's Bay and Marlborough fruit. Bright, light yellow-green, with a very rich, fresh, ripe, toasty bouquet, it is a seductive amalgam of highly concentrated tropical/citrus fruit flavours with classy oak. A powerful, high impact wine, still in its infancy, it deserves cellaring to at least 1999.

VILLA MARIA	VINTAGE	96	95	94	93	92	91	90
RES. MARL.	WR		6	5	7	5	6	6	6
CHARDONNAY	DRINK		97-00+	97-00	97-00	97-00	97-9	P	P

DRY $23 AV

☆☆☆☆⯪

With its rich, slightly mealy, citric-fruit flavoured palate and firm, authoritative finish, this is a distinguished wine, not voluptuous like its Reserve Barrique Fermented stablemate but concentrated and steely. The 1994 vintage is majestic, building beautifully in the bottle, with mouth-encircling grapefruit, oak and lees flavours and a sustained, taut finish. The '95 (***1/2) is scented and lively, with strong citrusy fruit and well-integrated oak, but lacks the power of the memorable '94. Grown in the Waldron vineyard and 80 per cent barrel-fermented, it is a pale, immaculate wine, attractively fresh and crisp, and still very youthful; open 1998 onwards.

VOSS
ESTATE
CHARDONNAY

DRY $17 AV

(☆☆☆)

The non-reserve wine from 1996 (***) was grown in Martinborough's Craighall vineyard, harvested at a very ripe 24° brix and lightly oaked. Tasted shortly after bottling, it revealed good depth of grapefruit and lemon flavours, with subtle wood influence and a firm, tight finish. It lacks the exciting power of its Reserve stablemate (below) but is still a satisfying wine for drinking during 1998.

VOSS EST.	VINTAGE	96	95	94	93	92
RESERVE	WR		6	6	7	4	6
CHARDONNAY	DRINK		98-01	97-01	97-00	P	P

DRY $24 AV

(☆☆☆☆⯪)

The 1994 vintage – Voss' first Martinborough-grown Chardonnay – is a beauty: a fat, succulent wine with a mealy, oaky bouquet, savoury, buttery palate and a very rich, trailing finish. The '95 is also powerful, with intense, lush flavour. The 1996 (*****) is outstanding. Already delicious, yet built to last, it's a light yellow wine with a rich, oaky, mealy fragrance.

Richly alcoholic (14 per cent), it possesses an exciting concentration of peachy, oaky, complex, well-spined flavour. This is a power-packed wine, full of character.

WAIMATA	VINTAGE	95	94		DRY $25 -V
VINEYARD RES.	WR	6	5	
CHARDONNAY	DRINK	97-9	97-8		(☆☆☆☆⯪)

Produced by the students and staff of the winemaking course at Tairawhiti Polytechnic, this wine is grown on the banks of Gisborne's Waimata River, hand-picked, whole bunch-pressed, and fermented and lees-aged in new French oak barriques. The 1994 vintage is a full, soft wine with good depth of ripe, nutty flavour, drinking well now. The '95 (****) is a delicious wine, still ascending. Bright yellow, with a rich, toasty fragrance, it is a powerful (13.5 per cent alcohol) citrusy wine, fat, lush and creamy.

WAIPARA	VINTAGE	96	95	DRY $17 AV
DOWNS	WR	4	6	
CHARDONNAY	DRINK	97-8 P		☆ ☆☆

This is consistently the most successful wine grown at Keith and Ruth Berry's farm at Waipara. The 1995 vintage, matured in American and French oak casks, is pale yellow, fragrant and buttery, with plenty of savoury, citrusy, soft flavour. In the search for "greater fruit character", the '96 (***), produced by consultant winemaker Mark Rattray, was fermented in a lower percentage of new oak than in the past. It's a delicate, restrained wine with fresh, savoury, appetisingly crisp flavours, worth keeping until 1998.

WAIPARA	VINTAGE	96	95	94	93	92	91	90	DRY $21 -V
SPRINGS	WR	6	6	4	5	6	6	6	
CHARDONNAY	DRINK	98-00	97-8 P	P	P	P	P		☆ ☆☆⯪

The fleshy, soft 1995 vintage of this North Canterbury wine is a weighty style (14 per cent alcohol), with strong, butterscotch-like, honied flavours in a lush, forward style. The '96 (****) was harvested ripe (24° brix), and fermented and lees-aged for eight months in French oak barriques. It's a powerful wine, structured for a long life, with mouthfilling body and a tight, elegant palate revealing excellent depth of crisp, mealy, creamy flavour.

WAIPARA	VINTAGE	96	95	DRY $23 -V
WEST	WR	6	4	
CHARDONNAY	DRINK	97-00	97-8	(☆☆☆☆⯪)

Clearly superior to the winery's Riesling and Sauvignon Blanc of the same vintage, the '96 (***½) is a muscular wine (14 per cent alcohol) with a fragrant, nutty, cheesy, "malo"-influenced bouquet. Fermented and matured in wood, it is a fresh, crisp wine with plenty of appley, nutty, mealy flavour, and well worth cellaring.

WAIRAU		DRY $22 -V
RIVER		
CHARDONNAY		☆☆☆⯪

A consistently good Marlborough wine, although less striking than its Sauvignon Blanc stablemate. The 1994 vintage is fleshy and buttery, slightly mealy, soft and ready. Light yellow in hue, the '96 (****) is robust, smooth and vibrantly fruity, with ripe melon/citrus flavours and well-balanced toasty oak. A rich, full-flavoured wine, French oak-aged for six months, it is already a lovely mouthful, but capable of aging well.

WAIRAU RIVER
RICHMOND RIDGE
CHARDONNAY

DRY $13 V+

(☆☆☆)

The '96 vintage (***) of this Marlborough winery's second-tier Chardonnay is great value. Matured for three months in two and three-year-old French oak casks, it's a light yellow wine, fresh and crisp, with good depth of well-ripened, slightly buttery, melon/citrus flavour in a simple but very attractive style. Ready.

WEST BROOK
BARRIQUE FERMENTED
CHARDONNAY

DRY $19 AV

☆☆☆☆

The 1995 vintage is a voluptuous Gisborne wine, bright yellow, with the fragrant aromas of ripe fruit and toasty oak. It's a powerful wine, strongly oaked, with concentrated fruit flavours in a lush, creamy, buttery, rounded style. The elegant, beautifully balanced '96 (****¹/₂) is a rare example of Chardonnay not just made but actually grown in Henderson, West Auckland. It is also further evidence of West Brook's rising star. French and American oak-matured for eight months, it reveals toasty wood aromas and a full, generous palate with excellent depth of savoury, ripe, citrusy, mealy flavour. Still youthful; open 1998–99.

WHITEHAVEN
MARLBOROUGH
CHARDONNAY

DRY $17 AV

(☆☆☆)

It's no surprise that Simon Waghorn, formerly chief winemaker at Corbans Gisborne Winery, knows how to make a good Chardonnay. The debut 1995 vintage of this wine, 50 per cent barrel-fermented, is a full, fresh, appley, slightly buttery wine, well-balanced and with good flavour depth. The '96 (***) is a very lightly oaked style, but was matured on its yeast lees for an extended period, with regular stirring. It's a full, soft wine, appley, vibrantly fruity and full of fresh, youthful appeal.

WHITEHAVEN
MENDOZA
CHARDONNAY

VINTAGE	95
WR	6
DRINK	97-8

DRY $24 -V

(☆☆☆☆)

The 1995 vintage (****) of this Marlborough Chardonnay is a stylish debut. Hand-picked and whole bunch-pressed, it was fermented in new French and American oak barriques and given extended lees aging. Ready now, it's a fragrant and complex wine with fresh, mouth-watering acidity, strong toasty oak, "malo"-derived milky/cheesy characters and excellent flavour depth.

WITHER HILLS
VIN. MARL.
CHARDONNAY

VINTAGE	96	95	94	93	92
WR	7	6	7	NM	6
DRINK	97-00	97-9	97-9	NM	97-8

DRY $25 V+

(☆ ☆☆☆☆ ☆)

The private label of Brent Marris, winemaker at Delegat's, this is an exceptionally classy wine. The '94 is a gorgeous wine. Fragrant and robust, with mouth-encircling flavour, the 1995 vintage (*****) is a very elegant style with sweet, ripe, highly concentrated fruit fleshed out with subtle, biscuity oak/lees characters and braced by fresh, lively acidity. This is an immaculate, astutely crafted wine, maturing superbly. The 1996 vintage, tasted in mid '97 as a representative barrel sample, looked extremely promising – a bold, citrusy, savoury, notably rich-flavoured and tautly structured wine with the power to flourish over the long haul.

Chenin Blanc

Looking for a good, full-bodied dry white wine at a price you can afford to drink every night? Try Chenin Blanc, or one of the several Chenin Blanc/Chardonnay blends.

A top New Zealand Chenin Blanc is fresh and buoyantly fruity, with good depth of melon and pineapple-evoking flavours and a crisp, racy finish. In New Zealand's cool climate for grapegrowing, the variety's naturally high acidity (an asset in the warmer viticultural regions of South Africa, the United States and Australia) can be a distinct handicap. But when the grapes achieve full ripeness here, this classic grape of Vouvray, in France's Loire Valley, yields sturdy wines that are satisfying in their youth yet can mature for many years, gradually unfolding a delicious honied richness.

Only two wineries have consistently made top-class Chenin Blancs: Collards and The Millton Vineyard, with Esk Valley hard on their heels. Seibel and Chifney also champion the grape. Other growers, put off by the variety's late-ripening nature and the susceptibility of its tight bunches to Botrytis rot, have recently uprooted their vines. According to the latest national vineyard survey, the area of bearing Chenin Blanc vines will drop between 1996 and 1999 from 143 hectares to 125 hectares.

Chenin Blanc is the country's seventh most widely planted white grape variety, with plantings concentrated on the east coast of the North Island. In the future, winemakers who plant their Chenin Blanc in the warmest, sunniest vineyard sites and crop their vines lightly can be expected to produce the ripest, most concentrated wines.

Don't overlook the Chenin Blanc/Chardonnays – notably from Matua Valley, Villa Maria, Vidal and Pleasant Valley – which offer highly enjoyable anytime drinking and great value.

AKARANGI CHENIN BLANC

DRY $10 -V

☆☆

Those vintages I have tasted of this Havelock North wine have tended to be austere, with biting acidity and slightly under-ripe flavours, or light and lacking flavour depth.

CHIFNEY CHENIN BLANC

DRY 16 AV

☆☆☆☆

A consistently attractive Martinborough wine, grown further south than most New Zealand Chenin Blancs, and one of the highlights of the Chifney range. The 1996 vintage (***¹/₂) underwent a partial malolactic fermentation and was matured for nine months in French and American oak casks. It's a full, vibrant, clearly varietal, strong-flavoured wine. The nutty wood enriches the palate but doesn't subdue the crisp, fresh fruit characters. Good drinking now onwards.

CHIFNEY CHENIN BLANC/CHARD. RESERVE

MED $15 V+

(☆☆☆☆)

The 1996 vintage (***¹/₂) of this distinctive Martinborough wine is a medium-sweet blend of Chenin Blanc with some noble rot infection and oak-aged Chardonnay. Full-bodied, with peachy, slightly honied flavours and balanced acidity, it's a very easy-drinking and characterful wine, already attractive but worth keeping to 1998–99.

COLLARDS H.B. CHENIN BLANC

DRY $13 V+

☆☆☆☆☆

VINTAGE	97	96	95	94	93	92	91	90
WR	7	7	6	7	7	7	6	6
DRINK	98-01	97-00	P	97-8	97-8	97-8	P	P

If I had to select just one modestly priced wine for my house dry white, this could well be it. Given a very restrained touch of wood, it is a notably rich, vibrantly fruity wine that consistently rivals The Millton Vineyard's at the top of New Zealand's Chenin Blanc tree. Ready now, the yellow-hued '95 is not a top vintage, but still lively, firm and dry, with satisfying depth of lemony, limey, slightly toasty flavour. The '96 (*****), which includes a small proportion of Te Kauwhata fruit, is a classy wine, brimming with youthful charm. Mouthfilling and richly scented, it's deliciously pure, ripe and fruity, with lots of fresh, crisp, zingy flavour. Enjoy now or cellar for a year or two.

COLLARDS SUM. CHENIN/ CHARDONNAY

DRY $11 V+

(☆☆☆☆)

VINTAGE	97	96
WR	6	6
DRINK	97-8	97-8

This wine has replaced the Private Bin Dry White as the all-purpose dry white in the Collards range. The ripely scented, vibrantly fruity debut 1996 vintage (***¹/₂) is a fractionally off-dry wine, blended from Hawke's Bay, Marlborough and Auckland grapes. Full of youthful appeal, it's fleshy, ripe-tasting, and deliciously well-balanced and fresh.

DAN. SCHUSTER	VINTAGE	96	95	94	93
H.B. CHENIN	WR		7	5	NM 7
BLANC	DRINK		98-9	97-9	NM P

DRY $16 AV

(☆ ☆☆☆⯪)

In 1993, Canterbury winemaker Danny Schuster replaced his Pinot Blanc with a wood-aged Hawke's Bay Chenin Blanc. The 1996 vintage (****), the best yet, is also the last of this label. Barrel-fermented and lees-aged, it's a distinctive wine with a toasty, fresh bouquet. Dry, with excellent depth of pineappley, leesy, slightly buttery flavour, it's a complex style, very approachable now but likely to develop well with cellaring.

ESK VALLEY	VINTAGE	96	95	94	93	92	91	90
CHEN. BLANC	WR		6	5	7	5	6	6	5
WOOD AGED	DRINK	97-00	97-8	97-00+	97-8	P	P	P

DRY $12 V+

☆ ☆☆☆⯪

A great value Hawke's Bay wine. It matures well: the '94 is still developing, with rich, ripe, rounded, slightly honied flavours. The fleshy 1995 vintage was matured for three months in French and American oak casks. Light yellow, it is not intensely flavoured, but has well-balanced acidity and a touch of complexity from the toasty oak seasoning. The '96 (****¹/₂) is a full-bodied, lively wine with a slightly creamy texture and very good depth of savoury, appley flavour.

LINCOLN
CHEN.BLANC/
CHARDONNAY

DRY $10 V+

(☆ ☆☆☆)

Here's a bargain! Drinking well now, the 1995 vintage (***) of this Hawke's Bay wine is a wood-matured blend of 70 per cent Chenin Blanc and 30 per cent Chardonnay. Bone-dry (unusual for Chenin Blanc), it is pale straw, with good weight and a toasty, firm, slightly complex palate. A great buy at $10.

MATAWHERO
EST. CHENIN
BLANC

DRY $15 AV

(☆ ☆☆☆)

The characterful 1995 vintage (***) of this crisp Gisborne dry white is light yellow, its strongly fruity, slightly honeyish flavours underpinned by vigorous acidity. Good drinking from now onwards.

MATUA	VINTAGE	96
CHENIN BLANC/	WR	6
CHARDONNAY	DRINK	98

DRY $11 V+

☆ ☆☆☆

This fresh, fruity dryish white is typically medium to full-bodied, satisfyingly full-flavoured, and sharply priced. Maturing well, the 1995 vintage (***) is a Gisborne blend of 70 per cent Chenin Blanc and 30 per cent Chardonnay. A decent all-purpose wine with satisfying depth of fresh, lively, fractionally off-dry flavour, it's developing a touch of complexity with age.

MILLS REEF
RES. CHENIN
BLANC

DRY $19 -V

(☆☆☆⟡)

The oak-aged 1995 vintage (***½) is a Hawke's Bay wine, maturing well. A full-bodied dry wine with firm acidity adding spine to its strong, appley, nutty flavours, it's a fairly complex style for drinking now onwards.

MILLTON VINE.,
THE, CHENIN
BLANC DRY

VINTAGE	96	95	94	93	92	91	90
WR	5	NM	6	6	7	6	5
DRINK	97-00	NM	97-00	97-9	97-9	97-9	P

M/DRY $20 AV

☆☆☆☆☆

This Gisborne wine rivals Collards' for the title of New Zealand's champion Chenin Blanc. Winemaker James Millton says he aims for "honey, acidity and almond flavours" – and he gets them. Barrel-fermented in French oak casks, new and old, it is typically a rich wine with restrained wood and strong, pineappley, slightly honeyish flavour. The 1994 vintage is a full, succulent, tropical-fruit-flavoured wine with a lingering, lush finish. The '96 (****) is bright yellow, with a highly scented, honeyish bouquet. It's slightly less weighty, lush and intense than the top vintages, but still richly flavoured, with crisp tropical-fruit characters, oak and honey adding up to an absorbing wine.

PLEASANT
VAL. CHENIN/
CHARDONNAY

VINTAGE	95
WR	4
DRINK	97-8

M/DRY $11 V+

(☆☆☆)

This unwooded Hawke's Bay wine hangs its hat on its vibrant, tangy fruit flavours. The '95 (***) is still fresh, its appley, slightly sweet flavours underpinned by crisp acidity. A good all-purpose white.

RONGOPAI
TE KAUWHATA
CHENIN BLANC

M/DRY $15 V+

(☆☆☆⟡)

The fleshy, generous 1995 vintage of this Te Kauwhata wine is a medium-dry style with bright, full-yellow colour and pleasing depth of toasty, slightly honeyish, ripe flavour. Delicious now, the '96 (****) is a pale, scented, weighty wine, fractionally off-dry, with loads of fresh, appley flavour in a crisp, vibrantly fruity style. This is a charming wine revealing excellent ripeness and sharply defined varietal character.

SALUT!
CHENIN BLANC/
SÉMILLON

M/DRY $8 V+

(☆☆⟡)

This non-vintage, pale, crisp, rather Sauvignon-like wine from Montana exhibits green-edged, clearly herbaceous aromas and a light, dryish, grassy palate. Re-tasted in 1997, it was not intense, but a decent dryish white, with the grassy Sémillon characters very evident.

SEIBEL CELLARMASTER'S RESERVE CHENIN BLANC

M/DRY $15 AV

(☆☆☆✓)

Penetrating and lively, the 1995 vintage (***½) of this mouthfilling Hawke's Bay wine was given "extended lees maturation and subtle oaking". A dryish style, it's very crisp and appley, with a touch of complexity, offering very satisfying drinking.

SEIBEL CHENIN BLANC MEDIUM-DRY

VINTAGE	94
WR	6
DRINK	96-10

M/DRY $12 AV

(☆☆☆)

Norbert Seibel made Corbans' acclaimed 1976 Chenin Blanc and still champions the grape. His 1994 vintage (***), like the '76 grown at Tolaga Bay, north of Gisborne, is a non-wooded wine, medium-bodied (10.5 per cent alcohol), fractionally sweet and full of character, with peachy, slightly honeyish flavour and a mouth-wateringly crisp finish.

TWIN ISLANDS H.B. CHENIN BLANC

M/DRY $10 V+

(☆☆☆✓)

The outpouring of fresh, ripe scents from the 1996 vintage (***½) is instantly appealing. So is the full, very fresh and pure palate, with its basket-of-fruit flavours and fractionally off-dry, smooth finish. Stunning value from the wine distributor, Negociants.

VIDAL CHENIN BLANC/ CHARDONNAY

VINTAGE	95	94
WR	5	5
DRINK	97-8	97-8

DRY $10 V+

(☆☆☆)

I can't think of a better-value dry white than the '95 vintage (****). A Hawke's Bay blend of 85 per cent Chenin Blanc and 15 per cent Chardonnay, oak-aged for three months, it's light gold and richly fragrant. The palate is full, with deep flavour, a touch of complexity and a beguiling creaminess of texture. Seemingly at its peak, it offers delicious, bargain-priced drinking.

VILLA MARIA PRI. BIN CHEN. BLANC/CHARD.

VINTAGE	96	95	94	93	92	91	90
WR	5	5	6	5	6	5	5
DRINK	97-9	97-9	97-8	P	P	P	P

M/DRY $10 V+

☆☆☆

A briefly oak-aged Hawke's Bay wine, not complex but offering plenty of character in a fruity, drink-young style. The '96 (***) offers plenty of flavour for $10. Most of the final blend was handled in stainless steel, but 25 per cent was matured for three months in new and one-year-old casks. It's a fresh, full-bodied wine, buoyantly fruity, with a sliver of sweetness amid its apple/melon flavours, balanced by lively acidity.

WEST BROOK H.B CHENIN BLANC

M/DRY $11 V+

(☆☆☆)

The '95 vintage of this well-priced wine offers fresh, buoyant, slightly sweet apple/lemon flavours, crisp and well-balanced. The vibrant '96 (***) is a very easy-drinking wine, pale, fresh and slightly sweet. Medium to full-bodied, it is not intense but clearly varietal, with delicate, appley, citrusy flavours and balanced acidity. Drink now or cellar.

Generic And Branded White Wines

Waimanu, Triple Peaks, Crystal Creek, Shipwreck Bay White . . . the past few years have brought a flow of new, cheap, non-varietally labelled whites onto the market. Are winemakers catering for a growing demand for lower-priced bottled wine, or are they looking for an outlet for grapes, like Chenin Blanc and (until recently) Riesling, that are otherwise hard to sell? Are they using these cheaper wines as an outlet for harder-pressed, coarser juice ("pressings"), or are they eager to target supermarket customers with strong, distinctive brands that stand out from the bewildering array of varietal wines? Whatever the answer is – and it's probably all of those things – competition in the "cheap and cheerful" market is hotting up.

"Varietal" labelling burst into fashion in New Zealand in the 1970s. Previously, European "generic" names had been popular: Corbans Claret, Villa Maria Hock, Montana Moselle. These antipodean "clarets" and "hocks" were typically made from coarse, low-grade hybrid grapes. When finer varieties like Cabernet Sauvignon and Müller-Thurgau started to come on stream in commercial volumes, wine producers eagerly switched to varietal labelling: prestige names like Cabernet Sauvignon were a valuable sales aid.

A few "Chablis" labels still survive, although the simple name "Dry White" is more common (in both senses of the word) and far more accurate. Fortunately, the ranks of winemakers who still consciously ape European wine labels are fast shrinking. If New Zealand and the EC are finally able to conclude their long-running negotiations over a wine treaty that would ban copying of each other's geographically based wine names, traditional European names will disappear altogether from our labels.

Branded wines (like Blenheimer and Chasseur) include some of New Zealand's largest-volume cask wines. These are the labels wine buffs imagine they are familiar with to the point of boredom – but often haven't tasted for 10 years.

BABICH
CLASSIC
DRY

DRY $9 V+

(☆☆☆)

This bone-dry wine has long (starting under the old "Dry White" label) been one of Babich's more popular lines. Typically a blend of Sylvaner, Riesling and Müller-Thurgau, grown in Gisborne and Hawke's Bay, its appeal rests on its fresh, clean, uncomplicated, appetisingly crisp flavour, total dryness, and sharp price.

BABICH FUMÉ VERT

VINTAGE	96	95	94	93	92	91	90
WR	6	6	7	6	7	7	4
DRINK	98-9	97-00	97-9	97-8	P	P	P

M/DRY $11 V+

☆☆☆

This is Babich's most popular wine – and with its flavoursome, easy-drinking style, it's easy to see why. Fumé vert means "smoky green", which aptly sums up the wine's style. The typically zesty '95 is a Gisborne-grown blend of 60 per cent Sémillon, 20 per cent Sauvignon Blanc and 20 per cent Chardonnay. It's a seductive mouthful, with delicate, lemony, gently herbaceous flavours, slightly sweet and persistent. The 1996 vintage (***) is very crisp and fresh, with an almost imperceptible touch of sweetness smoothing its delicate citrus/green capsicum flavours.

BLACK RIDGE EARNSCLEUGH RISE

M/DRY $12 -V

(☆☆☆)

Based predominantly on the Breidecker variety, the Alexandra winery's estate-grown blend is typically pale, floral and light, its mild, citrusy flavours harbouring a distinct splash of sweetness.

BLENHEIM RIDGE CHABLISSE

M/DRY $15 3L AV

☆☆

Drier and slightly more flavoursome than its stablemate, Blenheimer, Montana's Chablisse is based on Müller-Thurgau and Sauvignon Blanc, grown in Marlborough and Gisborne. A cask wine, it is typically crisp, with slightly coarse, green-edged flavours; a decent, dryish white with enough flavour and liveliness to be interesting.

BLENHEIMER MEDIUM WHITE

MED $15 3L AV

☆☆

For a multitude of New Zealanders, since the 1970s Montana's Müller-Thurgau-based Blenheimer has served as a fruity, gently sweet, easy entry to the world of wine. It's no longer available as a bottled wine, but the cask wine I tasted was light, fresh, clean and crisp – above average for a bulk wine.

BRAJKOVICH DRY WHITE

DRY $9 V+

(☆☆☆)

This non-vintage wine from Kumeu River is a rarity: a table wine based principally on the Spanish sherry grape, Palomino (with a small splash of Chardonnay and Sauvignon Blanc). Kumeu-grown, it is a full, reasonably full-flavoured wine, lemony, dry and zesty; a very decent quaffer.

CHASSEUR
DRY

M/DRY $15 3L AV
☆☆

No longer sold in bottles, this is a light (9.5 per cent alcohol), dryish rather than bone-dry cask wine. It's typically clean and pleasant, without any obvious varietal characteristics. The wine I last tasted was better than average for a cask – crisp and vigorous, lemony and slightly spicy, with a touch of flavour.

CHASSEUR
MEDIUM

MED $15 3L AV
☆☆

This old favourite from Cooks (now Corbans) is a popular cask wine in supermarkets. The pale, floral wine I tasted lacked flavour depth but was fresher than most casks. It is lightly scented, delicately flavoured and juicy, with a sweetish finish.

C.J. PASK
ROY'S HILL
WHITE

VINTAGE	96	95	94	93	92	91
WR		6	6	7	6	5	5
DRINK		99	98	99	98	P	P

DRY $11 AV
☆☆☆

C.J. Pask's cheapest white wine, this is a dry, non-wooded style based on Hawke's Bay Chenin Blanc. The '95 is a solid wine with reasonable depth of apple/lemon flavours, fresh and zingy. The 1996 vintage (***) is one of the best yet. A satisfying, very well-balanced wine, it is fresh, lively and flavourful, with a steely, not quite bone-dry finish.

COLLARDS
PRIVATE BIN
DRY WHITE

VINTAGE	95	94	93	92	91	90
WR	6	6	6	7	6	6
DRINK	P	P	P	P	P	P

DRY $10 V+
☆☆☆

Recently replaced by Summerfields Chenin/Chardonnay, for many years this was the quaffing dry white in the Collards range. The last 1995 vintage (***) is based principally on Chenin Blanc and Chardonnay, drawn from Hawke's Bay, Marlborough and Auckland. Bright, light lemon/green, with a slightly honeyish fragrance, it offers pleasing depth of crisp, citrusy, melon-like flavours. Ready.

COOPERS
CLASSIC
DRY

VINTAGE	96	95	94	93	92	91	90
WR	5	5	6	5	4	5	4
DRINK	97-8	P	P	P	P	P	P

DRY $10 V+
☆☆☆

Coopers Creek's quaffing wine is consistently one of the best $10 dry whites on the market. The 1996 vintage (***) is a grassy, tangy blend of two-thirds Sémillon and one-third Chardonnay, grown in Gisborne and handled entirely in stainless steel. Fresh and herbaceous on the nose, it offers lots of brisk, green-edged, dry flavour.

CORBANS
WAIMANU

M/DRY $9 V+
(☆☆☆)

This vibrantly fruity, medium-bodied, non-vintage wine is based principally on Sauvignon

Blanc , blended with Chenin Blanc and Riesling. The attractive, fresh, fruity bouquet leads into a slightly sweet, reasonably ripe palate with good depth of flavour – limey and citrusy, with a moderately crisp finish. Fine value.

COUNTRY DRY WHITE

M/DRY $15 3L -V

(☆⭒)

One of the most popular cask wines in supermarkets, this off-dry wine is a blend of New Zealand and imported wine, marketed by Montana under its Woodhill's brand. The wine I tasted was pale, medium-bodied and very plain – serviceable, but nothing more.

COUNTRY MEDIUM WHITE

MED $15 3L AV

(☆☆)

Country Medium enjoys huge popularity in supermarkets. Marketed by Montana under its Woodhill's brand, the cask wine I tasted was a blend of imported and New Zealand wine, citrusy, appley and soft. It lacked fragrance and the flavour was slightly coarse, but that's typical of cask wines and the sweetness helped to keep things pleasant, if uninspiring.

FAREWELL SPIT

M/DRY $8 V+

(☆☆⭒)

Seifried Estate's slightly sweet, non-vintage quaffer is blended from Riesling, Chardonnay and Sauvignon Blanc. It's a pale, light wine with Riesling-like aromas and fresh, lively, lemony, slightly green-edged flavours.

GLENMARK TRIPLE PEAKS

MED $10 V+

(☆☆⭒)

This label has replaced the Waipara White in Glenmark's range. The fresh, vigorous, slightly honeyish 1994 vintage (***¹/₂), blended from Waipara Riesling and Müller-Thurgau, balances a splash of sweetness with lively acidity.

GLENMARK TRIPLE PEAKS DRY

M/DRY $10 V+

(☆☆☆)

Great value. The light, zesty 1994 vintage (***), blended from Waipara Riesling and Müller-Thurgau, smells and tastes like Riesling, with a scented, lemony bouquet and good depth of lively, citrusy flavour, semi-dry and honeyish. Ready.

HUNTER'S ESTATE DRY WHITE

M/DRY $12 AV

☆☆☆

Typically floral, fresh and tangy, it is a Marlborough blend of Riesling and Sauvignon Blanc, with more flavour interest than most "dry whites", but also higher-priced. The wine I tasted in 1997 was citrusy and slightly grassy in a fresh, lively, flavoursome style.

LIEBESTRAUM

MED $15 3L AV

☆☆

This long-popular Corbans brand is a blend of Australian and New Zealand wine. When I last encountered it in a lineup of cask wines, it was distinctly sweet, citrusy and crisp, with medium body and light flavour. No excitement here, but nor is there anything to object to, and the price is sharp.

LONGBUSH KAHURANGI

MED $11 AV

(☆☆☆)

A pale, perfumed, Gisborne blend of Müller-Thurgau and Muscat that is light, juicy and crisp in a totally undemanding, very easy-drinking style. The 1995 vintage (**¹/₂), "perfect for all occasions", is a charming, flavoursome wine, light, crisp and grapey – ideal if you have a sweet tooth.

MATUA WHITE HILL

VINTAGE	95
WR	5
DRINK	P

M/DRY $8 V+

(☆☆☆)

White Hill (named after a Kumeu landmark) has replaced Matua Valley's long-popular Chablis as an enjoyable, dryish quaffer. Blended from Chenin Blanc (77 per cent), Riesling (15 per cent) and Chardonnay (8 per cent), the 1995 vintage (**¹/₂) is a medium-bodied wine with Chenin Blanc's fruity, citrus/melon flavours to the fore and a touch of sweetness to give an easy-drinking character. It's still fresh and lively, and maturing well.

MELNESS FLORAL

VINTAGE	95
WR	5
DRINK	97-05

M/DRY $14 AV

(☆☆☆☆)

"Floral" refers to the aromatic grape varieties this slightly sweet Canterbury wine was blended from: Riesling, Gewürztraminer and Morio-Muskat. The 1995 vintage (***¹/₂) is very attractive. Bright, light yellow, with fragrant citrus/spice aromas, it's a very fruity, slightly honied wine with very good depth of lemon and spice flavours and refreshing acidity.

Mission White Mirage

M/DRY $9 V+

☆☆½

From White Burgundy to White Meritage to White Mirage – the name has changed in the past few years, but the wine has stayed much the same. Matured for eight months in older barrels, it's typically a medium-bodied wine, fractionally sweet and smooth-flowing; a good all-purpose white, of wide appeal.

Misty Peak

M/DRY $9 V+

(☆☆½)

Eye-catchingly packaged in a tall, frosted bottle, Montana's medium-dry white is a blend of Müller-Thurgau, Riesling and Gewürztraminer, grown in Gisborne, Hawke's Bay and Marlborough. It's a pleasant, mild, medium-bodied wine, fresh and crisp, with citrusy, lightly spiced flavours, a splash of sweetness and lively acidity.

Nobilo White Cloud

VINTAGE	96	95
WR	6	5
DRINK	97-8	P

MED $9 V+

☆☆☆

Widely exported, White Cloud is also one of the hottest-selling bottled white wines in local supermarkets. Müller-Thurgau-based, with a touch of Sauvignon Blanc, and sweetened with Muscat Dr Hogg, it is grown in Gisborne, Hawke's Bay and Marlborough. Fragrant, grapey, clean and fresh, it is a very easy-drinking style. The 1996 vintage (***) is attractively full and flavoursome, with a lemony, slightly grassy bouquet and smooth, slightly sweet finish.

Okahu Est. Ninety Mile White

VINTAGE	96	95	94	93
WR	6	4	6	5
DRINK	97-01	97-8	96-8	P

DRY $19 -V

(☆☆☆½)

The 1996 vintage (***½) of this weighty dry white is a blend of 40 per cent Sémillon, estate-grown in Northland, with 60 per cent Chardonnay from Te Hana, north of Auckland. Eighty per cent of the wine was matured for seven months in new and one-year-old French oak barriques. It's a fresh, crisp, easy-drinking style, only mildly herbaceous, with a touch of complexity and good depth of ripe, citrusy, peachy, slightly leesy flavour.

Okahu Est. Shipwreck Bay White

M/DRY $16 -V

(☆☆☆)

Launched from the 1996 vintage (***), this distinctive new wine is a lightly wooded, off-dry, 50/50 mix of two German varieties, Arnsburger and GM 312-53, estate-grown at Kaitaia, with tank-fermented Chardonnay from Te Hana (just north of Wellsford). The bouquet is slightly toasty; the palate fresh, lively and skilfully balanced, with moderate acidity, a splash of sweetness and plenty of flavour.

OLD COACH **ROAD CLASSIC** **DRY WHITE**	VINTAGE 96 WR 5 DRINK 97-8	M/DRY $9 V+ ☆☆☆

Typically a great buy from Seifried Estate. The 1996 vintage (***) is a lively quaffer blended from Nelson Sauvignon Blanc and Riesling. Lightly scented, it's a dryish rather than bone-dry wine with good depth of fresh, crisp, lemony, gently herbaceous flavour. Drink young. A "steal" at under $10.

OLD COACH **ROAD WHITE** **AUTUMN**	VINTAGE 96 WR 5 DRINK 97-8	M/DRY $9 V+ (☆☆☆)

Seifried's thoroughly pleasant medium-dry white from 1996 (***) is a blend of Gewürztraminer and Riesling in which the Gewürztraminer makes its presence well felt. Lightly fragrant, fruity and soft, it exhibits a spicy bouquet and delicate fruit characters. Plenty of character for a slightly sweet, sub-$10 quaffer.

RIPPON VINE. **HOTERE** **WHITE WINE**	DRY $12 -V (☆☆☆)

Cultivated on the shores of Lake Wanaka in the Southern Alps, this wine is made "for summer drinking, not sipping". Tasting the 1996 vintage (**¹/₂), a blend of Müller-Thurgau, Breidecker and Chenin Blanc, is like biting a Granny Smith apple. It's a light (10 per cent alcohol) and lively wine, pale, with green-edged flavours and racy acidity.

ST AMAND **CHABLIS**	M/DRY $15 3L AV ☆☆

A safe bet for the medium-wine drinker looking to go a bit drier, this non-vintage wine is a Corbans blend. The cask wine I tasted was light, slightly sweet, clean and mild-flavoured, vaguely citrusy, but lacking depth of character.

ST AUBYNS **DRY** **WHITE**	M/DRY $8 V+ (☆☆☆)

This bottom-rung Villa Maria wine is ideal when you simply want a glass of no-fuss, off-dry white with reasonable body and flavour and a modest price-tag. It is grown principally in Gisborne, and tastes and smells like its predominant variety, Müller-Thurgau. Pale yellow, the 1996 vintage (**¹/₂) lacks fragrance, but is a well-balanced wine with citrusy, rounded flavours.

St Aubyns Medium White

`MED $8 AV`

(☆☆)

I tasted the 1996 vintage (**) of Villa Maria's low-priced quaffer this year in a blind tasting of blended medium whites. My brief notes read: "Lacks fragrance. Fruity, but a bit dull, sugary and plain."

St Helena South. Alps Dry White

`M/DRY $8 V+`

(☆☆⯪)

With 3000 cases produced each year, this cheap wine is one of the Canterbury winery's major lines. The 1996 vintage (**½) is a Canterbury wine based on "the pressings of Chardonnay, Pinot Blanc and Riesling," says proprietor Robin Mundy. It's a dryish rather than bone-dry wine, light and fresh, with crisp, tangy, green-edged flavours.

St Jerome Estate Dry White

`DRY $10 AV`

☆☆⯪

The 1996 vintage (***), based on Breidecker grapes grown at the Henderson estate vineyard, is the last of this line; the vines have been uprooted. Fractionally off-dry, it's a characterful, very easy-drinking wine, pleasantly fruity, ripe and smooth.

Te Mata Oak Aged Dry White

VINTAGE	96	95	94
WR	7	6	7
DRINK	98-9	97-8	P

`DRY $13 V+`

☆☆☆☆⯪

With its humble name, this is an easily overlooked wine in the Te Mata range, but it always offers good value. Typically a blend of Hawke's Bay Chardonnay and Sauvignon Blanc, with a portion of the final blend fermented and matured in oak, it is fresh, clean and slightly herbaceous, with plenty of appley, lemony, tangy flavour. Now only sold at the winery.

Waitiri Dry White

`MED $11 AV`

(☆☆⯪)

Designed for easy summer sipping, Gibbston Valley's 1995 vintage wine (**½) is a 2:1 blend of Marlborough Müller-Thurgau and Riesling, slightly sweet, with fresh, light, lemony, limey flavours. Ready.

Wohnsiedler Classic Dry White

`M/DRY $6 V+`

(☆☆)

Tasted in 1997, Montana's cheap, non-vintage quaffer is a plain but solid wine, shy on the nose, with light body and moderate depth of clean, smooth, dryish flavour.

Gewürztraminer

Don't expect an influx of new Gewürztraminer labels from the 1997 vintage. The total crop was only 510 tonnes – down by over 30 per cent on 1996, and less than one per cent of the total grape harvest.

White wines are commonly divided by winemakers into "aromatic" and "non-aromatic" classes. Chardonnay, for instance, is a non-aromatic variety: its fruit aromas are restrained rather than piercing. Gewürztraminer, by contrast, is an intensely aromatic variety: its fruit aromas can erupt out of the glass and swamp your senses.

Riesling, too, can pour forth a ravishing scent. In New Zealand these two highly aromatic varieties are experiencing contrasting fortunes. Riesling's popularity is at last on the surge; Gewürztraminer's is on the wane. Between 1983 and 1995, plantings of Riesling vines in this country rose by 190 per cent; those of Gewürztraminer more than halved (although the area of bearing vines is projected to expand slightly between 1996 and 1999, from 92 to 104 hectares). A key problem is that Gewürztraminer is a temperamental performer in the vineyard, being particularly vulnerable to adverse weather at flowering, which can decimate crop yields.

The majority of Gewürztraminer's plantings are in Marlborough and Hawke's Bay, with other significant pockets in Gisborne and Central Otago. Gisborne has traditionally been the source of New Zealand's finest Gewürztraminers, but most other regions are also succeeding in producing classy wines.

Gewürztraminer is a high-impact wine, brimming with scents and flavours. "Spicy" is the most common adjective used to pinpoint its distinctive, heady aromas and flavours; tasters also find nuances of gingerbread, freshly ground black pepper, cinnamon, cloves, mint, lychees and mangoes. Once you've tasted one or two Gewürztraminers, you won't have any trouble recognising it in a "blind" tasting – it's one of the most forthright, distinctive grape varieties of all.

The wine-growers of Alsace have long excelled with Gewürztraminer, but New Zealand's are rightly regarded as among the most intensely varietal in the world.

BABICH	VINTAGE	96	95	94	93	92	91	90	M/DRY $11 V+
GISBORNE	WR	6	5	7	5	6	6	6	
GEWÜRZTRAM.	DRINK	98	97-8	97-8	P	P	P	P	☆☆☆

Typically a fruity, dryish wine of good (occasionally excellent) quality, sharply priced. The 1994 vintage has strong, lemony, well-spiced flavour and a powerful finish, but the '95 is less exciting: medium-bodied and crisp, with citrusy, moderately spicy flavour. The 1996 vintage (***) is typical of the label – not intense but crisp, lively and well-balanced, with citrusy, ripe, gently spicy flavours.

BLACK	VINTAGE	96	95	94	93	92	91	90	DRY $16 -V
RIDGE	WR	6	7	7	6	4	3	4	
GEWÜRZTRAM.	DRINK	97-00+	97-00+	97-00+	97-00	97-8	P	P	(☆ ☆ ☆)

The 1994 and 1995 vintages from this Alexandra vineyard are big wines with a fresh, spicy fragrance and a touch of varietal bitterness amid their strongly peppery flavours. The '96 (***1/2) is a very characterful wine. Pale, with a spicy, slightly milky bouquet, it is a full-bodied, still very youthful, distinctly cool-climate style with strong, green apple and spice, fractionally off-dry flavours underpinned by lively acidity. It should age well.

BROOKFIELDS	VINTAGE	96	95	DRY $19 AV
GEWÜRZTRAM.	WR	7	6	(☆ ☆ ☆ ☆ ☆)
	DRINK	99	98+	

Robust, bone-dry Gewürztraminers are rare in New Zealand, which makes Brookfields' all the more welcome. Grown in stony soils in Ohiti Road, at the back of Roy's Hill near Fernhill, it is an impressively weighty wine with deep, lingering flavours. The '95 is a "serious" style of Gewürztraminer, fleshy and dry, with plenty of gingery, spicy flavour. The '96 (*****) is outstanding. Bold, with a heady perfume, great weight in the mouth (14 per cent alcohol) and a powerful surge of dry, concentrated, deeply spicy flavour, it is a pungent, memorable wine that will richly repay cellaring.

CHARD FARM GEWÜRZTRAM.

DRY $15 -V

☆☆☆

Gewürztraminer looks promising at this extraordinary vineyard site near Queenstown. The '95 is aromatic, crisp and fresh, with plenty of lemony, spicy, medium-dry flavour. The 1996 vintage (**1/2) is a pale, light wine with slightly green-edged flavours lacking full ripeness, but fresh and lively, with a lightly spiced, fractionally off-dry finish.

CHIFNEY GEWÜRZTRAM.

M/DRY $18 AV

(☆☆☆☆)

Gewürztraminer is emerging as a Chifney success story. The 1995 vintage is a bold, very ripe, upfront style with a heady, musky fragrance, high alcohol and loads of soft, spicy flavour. Stan Chifney died in mid 1996, not long after making the '96 (****1/2) – one of his best Martinborough wines. Harbouring a whopping 14.5 per cent alcohol, it's a pale-straw, distinctly medium style, vibrantly fruity, firm and very powerful, with a delightful depth of rich, ripe, lychees-like flavour. Drink 1998–2000.

CRAB FARM GEWÜRZTRAMINER

DRY $15 AV

☆☆☆

At its best, this Bay View, Hawke's Bay wine is full of varietal character. The 1995 vintage (***1/2) was grown in Crab Farm's estate vineyard and the nearby (but recently uprooted) Brownlie vineyard. It's maturing well, with lifted, lemony, spicy aromas that lead into a medium to full-bodied palate with lively, citrusy, peppery flavours, dry and crisp, with good length.

CROSS ROADS GEWÜRZTRAMINER

M/DRY $14 AV

(☆☆☆)

The 1995 vintage of this Hawke's Bay wine is a generous, ripe-tasting wine with lots of citrusy, spicy flavour, crisp, dryish and lingering. The '96 reveals a ripe fragrance of lychees and peaches, with crisp, slightly sweet, ripe, gingery flavours of quite good depth. The '97 (***½) is pale, with ripe fruit aromas and a full palate with plenty of crisp, spicy, slightly sweet flavour.

DRY RIVER GEWÜRZTRAM.

VINTAGE	97	96	95	94	93	92	91	90
WR	6	7	NM	6	NM	7	7	6
DRINK	98-02	98-02	NM	97-9	NM	97-8	P	P

M/DRY $21 AV

☆☆☆☆☆

This stylish, exceptionally full-flavoured yet wonderfully delicate Martinborough Gewürztraminer is the country's finest. In its youth, it typically displays lifted orange-peel fruit aromas, with a tight, well-spiced palate, rich in alcohol. There was no dry wine from 1995; the small crop all went to a late harvest style. The 1996 vintage (*****) is another splendid wine; arguably the greatest yet. Estate-grown, it is a lovely marriage of power and finesse, with mouthfilling body (13.7 per cent alcohol), very refined citrus/spice flavours and a lingering, very rich finish. Clearly New Zealand's classiest Gewürztraminer, it is enormously drinkable in its youth, but set for a long and graceful life in the cellar.

ESKDALE GEWÜRZTRAM.

VINTAGE	95	94	93	92	91	90
WR	4	5	NM	NM	5	7
DRINK	97-8	P	NM	NM	P	P

DRY $20 AV

☆☆☆☆½

Typically made from very ripe, late harvested fruit grown in the Esk Valley, Kim Salonius's wine bursts with character. Most vintages display mouthfilling body and a pungent, lingering spiciness; in some years *Botrytis* adds a honeyish intensity. The 1994 vintage is truly exciting drinking, with a gorgeous spread of peppery, citrusy, slightly earthy and honeyish flavour. The 1995 (***½) is firm and well-spiced, but less rich, less striking than the '94.

GATEHOUSE CANTERBURY GEWÜRZTRAMINER

DRY $14 V+

(☆☆☆☆)

I was initially unimpressed with the 1995 vintage (****) of this West Melton wine, but have scored it highly in recent tastings. It's a mouthfilling, very characterful wine with a pungent, spicy, rather Alsace-like fragrance, powerful surge of lemony, appley, spicy, slightly earthy flavour and a well-rounded, dryish finish. It should be long-lived.

GLENMARK GEWÜRZTRAMINER

M/DRY $18 -V

☆☆☆½

At its best, this Waipara, North Canterbury wine displays a lifted peppery/floral bouquet, lively acidity and positive spiciness. The '95 has a lovely, perfumed, richly peppery bouquet and real power through the palate, with good weight, strong, ripe, gingerbread and black-pepper flavours and a rounded, long finish. The 1996 vintage (***) is less memorable, but a full-bodied wine (harbouring 13.5 per cent alcohol), ripe and rounded, with good depth of citrusy, gingery flavours and a slightly sweet finish.

	VINTAGE	96	95	94	93	92	91	90	M/DRY $18 AV
GROVE	WR	6	6	6	5	NM	4	NM	
MILL									☆☆☆☆
GEWÜRZTRAM.	DRINK	98+	98+	97+	P	NM	P	NM	

This Marlborough wine is one of the country's best Gewürztraminers. The '95 (10 per cent Pinot Gris) is highly perfumed, with gentle, appley, well-spiced flavours and a surprisingly high level of sweetness; an attractive, cool-climate style that typically ages well. The '96 (***¹/₂) is a big, well-ripened, musky wine, medium-dry. A partial malolactic fermentation has contributed to its very fruity, smooth feel on the palate. Almost flabby, yet flavoursome and slightly lush, this is a distinctive and attractive wine.

	VINTAGE	96	95	94	93	92	91	90	M/DRY $17 AV
HUNTER'S	WR	5	4	4	4	4	5	4	☆☆☆☆⟩
GEWÜRZTRAM.	DRINK	99	98	P	P	P	P	P	

Hunter's produces a good Marlborough Gewürztraminer, with plenty of weight and tangy, spicy/citric fruit flavours. Richer than most past vintages, the '96 is a very stylish wine. Tightly built, with an impressive depth of fresh, crisp flavour, lemony, spicy, dryish and persistent, it is a powerful yet delicate wine that should blossom with age. The '97 (***) is a finely balanced wine with youthful, citrusy, moderately spicy flavours and a slightly sweet finish; open 1998–99.

JOHANNESHOF MARLBOROUGH GEWÜRZTRAMINER

M/DRY $16 AV

(☆☆☆☆⟩)

The 1995 vintage is the finest wine I've tasted from this tiny producer. It's highly varietal, pale and perfumed, with fullness of body and excellent depth of lemony, spicy flavour, delicate and lingering. The '96 (***¹/₂) is a high impact wine – yellow-hued, with an exotic, ripe, gingery, peppery perfume. Full-bodied, it's slightly phenolic (hard) on the palate, but already very expressive, with loads of dryish, well-spiced flavour.

KAWARAU ESTATE GEWÜRZTRAMINER

M/DRY $12 AV

(☆☆☆)

The exciting but rare (only 25 cases were produced) 1994 debut is a classy wine with a rich, deep, intensely spicy bouquet, mouthfilling body and concentrated, peppery flavour. The '96 (**¹/₂), again grown organically in the company's Morven Hill vineyard, overlooking Lake Hayes, near Queenstown, lacks the power and richness of its predecessor, but is realistically priced. Stop-fermented to retain slight sweetness, it reveals a delicate, lightly spicy fragrance and restrained, crisp, lemony, gently spiced flavours. Open 1998.

	VINTAGE	95	94	M/DRY $16 -V
KEMBLEFIELD	WR	5	6	
GEWÜRZTRAM.	DRINK	97-8	97-8	(☆☆⟩)

The 1995 vintage of this Hawke's Bay wine lacks the richness and character of the '94. It's a so-so wine, with a restrained bouquet. The palate is crisp and moderately varietal, more citrusy than spicy, with a fairly short finish. The '96 (**¹/₂) is a full-bodied wine with citrusy, earthy flavours and a slightly hard finish.

LAWSON'S DRY	VINTAGE	96	95	94
HILLS	WR	5	6	6
GEWÜRZTRAM.	DRINK	97-9	97-00	97-00

M/DRY $18 AV

☆☆☆☆

Consistently one of Marlborough's – and New Zealand's – top Gewürztraminers. Full of character, the 1995 vintage is a robust, rich wine, full bloomed, ripe and flavourful in a slightly sweet, citrusy, strongly peppery style with rounded acidity and a long finish. The '96 (****) is weighty yet delicate, with deep, positively spicy, citrusy flavour and power right through the palate. An off-dry style, it's crisp, tightly structured and still very youthful; cellar until 1998–99.

LINCOLN	VINTAGE	96
GISBORNE	WR	5
GEWÜRZTRAM.	DRINK	97-00

M/DRY $12 AV

(☆☆☆)

The 1996 vintage (***1/2) is an appealing wine, sharply priced. An easy-drinking, medium-dry style with good weight and depth of ripe, crisp, citrusy, positively spicy flavour, it offers fine drinking now, but should also age well.

LINDEN	VINTAGE	95
ESTATE	WR	4
GEWÜRZTRAM.	DRINK	00+

M/DRY $17 -V

(☆☆☆)

Estate-grown in the Esk Valley, the 1995 vintage (***) of this dryish Hawke's Bay wine is a mouthfilling style, with the distinctive, milky/cheesy characters of malolactic fermentation and good depth of citrusy, spicy, lingering flavour.

LINTZ EST.	VINTAGE	97	96	95	94	93	92	91
SPICY	WR	6	7	7	7	5	6	5
TRAMINER	DRINK	98-01	98-01	97-9	98-00	97-8	P	P

M/DRY $20 -V

☆☆☆☆

Martinborough winemaker Chris Lintz produces a full-flavoured, very upfront style of Gewürztraminer. The '95 possesses a very pungent bouquet. The palate is full (13 per cent alcohol) and forward in style, with fairly rich, peachy-ripe, moderately spicy flavours and a semi-dry, soft finish. The exotically perfumed '96 (****) is very fruity and forthcoming in its youth, with strong citrusy, spicy flavours and a slightly sweet, long finish.

LONGBUSH
WOOD. RES.
GEWÜRZTRAMINER

M/DRY $18 -V

(☆☆☆)

The punchy 1995 vintage (***) from the Longbush winery in Gisborne is deep gold, with a toasty, spicy bouquet. It's a very forward, slightly sweet style with plenty of gingery, honied, very soft flavour. Drink now.

LONGRIDGE	VINTAGE	96	95	94	93	92	91	90
OF H.B.	WR	7	5	7	7	5	6	5
GEWÜRZTRAM.	DRINK	97-05	97-04	97-05	97-00	97-00	97-00	97-8

M/DRY $14 V+

☆☆☆☆

From one vintage to the next, this is a superior, bargain-priced wine. The 1995 vintage, grown at Omaranui, is light gold, mouthfilling and ripe, with excellent depth of positively spicy, dryish flavour. The floral, well-spiced bouquet of the '96 (****) leads into an off-dry, well balanced palate with a powerful surge of ripe, peppery, gingery flavours. Why pay more?

LONGVIEW ESTATE GEWÜRZTRAMINER

DRY $14 AV

(☆☆☆)

The rich, citrusy/spicy fragrance of the 1995 vintage of this Northland wine is enticing. The palate is mouthfilling, with strong, ripe flavours of exotic fruits and ginger but also a touch of hardness on the finish. The '96 (***) is less rich but softer and more delicate, with clean, clearly varietal although not pungent lemon/spice flavours.

MATAWHERO GEWÜRZTRAMINER

DRY $22 -V

☆☆☆☆⅟

An acclaimed Gisborne wine in the early 1980s, when it was arrestingly perfumed and concentrated, since then its style has offered less pungent varietal character and a very soft finish. At a vertical tasting late last year of the 1987–94 vintages, the wines from the early–mid '90s were superior to those of the late '80s. The light yellow 1994 vintage (***¹/₂) is a distinctive wine with a musky bouquet and good depth of peachy, peppery flavours in a dry, weighty, well-rounded style, maturing well.

MATUA	VINTAGE	97	96	95	94	93	92	91
HAWKE'S BAY	WR	7	7	5	6	5	5	7
GEWÜRZTRAM.	DRINK	97-00	97-9	98	99	P	P	P

M/DRY $13 V+

☆☆☆☆

An easy-drinking, medium-dry wine that offers top value. The 1996 vintage is a classy wine, with delicacy and immaculate balance the keynotes. The subtle varietal fragrance leads into a fresh, clean palate with excellent depth of lemony, spicy, crisp flavour, fractionally off-dry and lingering. This is a stylish, gentle, ripe-tasting wine, built to last. The 1997 vintage (****) is another success; the equal of the '96. Already delicious, it's a soft, ripe, medium-dry style with good body and strong, lychees-like, well-spiced flavours, beautifully balanced and long.

MERLEN GEWÜRZTRAMINER

M/DRY $18 -V

(☆☆☆☆⅟)

Typically a fragrant and richly flavoured Marlborough wine, citrusy and spicy, fresh and crisp. The 1995 vintage is less lush than the bold, richly perfumed '94, but still a well-balanced, slightly sweet wine, citrusy and crisp, with plenty of varietal spiciness. The '96 (***¹/₂) is a full-bodied, ripe-tasting wine, richly scented, with plenty of flavour and a spicy, slightly sweet finish. It is opening out well with bottle-age; open 1998 onwards.

MISSION GEWÜRZTRAM.	VINTAGE	96	95	94	93	92
	WR	6	5	4	3	5
	DRINK	98-02	97-00	97-8	P	P

M/DRY $10 V+

☆☆☆

An easy-drinking Hawke's Bay style, typically fruity, citrusy, fresh and crisp. Is the 1995 vintage (****) the best-value Gewürz on the market? It could pass for Alsace. Bright, light-yellow in hue, it's a fractionally off-dry wine with impressive weight and an abundance of earthy, spicy, rounded flavour. Aging extremely well.

MISSION JEWELSTONE GEWÜRZTRAMINER DRY

DRY $18 -V

(☆☆☆☆)

The 1994 vintage (***¹/₂) is a serious style of Hawke's Bay Gewürz – robust (13.5 per cent alcohol) and bone-dry. Pale yellow, it reveals a slightly phenolic, bitter finish, but balanced acidity and good depth of lemony, spicy, slightly earthy flavour.

MONTANA PATU.EST. GEWÜRZTRAM.	VINTAGE	96	95	94	93
	WR	7	6	7	7
	DRINK	97-00	97-00	97+	97+

M/DRY $22 AV

(☆☆☆☆☆)

The 1995 vintage is a high-impact Gisborne wine with a powerful, musky perfume and golden colour. Robust, with a hint of honey amid its dryish, very strong, gingerbread and mango-like flavours, it offers good drinking from now onwards, but is slightly less memorable than the lush, rich and creamy '93 and '94 vintages. The 1996 (*****) sets a new standard for the label. Bright yellow,it is richly perfumed and weighty, very elegant and persistent, with greater delicacy and finesse than its predecessors. Already delicious, it offers a lovely spread of spicy, citrusy, honeyish flavour, slightly sweet and concentrated. The '97, tasted just before bottling, looks likely to be a repeat of the '96 – a notably big wine with excellent mouthfeel and texture and a lovely richness of citrus/spice flavours, very concentrated and long.

NOBILO MARLBOROUGH GEWÜRZTRAM.	VINTAGE	96
	WR	7
	DRINK	97-9

M/DRY $18 AV

(☆☆☆☆☆)

The 1996 vintage is a pricey Gewürz – but worth it. Nobilo's first Marlborough Gewürztraminer, it's an excellent debut. Pale, it's highly varietal and weighty (13 per cent alcohol), yet subtle and delicate, with impressive depth of lovely, ripe, slightly sweet apple/spice flavours. Highly enjoyable now, it should also richly reward cellaring.

OHINEMURI ESTATE GEWÜRZTRAM.	VINTAGE	96	95
	WR	6	6
	DRINK	97-9	97-8

M/DRY $16 AV

☆☆☆☆

The '95 is a very easy-drinking style, light yellow, with a quite rich, ripe bouquet and a sliver of sweetness amid its very fruity, moderately spicy, crisp flavours. The '96 (***¹/₂) is based on Gisborne grapes. The pungent, musky perfume leads into a fresh, flavourful wine, ripely fruity, with lychees-like flavours, a distinct splash of sweetness and balanced acidity.

	VINTAGE	96	95	94	93	92	91	90
PHOENIX	WR	4	6	6	NM	NM	5	7
GEWÜRZTRAM.	DRINK	98-9	97-8	P	NM	NM	P	P

M/DRY $14 V+

☆☆☆☆⯪

This Gisborne wine stands out in the Pacific range. Grown in the Thomas vineyard and made in a slightly sweet style, top vintages are pungently spiced, with a full-bloomed fragrance and very concentrated peppery, lychee-like flavours. The 1994 vintage lacked freshness, but the '95 is a return to top form. Yellow, with a musky perfume, it is weighty, slightly honeyish and rich; an exciting mouthful. The grapes for the 1996 vintage were adversely affected by rain and picked early. Pale and crisp, with a distinct splash of sweetness and lightly spicy flavour, it lacks richness. The '97 (*****) is outstanding, with a full-bloomed, musky perfume, richness of body and lovely depth of crisp, peppery, gingery flavour.

	VINTAGE	96
PLEASANT	WR	4
VAL. GIS.		
GEWÜRZTRAM.	DRINK	P

MED $13 V+

(☆☆☆)

The 1995 vintage is a pleasantly fruity wine with a distinct touch of sweetness, citrusy, lightly spiced flavours and a soft finish – a very easy-drinking style. Good drinking now, the yellow-hued '96 (***¹/₂) is a full-bodied, rounded wine, medium-dry, with a richly spicy fragrance and good depth and persistence of ripe, cinnamon and mango-evoking flavours.

	VINTAGE	96	95	94
REVINGTON	WR	4	4	7
VINEYARD				
GEWÜRZTRAM.	DRINK	97-9	97-8	97-04

DRY $18 AV

☆☆☆☆⯪

The Revington Vineyard in Gisborne's Ormond Valley yields some of the country's top Gewürztraminers. The 1994 vintage is magnificent – a powerful, classically structured wine, fleshy and dry, citrusy and intensely spicy, with a very good future. Ross Revington views the golden, gingery, soft '95 as "a stop-gap vintage, to be drunk while waiting for the better vintages to come round". The '96 (***¹/₂) is a light-yellow wine with a musky perfume. The palate is full, gingery and flavoursome, with a firm, bone-dry finish. Although it lacks the memorable quality of some past vintages, this is still a good wine with plenty of character.

RIPPON
VINEYARD
GEWÜRZTRAMINER

M/DRY $17 -V

☆☆☆

The 1995 vintage of this Lake Wanaka wine displays a fresh, lightly spicy fragrance and a dryish, crisp and delicate palate. Still in its infancy, the pale '96 (***) reveals spicy, slightly apricot-like aromas, good body, and a lightly peppery, crisp, slightly sweet palate. Leave it until at least 1998.

	VINTAGE	96
ST JEROME	WR	7
H.B.		
GEWÜRZTRAM.	DRINK	97-02

MED $16 -V

☆☆☆

Gewürztraminer is one of this small Henderson winery's strengths. The easy-drinking, very fruity '95 is a medium style with soft, pleasantly ripe, well-spiced flavours and some richness. The 1996 vintage (***¹/₂) is a forward, attractive wine with good weight, plentiful sweetness (20 grams/litre) and soft, ripe, lushly fruity flavour.

SAINTS	VINTAGE	96		M/DRY $16 AV
GISBORNE	WR	7		
GEWÜRZTRAM.	DRINK	97-00		(☆ ☆☆☆)

The 1995 vintage, grown by Montana in Hawke's Bay, is a golden, very full-flavoured wine with clean *Botrytis* influence and quite rich, complex flavours. The '96 (****) was grown at Patutahi in Gisborne. Produced in a slightly sweet style, this is a soft, rich wine with a well-spiced fragrance, pleasing intensity of gingerbread-evoking flavour, and a well-rounded, lingering finish. Already very enjoyable. The '97, tasted prior to bottling, looked good – strongly aromatic and ripe, with spicy, gingery flavours, lively acidity and a long finish.

SANDIHURST	VINTAGE	95		DRY $18 AV
RESERVE	WR	5		
GEWÜRZTRAM.	DRINK	97-8		(☆ ☆☆☆)

Proprietor John Brough was chuffed when his 1995 vintage (****), estate-grown at West Melton, won a silver medal in London – and deservedly so. This is a serious, satisfying style of Gewürztraminer. Pale lemon-green, it is perfumed, weighty and dry, its very persistent, well-spiced flavours cut with fresh acidity. One of the finest South Island Gewürztraminers yet.

SEIBEL GIS.		M/DRY $13 AV
GEWÜRZTRAMINER		
SEMI-DRY		☆☆☆

Light yellow, with fragrant aromas of cinnamon and gingerbread, the 1995 vintage (***) is a full, medium-dry style with a strong, peppery fragrance and plenty of crisp, clearly varietal flavour.

SEIFRIED	VINTAGE	96	95	94	93	92	91	90	M/DRY $13 AV
NELSON	WR	5	4	5	6	5	5	5	
GEWÜRZTRAM.	DRINK	97-00 P		97-8 P		P	P	P	☆☆☆

Gewürztraminer is represented in the Seifried range in two styles: medium-dry and the sweet Ice Wine. This is typically a floral, well-spiced, crisp wine, very easy-drinking. The 1996 vintage is a clearly varietal, well-structured wine, firm and dryish, with persistent lemon/spice flavours and good acid spine. A very sound wine with aging potential, and priced right. The '97 (***½) is a well balanced wine with fairly rich, crisp, well-spiced flavour.

	VINTAGE	97	96	95	94	M/DRY $12 AV
SOLJANS	WR	6	5	6	6	
GEWÜRZTRAM.	DRINK	97-00	97-8	P	P	☆☆⯪

An off-dry style based on Gisborne or Hawke's Bay fruit. The 1996 vintage, grown in Hawke's Bay, is a soft, very undemanding wine for current consumption. The bouquet is floral and musky; the palate ripely fruity, slightly sweet and rounded, with citrusy, pleasantly spicy flavours. The '97 (***½), grown in Gisborne, is a solid but plain wine with restrained, slightly sweet flavour.

	VINTAGE	96	95	94	93	92	91	90	M/DRY $20 AV
STONECROFT	WR	6	7	6	NM	NM	6	5	☆☆☆☆⯪
GEWÜRZTRAM.	DRINK	98+	97+	97+	NM	NM	P	P	

The Gewürztraminers from this tiny Hawke's Bay winery are always striking and among the finest in the country. The '95 is a lovely mouthful: weighty (13.5 per cent alcohol), with a rich spread of lychee, spice and gingerbread-evoking flavours, already delicious. The powerful '96 (*****) has a ravishingly perfumed bouquet, reminiscent of Muscat and roses. The palate is robust (13.5 per cent alcohol), with a rich surge of very ripe, gingery flavour and a rounded, long finish.

TE WHARE RA
DUKE OF MARL.
GEWÜRZTRAMINER

M/DRY $18 AV

☆☆☆☆

Powerful, ripe and rich, this wine typically packs more character into the glass than most other Gewürztraminers from the region. The heady '95 is yellow-hued, with a rich perfume of honey and spices and a robust palate overflowing with slightly sweet, peppery, honeyish flavour. The '96 (****) is another very characterful wine, ripely scented and weighty, with lovely citrus/spice flavours and a slightly sweet, soft finish.

	VINTAGE	96	95	M/DRY $14 AV
TORLESSE	WR	7	5	(☆☆☆)
MARLBOROUGH	DRINK	98-00	97-8	
GEWÜRZTRAM.				

The 1995 vintage is slightly overshadowed by its Waipara stablemate (below). Ready now, it is a golden, toasty, dryish wine with an abundance of gingery, well-spiced, softening flavour. The '96 (***) is a strongly varietal wine with a ripe, peppery fragrance and crisp, citrusy, positively spicy flavours.

	VINTAGE	96	95	M/DRY $14 AV
TORLESSE	WR	6	6	(☆☆☆)
WAIPARA	DRINK	98-00	P	
GEWÜRZTRAM.				

Grown in winemaker Kym Rayner's vineyard in North Canterbury, the 1995 vintage is a perfumed, full, slightly creamy wine with plenty of peppery flavour and a long, well-spiced finish. Rounded and rich, weighty and dry, it is a subtle, classy wine. The '96 (***) is slightly less impressive, but fresh and lively, with an aromatic, spicy/gingery nose and crisp, slightly sweet, moderately spicy palate.

	VINTAGE	96	95	94	93	92	M/DRY $14 V+
	WR	5	6	6	6	5	☆☆☆⯪
VIDAL	DRINK	97-9	97-8	97-8	P	P	
GEWÜRZTRAM.							

Typically a good, bargain-priced Hawke's Bay wine, crisp, with spicy/citric flavours and a hint of sweetness for easy drinking. The 1995 vintage is Vidal's best lower-tier Gewürztraminer since the memorable '89 – a perfumed, rich, medium-dry style with lush, ripe, smooth flavours and a long, peppery finish. The '96 (****½) is a "commercial" style with a very smooth-flowing sweetness, but it also shows good personality. The bouquet is spicy; the palate full, ripe and pleasantly peppery, with a firm, crisp finish. Fine value.

VIDAL	VINTAGE	95	94	93	92	91
RESERVE	WR	7	6	NM	5	6
GEWÜRZTRAM.	DRINK	97-00	97-8	NM	P	P

M/DRY $17 AV

☆☆☆☆

This top-tier wine is typically more restrained in its youth than the standard label (above), but flourishes in the cellar. The 1994 vintage is pale, with delicate but impressively intense, lemony, appley, clearly spicy flavours and a tight, crisp, lingering finish. The '95 (***½) is a restrained, delicate wine, still unfolding. Grown at Omaranui in Hawke's Bay, it's full-bodied, with crisp, lemony, clearly spiced flavour and a dryish finish. Leave it for a year or two.

VILLA MARIA	VINTAGE	97	96	95	94	93	92	91	90
PRIVATE BIN	WR		5	7	5	6	6	5	6	4
GEWÜRZTRAM.	DRINK	97-8	97-8	P	P	P	P	P	P

M/DRY $11 V+

☆☆☆☆

This long-popular wine is usually (but not always) made from Gisborne grapes in a floral, fruity, well-spiced, medium-dry style that is easy-drinking and priced sharply. The gold medal 1996 vintage was one of the royal bargains of the year. It's a powerful, intensely varietal wine with a voluminous, peppery, gingery fragrance. Highly expressive in its youth, it is mouthfilling, ripe, citrusy, spicy and crisp, with delicious flavour depth and a long, rich finish. The '97 (***) is good but less exciting. A crisp, stylish blend of Marlborough and Hawke's Bay grapes, stop-fermented with a touch of sweetness, it's a clearly varietal wine with delicate spice/lemon flavours.

WEST BROOK	VINTAGE	95	94	93	92	91	90
HAWKE'S BAY	WR	6	5	NM	NM	NM	6
GEWÜRZTRAM.	DRINK	97-00	97-00	NM	NM	NM	P

M/DRY $14 V+

☆☆☆½

A consistently satisfying wine, well-priced. Drinking well now, the '95 (***½) is a characterful, light-gold wine with rich, gingery aromas. Stop-fermented with a distinct touch of sweetness, it's full-bodied and smooth, with pleasing depth of spicy, slightly honeyish flavour.

Müller-Thurgau

Dedicated wine buffs may look down their noses at it, but Müller-Thurgau is still this country's third most important variety in terms of tonnes harvested (9739 tonnes in 1997, 16.7 per cent of the total grape crop). Every country has its "vin ordinaire" grape varieties: the south of France its endless tracts of red Carignan and white Ugni Blanc; Australia its ubiquitous Sultana and Trebbiano (Ugni Blanc); New Zealand its highly prolific Müller-Thurgau.

Professor Hermann Müller, a native of the Swiss canton of Thurgau, who worked at the Geisenheim viticultural station in Germany, wrote in 1882 of the benefits of "combining the superb characteristics of the Riesling grape with the reliable early maturing qualities of the Sylvaner". The variety Müller created (most likely a crossing of Riesling and Sylvaner, as he intended, but possibly of two different Rieslings) became extremely popular in Germany after the Second World War. Müller-Thurgau was prized by German growers not for the Riesling-like quality of its wine (it is far blander) but for its ability to ripen early with bumper crops.

In New Zealand, where plantings started to snowball in the early 1970s, by 1975 the same qualities had made it our most widely planted variety. Müller-Thurgau (once commonly known here as Riesling-Sylvaner) is still number three in terms of area of bearing vines, but by 1999 will have dropped to fifth position, and is destined to fall further.

Müller-Thurgau's rapid decline in recent years reflects New Zealand's mounting success with more prestigious varieties like Chardonnay and Sauvignon Blanc, and the move by Montana and Corbans to import cheap bulk wine from Australia, Spain and Chile. The remaining vines are concentrated in three regions: Gisborne, Hawke's Bay and Marlborough.

Müller-Thurgau is still the pool from which a substantial proportion of New Zealand's cask wine is drawn. Those accustomed to Riesling's deeper flavours often find Müller-Thurgau too mild ("Müller, Müller everywhere, and not a drop to drink," Australian wine writer James Halliday recalls thinking at the 1983 Easter Show Wine Competition) but the finest bottled wines offer enjoyable, light drinking at a sharp price.

Müller-Thurgau should be drunk young, at six to 18 months old, when its garden-fresh aromas are in full flower. Most labels are made slightly sweet, to maximise their commercial appeal. It is typically a fruity wine, with pleasant citric-fruit flavours which are akin to, but lack the penetration of, Riesling. Flab is a common problem: for the wine to be lively, crisp acidity is essential.

CORBANS WHITE LABEL SELECTION MÜLLER-THURGAU

MED $7 V+

(☆☆☆)

The first 1995 vintage is mouthfilling for Müller-Thurgau (12 per cent alcohol), with ripe, juicy, citrusy flavours, a distinct dollop of sweetness and a fairly soft finish. The very good '96 (***1/2) is a pale Marlborough wine with fresh lemon/lime scents and a tangy, flavourful palate. It's a very characterful, springy wine for Müller-Thurgau, lively and crisp, with a well-balanced touch of sweetness and lots of thirst-quenching appeal. A great buy.

GIESEN MÜLLER-THURGAU

MED $9 V+

(☆☆☆)

The 1996 vintage (***) is a pale, fresh, well-balanced wine with lemon/lime-juice aromas, a distinct splash of sweetness and clean, crisp finish.

NICKS HEAD MÜLLER-THURGAU/ MUSCAT

MED $8 V+

(☆☆☆)

This non-vintage wine from the Longbush winery at Gisborne is a light, undemanding, distinctly medium blend of 70 percent Müller-Thurgau and 30 per cent Muscat. It adopts the same varietal recipe and is made in the same style as the winery's popular Kahurangi. Fresh and fruity, it's a pleasant, no-fuss thirst quencher with appley, lemony flavours, a splash of sweetness and gentle acidity.

NOBILO FALL HARVEST RIESLING-SYLVAN.

VINTAGE	96
WR	7
DRINK	97-8

M/DRY $11 AV

(☆☆☆☆)

The debut 1996 vintage (***1/2) is pricey for Müller-Thurgau (which the wine is, despite the confusing use of a widely discarded synonym), but it offers good quality. It's a markedly drier style than Nobilo Müller-Thurgau (below). Grown in Hawke's Bay, it's ripely scented and slightly spritzig, with a very seductive balance of juicy, citrusy fruit, light sweetness and crispness.

NOBILO MÜLLER-THURGAU

MED $7 V+

☆☆☆

A light, gently sweet Gisborne wine that enjoyed runaway popularity in the 1970s, but of late its sales have been overtaken by Nobilo's White Cloud. Top vintages can still be surprisingly good. The '95 is a characterful wine with some richness, its strong, citrusy fruit flavours harbouring a touch of sweetness, with good acid adding liveliness and balance. The solid but less charming 1996 vintage (**1/2) offers smooth, easy drinking, with moderate depth of soft, sweetish, slightly honeyish flavours.

PLEASANT VAL.
GISBORNE
MÜLLER-THURGAU

`MED $9 V+`

(☆☆☆⯨)

The 1995 vintage (***¹/₂) is a very decent "Müller" – full, fresh, lively, fruity and juicy, with plenty of ripe, citrusy flavour, a splash of sweetness and enough acidity to keep things interesting.

ST HELENA
CANT. PLAINS
MÜLLER-THURGAU

`MED $8 V+`

☆☆⯨

This Canterbury winery produces a slightly drier style of Müller-Thurgau than most. At its best, this is a fresh, floral, fruity wine, its gentle splash of sweetness underpinned by lively, crisp acidity. The non-vintage wine (***) I tasted in 1997 was based on Canterbury grapes, grown in 1996. It's very appealing – light and well-balanced, with fresh, slightly limey flavours, tangy and refreshing.

TORLESSE
MÜLLER-THURGAU

`MED $8 V+`

(☆☆☆)

Still lively, the '95 vintage (***) is a characterful Marlborough wine, light (10 per cent alcohol), with fresh, crisp acid enlivening its fruity, slightly honied flavour.

VIDAL
MÜLLER-
THURGAU

VINTAGE	97	96	95	94
WR	6	6	6	6
DRINK	97-8	P	P	P

`M/DRY $7 V+`

☆☆☆⯨

This Hawke's Bay wine is one of the country's top Müller-Thurgaus, and superb value. If you've forgotten how seductive Müller-Thurgau can be, try the '97 (***¹/₂), which is full of youthful charm. Delicious drinking by late June, only three months after the vintage, it's a full, juicy, ripe-tasting wine with very good depth of flavour, all sweetness and grapiness. Drink it as young as possible.

VILLA MARIA
PRIVATE BIN
MÜLLER-THUR.

VINTAGE	97	96	95	94
WR	5	6	5	5
DRINK	97-8	97-8	P	P

`MED $7 V+`

☆☆☆

Top vintages of this Gisborne-grown label are rewardingly scented and crisp, with grapey freshness, slight sweetness and mouth-watering crisp acidity. The 1995 vintage was the first to be stop-fermented, rather than backblended, "to retain more fruit character with natural sugar". The '97 (***) is very fresh and juicy, with delicate apple/lemon flavours and a well-balanced, gently sweet, crisp finish. If you like this, don't miss the Vidal wine (above).

WOHNSIEDLER
MÜLLER-THURGAU

`MED $6 V+`

(☆☆☆⯨)

Wohnsiedler won a gold medal or two for Montana many moons ago, but is now a solid quaffer marketed in bottles and casks. Based on Gisborne grapes, it is stop-fermented with a definite touch of sweetness, counterpoised by refreshing acidity. One can't argue with its quality and value. The non-vintage (***) wine I tasted in 1997 is sweeter than many Müller-Thurgaus, but offered good sugar/acid balance and pleasing depth of fresh, ripe, juicy flavour.

Muscat and Morio-Muskat

Muscat Dr Hogg, an old English table grape, is Gisborne's third most extensively planted variety (and New Zealand's ninth). It is rarely marketed as a varietal wine (although The Millton Vineyard's richly perfumed, light and charming Muscat 1995 showed what can be done). In New Zealand's cool climate, it ripens late in the season, without the lushness and intensity of Muscat grown in warmer regions. The grapes are usually blended with Müller-Thurgau, both in medium white wines and Asti-type bubblies, adding a musky, aromatic, fruity richness to the wines' bouquet and flavour.

Peter Morio's German crossing of Sylvaner and Pinot Blanc, two relatively subdued parents, produced a sibling so unexpectedly blowsy in aroma that it was labelled **Morio-Muskat**.

MERLEN MORIO-MUSKAT

MED $15 AV

(☆☆☆)

"There aren't many medium wines in Marlborough," notes winemaker Almuth Lorenz. "This wine is for average people looking for a 5 o'clock drink." Slightly sweeter than most Müller-Thurgaus (with 35 grams/litre of residual sugar) it is typically a charmingly floral and fruity wine with slightly spicy and pineappley, soft flavour. A good aperitif.

ST GEORGE ESTATE JULY MUSCAT

MED $11 AV

☆☆½

If you like Müller-Thurgau, you'll adore this. Martin Elliott's very fruity Hawke's Bay wine typically has a fresh, voluminous scent and a lively, slightly sweet, soft, totally undemanding flavour.

Osteiner

This crossing of Riesling and Sylvaner is a rarity not only in New Zealand, but also in its native Germany.

M/DRY $13 -V

RIPPON OSTEINER   ☆☆☆

This typically fragile Lake Wanaka wine could be mistaken in some years for a light Müller-Thurgau. Not so the 1995 – a light, lively, rather Riesling-like wine with quite good depth of lemon/lime flavours, a hint of sweetness and zingy acidity. The '96 (***¹/₂) is similar. It's a pale, light wine with a cool-climate vivacity, fresh, lemony flavours and a slightly sweet, tangy finish. Essentially a pleasant quaffer, with scarcity pushing up the price.

Pinot Blanc

If you love Chardonnay, you'll also savour Pinot Blanc. A white mutation of Pinot Noir, Pinot Blanc is highly regarded in Italy and California for its generous extract and moderate acidity, although in Alsace and Germany, the more aromatic Pinot Gris finds greater favour. With its fullness of weight and restrained, appley aroma, Pinot Blanc can easily be mistaken for Chardonnay in a blind tasting. Plantings are scarce in New Zealand, with 28 hectares of bearing vines in 1997, concentrated largely in Marlborough.

DRY $10 V+

ST HELENA PINOT BLANC   ☆☆☆☆

VINTAGE	96	95	94	93	92	91	90
WR	5	5	6	6	6	5	7
DRINK	97-8	P	P	P	P	P	P

This estate-grown Canterbury wine is typically weighty, with plenty of fresh, slightly earthy, savoury and flinty flavour. Don't miss the 1996 vintage (****). Lightly oaked, it tastes like a cross of Chardonnay and Gewürztraminer – full bodied and savoury. The bouquet is earthy and well-spiced, with hints of stone-fruits; the palate powerful, with impressively concentrated, delicate flavour and a rich, dryish, persistent finish. I can't recall a better vintage of this label. It's still youthful; open 1998. At just under $10, an exceptional buy.

Pinot Gris

Pinot Gris is a low-profile variety in New Zealand (covering only 0.4 per cent of the national producing vineyard) but the vine is spreading fast, reflecting the winemakers' increasing interest in the high quality of its wine (see the Variety Focus, page 19).

This year's guide features six new labels, adding to the six new arrivals last year. Like Pinot Blanc a mutation of Pinot Noir, Pinot Gris has skin colours ranging from blue-grey to reddish-pink, sturdy extract, a fairly subtle, spicy aroma, and a slow-building flavour of stone-fruits and a hint of earthiness. Popular in Germany, Alsace and Italy, it is still largely unknown here, but likely to play a more important role in future. The majority of plantings are found in Marlborough, Otago and Canterbury, where the fairly low acidity of Pinot Gris is a distinct asset, but there are also significant pockets in Hawke's Bay and Martinborough.

BROOKFIELDS PINOT GRIS

VINTAGE	96	95
WR	7	6
DRINK	99	98+

M/DRY $17 AV

☆ ☆-☆ ☆ ☆ ☆

I'm not a fan of Hawke's Bay winemaker Peter Robertson's 1994 and 1995 vintages, but the '96 (****) is a huge improvement. Grown in Ohiti Road and not oak-aged, it's a bold, dryish wine, pale but highly varietal, with rich, concentrated flavours – peachy, spicy, savoury, long. It should age splendidly.

CHARD FARM PINOT GRIGIO

DRY $18 -V

(☆ ☆ ☆)

Barrel-fermented and lees-aged, the 1995 vintage of this Central Otago wine is a delicious and complex wine, weighty and brimming with flavour. Pale, with a slightly creamy texture, the '96 (***½) is an appley, spicy, earthy, crisp wine with reasonable flavour depth, but it lacks the beguiling richness of the '95.

DRY RIVER PINOT GRIS

VINTAGE	97	96	95	94	93	92	91	90
WR	7	NM	6	7	6	7	6	6
DRINK	01-05	NM	98-4	98-2	97-9	97-8	P	P

DRY $28 AV

☆ ☆ ☆ ☆ ☆

The most acclaimed Pinot Gris in the country, this is a powerful, dry Martinborough wine with a subtle, peachy/earthy aroma and extraordinarily concentrated stone-fruit flavours. At least four years' bottle-aging is needed to unfold the wine's full majesty – opened in late 1996, the '91 was a truly memorable mouthful, with great intensity and finesse. The 1995 vintage, grown in the estate vineyard, is a strapping (14 per cent alcohol) wine. Bold, savoury, spicy, citrusy and earthy, crisp and lingering, in its youth it is less lush and expressive than the '94, but tightly structured. No dry wine flowed from the 1996 vintage (see Dry River Pinot Gris Selection in the Sweet White Wines section) but a dry style was made in 1997.

GIBBSTON VAL. CENTRAL OTAGO PINOT GRIS

VINTAGE	96	95	94	93	92	91	90
WR	NM	6	6	6	6	5	3
DRINK	NM	97-00	97-00	P	P	P	P

D-MED $19 -V

☆ ☆ ☆

Pale and aromatic, the 1995 vintage (which includes 10 per cent Gewürztraminer) shows good concentration of peachy, earthy flavour, an obvious splash of sweetness and high acidity. **Crisp and tight in its youth, it should be in peak condition from now onwards.**

	VINTAGE	96	95			M/DRY $15 V+
GIESEN						
PINOT	WR	NM	4			(☆☆☆☆⸮)
GRIS	DRINK	NM	97-9			

Launched from the 1995 vintage (***¹/₂) , this Canterbury wine was made in an off-dry style. It's easy to enjoy – aromatic and weighty, with clearcut varietal character, very good depth of ripe, peachy, earthy flavour and a slightly sweet, crisp finish. Ready; no rush.

	VINTAGE	97	96	95	94	MED $19 AV
GROVE MILL						
PINOT	WR	6	6	6	6	(☆☆☆☆)
GRIS	DRINK	97+	97+	P	P	

Grove Mill is playing a key role in the emergence of Pinot Gris in Marlborough. The deliciously rich-flavoured 1996 vintage is weighty, ripe-tasting and peachy, with smoothness from a partial malolactic fermentation and plentiful (23 grams/litre) sweetness. The '97 (****) is again a lovely wine, although I'd prefer a drier style. The fresh-scented bouquet leads into a mouthfilling , very easy-drinking wine with rich, ripe, peachy, spicy, rounded flavour, a distinct splash of sweetness, and delicious delicacy and depth.

	VINTAGE	96	DRY $15 V+
HUNTAWAY			
RES. GISBORNE	WR	6	(☆☆☆☆)
PINOT GRIS	DRINK	97-9	

The first 1996 vintage (****) is a deliciously ripe-tasting, delicate, vibrantly fruity wine from Corbans. The colour is bright yellow-green; the flavour rich, citrusy, peachy and slightly nutty, with a smooth, persistent finish. It's enjoyable now, but won't break into full stride until 1998.

	M/DRY $12 V+
LARCOMB	
PINOT	(☆☆☆☆⸮)
GRIS	

Grown south of Christchurch, the 1995 vintage (***¹/₂) is an appealing, light yellow wine, fleshy, with slightly earthy and spicy, dry, well-rounded, persistent flavour.

	DRY $15 AV
LINDEN EST.	
GISBORNE	(☆☆☆☆⸮)
PINOT GRIS	

The debut 1996 vintage (***¹/₂) is well worth buying. A fat, light gold wine with very satisfying fullness of body and depth of ripe, peachy, slightly buttery, well-rounded flavour, it is maturing well; open 1998.

MARGRAIN	VINTAGE	96
PINOT	WR	7
GRIS	DRINK	98-02+

M/DRY $25 -V

(☆☆☆☆⯪)

If the standard of the excellent 1996 vintage (****½) is repeated, this will be an exciting label to follow. A big, rich-flavoured Martinborough wine, it was not matured in oak, but aged on its yeast lees in stainless steel tanks. Intensely varietal, with searching, peachy, lemony, slightly earthy flavours and firm acidity, balanced by a hint of sweetness, it is powerful and concentrated, with richness right through the palate.

MARTINBORO.	VINTAGE	96
VINEYARD	WR	6
PINOT GRIS	DRINK	99

M/DRY $22 AV

(☆☆☆☆☆)

For his first 1996 vintage (*****), winemaker Larry McKenna aimed for "a Burgundian style with complexity, texture and weight" – and hit the target with ease. (Small pockets of Pinot Gris can be found in Burgundy.) Fermented with natural yeasts and matured for 10 months in old oak casks, it's a bright, light yellow, mouthfilling wine with a fat, rich palate – weighty, peachy, nutty, dryish, rounded and long.

MISSION
JEWELSTONE
PINOT GRIGIO

DRY $18 AV

(☆☆☆☆)

The strapping (13.5 per cent alcohol) 1995 vintage (****) of this Hawke's Bay wine was made from the first crop off young vines at Greenmeadows. It's full-bodied and fresh, with impressively rich, appley, earthy, nutty flavours, a touch of lees-aging complexity and a dry, slightly tannic finish. It should be very long-lived.

MISSION	VINTAGE	96	95	94	93	92
PINOT	WR	5	5	6	4	6
GRIS	DRINK	98-00	97-8	97-8	P	P

M/DRY $10 V+

☆☆☆

The Mission has long been a standard-bearer for Pinot Gris. This is typically a tangy, easy-drinking, full-bodied wine with hints of apricots and earth and a slightly sweet finish. The 1995 vintage (***), grown in Gisborne, is the cheapest New Zealand Pinot Gris available, and it's great value. Slightly pink-hued, it's an off-dry style, fleshy and clearly varietal, with plenty of crisp, earthy, spicy, stone-fruit flavour.

ST HELENA	VINTAGE	96
PINOT	WR	5
GRIS	DRINK	97-00

M/DRY $13 AV

☆☆☆

The 1995 vintage, estate-grown in Canterbury and 20 per cent barrel-fermented, is a gutsy wine with a fresh, slightly earthy fragrance and loads of flavour. The '96 (***½), also partly oak-matured, is a slightly off-dry style, full-bodied and fresh, with reasonable depth of peachy, spicy flavour.

SANDIHURST
PINOT
GRIS

M/DRY $13 AV

(☆☆☆)

Pale, with fullness of body and a whisker of sweetness, the 1995 vintage (***) of this Canterbury wine is an easy-drinking style with attractive, appley, earthy flavours and an appetisingly crisp finish. Open 1997–98.

SANDIHURST
RESERVE
PINOT GRIS

VINTAGE	95
WR	5
DRINK	97-9

DRY $18 AV

(☆☆☆½)

Sandihurst's reserve label from 1995 (***½) is a partly barrel-fermented Canterbury wine, richer-flavoured and drier than the non-reserve wine (above). Mouthfilling and strongly varietal, it offers very good depth of peachy, spicy flavour and a crisp, dry finish.

SHALIMAR
ESTATE
PINOT GRIS

DRY $14 -V

(☆☆)

The debut 1994 vintage of this Gisborne wine was very plain, but the '96 (**½) is more attractive. It's a crisp, still very youthful wine, with a slightly green-edged nose and palate. Open 1998.

SHINGLE PEAK
MARLBOROUGH
PINOT GRIS

VINTAGE	96
WR	5
DRINK	97-00

M/DRY $15 V+

(☆☆☆½)

Matua Valley's 1995 vintage was an auspicious debut – a weighty, partly barrel-fermented, off-dry wine with good extract (stuffing) and impressive depth of flinty, spicy flavour, firm and long. The partly oak-aged '96 (***) is also an attractive wine, although some of the richer characters of Pinot Gris elude it. Pale lemon-green in hue, with a fresh, floral fragrance, it's citrusy, slightly spicy and crisp, with a touch of tannin often found in Pinot Gris, a fractionally off-dry finish and good weight. Not yet the great Marlborough Pinot Gris, but a very decent wine, priced right.

TORLESSE
CANTER.
PINOT GRIS

VINTAGE	95
WR	5
DRINK	97-8

DRY $14 V+

(☆☆☆½)

Ready now, the full, soft 1995 vintage (***½) is Torlesse's first Pinot Gris. Grown at Yaldhurst and oak-matured for six months, it is straw coloured, with a peachy-ripe bouquet and generous palate – weighty, rich and mellow.

Riesling

The 25 new labels in this year's guide tell their own story about the growing popularity of Riesling in New Zealand. It's not exactly the wine name on everyone's lips, but Riesling sales soared by 500 per cent between 1991 and 1996, rising from 3 per cent to 9 per cent of total bottled white wine sales. Captivated by Chardonnay and Sauvignon Blanc, Kiwi wine lovers for many years ignored this country's equally delightful Rieslings. At last, Riesling is starting to achieve the profile and popularity it richly deserves.

If you prefer wines that "knock your socks off", you probably have yet to be entranced by Riesling's fragile charms. Ravishing perfume, lightness and flavour delicacy are the hallmarks of the greatest New Zealand Rieslings. Scentedness and flavour intensity, rather than mouthfilling body, are the winemaker's goals for Riesling.

Riesling is regarded around the world as Chardonnay's great rival in the white-wine quality stakes, well ahead of Sauvignon Blanc. So what took New Zealand wine lovers so long to appreciate Riesling's lofty stature?

Several factors have until recently tethered Riesling's popularity. The long-lived confusion over names ("Riesling-Sylvaner" is the humbler Müller-Thurgau; "Rhine Riesling" is a synonym for the true Riesling) has hardly helped Riesling build a distinctive identity. Riesling is often made fractionally sweet to balance the grape's natural steely acidity; this hint of sweetness runs counter to the current fashion for bone-dry wines. And Riesling demands time to unfold its full glories; drunk in its infancy, as it often is, it may not taste greatly superior to the blander, but cheaper, Müller-Thurgau.

Riesling ranks as New Zealand's fourth most extensively planted white-wine variety. Reflecting the winemakers' intensifying interest in the great grape of Germany, between 1996 and 1999 the total area of bearing vines will expand by over 40 per cent. Plantings are light in Gisborne and (according to the 1996 national vineyard survey) non-existent in Auckland. A classic cool-climate variety, Riesling is particularly well suited to the cooler growing temperatures and lower humidity of the South Island. Its stronghold is Marlborough, where over half of all the vines are concentrated, but the grape is also well established in Hawke's Bay, the Wairarapa, Nelson, Canterbury and Central Otago.

Riesling styles vary markedly around the world. New Zealand's Rieslings veer occasionally towards the robust, mouthfilling, dry styles of Alsace and Australia, but more often towards the classic German style: light and elegant, relying on their garden-fresh, summery scents and exquisite balance of fruit, sweetness and acidity for their appeal.

| *ALLAN SCOTT* *MARLBOROUGH* *RIESLING* | VINTAGE 96 95
WR   6   6
DRINK   97-01 97-8 | M/DRY $15 V+
☆☆☆☆ |

Top vintages of this wine can be highly impressive. The '95 is weighty, flavoursome and slightly honeyish, but lacks the seductive fragrance and vigour of this wine at its best. The '96 (****¹/₂) is fine value. It's a classic Marlborough style, scented and lively, with a whisker of sweetness amid its fresh, tangy, incisive lemon/lime flavours. It's excellent now, but also well worth cellaring.

| *BABICH* *HAWKES BAY* *RIESLING* | VINTAGE 96 95 94 93 92 91 90
WR   6   5   6   7   5   5   5
DRINK   98-9 P 97-8 P P P P | M/DRY $12 V+
☆☆☆ |

Typically a well-crafted and well-priced wine, although it lacks the power of South Island Rieslings. The '95 is an attractive mouthful, with lots of fresh, appley, lemony flavour, a hint of sweetness and appetising acidity. The '96 (***) is crisp and lively, with fresh lemon/lime flavours, not intense, but delicate and finely balanced. It's maturing gracefully and worth holding until 1998–99.

| *BLACK* *GECKO* *RIESLING* | | M/DRY $10 AV
(☆☆☆) |

Montana's crisp blend of Marlborough Riesling and Gewürztraminer is light, fresh and slightly sweet, with lively but not intense apple/lemon flavours and a touch of spice. A solid quaffer, priced right.

| *BLACK* *RIDGE* *RIESLING* | VINTAGE 96
WR   5
DRINK   97-00+ | M/DRY $16 -V
(☆☆☆) |

This fragile wine from the world's southernmost winery at Alexandra displays green-appley aromas and a crisp, fresh, Mosel-like delicacy. The '95 is mouth-wateringly crisp, clean and delicately flavoured, with good length. The '96 (**¹/₂) is a pale, appley, tangy wine, fresh and dryish, with green-tinged flavours that suggest a slight lack of fruit ripeness. Pricey, but worthwhile.

| *BLUE* *ROCK* *RIESLING* | | D-M/DRY $16 -V
(☆☆☆) |

Those vintages I have tasted (1994, 1995) of this Martinborough wine have been solid but plain, either lacking flavour depth or austere, with green-edged characters and a high-acid finish.

VINTAGE	96	95	94	93	92
CAIRNBRAE RIESLING WR	7	5	6	5	5
DRINK	98	P	97-9	P	P

M/DRY $14 V+

(☆☆☆☆)

The '95 lacks its customary perfume but is fruity and juicy, its distinct splash of sweetness supported by plenty of acidity. The '96 (***) is a very solid Marlborough wine. Elegant, with nicely balanced citrus/apple flavours, crisp, slightly sweet and lively, it looks capable of opening out quite well over the next year or two.

CHANCELLOR MARLBOROUGH RIESLING

M/DRY $14 AV

(☆☆☆)

Still tight and youthful, the 1996 vintage (***) is a tangy, citrusy, flavoursome Riesling with a drier finish than most. It was produced at the Allan Scott winery, part-owner of Waipara Estates, owner of the Chancellor brand. Open 1998 onwards.

CHARD FARM RIESLING

M/DRY $14 AV

(☆☆☆)

The off-dry 1995 vintage, based predominantly on Bannockburn fruit, is a copybook Riesling – crisp and intense, with rich lemon/lime flavours, freshness and zing. The '96 (***1/2) is less exciting; a pale, crisp and tangy, distinctly green-edged wine, not giving much away in its youth, but with cool-climate delicacy and briskness. Open mid 1998 onwards.

VINTAGE	96
CLEARVIEW EST. BLACK WR	5
REEF RIESLING DRINK	97-9

M/DRY $16 -V

☆☆☆

This tiny Te Awanga, Hawke's Bay winery is best known for Chardonnay, but the fresh, penetrating 1995 vintage showed winemaker Tim Turvey can also spin a good Riesling: incisive, slightly sweet and zesty. The '96 (***) is also enjoyable, with fullness of body and strong, lemony flavour, fresh and tangy.

VINTAGE	97	96	95	94	93	92	91	90
COLLARDS QUEEN CHARL. WR	7	6	NM	7	6	7	6	NM
RIESLING DRINK	98-01	97-9	NM	97-9	97-8	97-8	P	NM

M/DRY $13 V+

☆☆☆☆☆

A consistently classy wine and a wonderful bargain. In the past known as Marlborough Riesling, since the 1996 vintage it has been labelled Queen Charlotte. Tasted this year, the '93 is at the peak of its powers – ravishingly perfumed and exceptionally intense. The 1994 vintage is also top-flight: richly scented and awash with delicate, fractionally sweet lemon/lime flavours, racy and lingering. There is no 1995. The '96 (****1/2) is a typically impressive Collards Riesling. A beautifully balanced medium-dry style, it is lemon-scented, with strong lemon/lime-juice flavours, good acid spine and a long finish.

COLLARDS RHINE RIESLING	VINTAGE	97	96	95	94	93	92	91	90	MED $13 V+
	WR		6	6	5	7	7	7	6	☆☆☆☆⯪
	DRINK		98-00	98-9	97-98	97-99	97-8	P	P	P

Typically a ravishingly scented, deep-flavoured wine, its delicate sweetness (almost twice that of its Queen Charlotte stablemate) balanced by mouth-watering acidity. Good now, the flavourful, easy-drinking 1995 vintage is crisp and lively, delicate and citrusy. The instantly likeable '96 (****½) is a distinctly medium blend of Hawke's Bay and Auckland fruit (this vintage without its customary part-Marlborough content). It's full, with fresh, delicate, but not highly concentrated citrus/lime flavours and good balance of fruit, acidity and sweetness.

COOPERS CREEK HAWKE'S BAY RIESLING	VINTAGE	97	96	95	94	93	92	91	90	M/DRY $14 V+
	WR		5	6	4	5	6	5	7	7	☆☆☆☆☆
	DRINK		98-9	00-05	P		97-98	P	P	P

For a wine that has enjoyed glowing success on the show circuit, this Hawke's Bay beauty is very modestly priced. It's a fractionally off-dry style, typically ravishingly fragrant, with fresh, strong lemon/lime flavours, a touch of honey and good, tart acidity. The '95 is less perfumed, delicate and intense than usual, with a slightly hard finish. The '96 vintage (*****½) is much more impressive, with floral/honey scents and a deliciously fresh and springy palate – full-flavoured, crisp, poised, long.

COOPERS CREEK RES. HAWKE'S BAY RIESLING		MED $19 AV
		(☆☆☆☆☆)

Grown in the same Clive vineyard (Jim Scotland's) as the "standard" label, winemaker Kim Crawford describes his first reserve Riesling from the 1996 vintage (*****) as a "limited volume wine, which will only be produced in good years". A medium style, significantly sweeter than the "standard" label (above), it's still very fresh and crisp, but an immaculate wine with enticing honey/pear aromas, good weight and piercing, slightly honeyish lemon/lime flavours, lively and long. Open 1998 onwards.

CORB. PRI. BIN AMBERLEY RIESLING	VINTAGE	94	93	92	91	90	DRY $17 V+
	WR		7	6	6	7	6	☆☆☆☆☆
	DRINK		98-04	98-00	97-00	97-00	97-8

Launched from the 1993 vintage, this is the famous Robard & Butler Amberley Rhine Riesling under a new label. The grapes are grown at Waipara, not Amberley, in North Canterbury. The 1993 vintage has excellent harmony and length, with deep, honeyish flavours. The '94 (****½) is bright, light yellow, with a lemony, slightly honied fragrance. It's a distinctively fleshy, mouthfilling , generous wine with intense, citrusy, toasty, spicy, honeyish flavours enlivened by fresh, racy acidity. Characterful, rich wine, already delicious. (Note: the pre-1993 vintage ratings apply to the Robard & Butler-labelled wine.)

CORBANS WHITE LABEL JOHAN. RIESLING	VINTAGE	96	95	94	93	92	91	M/DRY $8 V+
	WR	6	NM	7	6	6	7	
	DRINK	97-9	NM	97-9	97-8	P	P	☆☆☆

Johannisberg Riesling is a synonym, commonly used in the US, for Riesling. A two star-plus wine at a one-star price, it was going to be phased out after the 1994 vintage, but it's back from '96 (**¹/₂). Grown in Marlborough, it's a pale wine with fresh lemon/lime aromas, medium body and clean, crisp, appley flavours with moderate depth.

COVELL ESTATE RIESLING	VINTAGE	96	95	94	DRY $16 -V
	WR	5	NM	5	
	DRINK	97-00+	NM	97-9	(☆☆☆)

Organically grown at Galatea, near Murupara, in the inland Bay of Plenty, the rare 1994 vintage was 20 per cent aged in new oak casks. Pale, with spine-tingling acidity, it's an austere wine, clearly varietal, with dry, appley flavours, and is very much a food wine.

CROSS ROADS DRY RIESLING	VINTAGE	96	95	94	93	92	91	90	M/DRY $14 V+
	WR	7	6	5	NM	7	6	6	
	DRINK	97-02	97-9	97-8	NM	97-00	97-8	P	☆☆☆☆

Maturing well, the 1995 vintage is a full, flavoursome wine, grown at the highly rated Yates vineyard in Hawke's Bay. Still very lively, it offers ripe, grapefruit-like aromas and flavours in a dryish style, crisp and long. The 96 (***¹/₂) should also mature well. It's a tense wine with good depth of vibrant, grapefruit and lemon flavours, a hint of honey and a fractionally sweet, freshly acidic finish.

CROSS ROADS RIESLING	MED $12 V+
	(☆☆☆☆)

The 1996 vintage (***¹/₂) is a very solid Hawke's Bay wine, fresh, crisp and balanced, with pleasing depth of slightly sweet, lemony, limey, lingering flavour. It's still tight; open 1998 onwards. Good value.

DARJON RIESLING	M/DRY $15 AV
	(☆☆☆)

The debut 1995 vintage (***) , estate-grown at Swannanoa in Canterbury, is full of charm. Pale, with fresh, floral scents, it has an appealing delicacy and harmony of slightly honeyish, citrusy flavours, slight sweetness and lively acidity. This is a lighter style of Riesling, offering good drinking.

DE REDCLIFFE DRY RIESLING	VINTAGE	96	95	DRY $14 -V
	WR	7	5	
	DRINK	97-8	P	(☆☆)

The 1995 vintage of this Marlborough wine is light-bodied (10 per cent alcohol), with quite good depth of green-edged, freshly acidic flavour. It's a slightly austere style, but lively and forward, offering sound drinking now.

DE REDCLIFFE	VINTAGE	97	96	95	94	93	92	91	90	MED $14 V+
MARLBOROUGH	WR		7	7	NM	6	6	NM	7	NM	☆☆☆☆☆
RIESLING	DRINK		98-9	97-8	NM	P	P	NM	P	NM	

This consistently flavour-packed and zingy wine is one of the highlights of the De Redcliffe range. The 1996 vintage (****) is again impressive. Pale, with a scented, limey, lemony fragrance, it is attractively full and tangy, with lots of fresh, delicate, lively flavour, a well-integrated touch of sweetness and long finish. Already very expressive; drink now onwards.

DE REDCLIFFE	VINTAGE	95	M/DRY $11 AV
TE KAUWHATA	WR	4	(☆☆☆)
RIESLING	DRINK	P	

The golden 1995 vintage (**1/2), grown in Ross Goodin's vineyard, is a very forward, slightly honeyish, light-bodied wine (only 9.5 per cent alcohol) with slight sweetness, moderate flavour depth and a soft finish. Drink up.

DRY RIVER	VINTAGE	97	96	95	94	93	92	91	90	M/DRY $19 V+
RIESLING	WR	7	7	6	6	7	7	7	7	☆☆☆☆☆
CRAIGHALL EST.	DRINK	01-06	00-06	99-04	97-02	97-00	97-00	97-00	P	

One of New Zealand's great Rieslings, this Martinborough wine is typically fragile and beautiful, in most years with only a touch of sweetness. The '96, labelled Craighall Dry, is a classic, with exceptional flavour depth and Alsace-like body and power. Bright, light yellow-green, it is a strikingly full-bodied, rich wine, with great weight in the mouth and piercing lemon/lime flavours, tangy and superbly sustained. It carries the dry style effortlessly. Exciting stuff. A sweeter style, the 1997 vintage (*****) is beautifully scented, with incisive lemon/lime flavours, *Botrytis*-derived honey characters, and lovely poise and delicacy. It is already delicious, but also ideal for medium and long-term cellaring.

ESK	VINTAGE	97	96	M/DRY $14 V+
VALLEY	WR	6	6	(☆☆☆☆)
RIESLING	DRINK	97-00	97-9	

This Hawke's Bay winery's debut Riesling from 1996 (***1/2) is a blend of Takapau (Central Hawke's Bay) and riper Ohiti Road material. Slightly honied on the nose, it is weighty and vibrantly fruity, with firm, well-sprung acidity and a splash of sweetness giving an easy-drinking appeal. A strong-flavoured wine, well worth cellaring.

FORREST EST.	VINTAGE	97	96	95	94	DRY $15 V+
MARLBOROUGH	WR	6	5	NM	6	☆☆☆☆☆
RIESLING	DRINK	00+	97+	NM	P	

John Forrest believes Riesling will one day be Marlborough's greatest wine, and his own wine is helping the cause. It wasn't made in 1995 but the '96 is instantly appealing. Pale and youthful, it reveals a fresh, floral, highly scented bouquet and zingy, ripe, dryish lemon/lime flavours, deliciously crisp and intense. The '97 (****1/2) looked lovely in its extreme youth, with a deeply scented bouquet, and deliciously fresh, vibrant, ripe, dryish flavour.

FRAMINGHAM RIESLING CLASSIC DRY

M/DRY $17 AV

(☆☆☆☆)

Grown at Renwick by Rex and Paula Brooke-Taylor, owners of the Framingham vineyard, this is a consistently delightful Marlborough wine. The 1995 vintage is beautifully scented, with fresh, intense, slightly honeyish flavours, dryish rather than bone-dry; a great effort for a '95. With 10 grams per litre of residual sugar, the 1996 (****) is a medium-dry rather than dry style, with pure, delicate flavours, ripe, balanced and sustained. Charming now, it also offers good cellar potential.

FRAMINGHAM MEDIUM RIESLING

MED $17 AV

(☆☆☆☆)

Pale, with fresh, steely, appley aromas, the 1995 vintage of Rex and Paula Brooke-Taylor's Marlborough wine is a distinctly medium style with strong, appley, lemony, slightly honeyish flavours, not highly concentrated but well balanced. The '96 (****1/2) is a delicious wine, full-flavoured and zesty, with a touch of honey enriching its ripe citrusy characters. A medium style with lovely balance and intensity, it should richly reward cellaring.

GATEHOUSE CANTERBURY RIESLING

MED $13 AV

(☆☆⚬)

Tasted recently, the '91 (labelled Riesling Dry) is a solid although unmemorable Canterbury wine, carrying the dry style well, with reasonable depth of crisp, grapefruit/lime flavour. The 1994 vintage is pale, with tense, appley, slightly sweet flavour; a characterful wine, developing well. The '95 (**1/2) is more fragrant, full and fresh, with an inviting, lemony, slightly honeyish bouquet, but the flavour lacks delicacy, with a touch of phenolic hardness.

GIBBSTON VALLEY OTAGO RIESLING

VINTAGE	96	95	94	93	92	91	90
WR	3	7	5	6	5	5	4
DRINK	97-8	97-00	97-9	P	P	P	P

MED $19 -V

☆☆☆☆

The '95 is a fresh, springy, dryish wine, full-bodied, with penetrating lime/citrus-fruit flavours, packed with aging potential. The sweeter 1996 vintage (****), grown at Gibbston and Bannockburn, is pricey – but the quality is there. The fresh, lifted lime-juice aromas are inviting; so is the deliciously zesty palate – all freshness and liveliness and awash with lemon and lime-like flavours. A classic cool-climate medium Riesling, delicate and intense.

GIESEN CANTERBURY RIESLING

MED $12 V+

(☆☆☆⚬)

Still youthful, the highly appealing 1996 vintage (***1/2) has a slightly honeyish fragrance, reflecting the influence of noble rot. Based on fruit off low-cropping vines (6 tonnes/hectare) at Burnham, south-west of Christchurch, it is a delicate wine with good depth of crisp, lemon/lime flavour in a distinctly medium style. "Give it time," urges winemaker Marcel Giesen. Open 1998 onwards.

GIESEN CANT. RIESLING EXTRA DRY	VINTAGE	93	92	91	DRY $15 AV
	WR	4	NM	6	☆☆☆⟡
	DRINK	97-02	NM	97-9	

Estate-grown at Burnham, south-west of Christchurch, the 1993 vintage (***1/2) is an unflinchingly bone-dry style from a notably cool season. Light yellow, with a developed, limey, toasty fragrance, it's an austere wine with piercing, well-concentrated apple/lemon flavours laced with spiky acidity. Forget the aperitif role, it's very much a food wine. "I recommend oysters as a good match," says winemaker Marcel Giesen, "without the lemon wedges."

GLADSTONE RIESLING	VINTAGE	96	95	94	93	92	91	M/DRY $17 AV
	WR	6	6	6	5	4	6	☆☆☆☆
	DRINK	97-00	97-06	97-00	97-9	97-9	97-8	

Intensely floral and tangy, this classy Wairarapa wine has been one of the finest Rieslings made in the North Island. The '95 is lighter and less intense than usual, but still delicate, crisp and harmonious. The statuesque 1996 vintage (****) is an extraordinarily high alcohol (14 per cent) style. Still a baby, it's a fragrant, slightly sweet and honied wine with a rich surge of lemon/tropical fruit flavours, very fresh and lively. A notably powerful wine, it should age splendidly.

GLENMARK RIESLING DRY	VINTAGE	95	94	93	92	DRY $14 V+
	WR	7	7	NM	5	☆☆☆⟡
	DRINK	98-01	97-00	NM	97-8	

John McCaskey's Waipara, North Canterbury Rieslings age gracefully. From a tiny crop of "really ripe" grapes, the 1994, labelled "Proprietors Reserve", is a delightfully fragrant wine, full in body, slightly spicy on the nose and palate, with good balance and lingering, lemony, appetisingly crisp flavour. The '95 (***1/2) has a scented, honeyish fragrance and good depth of limey flavour, steely, fresh and delicate. It needs time; open 1998 onwards.

GLENMARK RIESLING MEDIUM		MED $14 AV
		(☆☆☆)

The 1995 vintage (***1/2) of this North Canterbury Riesling is essentially the same wine as the Riesling Dry (above), only made in a sweeter style. More forward in its appeal, it's a characterful, strongly varietal wine with well-concentrated lemon/lime flavours.

GLOVER'S RICH. DRY RIESLING	VINTAGE	96	DRY $17 -V
	WR	7	(☆☆☆)
	DRINK	98-03	

Dave Glover's 1995 Riesling (not labelled Dry) is an austere mouthful, with green-appley, limey flavours, lacking real ripeness, and a high-acid finish. The '96 (***1/2) is much more attractive, although its total dryness and lively acidity still give it a touch of austerity. It's freshly scented, with strong citrusy, limey flavours, tangy and lingering. A good food wine, worth cellaring.

GROVE MILL RIESLING	VINTAGE	96	95	94	93	92	91	90	MED $16 V+
	WR	7	5	7	6	6	7	3	
	DRINK	98+	P	98+	P	P	P	P	☆☆☆☆☆

A very classy Marlborough label, typically exquisitely well-balanced, with piercing flavour and a distinct touch of sweetness. The '95 is not a classic wine for the long haul – delicate, appley and honeyish, but lacking its customary zing and with a slightly weak finish. Produced in a distinctly medium style, the 1996 vintage (*****) is a beautifully perfumed wine. The palate is very stylish, with ripe, penetrating citrus/lime flavours interwoven with abundant sweetness and fresh, lively acidity. An immaculate wine, already delicious, for drinking now to 2000.

HIGHFIELD EST. MARLBOROUGH DRY RIESLING	VINTAGE	97	96	95	94	93	92	91	90	M/DRY $14 AV
	WR	6	6	NM	5	4	4	6		
	DRINK	97-00	97-00	NM	97-9	P	P	97-00	P	☆☆☆

The 1996 vintage of this Marlborough wine is not intense, but floral and delicate, with quite good depth of ripe, lemony, appley, slightly sweet flavour. The '97 (***) is fresh and ripely flavoured in a crisp, off-dry style. (The fully dry Elstree Brut Reserve Riesling 1997 (****¹/₂) is a powerful, robust wine with fresh, searching lemon/lime flavours; open mid 1998 onwards.)

HUNTER'S RIESLING	VINTAGE	96	95	94	93	92	91	90	M/DRY $16 AV
	WR	5	NM	5	4	4	5	4	
	DRINK	98	NM	P	P	P	P	P	☆☆☆☆¹

This Marlborough wine doesn't scale the heights of its Sauvignon Blanc stablemate, yet is still consistently good. There is no '95. The 1996 vintage (****¹/₂) is one of the best, with a fresh, lifted bouquet, good depth of zingy lemon/lime flavours, immaculate sugar/acid balance and a slightly off-dry finish.

JACKMAN RIDGE RIESLING	VINTAGE	95	94	M/DRY $10 AV
	WR	5	6	
	DRINK	P	P	(☆☆☆)

Tart and dryish, with moderate flavour depth, this Marlborough wine is typically no match for the company's fractionally higher-priced Riesling under the Montana Marlborough label. The solid 1995 vintage (**¹/₂) has a slightly honied nose, with the kerosene-like character of mature Riesling. On the palate, it's light, crisp and lemony, but lacks real depth. Ready.

JOHANNESHOF MARLBOROUGH RIESLING	VINTAGE	96	MED $17 -V
	WR	4	
	DRINK	97-00	(☆☆☆)

The 1996 vintage (***) from this tiny Korokipo winery is fresh and tart, with green apple aromas. It's a medium style, juicy and limey, with tense acidity and plenty of flavour.

LAKE CHALICE RIESLING

M/DRY $15 -V

(☆☆⯪)

The 1994 vintage (the best yet) of this Marlborough wine is hefty, vivacious and full of limey, lemony flavour. The '95 is shy and slightly austere, with lemony flavours and a freshly acidic finish. The 1996 (**¹/₂) is disappointing for the vintage – full-bodied (over 13 per cent alcohol) but pale and restrained on the nose, with very crisp lemon/lime flavours of moderate depth.

LANGDALE RIESLING

M/DRY $14 -V

(☆☆⯪)

The '95, estate-grown at West Melton, is a fragile wine, lightly floral, with clean, fresh, delicate flavours in a slightly sweet, invigoratingly crisp style. The 1996 vintage (**¹/₂) is light, crisp and medium-dry, with a green-edged bouquet and reasonable depth of appley, limey, slightly honied flavour. It's a solid wine, but lacks intensity.

LARCOMB RIESLING

M/DRY $12 V+

(☆☆☆☆)

Grown at Rolleston, south-west of Christchurch, the 1995 vintage (****) is a very seductive, gentle, rather Germanic wine. Light yellow, with a slightly honied bouquet, it is a medium-dry style, ripe, concentrated, delicately flavoured and finely balanced. A great buy.

LAWSON'S DRY HILLS MARL. RIESLING

VINTAGE	96	95	94
WR	6	NM	6
DRINK	97-01	NM	97-8

MED $16 AV

(☆☆☆☆)

The first 1994 vintage was eye-catchingly good – a full-bloomed wine with intense lemon, melon and apple-like flavours and moderate acidity, carrying the dry style well. The sweeter '96 (****) is a stylish and richly flavoured wine. Grown in the Hutchinson vineyard in the heart of the Wairau Valley, it is a full-bodied medium style with finely tuned acidity and a lovely spread of lemon/lime flavours, penetrating and long.

LINCOLN MARLBOROUGH RIESLING

VINTAGE	96
WR	6
DRINK	97-9

M/DRY $12 AV

(☆☆⯪)

The 1996 vintage (**¹/₂) is a solid wine with appley, green-edged aromas and flavours and a slightly sweet, very crisp finish. Priced right.

LINCOLN RESERVE RIESLING

M/DRY $11 375ML -V

(☆☆☆☆)

Still available, the '92 vintage of this dryish Hawke's Bay wine was released in 1995 in half bottles. Light gold in hue, it is a vigorous, very well-balanced wine with a powerful surge of toasty, limey, concentrated flavour, now starting to round out.

LINTZ
RIESLING
DRY

DRY $18 V+

(☆☆☆☆☆)

The 1996 vintage (*****) is a super Martinborough wine, fully deserving its gold at the 1997 Liquorland Royal Easter Wine Show. Very impressive in its youth, it is intensely fragrant, weighty and crammed with fractionally honied lemon/lime flavours, very long and rich. A striking wine, offering lovely drinking now to 2000+.

LINTZ
ST ANTHONY
RIESLING

MED $22 -V

(☆☆☆☆)

Described as an "auslese style" by winemaker Chris Lintz, the 1996 vintage (***¹/₂) is a single-vineyard Martinborough wine, based on *Botrytis*-affected fruit. A medium style with a bright, light yellow/green hue, it possesses attractive floral/honey aromas and plenty of citrusy, spicy, honied, but slightly hard flavour, lacking the delicacy and sheer class of its Riesling Dry stablemate (above). There is no '97.

LONE TREE
MARLBOROUGH
RIESLING

M/DRY $9 V+

(☆☆☆☆)

An exceptional buy from Corbans – a characterful, flavourful, non-vintage Riesling for well under $10. Pale lemon-green, with a fresh, limey fragrance, it's a very harmonious wine with a delicious balance of penetrating lemon/lime flavour, slight sweetness and lively acidity.

LONGBUSH
RHINE
RIESLING

M/DRY $15 AV

(☆☆☆)

The minerally, kerosene-like character of some aged Rieslings can be detected on the nose and palate of the 1993 vintage (***) of this Gisborne wine. Still available, it's a characterful wine – citrusy and crisp, slightly sweet and firm, with good depth. Drink now.

LONGBUSH
RIESLING
BOTRYTISED

M/DRY $15 AV

(☆☆☆)

The 1995 vintage of this Gisborne wine (***) was made from late-harvested grapes, 30 per cent *Botrytis*-infected. Produced in a medium-dry style, it is yellow-hued, with a fairly restrained bouquet and pleasant but not concentrated flavours – crisp and appley, with a touch of honey. Drink now.

MARTINBOROUGH	VINTAGE	97	96	95	**M/DRY $16 AV**
VINEYARD	WR	6	6	4	
RIESLING	DRINK	99+	98+	P	(☆☆☆☆☆)

The bright yellow, highly perfumed '95 is a sweeter style than usual, with *Botrytis* characters adding a marmalade-like richness. The 1996 vintage is a weighty, piercing, dryish wine with strong, ripe flavours and tangy acids, drinking well already but offering excellent cellar potential. The medium-dry '97 (****¹/₂) is tight and deep-flavoured, with lively acidity underpinning its piercing lemon/lime flavours; give it time.

	VINTAGE	94	**M/DRY $14 -V**
MELNESS	WR	5	
RIESLING	DRINK	97-04	(☆☆☆)

Still on sale in 1997, the '94 vintage (**¹/₂) from this tiny Canterbury winery was grown in Marlborough. The bouquet is shy; the palate medium-bodied, with lemony, slightly sweet, softening flavour. A solid but plain wine, ready now.

MERLEN	**MED $14 V+**
MARLBOROUGH	
RIESLING	☆☆☆☆

Almuth Lorenz's recent vintages are her best. Strong, ripe, grapefruit and slightly honied flavours hold sway in the full-bodied and characterful 1996 vintage, produced in a distinctly medium style supported by racy acidity. It's full of drink-young charm; open now onwards. The '97 (****) also looks full of promise, with springy, slightly sweet lemon/lime flavours of excellent depth.

MILLS REEF	VINTAGE	96	95	94	**M/DRY $18 V+**
ELSPETH	WR	7	NM	7	
RIESLING	DRINK	98-01	NM	97-00	(☆☆☆☆☆)

Mills Reef's top Hawke's Bay Riesling is among the region's finest. Full of character and now approaching the height of its powers, the 1994 vintage is a bold wine, deliciously perfumed and poised. Light yellow, it is rich and mouthfilling, with strong, ripe grapefruit-like flavour, slight sweetness and good acid balance. There is no '95. The 1996 vintage (****¹/₂) is again a powerful style, with a full-bloomed fragrance and excellent weight and depth of flavour, dryish and rich.

MILLS REEF	VINTAGE	96	95	94	**M/DRY $12 AV**
MOFFAT ROAD	WR	5	6	6	
RIESLING	DRINK	00	97-9	97-00	(☆☆☆)

Until recently this Hawke's Bay wine was sold under the Mere Road brand (after the road in Hawke's Bay where Mills Reef owns a vineyard), but is now named after the Tauranga road where the winery is sited. It's a slightly sweeter style than its stablemates (above), produced in an easy-drinking style. The 1996 vintage (**¹/₂) is a pale lemon-green, pleasant but not intense wine, lightly fragrant, with juicy, lemony, appley flavours and good sugar/acid balance.

MILLS REEF	VINTAGE	96	95	94				**M/DRY $15 V+**
RESERVE	WR	6	7	7				
RIESLING	DRINK	98-00	97-00	97-9				(☆☆☆☆⯪)

The stylish '95 vintage of Mills Reef's middle-tier Hawke's Bay Riesling is scented and light, its zesty, citrusy flavours mingled with ripe, passionfruit-like characters. The '96 (***¹/₂) is a full, weighty wine with good depth of fresh, delicate lemon/apple flavours, balanced acidity and enough power to age well.

MILLTON VINE.,	VINTAGE	96	95	94	93	92	91	90	**M/DRY $19 AV**
THE, RIESLING	WR	6	NM	7	5	7	6	6	
OPOU VINEYARD	DRINK	98-02	NM	97-04	97-00	97-00	P	P	☆☆☆☆☆

This Gisborne winery produces a classy Riesling, more honeyish and opulent than the brisk, limey Rieslings of Marlborough. The 1994 vintage sees the label in top form: ravishingly perfumed, with a deliciously intense surge of delicate, lemony, honeyish flavours. There is no 1995. The '96 (****) is a medium style, strong-flavoured and lively, but slightly less arresting than the finest vintages. Light yellow, with a honeyish bouquet, it is a light (10.5 per cent alcohol) wine with excellent depth of grapefruit, lime and honey flavours and a crisp, slightly sweet finish.

MISSION	VINTAGE	96	95	94	93	92			**M/DRY $12 V+**
HAWKE'S BAY	WR	6	6	6	5	5			
RIESLING	DRINK	97-05	97-02	97-00	97-00	P			☆☆☆☆

Mission's bargain-priced Hawke's Bay Rieslings have made a big splash since the first, gold medal 1992 vintage. The slightly honied '95 is a beautifully perfumed, medium-sweet wine with plenty of lemony, limey, invigoratingly crisp flavour. The fresh, lemony scents of the 1996 vintage (****) lead into a delicate, medium-dry palate, citrusy, limey and deftly balanced, with springy acidity and very good length.

MONTANA	VINTAGE	97	96	95	94	93	92	91	90	**M/DRY $12 V+**
MARLBOROUGH	WR	6	7	5	7	5	5	6	6	
RIESLING	DRINK	97-00+	97-00+	97-00+	97-00+	97-00+	97-00+	97-00	97-00	☆☆☆☆

One of New Zealand's greatest wine bargains, this beauty matures splendidly for a decade or longer. The '96 (****) is slightly less concentrated than the country's greatest Rieslings, but a lot cheaper. It's an intensely varietal wine, vivacious and springy, with fullness of body and strong, slightly sweet lemon/lime flavours, well balanced for early drinking but set to mature well. (The 1997 vintage, tasted just prior to bottling, looked promising, with a lemon/green hue, fresh floral/citrus aromas and ripe, slightly sweet, frisky flavour.)

MOUTERE		**DRY $15 AV**
HILLS NELSON		
RIESLING		(☆☆☆)

The slightly austere, rather Mosel-like 1996 vintage (***) was grown on the Waimea Plains. Pale and light (10 per cent alcohol), it's a clean, fractionally off-dry wine with high acidity and good depth of appley flavours. A very tense wine, it should open out well with age.

NEUDORF
NELSON
RIESLING

VINTAGE	96	95	94	93	92	91	90
WR	6	NM	6	5	6	6	6
DRINK	98-04	NM	97-00+	97-00	97-9	97-8	97-8

DRY $16 V+

☆☆☆☆☆

A copybook, cool-climate style, this wine is typically intensely floral, fresh and frisky, with an exciting concentration of lemon/lime flavours, zingy acids and great length. There is no 1995. "A fistful of flowers on the nose" is proprietor Judy Finn's description of the '96 (****). This fresh, tangy wine was grown at Upper Moutere and Brightwater and aged on its light yeast lees for three months to add complexity. It's a full-flavoured, almost fully dry wine, zesty and beautifully balanced, but less strikingly aromatic and concentrated than the best of past vintages.

NGA
WAKA
RIESLING

VINTAGE	96	95	94	93
WR	6	6	6	5
DRINK	97+	97+	97+	97+

MED $19 AV

☆☆☆☆⯪

The 1993 to 1995 vintages are austere, bone-dry Martinborough wines of high quality. The '95 is impressively concentrated in flavour, taut and crisp, with great aging potential. The 1996 vintage (*****) is a style departure, with a distinct dollop of sweetness. "The high brix at harvest gave the options of a high alcohol, dry wine or an off-dry, slightly lower alcohol wine," says winemaker Roger Parkinson. "In the end the yeast made the decision for me!" Still very youthful, it's an immaculate wine with a rich, ripe, slightly honied fragrance and very fresh, crisp palate, its lush tropical-fruit flavours very tight and intense. It should be superb around 1999.

OHINEMURI
ESTATE
RIESLING

VINTAGE	96	95
WR	6	5
DRINK	97-00	97-00

M/DRY $15 V+

☆☆☆⯪

German winemaker Horst Hillerich makes a consistently impressive Riesling. The 1995 vintage, a distinctly medium style made from Hawke's Bay grapes, is freshly scented, with plenty of lemony, limey flavour and good acid spine. The '96 (****), grown in Gisborne and lees-aged for six weeks, is one of the best yet. It's a beautifully crafted wine, light (10.5 per cent alcohol), very fresh and delicate, with citrusy, slightly honied flavours, crisp and long.

OMAKA SPRINGS
MARLBOROUGH
RIESLING

M/DRY $9 V+

(☆☆⯪)

The first 1995 vintage reflects the exceptionally wet harvest in its lack of flavour depth. Green apples and limes spring to mind when you sip it. The '96 (**½) is pale, with a light bouquet. It's solid but plain, with a clean, lemony, dryish palate, firm acid spine and moderate flavour depth. A bargain at its reduced price (previously $14).

PALLISER
ESTATE
RIESLING

M/DRY $18 AV

☆☆☆☆☆

Martinborough winemaker Allan Johnson's Rieslings are consistently top-flight. The '95, made in small volumes, is a slightly more austere style than usual, its clean, dryish, citrusy, appley flavours showing good depth, but less concentration than in most years. The '96 (*****) is typically classy. A medium-dry style made from fruit with a "light" level of *Botrytis*, it is beautifully scented, with intense, zingy lemon/lime flavours and a long, racy finish. It's a tightly structured, immaculate, penetrating wine, brimming with varietal character.

PEGASUS	VINTAGE	95		**MED $21 AV**
BAY	WR	7		
ARIA	DRINK	97-07		(☆☆☆☆☆)

Compared by the winery to an Alsace *vendange tardive* (late harvest) style, the 1995 vintage (*****) is a superb North Canterbury wine. It's yellow-hued, with a honeyish, limey fragrance. The flavour is a lovely harmony of rich, grapefruit, lime and nectarine characters, sweetness and *Botrytis*-derived honeyishness, with beautiful poise and intensity, lively acidity and a long, spreading finish. It should be very long-lived.

PEGASUS	VINTAGE	96	95	94	**M/DRY $18 V+**
BAY	WR	7	7	5	
RIESLING	DRINK	97-07	97-06	97-04	(☆☆☆☆☆)

More expressive in its youth than many Canterbury Rieslings, the first 1994 vintage is a vibrantly fruity, delicious Waipara wine, tangy, slightly sweet and packed with lemony, slightly limey fruit flavours. The '95, based on partly *Botrytis*-infected grapes, is even finer. Light yellow-hued, it is a beautifully balanced, medium-dry wine with very rich, crisp, slightly honeyish flavour, offering top-flight drinking over the next few years. The '96 (*****) is a ravishingly beautiful wine with a richly honied bouquet, intense lemon/lime flavours, lively acidity, and superb harmony and length.

	VINTAGE	96	95	94	93	92
PELORUS	WR	5	3	6	6	3
RIESLING	DRINK	97-00 P		97-8 P		P

MED $16 AV

(☆☆☆☆)

A rising star of Nelson wine is Andrew Greenhough and Jenny Wheeler's Pelorus winery south of Richmond. At its best (as in the gold medal 1993 and 1994 vintages), the Riesling is strikingly perfumed, incisively flavoured and zesty. I haven't tasted the '95, but it wasn't a favourable vintage for Riesling in Nelson. The estate-grown 1996 vintage (***½) is a medium style with appetisingly crisp, lemony, persistent flavours, but less striking than the '93 and '94.

PLEAS. VAL. SIG.	VINTAGE	96	**M/DRY $14 V+**
SEL. WAIRARAPA	WR	7	
RIESLING	DRINK	97-9	(☆☆☆☆)

The first 1996 vintage (***½) is an extremely rare instance of Wairarapa (in this case, Masterton) grapes sold to a winery outside the region. Its cool-climate vigour is appealing; so are the fresh-scented bouquet and lively lemon/passionfruit flavours.

POUPARE	**M/DRY $14 -V**
PARK	
RIESLING	(☆☆☆)

At over 13 per cent alcohol, the first 1994 vintage of this Gisborne wine packs a powerful punch for Riesling. It's a big, juicy, medium style with some rich fruit flavours, but also lacks a bit of freshness and zing. The '96 vintage (**¹/₂) is more attractive – a pleasant, slightly sweet but not intense wine with ripe lemony flavours.

RIPPON VINEYARD RIESLING

DRY $22 -V

(☆☆☆)

In its youth, this rare (and expensive) Lake Wanaka wine is typically restrained, with pure, delicate apple/lemon flavours and invigorating acidity. The 1995 vintage is fresh and frisky, with good depth of limey, slightly sweet flavour, well-balanced and persistent. The pale '96 (**¹/₂), likened by the winery to a Mosel, is a slightly austere, steely, full-bodied wine with green apple flavours and a dry, freshly acidic finish. Open 1998 onwards.

ROB. & BUT. MARL. DRY RIESLING

VINTAGE	95	94
WR	6	7
DRINK	00	00

M/DRY $10 V+

(☆ ☆☆)

The 1994 vintage, labelled as Marlborough Riesling, was a top buy – a generous, ripely flavoured wine, medium in style, with good depth of well-balanced, grapefruit-like, now-softening flavour. The '95 (**¹/₂), labelled Dry Riesling, is a solid but more austere wine, light (10.5 per cent alcohol) and lacking full ripeness, with appley, steely, slightly honied flavours and an off-dry finish.

RONGOPAI TE KAUWHATA RIESLING

DRY $18 -V

(☆☆⛧)

The 1996 vintage (**¹/₂) lacks the magic of the Rieslings of the south. A pale wine with fresh, lemony scents, it possesses quite good depth of apple/citrus flavours and firm acidity, carrying the dry style well, but it's less aromatic, zesty and piercing than South Island Rieslings. Open 1998.

ROSEBANK MARLBOROUGH RIESLING

VINTAGE	94	93
WR	6	6
DRINK	97-9	97-9

M/DRY $12 V+

(☆ ☆☆⛧)

The bargain-priced, multiple award-winning 1994 vintage (****) is aging splendidly. Bright, light yellow, it is scented, citrusy and slightly toasty on the nose, with a cool-climate intensity of flavour, dryish, zesty and lingering.

SAINT CLAIR MARLBOROUGH RIESLING

VINTAGE	96	95	94
WR	7	6	6
DRINK	97-05 P	P	

MED $15 V+

(☆ ☆☆☆)

The '95 is very impressive for the vintage. Grown by Neal Ibbotson and made by Kim Crawford, it is full and freshly aromatic, with a harmonious balance of fruit, fractional sweetness and acidity, and lots of passionfruit/lemon flavour, ripe and zesty. The '96 (*****¹/₂) is a notably ripe style: my sample bottle was wrapped in wallpaper with a brick design, to underline the high brix (sugar content) of the grapes! Packed with rich tropical-fruit characters in an intense, lush style harbouring an abundance of sweetness (28 grams/litre), it's a delicious mouthful, for drinking anytime from now onwards.

	VINTAGE	96	95	94	93	92	91	90
ST HELENA	WR	6	5	4	5	NM	4	5
RIESLING	DRINK	97-9	P	P	P	NM	P	P

MED $10 V+

☆☆☆

In favourable vintages, St Helena produces a quite Mosel-like Canterbury wine, fresh and vibrant, with piquant acidity. The '95 is a pale, light, medium-dry wine with moderate depth of crisp, delicate green apple flavours. The 1996 vintage (****) is a big step up, and the best St Helena Riesling I've tasted. The slightly honied bouquet leads into a beautifully balanced wine with strong lemon/lime flavours, a distinct touch of *Botrytis*-derived richness, well-integrated sweetness (15 grams/litre) and lively acidity. Poised, delicate and lingering, this is a top vintage at a giveaway price.

ST JEROME
RHINE
RIESL. MED.

MED $15 AV

☆☆☆

The fresh, lemon-scented, strongly citrusy 1995 vintage (***) is a 2:1 blend of Marlborough and West Auckland fruit. It's lively and slightly honeyish, with a slightly sweet, appetisingly crisp finish.

SALUT!
RIESLING/
TRAMINER

MED $8 V+

(☆☆☆)

The non-vintage wine on the market in 1997, produced by Montana, is not the "exotic, heady" wine claimed on the back label. But what can you expect for $8? It's a solid, easy-drinking medium white, lightly fragrant, with a reasonable depth of crisp, lemony flavour and a touch of spiciness adding interest.

SANDIHURST
RIESLING

M/DRY $13 -V

(☆☆☆)

Those vintages I have tasted of this West Melton, Canterbury wine have been sound, although not memorable. The '93, tasted last year, was bright yellow, with light body (10 per cent alcohol) and fully mature, slightly honeyish, soft flavour. The 1996 vintage (**¹/₂) is a springy, medium wine, slightly unripe-tasting, but offering plenty of green-edged, invigoratingly crisp flavour.

SEIBEL LIMITED
EDIT. WHITE
RIESL. CLAS. DRY

DRY $14 V+

(☆☆☆☆)

Formerly labelled as White Riesling Barrel Fermented, the 1994 vintage (***¹/₂) was grown in Gisborne, and then barrel-fermented and lees-aged for two years in seasoned (or in Norbert Seibel's words, "wine-sweetened") casks. It's a complex, toasty wine, light yellow, mingling strong, limey Riesling fruit flavours with slightly nutty oak. A very distinctive dry wine, it's richly fragrant and rounded, and drinking well right now.

SEIBEL LIMITED EDIT. WHITE RIESL. SEMI-DRY	VINTAGE	95	94	93	92	91	90		MED $14 V+
	WR	6	6	NM	NM	6	7		☆☆☆☆
	DRINK	97-05	97-05	NM	NM	97-05	97-8		

Aging well, the '94 (labelled Seibel White Riesling Medium Dry) is a pale Gisborne wine with a distinct splash of sweetness. Light-bodied (10.5 per cent alcohol), it's delicate and finely balanced, with crisp, engaging acidity underpinning its fresh, appley flavour. The 1995 (****) is also maturing splendidly. This pale, light Marlborough wine is a very elegant style with fresh, tight, lemony, slightly sweet flavours, springy and well-balanced.

SEIFRIED NELSON RIESLING	VINTAGE	96	95	94	93	92	91	90	M/DRY $13 V+
	WR		5	4	5	6	5	6	5	☆☆☆↓
	DRINK		97-02	97-8	97-9	P	P	P	P	

Seifried whites are going from strength to strength. Maturing well, the '95 is a very good effort from a poor vintage. A medium-dry style, it offers pleasing depth of vigorous, citrusy fruit flavour and a well-balanced, quite rich finish. The lemon-green 1996 vintage (***1/2) is full-bodied and ripe-tasting, with fresh, lemony scents. With its lively acidity and pleasing depth of finely balanced flavour, it should age well, although it's already an attractive mouthful.

SEIFRIED EST. RIESLING DRY	VINTAGE	96	95	94	93	92	91	90	DRY $13 V+
	WR		5	4	6	7	5	7	5	☆☆☆☆
	DRINK		97-02	97-9	98-9	97-8	P	P	P	

A jewel of the Seifried range. Bone-dry, it is sharper and more austere than most New Zealand Rieslings, yet in top years delivers generous, pure, fresh flavours. Opened early in 1997, the '89 was maturing well, with strong, crisp, limey, toasty flavours. Aromatic, with loads of flavour, the lovely 1994 vintage is a powerful Nelson wine with concentrated lemon/lime characters and a long, rich, zingy finish. However, the pale, steely '95 (**1/2) is lean, green-edged and lacks the richness of Seifried Rieslings at their best.

SELAKS MARLBOROUGH RIESLING	VINTAGE	96	95	94	93	92	91	M/DRY $14 V+
	WR	7	NM	6	6	6	6	☆☆☆☆
	DRINK	97-01	NM	97-8	P	P	P	

Selaks are Sauvignon Blanc wizards, but their Rieslings can also be spellbinding. The steely 1994 vintage was shy in its youth but has flourished with bottle-age, developing toasty, lemon/lime characters on the nose and incisive, green apple and lime-like flavours. Very fresh and flavourful, the '96 (****) is a seductive wine, already drinking well. Full-bodied (13 per cent alcohol), it reveals strong, floral, citrusy scents and a rich, ripe, lively palate, zingy, slightly sweet and long. A great buy.

SELAKS RIESLING DRY	VINTAGE	96	95	94	93	M/DRY $14 V+
	WR	7	6	NM	6	(☆☆☆☆)
	DRINK	97-01	97-00	NM	97-8	

The 1995 vintage is one of the best Marlborough Rieslings of the vintage – very aromatic and chockfull of lemon/lime flavour, racy and long. The '96 (****) is a classy, full-bodied, ripe-tasting wine with very delicate citrusy flavours and a moderately crisp, slightly off-dry finish. It's still unfolding; open 1998 onwards.

SHERWOOD ESTATE RIESLING

M/DRY $12 AV

(☆☆☆⯨)

The 1995 vintage of this Canterbury wine is attractively fragrant, with racy acidity and good depth of lively, appley, slightly sweet flavour. The '96 (***1/2) is a lemony, slightly sweet style with reasonable flavour depth, balanced for easy drinking.

SHINGLE PEAK MARLBOROUGH RIESLING

VINTAGE	96	95	94	93	92
WR	6	5	6	5	6
DRINK	97-00+	97-8	97-9	97-8	P

M/DRY $13 V+

☆☆☆☆⯨

Matua Valley's Riesling is consistently attractive: an off-dry style with strong fruit flavours, tense underlying acidity and great drinkability. The '95 is a crisp and limey wine with a green-edged, dryish, rather tart finish. The 1996 (***) is a very solid wine, although it lacks the intensity of some past vintages. Full-bodied, with quite good depth of juicy, citrusy flavour, a splash of sweetness and balanced acidity, it's worth keeping another year or so to open out.

SOLJANS MARLBOROUGH RIESLING

VINTAGE	96	95
WR	6	6
DRINK	97-02	97-00

M/DRY $13 -V

(☆☆☆⯨)

The first 1996 vintage takes over from the former Soljans Rhine Riesling, based on Hawke's Bay fruit (of which the '95 is not intense but still enjoyable, with a floral, appley bouquet, fresh, lively, juicy palate and crisp, slightly sweet finish). The '96 (***1/2) is a full-bodied Marlborough wine with a restrained bouquet and reasonable depth of lemony, slightly sweet, crisp flavour. It's a solid wine, but lacks real zing and intensity.

STONE CREEK MARLBOROUGH RIESLING

VINTAGE	96	95
WR	5	5
DRINK	97-00	97-00

M/DRY $13 V+

(☆☆☆☆⯨)

Morton Estate's 1995 Riesling is light (10 per cent alcohol), with fresh, lifted, lemon/lime aromas, strong, slightly honeyish flavours, and a sliver of sweetness balanced by lively acidity. The '96 (***1/2) is also attractive, its fresh, appley fragrance leading into a lively palate with crisp, delicate, finely balanced flavours. The Stone Creek label is currently being phased out.

STONE.VINE. MARLBOROUGH RIESLING

VINTAGE	96	95	94	93	92	91	90
WR	7	6	7	7	6	6	7
DRINK	98-06	97-04	97-04	97-00	97-9	97-8	P

M/DRY $14 V+

☆☆☆☆☆

Of Corbans' four-label range of Stoneleigh Vineyard Marlborough wines, in quality terms this is the greatest success. Deliciously fragrant and full-flavoured in their youth, the wines mature gracefully for a decade, perhaps longer. The '95 is a characterful wine from a wet vintage. Light yellow, with a slightly toasty bouquet, it reveals an emerging hint of honey and lots of strongly citrusy, crisp, slightly sweet, vigorous flavour . It's a forward style, already drinking well. The '96 (*****), the first vintage to drop the word Rhine from the label, is an extremely classy wine – and a royal bargain. The bouquet is fresh and intense, with classic lemon, lime and honey aromas. Still a baby, it's a beautifully balanced medium style with tense, youthful acidity and very stylish lemon/lime flavours, rich and long. It's all there for great drinking 1999 onwards.

TE MANIA NELSON RIESLING			M/DRY $14 AV
VINTAGE	96		
WR	4		(☆ ☆☆☆)
DRINK	97-01		

The 1995 vintage, grown on the Waimea Plains, is a decent debut, with a scented, floral bouquet, light body and good depth of citrusy, slightly limey, crisp and lively flavour, with a long, slightly sweet finish. The fresh, lively '96 (***) is still tight and youthful, with slightly unripe aromas, but the palate offers good depth of crisp, slightly sweet, appley flavour.

TE WHARE RA DUKE OF MARL. RIESL.

MED $16 AV

☆☆☆☆

Allen Hogan produces gorgeous honey-sweet Rieslings, so it's no surprise his drier version is also absorbing. There is no 1995. The '96 (****), based on Brancott Valley fruit, is a big, fruity wine with bright, light yellow-green colour and a lemony, slightly musky fragrance. Strong, ripe tropical fruit flavours hold sway, with a distinct splash of sweetness, balanced acidity and a touch of honey. It's a very characterful wine, already highly appealing.

THREE SISTERS RIESLING		M/DRY $15 V+
VINTAGE	96	
WR	6	(☆ ☆☆☆ ⟋)
DRINK	98-04	

When Sir Richard Harrison, former speaker of the House of Representatives, opened several young Central Hawke's Bay wines to taste, the '96 Riesling (***1/2) was clearly the pick of the bunch. It's a rare wine – only 30 cases were produced. Grown in Harrison's own tiny vineyard at Takapau, it's a fragrant, clean, tautly structured wine, medium-dry, with a distinct touch of noble rot amid its well concentrated flavours.

TIMARA RIESLING

M/DRY $9 V+

(☆☆ ⟋)

A budget-priced wine made by Montana from Marlborough grapes, although that isn't mentioned on the label. The 1996 vintage (**1/2) is a very easy-drinking wine, less intense than Montana Marlborough Riesling, but a good buy. Floral and slightly honied on the nose, it's a full-bodied wine with ripe fruit flavours and good sugar/acid balance. As a cheap, all-purpose medium white, this is hard to beat.

TORLESSE WAIPARA RIESLING								M/DRY $13 V+
VINTAGE	96	95	94	93	92	91	90	
WR	6	5	7	6	NM	6	6	☆☆☆☆ ⟋
DRINK	98-06	97-8	97-00	97-8	NM	P	P	

This North Canterbury winery's dry Rieslings have been consistently good. Maturing solidly, the '95 (***1/2) was grown in winemaker Kym Rayner's vineyard. A delicate style with good depth of lemony, slightly honeyish flavour and a crisp, just off-dry finish, it's a lean, tight wine, still developing.

VILLA MARIA PRIVATE BIN RIESLING	VINTAGE	96	95	94	93	92	91	M/DRY $13 V+
	WR	5	4	6	6	5	5	
	DRINK	97-8	97-8	97-9	97-8	P	P	☆☆☆☆

A consistently delightful wine. The '95, an attractive blend of Marlborough (70 per cent) and Gisborne (30 per cent) fruit, is fragrant and ripe, with good depth of grapefruit and lime-like flavours, a dollop of sweetness and a crisp, lively, lingering finish. The '96 (*****) has been one of the great buys of 1996–97. Winner of a gold medal and trophy at the 1996 Liquorland Top 100, it's a Marlborough wine with a very fresh-scented, floral, limey bouquet. Full, with great vigour and depth of lemon/lime flavour and lovely sugar/acid balance, it's a bigger and richer wine than usual, with an exciting rush of flavour and exceptional quality for the price. Tasted in its extreme infancy, the '97 also looked promising, with fresh, lively acidity and rich lemon/apple flavours.

VILLA MARIA RESERVE RIESLING	VINTAGE	96	DRY $19 AV
	WR	7	
	DRINK	97-00+	(☆☆☆☆☆)

Villa Maria's first "reserve" Riesling, from the 1996 vintage (*****) richly deserves its status, rating among the greatest Rieslings ever to flow from the region. This is a splendidly powerful yet elegant Marlborough wine that should live for many years. Harvested at 23˚ brix from young vines in the Seddon Vineyard in the Awatere Valley, it's a weighty (13 per cent alcohol) style with arrestingly rich flavour – lemony, limey and slightly honeyish – and great poise and persistence.

WAIPARA WEST RIESLING	M/DRY $16 -V
	(☆☆☆)

The debut 1996 vintage (**¹/₂) is a pale, full-bodied, medium-dry wine, limey and tangy, with reasonable flavour depth, but it lacks a bit of ripeness, delicacy and varietal definition.

WAIPARA SPRINGS RIESLING	VINTAGE	96	95	94	93	M/DRY $14 AV
	WR	6	6	5	4	
	DRINK	98-06	97-05	97-00	P	(☆☆☆)

The estate-grown Riesling Dry 1995, based on ripe (23˚ brix) grapes, stop-fermented with a trace of residual sugar, is a good wine: fragrant and flavourful, with a crisp, very citrusy and lively palate. The '96 (***) is attractively fresh and aromatic, with plenty of limey, zingy flavour and a cool-climate vivacity and length.

WALKER ESTATE RIESLING	MED $16 -V
	(☆☆☆)

Slightly shy in its youth, the '96 vintage (**¹/₂) of this pale Martinborough wine is floral, with lemony, distinctly medium flavours underpinned by lively acidity. A solid wine, it could well open out with time.

WEST BROOK	VINTAGE 96	**M/DRY $14 V+**
MARLBOROUGH	WR 6	(☆ ☆☆☆☆)
RIESLING	DRINK 98-02	

The 1996 vintage (****) is a well-made wine, light yellow, with a pungent, limey bouquet. Full-bodied, slightly sweet and lively, with appetising acidity and strong lemon/lime flavours, it is a well-balanced, tightly structured wine with good varietal character and should age well. Fine value.

WHITEHAVEN	**M/DRY $15 V+**
MARLBOROUGH	(☆☆☆☆)
RIESLING	

The 1995 is lively and flavourful, with a touch of sweetness amid its attractively ripe and delicate, zesty lemon/lime characters. The '96 (****) is a classy single-vineyard wine grown in Conders Bend Road, Renwick. It's freshly scented, with ripe, delicate lemon/lime flavours to the fore, a sliver of sweetness, finely balanced acid and a long finish. Drink now onwards.

WINSLOW	VINTAGE 97 96 95 94	**M/DRY $18 AV**
RIESLING	WR 6 6 NM 6	(☆ ☆☆☆☆)
MEDIUM-DRY	DRINK 97-01 97-00 NM 97-8	

Perfumed and zippy, the 1994 vintage of this Martinborough wine is chock full of flavour in an invigorating, fractionally sweet style. There is no '95, but the 1996 (****) is again impressive. A medium-dry style based on very ripe grapes with 5 to 10 per cent noble rot infection, it is robust (13 per cent alcohol), with penetrating, appetisingly crisp lemon/lime flavours. A powerful, rich wine, well worth cellaring. (The 1997 St Vincent Riesling Dry (***1/2) promises to be a good food wine, with strong apple/lime flavours, tangy and dry, slightly austere in its youth, it needs time; open 1999 onwards.)

Sauvignon Blanc

Marlborough's strikingly aromatic and pungent Sauvignon Blancs continued to bask in the international limelight in 1997. Villa Maria Reserve Wairau Valley Sauvignon Blanc 1996 scooped the prestigious trophy for champion wine of the show at the 1997 Sydney International Wine Competition, triumphing over 1000 other entrants. Villa Maria Cellar Selection Sauvignon Blanc 1996 then won the trophy for best Sauvignon Blanc at the 1997 International Wine and Spirit Competition in London (giving New Zealand the trophy for the eighth time in the past nine years).

The rise to international stardom of New Zealand Sauvignon Blanc has been swift. The variety was first introduced to the country in the early 1970s; Matua Valley marketed the first varietal Sauvignon Blanc in 1974. Montana then planted sweeping vineyards in Marlborough, allowing Sauvignon Blanc to get into a full commercial swing in the early 1980s.

Sauvignon Blanc is New Zealand's second most widely planted variety (behind Chardonnay), in 1997 comprising 21 per cent of the bearing vineyard. Over two-thirds of all plantings are concentrated in Marlborough, with Hawke's Bay the other major stronghold. Plantings are expanding fast: between 1996 and 1999, the area of bearing Sauvignon Blanc vines is increasing by 45 per cent.

The flavour of New Zealand Sauvignon Blanc varies according to fruit ripeness. At the herbaceous, under-ripe end of the spectrum, vegetal and fresh-cut grass aromas hold sway; riper wines show capsicum, gooseberry and melon-like characters; very ripe fruit displays honeyish, tropical-fruit flavours.

Intensely herbaceous Sauvignon Blancs are not hard to make in New Zealand's cool-climate for viticulture. "The challenge faced by New Zealand winemakers is to keep those herbaceous characters in check," says Kevin Judd, winemaker at Cloudy Bay. "It would be foolish to suggest that these herbaceous notes detract from the wines; in fact I am sure that this fresh edge and intense varietal aroma are the reason for its recent international popularity. The better of these wines have these herbaceous characters in context and in balance with the more tropical fruit characters associated with riper fruit."

There are two key styles of Sauvignon Blanc produced in New Zealand. Wines fermented and matured in stainless steel (the most common) place their accent squarely on their fruit flavours, and are usually labelled as "Sauvignon Blanc". Wood-fermented and/or wood-matured styles are typically called "Sauvignon Blanc Oak Aged", "Reserve Sauvignon Blanc" or (decreasingly) "Fumé Blanc".

Another major style difference is regionally based: the rapier-like wines of Marlborough contrast with the softer, lusher, less pungently herbaceous wines of Hawke's Bay. These are wines to drink young (within a year or two of the vintage) while they are irresistibly fresh, tangy and piquant, although the more complex, oak-aged Hawke's Bay wines can mature well for several years.

AKARANGI SAUVIGNON BLANC

DRY $12 -V

☆☆

Pale and light, the 1995 vintage of this Hawke's Bay wine is limey and crisp, but its flavour is very shallow. The '96 (**) is a clean, light wine with a soft, restrained flavour.

ALLAN SCOTT MARLBOROUGH SAUVIGNON

VINTAGE	97	96	95
WR	7	7	5
DRINK	97-8	P	P

DRY $17 V+

☆☆☆☆½

Allan Scott aims for a "ripe, tropical not herbaceous" style of Sauvignon Blanc (like the French, he simply calls it "Sauvignon"). Every time I encountered the '96 in a blind tasting, it knocked my socks off. One of the top wines of the vintage, it's a classic Marlborough style with a fresh, lifted, voluminous bouquet. The palate boasts pure, ripe, exceptionally concentrated flavours underpinned by invigorating acidity, leading to a dry, superbly sustained finish. The 1997 vintage (****½), is a pale, highly scented wine, fractionally less intense than the '96, but very ripe, with excellent depth of passionfruit-like flavour, cut with fresh acidity.

ALPHA DOMUS SAUVIGNON BLANC

VINTAGE	97	96
WR	6	5
DRINK	97-9	97-8

M/DRY $15 V+

(☆☆☆☆½)

Grant Edmonds, formerly chief winemaker of Villa Maria, produced the first 1996 vintage of this Hawke's Bay wine. Fermented and lees-aged in stainless steel tanks, it is an instantly attractive style. The fresh, ripe aromas lead into a crisp, non-herbaceous palate with good depth of tropical-fruit flavours and a sliver of sweetness to balance its zesty acidity. A very easy-drinking and enjoyable wine. The '97 (****) is a very satisfying wine, fresh, weighty and rounded, with rich tropical/lime flavours and excellent length.

AZURE BAY SAUVIGNON BLANC/SÉMILLON

M/DRY $10 V+

(☆☆☆)

The 1996 vintage (***) is a remarkably good wine for just under $10. Grown by Montana in the Marlborough and Gisborne regions, it's attractively fresh and lively, with a pleasing depth of crisp, lemon/herbal flavours and a slightly sweet finish.

BABICH H.B. **SAUVIGNON** **BLANC**	VINTAGE	96	95	94	93	92	91	90	**DRY $12 V+**
	WR	6	6	7	6	7	5	NM	
	DRINK	97-8	P	97-8	P	P	P	NM	(☆☆☆)

A typical, always very easy-drinking Hawke's Bay style: full bodied, with fresh, lime and tropical fruit flavours, without pungent herbaceousness. The '96 is one of the most enjoyable vintages of this well-priced label. Mouthfilling, it's a riper style, strongly varietal, with satisfying depth of crisp, fresh, melon and lime-evoking flavours, offering good drinking right now. The 1997 vintage (**¹/₂) is a solid, very crisp wine with lemon/herbal flavours, but a bit less ripe and lighter than the '96.

BABICH MARA **ESTATE** **SAUVIGNON**	VINTAGE	96	95	94	93	**DRY $17 V+**
	WR	6	6	7	6	
	DRINK	97-00	97-8	97-9	P	(☆☆☆☆☆✫)

White Graves is the model for this barrel-fermented and lees-aged Hawke's Bay wine. The '95 is maturing splendidly. Grown in the Gimblett Road shingle country, it's a ripely fragrant, multi-faceted wine with impressive weight and flavour richness, a slightly creamy texture and a lovely harmony of melon/passionfruit characters, oak and acidity. The '96 (****¹/₂) has an oaky bouquet (full barrel-ferment, 15 per cent new wood) and rather Chardonnay-like palate, with good weight and depth of nutty, complex flavour. There's plenty of ripe, sweet fruit there, but it needs time to achieve balance; open 1998.

BABICH **MARLBOROUGH** **SAUV. BLANC**	VINTAGE	96	95	94	93	92	91	**DRY $12 V+**
	WR	6	5	7	6	7	7	
	DRINK	97-8	P	97-8	P	P	P	☆☆☆☆

This wine regularly offers four-star or better quality at a two-star price. The accent is on vigorous gooseberry and capsicum-like fruit flavours, underpinned by racy acidity. The '95 lacked its customary weight and flavour richness, but the '96 is a return to good form. Grown in the Rapaura district, it's fresh and ripely aromatic, with very good depth of pure, delicate, gooseberry/capsicum flavours, long and lively. The 1997 vintage (****) is also excellent, with ripe fruit aromas and lots of fresh, delicate, mouth-wateringly crisp flavour.

BIRCHWOOD **MARLBOROUGH** **SAUV. BLANC**	**DRY $12 V+**
	(☆☆☆✫)

Produced by Selaks exclusively for Foodtown, the '96 (***¹/₂) is a very lively wine with strong lemon/capsicum flavours, a fractionally off-dry finish and brisk acidity. Top value.

BRADSHAW **EST. SAUVIGNON** **BLANC**	**DRY $14 AV**
	(☆☆☆)

Estate-grown at Havelock North, the 1996 vintage (***) is a very decent wine with a fresh, ripe, lifted bouquet, generous body and good depth of melon/capsicum flavour, crisp and dry.

BRAJKOVICH SAUVIGNON

DRY $15 AV

☆☆☆

The switch from Gisborne to Kumeu fruit since 1993 has raised the interest level. Handled in stainless steel, this wine typically offers a scented, citrusy, ripely herbal bouquet and ripe tropical-fruit flavours in a very easy-drinking, rounded style.

BROOKFIELDS SAUVIGNON BLANC

VINTAGE	96	95	94	93	92	91	90
WR	6	6	7	7	7	6	6
DRINK	98	97+	P	P	P	P	P

DRY $17 AV

☆☆☆☆

This Hawke's Bay wine is a quite complex style, worth short-term cellaring. The '95, predominantly estate-grown, and oak-matured for two months, is less lush and intense than the striking '94, but still highly enjoyable – citrusy, toasty, crisp and flavourful, with some complexity and richness. The 1996 vintage (****) is a soft, weighty, rich-flavoured wine with ripe tropical fruit and oak aromas and a mealy, complex palate.

CAIRNBRAE OAK AGED SAUV. BLANC

VINTAGE	96
WR	6
DRINK	99

DRY $18 -V

(☆ ☆☆☆½)

A marriage of 90 per cent Marlborough Sauvignon Blanc and 10 per cent Sémillon, the 1996 vintage (***½) was matured for five months in American oak casks. It's a lightly wooded style, herbaceous and mouth-wateringly crisp in a dry, steely, appley, slightly austere style with searching flavours. A greener-edged wine than its non-wooded stablemate (below), reflecting the Sémillon influence, it's worth cellaring. This wine is being replaced by Cairnbrae's new Reserve Barrel Fermented Sauvignon Blanc label.

CAIRN. MARL. SAUVIGNON BLANC

VINTAGE	96	95	94	93
WR	6	5	7	6
DRINK	97-8	P	97-8	P

DRY $14 V+

(☆☆☆☆)

The keenly priced 1996 vintage (****) is brimful of appeal. It's a classic Marlborough style, fresh, lively and limey, with excellent vigour and flavour depth and a powerful finish. Tasted as a tank sample, the ripely scented '97 looked at least equally good, with excellent concentration of zingy, tropical fruit flavours, a herbal undercurrent and rich finish.

CHANCELLOR WAIPARA SAUVIGNON

VINTAGE	96
WR	5
DRINK	97-9

M/DRY $19 -V

(☆☆☆½)

Grown at Waipara in North Canterbury and made at the Marlborough winery of Waipara Estates' part-owner, Allan Scott, the debut 1995 vintage is an impressively aromatic and full-bodied wine with good depth of ripe flavour, crisp and lively. The '96 (****), 15 per cent French oak-fermented, is a freshly aromatic and zingy wine with good weight. The subtle use of wood adds a touch of complexity to its fresh, crisp, melon and green capsicum-like flavours.

CHARD FARM SAUVIGNON BLANC

M/DRY $17 AV

☆☆☆⟡

Sauvignon Blanc is emerging as one of Chard Farm's successes. The pale, aromatic and zingy 1996 vintage (***/₂) was partly fermented and lees-aged in new and one-year-old French oak barriques. This is an attractive Central Otago wine with good depth of dryish, delicate melon/capsicum flavours, cut with fresh acidity.

C.J. PASK SAUVIGNON BLANC

VINTAGE	97	96	95	94	93	92	91
WR		6	6	5	6	5	6	5
DRINK	98	P	P	P	P	P	P

DRY $14 V+

☆☆☆⟡

Hawke's Bay winemaker Kate Radburnd aims for "an easy-drinking style with its emphasis on tropical-fruit flavours and a tangy lift". The '95 was one of the better wines of the vintage. Fresh, lively and almost imperceptibly off-dry (stop-fermented at 4 grams/litre residual sugar), the '96 (***) is a highly approachable wine with good weight and crisp acidity underpinning its moderately ripe, slightly green-edged flavours.

CLEARVIEW EST. RESERVE FUMÉ BLANC

VINTAGE	96	95	94	93	92	91	90
WR	4	5	6	6	6	6	4
DRINK	97-9	97-9	P	P	P	P	P

DRY $18 AV

(☆☆☆☆)

Full of character, this Te Awanga wine is usually a very weighty, rich-flavoured, satisfying mouthful. The 1994 vintage is a typically bold style, awash with strong, ripe, tropical-fruit flavours, fleshed out with toasty oak. The '95 is less seductive – robust and complex in a ripe, non-herbaceous style, but the fruit flavours are less lush and rich than usual. (Note: the 1996, fermented and matured for 11 months in new and two-year-old French and American oak casks, has not been given Reserve status and is priced below the usual $21.)

CLOUDY BAY SAUVIGNON BLANC

VINTAGE	97	96	95	94	93	92	91	90
WR	6	6	4	6	4	5	6	4
DRINK	98	P	P	P	P	P	P	P

DRY $23 AV

☆☆☆☆☆

No other New Zealand wine has generated as much fervour around the world as Cloudy Bay Sauvignon Blanc. The irresistibly aromatic and zesty style and its rapier-like flavours stem, winemaker Kevin Judd is convinced, from "the fruit characters that are in the grapes when they arrive at the winery". The '95 is as excitingly intense as ever. The gorgeous 1996 vintage (*****) is an explosive Marlborough wine with a voluminous bouquet. Mouthfilling (13.5 per cent alcohol), it is a deliciously powerful wine with ripe, mouth-encircling flavour, arresting concentration, fresh, appetising acidity and a long, long finish. A great vintage of a great label.

COLLARDS MARL. SAUVIGNON BLANC

VINTAGE	97	96	95	94	93	92	91	90
WR	7	6	5	7	6	7	6	5
DRINK	97-9	97-8	P	P	P	P	P	P

DRY $15 V+

☆☆☆☆

Typically a verdant, crisp wine in the classic Marlborough mould. The '95 vintage is lighter than usual, with its fresh, limey flavours lacking their customary intensity. The pale, mouthfilling 1996 (****) is very appealing, with delicate, penetrating, clearly herbaceous but ripe flavours braced by lively acidity and an impressively long finish.

COLLARDS ROTH. VINE. SAUVIGNON BLANC

DRY $15 V+

☆☆☆☆⯪

VINTAGE	97	96	95	94	93	92	91	90
WR		7	7	6	7	7	7	6	6
DRINK		97-00	97-9	P		97-8	97-8	97-8	P	P

Grown in Collards' Rothesay Vineyard at Waimauku, West Auckland, at its best this non-wooded Sauvignon Blanc is outstandingly lush and robust. The 1995 is one of the top wines of the vintage, with more body and flavour than most. The '96 (*****) is a very seductive wine indeed. It's less intensely aromatic than southern styles, but certainly makes up for that on the palate. It's deliciously full and fresh, with a powerful surge of ripe, almost sweet-tasting fruit, good acid spine and a notably rich, persistent finish.

CONDERS BEND MARL. SAUVIGNON BLANC

DRY $16 V+

☆☆☆☆

Under the Conders Bend label, recently acquired by Delegat's, Craig Gass produced a consistently impressive Sauvignon Blanc – mouthfilling and lush. The '95 is one of the region's finest: fresh and lively, with plenty of limey, delicate flavour. The 1996 vintage (*****1/2) is a highly fragrant wine with a delightful depth of ripe, herbaceous flavour, fresh, crisp and deliciously long.

COOPERS CREEK GISBORNE FUMÉ BLANC

DRY $15 V+

☆☆☆☆

VINTAGE	95	94	93	92	91	90
WR		5	5	6	5	7	
DRINK	97-8	P	P	P	P	P	

The 1995 vintage (****) is a delightful wine. Bright, light lemon-green in hue, it is a highly fragrant blend of 80 per cent Sauvignon Blanc and 20 per cent Sémillon, French oak-aged for four months. Still fresh, it is full and lively on the palate, offering very good depth of ripe, melon/capsicum flavours, delicately seasoned with wood.

COOPERS CREEK MARL. SAUV. BLANC

DRY $14 V+

☆☆☆☆

VINTAGE	97	96	95	94	93	92	91	90
WR		6	6	5	7	5	5	6	4
DRINK		97-8	97-8	P	P	P	P	P	P

A consistently delightful wine, bargain-priced. The '96 is a deliciously rich wine with a hint of honeysuckle on the nose and a very full, tangy palate offering excellent depth of ripe, tropical fruit, gently herbaceous flavours. The 1997 vintage (****1/2) was on the shelves by early July. It's a drier wine than the '96, with fresh, lifted, sweet-fruit aromas and very ripe, crisp and lively, non-herbaceous flavours, redolent of passionfruit.

COOPERS CREEK MARL. OAK AGED SAUV. BLANC

DRY $19 V+

(☆☆☆☆⯪)

VINTAGE	96	95	94
WR		6	6	5
DRINK		97-9	P	97-8

This wine is based on the "pick" of the crop, fermented in tanks, then matured on its yeast lees for about six months in American oak casks. The '95 is superbly fragrant, with a touch of spicy oak and loads of fresh, crisp, ripe flavour, very lively and intense. The 1996 vintage (*****) is a splendidly lush and persistent wine, with wood and lees-aging characters interwoven with very ripe fruit. The bouquet of rich fruit and toasty oak leads into a soft, complex, deep-flavoured palate with delicious ripeness and roundness. Hard to resist in its youth, it should also mature well through 1998.

CORBANS EST.
H.B. SAUVIGNON
BLANC

DRY $11 AV

(☆☆⯨)

The first 1995 vintage of Corbans' budget-priced Sauvignon Blanc, grown in Gisborne, is fresh and clearly varietal, with a ripely herbaceous bouquet and plenty of tropical/herbal flavour. It's not intense, but very easy-drinking. The '96 (**¹/₂), is a light yellow wine with a slightly honied nose and smooth, lemony flavours, lacking real depth.

CORBANS PRI.
BIN MARL.
SAUVIGNON BLANC

DRY $19 -V

(☆☆☆⯨)

The slightly austere 1996 vintage (***¹/₂) could mature well, but slightly lacks the intensity I'd have expected of a Private Bin label. Pale, with delicate, limey scents, it's a medium-bodied, clearly varietal wine with highish acidity and dry, persistent apple/lime flavours. Worth keeping to mid-98.

CORBANS WHITE
LAB. SEL. SAUV.
BLANC/SÉMILLON

	VINTAGE	96	95
	WR	6	6
	DRINK	97-8	97-8

DRY $9 V+

(☆☆⯨)

The first 1995 vintage is fresh and crisp, with a clearly herbaceous bouquet and moderate depth of melon and herbal flavours. The 1996 vintage (**¹/₂) of this low-priced Gisborne quaffer is a blend of 70 per cent Sauvignon Blanc and 30 per cent Sémillon. It's a solid but plain wine, lacking fragrance, with clean, appley, green-tinged flavours and a dry, slightly sharp finish.

CRAB FARM
SAUVIGNON
BLANC

DRY $15 -V

☆☆⯨

A roaring success in the tiny Bay View winery's restaurant over summer, this non-wooded Hawke's Bay wine has been of varying quality. Some vintages have been ripe but lacked concentration. At its best, it is fleshy and full-flavoured, and a good example of the regional style.

CROSS
ROADS
SAUVIGNON

M/DRY $14 -V

(☆☆⯨)

The 1996 vintage (**¹/₂) is an unwooded Hawke's Bay wine produced in a medium-dry style. It lacks real freshness and fragrance on the nose, but offers reasonable depth of appley, lemony flavour in a very easy-drinking style.

CROSS ROADS	VINTAGE	96	95	94	93	92	91	90	DRY $14 AV
SAUVIGNON	WR	6	5	6	4	7	6	6	
OAK AGED	DRINK	97-00 P		96-9 P		97-00 P		P	☆☆☆

At its best, this is a bold Hawke's Bay wine intermingling ripe tropical-fruit and moderately herbal flavours with barrel-ferment complexity. The 1994 vintage is a delicious wine with fresh, lively, tropical-fruit flavours and oak complexity in a ripe, robust style. The '95 (**¹/₂) includes 15 per cent Sémillon. Pale and slightly austere, it lacks the power and richness of the '94, with a crisp, appley, slightly nutty flavour.

DASHWOOD	VINTAGE	97	96	95	94	93	92	91	90	DRY $17 AV
MARLBOROUGH	WR	6	7	5	7	4	4	6	6	
SAUV. BLANC	DRINK	97-8 P	P	P	P	P	P	P		☆☆☆☆

The Vavasour winery markets its drink-young, non-wooded Sauvignon Blanc under the Dashwood label. Grown in several Awatere Valley vineyards, the 1996 vintage is a powerful and intense, distinctly cool-climate wine. The bouquet is fresh, lifted and slightly grassy; the flavour brisk and incisive in a flinty, penetratingly herbaceous style with hints of tropical fruit, good length and a mouth-wateringly crisp finish. The '97 (****) is a typically zesty wine with fresh, crisp, ripely herbaceous flavours of excellent depth.

DE GYFFARDE	VINTAGE	96	95	DRY $15 AV
MARLBOROUGH	WR	5	4	
SAUV. BLANC	DRINK	97-8	P	(☆☆☆)

Grown in Rod and Di Lofthouse's vineyard in the Rapaura district, this wine is made on their behalf by Simon Waghorn at the Whitehaven winery. The 1996 vintage (****¹/₂) is a pale, ripely scented wine, with good depth of non-herbaceous, tropical fruit (melon and passionfruit) flavours, very ripe and delicate.

DELEGAT'S HB	VINTAGE	97	96	95	94	93	92	91	90	M/DRY $13 AV
SAUVIGNON	WR	6	5	5	6	5	6	5	6	
BLANC	DRINK	97-8	97-8	P	P	P	P	P	P	☆☆☆

This unwooded wine places its accent on round, ripe Hawke's Bay fruit flavours, in a very easy-drinking style. The 1996 vintage (***) is ripe and rounded, with melon-like flavours of good depth. The '97, tasted prior to bottling, showed lively melon and capsicum-like flavours, at the greener end of the spectrum for Hawke's Bay, but clearly varietal and of good depth.

DELEGAT'S PROP.	VINTAGE	96	95	94	93	92	91	90	DRY $18 V+
RES. OAK AGED	WR	7	6	7	6	7	6	6	
SAUV. BLANC	DRINK	97-00	97-8	P	P	P	P	P	☆☆☆☆☆

A very classy Hawke's Bay wine, packed with lush fruit flavours fleshed out with wood. Winemaker Brent Marris reserves the "pick" of the ripest grapes for this top label, blends it with some greener fruit for acid structure and balance, wood-ferments half the wine and then barrel-matures the lot for up to six months. The '96 is a delightful, full-bodied, very fresh and refreshing wine, beautifully scented and vibrantly fruity, with lively acidity and a wealth of tropical fruit flavours, subtly seasoned with oak. The 1997 vintage (****¹/₂) is an impressively weighty wine with loads of fresh, tangy, tropical fruit flavour and a subtle twist of oak.

DE REDCLIFFE MARL. SAUV. BLANC	VINTAGE	97	96	95
	WR	7	6	6
	DRINK	97-8	P	P

DRY $14 V+

(☆☆☆☆⯪)

Past vintages of this wine have been attractive, with strong, verdant flavour and a firm acid underlay. The '95 is a vigorous, slightly honeyish, full-flavoured wine, with more character than many 1995 Sauvignon Blancs. The 1996 vintage (****), released in mid 1997, is a very appealing wine, fleshy and ripely scented, with crisp, concentrated tropical fruit flavours, maturing gracefully.

DE REDCLIFFE RES. SAUVIGNON BLANC	VINTAGE	96
	WR	7
	DRINK	P

DRY $19 AV

(☆☆☆☆☆)

De Redcliffe's first reserve Sauvignon from the 1996 vintage (****) is a single-vineyard wine based on young, first-crop vines at Renwick, Marlborough. It displays an almost Hawke's Bay-like weight and richness, with mouthfilling body and a generous surge of ripely herbaceous, rounded flavour. An impressive debut.

DE REDCLIFFE SAUVIGNON BLANC/SÉMILLON	VINTAGE	96
	WR	6
	DRINK	97-8

DRY $16 V+

(☆☆☆☆☆)

The generous, deeply flavoured 1996 vintage (****) is a 50/50 blend of Marlborough Sauvignon Blanc and Auckland Sémillon, matured for four months in new French and German oak casks. The marriage is a happy one: this is an excellent wine, full of character, with a very attractive, slightly herbaceous, nutty bouquet. The palate is full-bodied, with ripe, tropical fruit flavours, considerable complexity and balanced acidity, delivering very satisfying drinking from now onwards.

DRY RIVER SAUVIGNON BLANC	VINTAGE	97	96	95	94	93	92	91	90
	WR	7	7	5	6	7	6	7	5
	DRINK	97-02	97-02	97-00	97-00	97-9	97-9	97-8	97-8

DRY $18 V+

☆☆☆☆⯪

Estate-grown in Martinborough, at its best this is an intense, cool-climate style, with an outpouring of lush, ripe fruit aromas and a mouth-wateringly crisp, vigorous palate. The 1995 is a slightly less ripe style, with strong lemon, passionfruit and green capsicum-like flavours and a long, tangy finish. The '96 is one of the finest yet. It's a very expressive wine with highly fragrant, ripe fruit aromas, impressive weight and depth of fresh, pure, delicate tropical fruit flavours and a crisp, long finish. The outstanding 1997 vintage (*****) is less pungently aromatic but more robust than most Marlborough Sauvignon Blancs. Weighty, with good acid spine, it is overflowing with fresh tropical fruit flavours in a very ripe, rich style.

ESK VALLEY SAUVIGNON BLANC	VINTAGE	97	96	95	94	93	92	91	90
	WR	6	6	5	7	5	5	6	5
	DRINK	97-8	P	P	P	P	P	P	P

DRY $13 V+

☆☆☆☆⯪

An unwooded, consistently above-average Hawke's Bay wine. In warmer vintages it is robust, with a rich, herbal but not pungently herbaceous flavour; cooler years produce a less powerful but zesty wine. The 1996 vintage is a fresh, delicate wine with limey aromas, good weight, and excellent depth of ripe melon/capsicum flavours, crisp and persistent. The '97 (***) is weighty, ripe and rounded, but in its infancy slightly less intense than the '96.

FAIR. DOWNS MARLBOROUGH SAUV. BLANC	VINTAGE	96					DRY $17 AV
	WR	6					(☆☆☆☆)
	DRINK	97-8					

Grown by Ken and Jill Small at the head of the Brancott Valley, and made by John Forrest, the 1996 vintage is an instantly likeable wine with fresh, ripe passionfruit/lime characters. It's fragrant and full-bodied, with crisp, penetrating flavour in a very clean and lively style. The '97 (****) is a boldly mouthfilling wine, freshly scented, with impressive depth of melon/herbal flavours and a lingering finish.

FORREST EST. MARLBOROUGH SAUV. BLANC	VINTAGE	97	96	95	94	93	92	DRY $16 V+
	WR	6	6	4	6	6	4	☆☆☆☆½
	DRINK	97+	97+	P	P	P	P	

John Forrest's unwooded Sauvignon Blanc is very fragrant and rich-flavoured, and of sharply rising quality in recent years. The fresh, vibrant, lifted bouquet affords a great introduction to the delicious 1996 vintage. On the palate, it is very clean and varietal, with ripe, concentrated fruit flavours in a full, lush, gently herbaceous, very elegant and well-balanced style. Tasted soon after bottling, the '97 (****1/2) is a repeat of the '96: a mouthfilling wine with very ripe passionfruit/lime flavours in a vibrant, lush, weighty style, long and rich.

GIBBSTON VAL. CENTRAL OTAGO SAUV. BLANC	VINTAGE	95	94	93	92	91	90	89	DRY $20 -V
	WR		6	5	5	6	5	4	☆☆☆
	DRINK	97-9	97-8	P	P	P	P	P	

Past vintages of this wine were stalky and tart when young, but with age rounded out into a broader, richer wine. The 1995 vintage (***1/2), fermented and matured for eight months in oak casks, is yellow hued, with mouthfilling body and lots of toasty, ripe, non-herbaceous flavour. Characterful, crisp and complex, this is the finest wine yet under this label.

GIBBSTON VAL. MARL. SAUVIGNON BLANC		DRY $18 AV
		(☆☆☆☆½)

This Central Otago winery doesn't produce a Marlborough Sauvignon Blanc every vintage, but when it does, they're always good. The '96 is a delicious mouthful, with fresh, zingy, tropical-fruit and green capsicum-like characters in a very ripe, flavourful and lingering style. The 1997 vintage (*****) is another beauty, with a voluminous bouquet and strikingly rich flavour – intense, limey and delicate, with racy acidity.

GIESEN MARL. SAUVIGNON BLANC		DRY $16 AV
		☆☆☆

The '95 is a weighty, moderately ripe wine with strong, crisp, honied flavours and a slightly grippy (hard) finish. The '96 (****), grown in the company's own Dillons Point vineyard in Marlborough, is the best vintage yet. Instantly appealing, it offers loads of ripe, tropical fruit and capsicum-like flavour, delicate and finely balanced, with fresh, appetising acidity and a deliciously long finish.

GILLAN MARL.
SAUVIGNON
BLANC

VINTAGE	97	96	95	94
WR		6	6	4	7
DRINK		98-9	98	P	P

DRY $16 V+

(☆ ☆☆☆☆)

The vibrant, lush 1994 vintage won the trophy for top Sauvignon Blanc at the Air New Zealand Wine Awards. The '95 is much less exciting, but still solid, with quite good depth of citrusy, green-edged, well-rounded flavour. The 1996 vintage (****) is an attractively ripe wine, yet it retains its cool-climate vigour and impact. Grown in the Eastfields vineyard near Blenheim, it is fresh and delicate, with strong, citrusy, limey aromas and flavours in a deliciously easy-drinking style.

GLADSTONE
FUMÉ
BLANC

VINTAGE	96
WR	7
DRINK	97-9

DRY $19 AV

(☆ ☆☆☆☆↗)

The lush, lovely 1996 vintage (*****/₂) of this Wairarapa wine was oak-matured for three months. It's a highly fragrant, very ripe style with a powerful surge of fresh, lively tropical fruit flavours and deftly balanced wood adding a creamy richness.

GLADSTONE
SAUVIGNON
BLANC

VINTAGE	96	95	94	93	92	91	90
WR	7	6	6	6	6	6	6
DRINK	98-9	P	P	P	P	P	P

DRY $18 V+

(☆ ☆☆☆☆↗)

The Gladstone style bursts with pure, delicate aromas and flavours in a clearly but not pungently herbaceous style. The 1996 vintage (*****) is top-flight. It's a notably ripe wine with a rich, beautifully scented bouquet. The palate is vibrantly fruity, with very fresh, delicate tropical fruit flavours and a slight herbal undercurrent. Crisp, immaculate, intense – this is a splendid Wairarapa wine.

GLENMARK
WEKA PLAINS
SAUVIGNON BLANC

DRY $21 -V

(☆☆☆↗)

"One row, one barrique," is how proprietor John McCaskey sums up the supply of this rare, oak-aged Waipara wine. Only 300 bottles were produced of the 1996 vintage (***¹/₂). It's a very satisfying wine, vibrantly fruity, with some complexity and lots of firm, fairly ripe, green-edged flavour.

GLOVER'S
MOUTERE
SAUV. BLANC

VINTAGE	96	95	94	93	92	91
WR	5	4	6	6	6	5
DRINK	97-9	97-8	97-8	P	P	P

DRY $17 -V

☆☆↗

Very much a food style, the bone-dry 1995 vintage is a high-acid wine with nettley, tangy flavour. The '96 (**¹/₂) has fresh, moderately ripe fruit aromas in a dry, flinty, green-edged style, more austere than most.

GOLDWAT. DOG POINT MARL. SAUV. BLANC

DRY $19 AV

(☆☆☆☆½)

It's pricey, but Goldwater's Marlborough wine is also classy. The 1996 vintage is based on the second crop off young vines in the Dog Point vineyard in the Brancott Valley. Ten per cent of the wine was barrel-fermented. It's a delicious wine, aromatic, full-bodied, very fresh and lively, with a surge of well-ripened melon/green capsicum flavours and a freshly acidic finish. The '97 (*****) is strikingly powerful. Richly fragrant, it is very ripe yet vivacious, with intense passionfruit/lime flavour, zingy acids and great weight.

GROVE MILL MARLBOROUGH SAUV. BLANC

VINTAGE	96	95	94	93	92	91	90
WR	7	5	5	4	7	5	4
DRINK	97-00 P	97-8 P	P	P	P	P	

DRY $18 V+

☆☆☆☆½

A classic regional style with penetrating flavour and invigorating acidity. The '95 has a herbaceous bouquet and plenty of flavour, but lacks its customary intensity. The 1996 vintage is a succulent wine with a rich, ripely herbal bouquet, mouthfilling body, a sliver of sweetness amid its concentrated, gooseberry and capsicum-like flavours, and lovely balance and vigour. The '97 (*****) is similar to the '96, with mouthfilling body and ripe tropical/capsicum flavours, very concentrated and persistent. (The 1997 Sanctuary Sauvignon Blanc (***½) is an enjoyable although not intense wine, with fresh, crisp, ripe, delicate flavours.)

GROVE MILL WINEMAKER'S RES. SAUVIGNON BLANC

DRY $21 -V

(☆☆☆☆)

The 1996 vintage (****) is an impressively rich Marlborough wine. Bright, light lemon-green in hue, it is fresh and highly aromatic on the nose. The palate is fleshy and buoyant, with an excellent depth of crisp, ripely herbaceous flavour.

HALF MOON BAY SAUVIGNON BLANC

VINTAGE	97	96	95
WR	5	6	5
DRINK	98-9	97-8	P

DRY $17 AV

(☆ ☆☆☆)

The first 1995 vintage of this lightly wooded Hawke's Bay wine from Negociants, the wine distributors, is skilfully made, with impressive body and flavour intensity. The ripely scented '96 (***½) is full-bodied, juicy and well-rounded, in a satisfyingly ripe style with pure, penetrating tropical/gooseberry flavours.

HAU ARIKI SAUVIGNON BLANC

DRY $17 -V

(☆☆☆)

Produced by the Hau Ariki marae at Martinborough, the barrel-aged 1995 vintage (***) is a yellow-hued, full-bodied wine with strong, toasty oak fleshing out its ripe gooseberryish flavours.

HAWKESBRIDGE WILLOW. VINE. SAUVIGNON BLANC

DRY $16 V+

(☆☆☆☆)

Mike and Judy Veal's Marlborough Sauvignon Blanc from 1994 was an auspicious debut, robust and incisively flavoured. The '95, however, was much lighter and less ripe. The immaculate 1996 vintage (****) marks a return to the standard of the '94. It's the sort of Sauvignon Blanc it's easy to drink a lot of, with mouthfilling body and a basket of ripe fruit flavours – pure, delicate and non-aggressive, with fresh, balanced acidity.

HIGHFIELD ELSTREE RESERVE SAUVIGNON BLANC

DRY $23 -V

(☆☆☆⯪)

This Marlborough winery's fully barrel-fermented Sauvignon Blanc from 1994 is a mouthfilling, creamy, oaky, complex style with ripe, soft fruit and cheesey, "malo"-derived characters on the nose and palate. Good, Chardonnay-like food wine. The '97 (****) is a much more fruit-driven style. It is a pale, scented wine with ripe, delicate, limey flavours, a slightly creamy texture and good weight. Open mid 1998 onwards.

HIGHFIELD MARLBOROUGH SAUV. BLANC

VINTAGE	97	96	95	94	93	92	91	90
WR	6	6	5	5	5	5	6	4
DRINK	97-00	97-9	P	P	97-8	97-8	97-8	P

M/DRY $16 AV

☆☆☆

Typically an attractive, easy-drinking wine, although not intense. The 1996 vintage has a fresh, ripe, scented bouquet and crisp, balanced tropical/lime flavours, moderately concentrated, with a sliver of sweetness adding to its very pleasant, undemanding style. The '97 (***) is not intense, but attractively fresh and zingy, with ripe passionfruit/lime flavours.

HUNTER'S MARLBOROUGH SAUV. BLANC

VINTAGE	96	95	94	93	92	91	90
WR	5	4	5	5	5	6	4
DRINK	97-8	P	P	P	P	P	P

DRY $20 AV

☆☆☆☆☆

Hunter's' ranking among New Zealand's most illustrious producers stems chiefly from the exceptional quality of this wine, which exhibits the "leap-out-of-the-glass" aromas of ripe, cool-climate grapes, uncluttered by any oak handling. The '95 lacks the sheer excitement of a top year, but displays delicate, lively, melon and herbal characters, not intense but true. The 1996 vintage was a bit closed in its youth but has opened up superbly, with mouthfilling body (13 per cent alcohol) and impressively rich, incisive gooseberry/capsicum flavours. Overshadowed in its extreme youth by more forward wines, the '97 (****) is a strong-flavoured, crisply herbaceous style that should reveal its typical class by early 1998.

HUNTER'S SAUV. BLANC OAK AGED

VINTAGE	96	95	94	93	92	91	90
WR	5	NM	5	5	5	6	4
DRINK	97-8	NM	P	P	P	P	P

DRY $22 AV

☆☆☆☆☆

Equally distinguished as its unwooded stablemate (above), this slightly higher-priced label is based on ripe, less-herbaceous Marlborough grapes of which a portion is wood-fermented and lees-aged; the rest is fermented and matured in stainless steel. It typically offers pure, deep, incisive fruit flavours, plenty of body and acidity, and well-judged, subtle wood handling. There was no '95. In its youth, the 1996 vintage (*****) is a slightly more oak-influenced style than in the past; 45 per cent spent eight months in new French oak barriques. Intense and vibrant, with pure, well-ripened tropical fruit flavours and nutty oak, it's a mouthfilling wine, still quite tight, offering splendid drinking through 1998.

HUNTER'S SPR. *CREEK VINE.* *SAU. BL/CHARD.*	VINTAGE	96	95	**DRY $15 AV**
	WR	5	5	(☆ ☆☆)
	DRINK	97-8	97-8	

Two-thirds Sauvignon Blanc, one-third Chardonnay is the varietal recipe for the thoroughly pleasant 1996 vintage (***) of this Marlborough wine, grown in the Spring Creek vineyard at Rapaura. Fragrant, with a ripely herbaceous bouquet, it is a faintly oaked wine (20 per cent was barrel-aged for six weeks) with good depth of passionfruit and melon-like flavours in a fresh, ripe, easy-drinking style.

JACKSON EST. *MARLBOROUGH* *SAUV. BLANC*	VINTAGE	96	**DRY $17 V+**
	WR	5	☆☆☆☆☆
	DRINK	97-8	

Every vintage, this label stands out. It is grown in John Stichbury's vineyard in the heart of the Wairau Valley, and made by Australian consultant Martin Shaw at Rapaura Vintners. The '95 is less exciting than usual, but still one of the more attractive wines of the vintage: fragrant, with good depth of moderately ripe, citrus/capsicum-like flavours, fresh and tangy. The 1996 vintage (*****) is a distinctively lush and mouthfilling wine, maturing superbly. Vibrantly fruity and zingy, with good extract and fruit concentration, it is a notably ripe-flavoured style with lovely vigour and depth.

KAWARAU EST. *SAUVIGNON* *BLANC*	**DRY $18 -V**
	(☆☆☆)

It doesn't scream at you, but it's easy to enjoy a second or third glass of the 1996 vintage (***) of this Central Otago wine. Grown in the company's Dunstan vineyard at Lowburn, north of Cromwell, and partly matured in French oak casks, it's a very clean, delicate wine with satisfying depth of flinty, nettley flavour, invigorating acidity and subtle oak influence.

KEMBLEFIELD *RES. SAUVIGNON* *BLANC*	**DRY $18 AV**
	(☆☆☆☆)

This is emerging as Kemblefield's finest wine. The '95 vintage is mouthfilling (14 per cent alcohol), with very good depth of ripe, quince and melon-like fruit flavours, complexity and a slightly creamy texture. The 1996 (****) is a powerful Hawke's Bay wine with a ripely herbaceous, oaky fragrance, plenty of muscle and a creamy-soft texture, giving great drinkability.

KEMBLEFIELD *SAUVIGNON* *BLANC*	**DRY $15 AV**
	(☆☆☆)

The 1995 vintage of this Hawke's Bay wine, Kemblefield's first unwooded Sauvignon Blanc, is moderately ripe but full-flavoured. The '96 (****1/2), made from bought-in grapes, is a satisfyingly full-bodied style with strong, ripe, delicate flavours and good length.

KERR FARM SAUVIGNON BLANC

DRY $15 AV

(☆☆☆)

The first 1996 vintage (***) of this Kumeu, West Auckland wine should win plenty of friends. Pale, with a fresh, ripely fragrant bouquet, it is a weighty style with good depth of non-aggressive, ripely herbal flavours in a crisp, very easy-drinking style.

KIM CRAWFORD AWATERE SAUVIGNON

VINTAGE	96
WR	6
DRINK	97-8

DRY $27 -V

(☆ ☆☆☆)

It needs time, but the debut 1996 vintage (****) should deliver rich, complex drinking in 1998. Grown in Marlborough's Awatere Valley, half the wine was handled in tanks. The rest was fermented and lees-aged for 10 months in oak, and given a softening malolactic fermentation. Pale yellow, with wood clearly in evidence on the nose, it's a full, rounded wine, still very fresh, with strong, ripe fruit flavours, oak richness and firm underlying acidity.

KIM CRAWFORD MARL. SAUV. BLANC

VINTAGE	96
WR	5
DRINK	97-8

DRY $17 V+

(☆☆☆☆☆)

The very classy '96 launched this new label from Coopers Creek's winemaker. It's a weighty, steely, dry wine, very intense, with lovely, ripely herbaceous flavours uncluttered by oak and a rich, very long finish. The '97 (*****) is also stunning. It is a notably bold, super-ripe wine with a delicious surge of fresh, crisp tropical/capsicum flavours and exceptional overall intensity.

KUMEU RIVER SAUVIGNON/ SÉMILLON

VINTAGE	96	95	94	93	92	91	90
WR	7	NM	7	7	7	6	5
DRINK	98-00	NM	P	P	P	P	P

DRY $22 AV

☆☆☆☆☆

Winemaker Michael Brajkovich aims to "ripen the Sauvignon grapes in our Kumeu vineyard fully, to reach beyond the more typical New Zealand grassy/vegetative aroma and achieve a fuller, fruitier, more aromatic style of wine with sufficient body and complexity to be able to mature in the bottle". It is typically a robust wine with ripe tropical and stone-fruit flavours, buttery "malo" influence, oak and lees-aging richness and a long, dry finish. The 1996 vintage (****1/2), only 10 per cent Sémillon, was fermented in older oak barrels and given a full, softening malolactic fermentation. It's a distinctive, subtle and complex wine, full and fresh, with ripe, quince-like flavours and a touch of butterscotch – a good drink-now or cellaring proposition.

LAKE CHALICE SAUVIGNON BLANC

VINTAGE	96
WR	5
DRINK	97-8

DRY $16 -V

(☆ ☆☆)

Named after a lake in the Richmond Range, on the northern side of the Wairau Plains, the 1995 vintage of this Marlborough wine is light in body and flavour. The '96 (**1/2) is a pale, herbaceous wine, fresh, clean and crisp, but its appley, green-edged flavours lack depth.

LANGDALE MARLB. SAUVIGNON BLANC

DRY $19 -V

(☆☆☆)

The 1996 vintage (**1/2) from this small West Melton winery is a solid wine with a hint of canned peas on the nose, full body, and quite good depth of smooth, ripe flavour, with a herbal undercurrent.

LARCOMB SAUVIGNON BLANC

M/DRY $12 V+

(☆☆☆)

Grown at Rolleston, south-west of Christchurch, the 1996 vintage (***) is quiet on the nose, but the palate shows good vigour, with a sliver of sweetness and good depth of melon/capsicum flavours.

LAWSON'S DRY HILLS MARL. SAUV. BLANC

VINTAGE	96	95	94
WR	6	4	5
DRINK	97-9	97-8	97-01

DRY $17 V+

☆☆☆☆☆

The '95 is a richly scented, subtle wine with an extra flavour dimension, slightly less powerful than in a top year, but with a real touch of class. The '96 is outstanding. Five per cent fermented in French oak barriques, and blended with 15 per cent Sémillon, it's deeply scented, very intense and zingy, with a lovely array of gooseberry/melon/capsicum flavours, fresh, authoritative acidity and a notably rich finish. The 1997 vintage (****1/2) is a notably ripe style with fresh, intense tropical fruit aromas and rich flavour, lively and lingering.

LIMEBURNERS BAY SAUVIGNON BLANC

DRY $13 AV

(☆☆☆)

Grown in West Auckland, the 1995 vintage of this non-oaked wine is not an intensely varietal style, but ripely herbal, with a well-rounded finish. The '96 (**1/2) is a pale, solid wine with reasonable depth of fresh, crisp, slightly grassy and appley flavours.

LINCOLN H.B. SAUVIGNON BLANC

DRY $12 V+

(☆☆☆)

The 1995 vintage (10 per cent Sémillon) is a solid, fruity, flavoursome wine, rounded and ready, with a distinct touch of *Botrytis*-derived honey characters. The '96 (**1/2) is a full-bodied style with moderately ripe, green-edged, very crisp flavour.

LINCOLN MARL. SAUVIGNON BLANC

VINTAGE	96
WR	4
DRINK	97-8

DRY $14 AV

(☆☆☆)

This West Auckland winery's first Marlborough Sauvignon, from the '95 vintage, has strong, herbaceous, slightly austere flavours and bracing acidity. The pale, green-edged 1996 (***) lacks the lushness and richness of fully ripe fruit, but offers plenty of grassy, appley, herbaceous flavour enlivened by racy acidity.

LINDEN EST. SAUVIGNON BLANC

DRY $15 AV

☆☆☆

Grown in the Esk Valley of Hawke's Bay and partly barrel-fermented, the 1995 vintage is a crisp, plain wine, lacking fruit richness, with appley, green-edged flavours and a slightly short finish. The '96 (***1/2) is a crisp, solid dry white, but cheesy, milky characters blur the varietal definition.

LINDEN EST. RESE. SAUVIGNON BLANC

DRY $18 AV

(☆☆☆☆)

The 1995 vintage of this Esk Valley wine, partly fermented and matured for three months in American oak barriques, displays ripe, sweet fruit characters, subtle wood seasoning and a tight, long finish. Still a baby, the '96 (****) is a bold, complex style of Sauvignon with a nutty, slightly buttery, "malo"-influenced bouquet. Weighty, fresh and crisp, with rich, well-ripened fruit flavours overlaid with wood, it's a very good food style, worth cellaring until 1998.

LINTZ EST. SAUVIGNON BLANC

VINTAGE	97	96	95	94	93	92	91
WR		7	6	7	6	7	5	5
DRINK		97-00	97-9	97-9	98-9	P	P	P

DRY $18 V+

☆☆☆☆☆

A robust, rich-flavoured style of Martinborough Sauvignon Blanc. The oak-aged '95 is a fleshy wine with savoury, appley, nutty, complex flavours and a long, steely finish. The 1996 vintage is the most memorable yet. Handled entirely in stainless steel tanks to enhance its varietal characters, it's a classic, intense cool-climate style with an enticing, ripely aromatic bouquet. The palate is fresh and immaculate, with rich, vibrant, appetisingly crisp melon/capsicum flavours, beautifully balanced and lingering. In its youth, the '97 (****) is a bold, high alcohol style, richly flavoured but needing time – open mid 1998 onwards.

LONGRIDGE OF H.B. SAUVIGNON BLANC OAK AGED

VINTAGE	96	95	94	93	92	91	90
WR		7	6	7	6	5	6	5
DRINK		97-00	97-9	97-8	P	P	P	P

DRY $13 V+

☆☆☆☆

A fine value wine from Corbans that is a full-bodied style with fresh, limey, tangy flavours. The '95 is unexpectedly good, with a depth of tropical fruit and distinctly herbaceous flavours, plus oak-derived complexity and richness. The '96 (***1/2) was grown at Oamaranui and matured for three months in French and American oak barriques. It's a fresh, flavourful, finely balanced wine with good depth of lemon/herbal characters and a subtle backdrop of oak.

MARK RAT. MARL SAUV. BLANC

VINTAGE	96
WR	6
DRINK	97-00

DRY $16 V+

(☆☆☆☆)

The bone-dry 1996 vintage (****) from this Waipara winemaker is highly appealing. It's a full, incisive wine with lifted, fresh, ripe scents, good weight, strong melon/capsicum flavours and a long, steely finish.

MARTINBOR. **VINEY. SAUV.** **BLANC**	VINTAGE	97	96	95	94	93	92	91	90	**DRY $17 V+**
	WR	6	6	5	6	5	5	5	5	
	DRINK	99	98	P	P	P	P	P	P	☆☆☆☆⯪

"We want to make more the Hawke's Bay than Marlborough style," says winemaker Larry McKenna. This fresh, dry wine is typically ripe and vibrantly fruity, with passionfruit and pineapple-evoking aromas and flavours and fresh, lively acidity. The 1996 vintage is one of the best yet – a lush, mouthfilling (13 per cent alcohol) wine with concentrated, lively, ripely herbal flavours and lovely balance and length. The '97 (****¹/₂) is weighty and ripely scented, with intense passionfruit/lime flavours and a crisp, dry, long finish.

MATUA H.B. **SAUVIGNON** **BLANC**	VINTAGE	96	95	94	93	92	91	90	**DRY $13 V+**
	WR	5	4	7	6	5	6	5	
	DRINK	97-8	P	P	P	P	P	P	☆☆☆

A consistently satisfying wine, and good value. The '95 veers more to green capsicum than riper flavours in a light, clean style which lacks weight and concentration but offers solid drinking. The 1996 vintage (***) is full-bodied and lively, although not intense, with ripe melon/capsicum flavours and a crisp, fractionally off-dry finish.

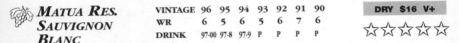

MATUA RES. **SAUVIGNON** **BLANC**	VINTAGE	96	95	94	93	92	91	90	**DRY $16 V+**
	WR	6	5	6	5	6	7	6	
	DRINK	97-00	97-8	97-9	P	P	P	P	☆☆☆☆☆

One of the country's top oak-aged Sauvignons, estate-grown at Waimauku. The '95 has a powerful surge of ripely herbal flavour, oak complexity and a long, subtle, creamy-rich finish. The 1996 vintage (****) was barrel-fermented, lees-aged for eight months and given a full, softening malolactic fermentation. Full-bodied and ripe, it is quite oaky on the nose, with rich, persistent fruit flavours fleshed out with wood and "malo"-derived complexities. An excellent wine, but slightly less lush and concentrated than the greatest vintages.

MERLEN **SAUVIGNON** **BLANC**	**DRY $15 V+**
	☆☆☆⯪

The standard of Almuth Lorenz's Marlborough wine has soared in recent vintages. The ultra-ripe 1994 is a distinctive, fleshy style with a basket of fruit characters, flavour-packed and rich. The greener-edged 1995 reveals a fresh, lively, herbaceous bouquet. One of the more successful '95s, it is delicate, flavoursome and tangy, with a lingering, well-balanced finish. The 1997 vintage (****¹/₂) is a crisp, lively wine with green capsicum/fresh-cut grass aromas and flavours.

MILLS REEF **ELSPETH** **SAUV. BLANC**	VINTAGE	96	95	94	93	92	**DRY $20 AV**
	WR	7	NM	7	6	7	
	DRINK	97-9	97-NM	97-8	P	P	☆☆☆☆⯪

Past vintages of Mills Reef's flagship Hawke's Bay Sauvignon have been a classy fumé style with mouth-filling body, oak richness and the power and structure to flourish in the cellar. The 1996 vintage (****¹/₂) was handled predominantly in tanks, with 30 per cent of the final blend fermented in oak and given a malolactic fermentation. Pale, with a slightly oaky fragrance, it is a very full-bodied wine with rich, ripe, rounded tropical fruit characters, well-integrated wood, a slightly creamy texture and almost Chardonnay-like power.

MILLS REEF	VINTAGE	96	95	94				M/DRY $12 AV
MOFFAT ROAD	WR	6	5	5				
SAUV. BLANC	DRINK	98	P	P				(☆☆½)

The full, ripe-tasting '94 got this lower-tier, slightly sweet Hawke's Bay label off to a good start. The 1995 vintage is less ripe, greener and more austere. With its fullness of body and reasonable depth of moderately ripe, limey, green-edged flavours, crisp and dryish, the '96 is a solid wine, priced right. The '97 (***½) is a solid wine, ripe-tasting and rounded, offering smooth, dryish, easy drinking.

MILLS REEF	VINTAGE	96	95	94				DRY $17 AV
RES. SAUVIGNON	WR	6	5	7				
BLANC	DRINK	97-9	97-8	P				(☆☆☆☆½)

The 1995 vintage is maturing gracefully, with plenty of slightly herbaceous, appley, figgy, complex flavour. The '96 (****) is a delicious wine. Grown in Hawke's Bay, with very subtle oak handling, it's attractively scented, fresh and ripe in a clearly varietal style with rich, vibrant, tropical/herbaceous flavours and an appetisingly crisp finish.

MILLTON VINE.,	VINTAGE	96	95	94	93	92	91	90	M/DRY $16 AV
THE,TE ARAI RIV.	WR		6	5	6	5	6	4	6
SAUV. BLANC	DRINK		97-8	P	97-8	P	P	P	P	☆☆☆☆½

James Millton produces fresh, buoyantly fruity Gisborne wines with "tropical, guava flavours". The '95 is less rich than the memorable '94, but still attractively scented, with loads of melon and lemon-like flavour, dry and crisp. The pale straw, oak-aged 1996 vintage (***) is an ideal food wine, with good body, lively acidity and plenty of ripe, dryish flavour.

MISSION EAST		M/DRY $11 AV
COAST SAUV.		
BLANC		(☆☆☆½)

The 1996 vintage, blended from Hawke's Bay and Gisborne fruit, is a ripe, smooth-flowing, slightly sweet style of Sauvignon Blanc with gently herbaceous, melon and lime-evoking flavours and moderate acidity. Easy, undemanding drinking. The '97 (**½) is a solid but restrained wine, with gentle lemon/lime flavours.

MISSION RES.	VINTAGE	95	94	93	DRY $13 V+
SAUVIGNON	WR	5	6	4	
BLANC	DRINK	97-8	P	P	☆☆☆

In the past labelled as Fumé Blanc, at its best this is one of the Mission's most characterful and flavour-packed wines. Grown in Hawke's Bay, part of the final blend is fermented in oak barriques. Wood adds spice to the mouthfilling, lively 1995 vintage (***). The bouquet mingles fresh, green capsicum-like aromas and nutty oak; the palate is vigorous and slightly austere, with loads of green-edged flavour and a very crisp finish.

MONTANA BRAN.	VINTAGE	95	94	93	92	91	DRY $24 -V
ESTATE SAUV.	WR		5	6	6	NM 7	
BLANC	DRINK		97-9	97-01	97-00	NM	97-00	☆☆☆☆

Promoted as a "complex style of Sauvignon Blanc", this wine lives up to its billing. Based on the "pick" of the crop from Montana's Brancott vineyard in Marlborough, with partial fermentation in French oak barrels, the 1995 vintage (****) is full-flavoured and well-rounded. Ripe fruit flavours are fleshed out with strong oak and lees-aging characters, creating a complex style with a long, soft finish.

MONTANA MARL.	VINTAGE	97	96	95	94	93	92	91	90	DRY $12 V+
SAUVIGNON	WR	7	7	5	7	6	5	7	4	
BLANC	DRINK	97-9	97-8	P	97-9+	97-8+	P	P	P	☆☆☆☆

This famous, bargain-priced label rests its case on the flavour explosion of slow-ripened Marlborough fruit – a breathtaking style of Sauvignon Blanc which this wine, more than any other, has introduced to wine lovers in key markets around the world. Recent vintages are less lush, more pungently herbaceous than some other Marlborough labels; "this is the style we can sell locally and the UK wants," reports Montana. The 1996 vintage sees the label in top form – aromatic and brisk, with incisive yet delicate, melon and green capsicum flavours, lively acidity and a lingering, satisfyingly dry finish. In its youth, the '97 (****) looks just as good. Not quite as concentrated as the region's greatest Sauvignons, it is nevertheless intensely varietal and very flavoursome, with a lovely, deep fragrance, fresh, penetrating gooseberry/capsicum flavours and a mouth-wateringly crisp finish. A wonderful buy.

MONTANA RES.	VINTAGE	96	DRY $17 V+
VINE. SEL.	WR	7	
SAUV. BLANC	DRINK	97-00	(☆☆☆☆☆)

Launched from the 1996 vintage (****1/2), this is a riper, less pungently herbaceous style of Marlborough Sauvignon Blanc than its famous stablemate (above). The '96 (****1/2) has a rich, intensely varietal bouquet, with good weight (13 per cent alcohol) and the lush, delicate, sweet-fruit characters of passionfruit and melons. Tasted prior to bottling, the 1997 vintage looked at least as good, with pure, notably ripe and concentrated fruit flavours and great length.

MORTON EST.	VINTAGE	97	96	95	94	93	92	91	90	M/DRY $14 AV
WHITE LAB. H.B.	WR	6	6	5	6	4	5	5	4	
SAUV. BLANC	DRINK	97-8	97-8	P	P	P	P	P	P	(☆☆☆)

Morton's "white label" wine is stop-fermented to retain a whisker of sweetness. The 1996 vintage (***) is an immediately attractive, green-tinged wine with a very fresh and vigorous palate with strong, pure, ripely herbaceous flavours braced by zingy acidity.

MORTON EST.		DRY $16 AV
WHITE LAB. OAK		
AGED SAUV. BLANC		(☆☆☆☆)

Launched from the 1996 vintage (***1/2), this Hawke's Bay wine was fermented and matured for four months on its yeast lees in French oak barriques. It's a stylish, ripe, non-herbaceous wine, freshly scented, with crisp, persistent melon-like flavours and well-integrated oak adding richness.

MOUNT LINTON MARL. SAUV. BLANC

VINTAGE	96	95	94
WR	6	5	5
DRINK	97-8	P	P

DRY $17 AV

(☆ ☆☆☆½)

It's not well known, but this wine is worth getting to know. Both the 1994 and 1995 vintages are rewarding. The 1996 vintage (***½) is a crisp, strongly herbaceous, mouthfilling wine, full-flavoured, with excellent vigour and persistence.

MOUNT RILEY MARL. SAUVIGNON

M/DRY $13 V+

(☆☆☆☆½)

Mount Riley is the second label of Allan Scott. For a lower-tier wine, the 1996 vintage is a great effort. Mouthfilling and zingy, ripe yet clearly herbaceous, it offers very good depth of tropical fruit/capsicum flavours. A delicious bargain. The '97 (****) is equally good, with ripe, searching flavours in a zesty, fractionally sweet, clearly herbaceous style.

MOUTERE HILLS MARLBOROUGH SAUVIGNON BLANC

M/DRY $16 AV

(☆☆☆)

The tasty and very distinctive 1996 vintage (***) from this tiny Nelson winery is a slightly sweet style, 40 per cent barrel-fermented. It's a fresh, lively wine with ripe fruit flavours wrapped in toasty oak, and appetising acidity to balance its distinct splash of sweetness. Drink now.

NAUTILUS HAWKE'S BAY SAUVIGNON BLANC

M/DRY $16 AV

(☆☆☆)

It's quiet on the nose, but the 1996 vintage (***) of this slightly off-dry wine is ripely herbaceous, crisp and quite flavoursome in an easy-drinking style with plenty of body.

NAUTILUS MARL. SAUVIGNON BLANC

VINTAGE	97	96	95	94	93	92
WR	5	5	4	7	4	5
DRINK	97-8	P	P	P	P	P

DRY $17 V+

☆☆☆☆☆

This label is a Marlborough classic. The 1994 vintage, winner of six gold medals around the world, was a gorgeous wine, with a lovely surge of passionfruit and capsicum-like flavours. The '96 is a lovely, easy-drinking wine with lots of class, although slightly less intense than the '94. Rich, sweet-fruit aromas lead into a mouthfilling, fruity, gentle wine with lush, ripe-tasting, passionfruit-like characters, underpinned by fresh, lively acidity. The pale, intense 1997 vintage (*****) is the best since '94. It is a mouthfilling wine, beautifully balanced and concentrated, with fresh, ripe passionfruit/capsicum aromas, sweet-fruit characters and a long, zesty finish.

NEUDORF MOUTERE FUMÉ BLANC

DRY $16 -V

(☆☆☆)

Toast and honey characters abound in the golden, deeply coloured 1995 vintage (***¹/₂), a Nelson blend of 85 per cent Sauvignon Blanc and 15 per cent Sémillon. Quite full-bodied in the mouth, yet only 10.5 per cent alcohol, it's a slightly complex, firmly structured wine, maturing reasonably but probably best opened now.

NEUDORF NEL. SAUVIGNON BLANC

VINTAGE	96	95	94	93	92	91	90
WR	6	5	6	5	5	6	5
DRINK	97-9	97-9	97-9	97-8	P	P	P

DRY $17 AV

☆☆☆☆

An immaculate Nelson wine, appetisingly fresh and zippy. The 1995 vintage, a 50/50 regional blend labelled Nelson/Marlborough, is full and very fruity, with plenty of crisp, gooseberryish flavour and a distinct touch of *Botrytis*-derived honey characters. The lovely 1996 vintage offers power through the palate, with richness of body and strong, vibrant gooseberry/melon fruit flavours, deliciously ripe and long. The '97 (***¹/₂) looked promising in its youth, with fullness of body and plenty of lively sweet-fruit flavour.

NGA WAKA SAUVIGNON BLANC

VINTAGE	97	96	95	94	93
WR	7	7	7	6	6
DRINK	97+	97+	P	P	P

DRY $22 AV

☆☆☆☆☆

Since the gorgeous, bone-dry gold medal 1993 vintage (which was drinking superbly in early '97) this Martinborough wine hasn't faltered. The '95 won the trophy for top Sauvignon Blanc at that year's Air New Zealand Wine Awards. The bouquet of the immaculate 1996 vintage is striking – packed with sweet, very ripe, passionfruit-like aromas. It's a beautifully structured and balanced wine, vivacious and buoyantly fruity, with intense, pure, gooseberry/capsicum flavours and a crisp, bone-dry, trailing finish. The '97 (*****) is another splendid wine – immaculate, lush and piercing. Pale, and beautifully scented, it is a mouthfilling wine with rich, intense tropical fruit flavours enlivened by racy acidity.

NGATARAWA CLASSIC SAUVIGNON BLANC

DRY $12 V+

(☆☆☆)

Ngatarawa's new, lower-tier Hawke's Bay Sauvignon Blanc from 1996 (***) is a decent, all-purpose, easy-drinking dry white. Light lemon-green in hue, it is a full-bodied wine mingling ripe tropical-fruit with greener, herbal flavours, fresh acidity and good depth.

NGATA. STABLES OAK AGED SAUV. BLANC

VINTAGE	96	95	94	93	92	91	90
WR	6	5	6	6	6	6	6
DRINK	P	P	P	P	P	P	P

DRY $15 AV

☆☆☆

Matured for two months in seasoned oak puncheons to "round the wine out", Alwyn Corban's 1996 vintage (***¹/₂) is his first Hawke's Bay Sauvignon Blanc since the 1980s to be oak-aged. It's a very flavoursome wine with a lifted, slightly nutty, herbaceous bouquet, fullness of body and plenty of crisp, slightly oaky flavour.

NOBILO FALL HAR. OAK AGED SAUV. BLANC	VINTAGE	96							M/DRY $13 AV
	WR	6							
	DRINK	97-8							(☆ ☆☆)

Grown in Marlborough, Nobilo's recently launched oak-matured wine from 1996 (***) is a fresh, crisp, medium-bodied style with a sliver of sweetness amid its citrusy, limey, zesty, very lightly wood-influenced flavours.

NOBILO FALL HARVEST SAUV. BLANC	VINTAGE	96							M/DRY $12 V+
	WR	6							
	DRINK	97-8							(☆ ☆☆)

Clearly pitched at the mainstream market, Nobilo's recently launched 1996 Marlborough Sauvignon Blanc (***) is a fractionally sweet, easy-drinking style, lightly fragrant, with fresh, ripe flavours and lively acidity. Sharply priced.

NOBILO MARL. SAUVIGNON BLANC	VINTAGE	96	95	94	93	92	91	90	89	DRY $14 V+
	WR	6	5	7	6	7	7	6	7	
	DRINK	97-8	P	P	P	P	P	P	P	☆☆☆☆☆

A classic Marlborough Sauvignon Blanc and consistently one of the top sub-$15 wines on the market. The '95 is one of the livelier wines of the vintage, with fresh, zippy lemon/capsicum flavours. Grown in the Matador vineyard at Rapaura, the '96 is full-bodied and flavour-packed, with pure, delicate, tropical and green capsicum-like characters and a zesty, sustained finish. Why pay more? The pale lemon-green 1997 vintage (****) is another sucess, with fresh, ripely herbaceous aromas and a vibrantly fruity palate, appetisingly crisp and flavourful.

NOBILO GRAND RESERVE SAUV. BLANC	VINTAGE	96							DRY $20 AV
	WR	7							
	DRINK	98-00							(☆☆☆☆☆)

Robust (13.5 per cent alcohol), with a powerful attack of piercing, steely flavour, the first 1996 vintage (*****) was made from the first pick of well-ripened (24° brix) grapes off young vines in Marlborough's Awatere Valley. The wine was fermented and matured on its gross lees for eight months in French and German oak barriques (30 per cent new), and 40 per cent was given a softening malolactic fermentation. The result is an excitingly intense wine with a rich, herbaceous bouquet, impressive weight and deep, flinty, lingering flavours, beautifully balanced.

ODYSSEY SAUVIGNON BLANC	VINTAGE	97	96						DRY $14 V+
	WR	5	5						
	DRINK	97-8	P						(☆ ☆☆☆)

Rebecca Salmond, winemaker at Pleasant Valley, produces consistently good wines under her own Odyssey label. Hawke's Bay-grown, the 1996 vintage (****) is a ripe-tasting, lively, fresh wine with generous, almost lush melon/lemon/capsicum flavours and a well-rounded finish.

OHINEMURI	VINTAGE	96	**DRY $18 AV**
EST. SAUVIGNON	WR	5	
BLANC	DRINK	97-9	☆☆☆

Karangahake Gorge winemaker Horst Hillerich barrel-fermented and lees-aged 25 per cent of his 1996 wine (***). Grown in Hawke's Bay, it's not an intensely varietal style, but satisfyingly full-bodied, with plenty of ripe, non-herbaceous, slightly nutty flavour.

OLD COACH	VINTAGE	96	95	**DRY $11 V+**
ROAD NELSON	WR	5	5	
SAUV. BLANC	DRINK	97-8	P	(☆☆☆)

Seifried Estate's second-string Sauvignon. The debut '95 offers incisive lemon/lime flavours and invigorating acidity, creating a very fresh and vigorous wine. The '96 is a strongly herbaceous, pungently varietal style with fresh-cut grass aromas and lots of crisp, nettley flavour. A great buy. In its youth, the zippy 1997 vintage (**¹/₂) looked slightly less impressive, with reasonable depth of ripe, melon/capsicum flavour.

OMAKA SPRINGS	VINTAGE	96	95	**M/DRY $11 AV**
MARL. SAUV.	WR	6	6	
BLANC	DRINK	97-8	P	☆☆✫

The first 1994 vintage was the best yet, with ripely herbal, penetrating flavour. The '95 is light, with a herbaceous bouquet and very crisp, grassy flavours harbouring a splash of sweetness. The low-priced '96 (**¹/₂) is a pale, medium-dry wine, not intense but pleasantly fresh, limey and zingy.

OYSTER BAY	VINTAGE	97	96	95	94	93	92	91	90	**DRY $17 V+**
MARLBOROUGH	WR	7	6	5	6	5	6	5	7	
SAUV. BLANC	DRINK	97-9	97-8	97-8	P	P	P	P	P	☆☆☆☆✫

Oyster Bay is a Delegat's brand, reserved for their Marlborough wines. The 1996 vintage (*****¹/₂) is a zesty, flavour-packed wine with good body, intense melon/capsicum characters and lively acidity in a very fresh, pure and penetrating style. It's maturing well. The 1997, tasted prior to bottling, looked likely to surpass the '96, with impressive weight and an explosion of lovely, ripe, zingy flavour.

PALLISER BAY	**DRY $18 -V**
OAK-AGED	
SAUVIGNON BLANC	(☆☆☆✫)

Winemaker Allan Johnson is a proven performer with Martinborough Sauvignon Blanc, and his first 1994 Hawke's Bay model was a stunner – substantial and rich. The crisp, herbaceous '95 is a good wine, but lacks the power and richness of its predecessor. The '96 (***), again based on Hawke's Bay fruit, was matured for six months in predominantly American oak casks. It's a fresh, firm wine, less concentrated than the '94, with creamy oak and ripe, rounded lemon/herbal flavours.

PALLISER EST. SAUVIGNON BLANC

M/DRY $20 AV

☆☆☆☆☆

Top vintages of this Martinborough wine (which rivals Nga Waka at the top of the district's Sauvignon Blanc tree) are excitingly deep-scented, mouthfilling and lush, with very ripe, almost sweet-tasting fruit flavours. The '95 stood out above the rest at the 1996 Liquorland Royal Easter Wine Show – highly scented, with a delicious surge of ripe, delicate, zesty flavour. The 1996 vintage (*****) is another classy wine. It's a distinctly cool-climate style, very fragrant, fresh and zingy, with an exquisite balance of firm, crisp acidity and lush, ripe, penetrating tropical fruit flavours.

PEGASUS BAY SAUVIGNON/ SÉMILLON

VINTAGE	96	95	94	93	92	91
WR	7	7	6	6	5	6
DRINK	97-02	97-01	97-00	P	P	P

DRY $20 AV

☆☆☆☆½

An emerging North Canterbury classic. The Sauvignon Blanc is fermented in tanks; the Sémillon is fermented and matured on its yeast lees in seasoned oak barrels and given a softening malolactic fermentation. The '95 is gorgeous, a rich, complex, mouthfilling style bursting with ripe, exotic fruit flavours. The 1996 vintage (*****) is slightly less opulent than the '95, but still very stylish and concentrated. It's a weighty wine, still youthful, with tight, intense fruit flavours, subtle oak/lees influence and a rich, well-spined finish.

PLEASANT VAL. H.B. SAUVIGNON BLANC/SÉMILLON

VINTAGE	96
WR	5
DRINK	P

M/DRY $12 V+

(☆ ☆☆☆)

Full-bodied and flavoursome, the 1996 vintage (***) is an 80/20 blend, well-ripened and fruity, with melon/grass flavours and a slightly off-dry finish balanced by firm acidity. Attractive, easy drinking.

PLEASANT VAL. SIG. SEL. AUCK. SAUV. BLANC

VINTAGE	95
WR	5
DRINK	P

DRY $13 AV

(☆ ☆☆☆)

The first 1995 vintage is a Hawke's Bay wine with limey flavours of moderate depth. For '96 (***) the grape source switched to Auckland and the quality rose. Grown at Kumeu, this is a weighty (13 per cent alcohol) wine with a pleasing depth of ripe melon/capsicum flavours and fresh, tangy acidity. (The new Yelas Winemaker's Reserve Marlborough Sauvignon Blanc 1997 (***) is a big wine (13.5 per cent alcohol) with ripe melon/herbal flavours and a rounded finish.)

PONDER EST. MARL. SAUV. BLANC

VINTAGE	96	95	94
WR	6	5	7
DRINK	97-8	P	97-8

DRY $16 AV

(☆ ☆☆☆)

Mike Ponder's debut 1994 vintage was vibrant and zingy, with good weight and ripe, penetrating gooseberry/capsicum flavours, braced by vigorous acidity. The '95 is a solid but plain wine: light, clean, crisp, slightly honied and grassy. The 1996 vintage is a pleasant, ripely fragrant wine with fresh, lively melon and green capsicum-like flavours, but it lacks the intensity many others achieved in '96. The '97 (****) is clearly superior to the '96, with markedly greater depth of bouquet, ripe, delicate flavour and a long, rich finish.

RICHMOND PLAINS SAUV. BLANC

DRY $16 AV

(☆☆☆)

The Holmes brothers' vineyard at Richmond in Nelson is one of only two in New Zealand to enjoy full Bio-Gro (certified organic) status. The 1995 vintage is fresh, clean, brisk, limey and green-edged, with plenty of flavour, especially for a '95. The '96 (***1/2) is another attractive wine, full-bodied and lively, with delicate, ripe, melon-like flavours and a well-balanced, lingering finish.

RIPPON VINE. SAUVIGNON BLANC

DRY $19 -V

(☆☆☆)

The breathtaking quality of the '92 has yet to be repeated, but this estate-grown, barrel-fermented wine from Lake Wanaka grapes is typically a grassy style with complexity and a lingering, freshly acidic finish. The pale, grassy 1996 vintage (***1/2) was 60 per cent fermented in new and old French oak barriques. It's a fragrant, springy wine with loads of herbaceous, oaky flavour, steely and long.

RIVERBED SAUVIGNON BLANC

DRY $18 -V

(☆☆☆)

John Webber, owner of the extensive Matador vineyard, had the 1996 vintage (***) produced on his behalf at Selaks' Marlborough winery. Matured in French oak barriques, it's an unusual style of Sauvignon – frisky, limey, almost Riesling-like – with persistent, slightly nutty flavours and taut acid spine. Currently a bit austere, it could well reward cellaring.

RIVERSIDE SAUVIGNON BLANC

M/DRY $15 -V

(☆☆)

Grown in the Dartmoor Valley of Hawke's Bay, the 1996 vintage (**) is a plain wine, lacking fragrance, with moderate depth of green apple flavours, crisp and slightly sweet. Drink up.

ROB. & BUT. GIS. SAUVIGNON BLANC

VINTAGE	96
WR	6
DRINK	97-8

DRY $10 V+

(☆☆½)

Fermented in stainless steel and lees-aged for three months, Corbans' sharply priced quaffer from the 1996 vintage (**1/2) is fresh and limey on the nose with slightly green flavours – crisp, appley and straightforward.

ROCKWOOD SAUVIGNON BLANC

DRY $12 AV

(☆☆⚬)

Produced by winemaker Tony Bish and the Mason brothers of Sacred Hill, the first 1995 vintage (***1/2) is a blend of 80 per cent Hawke's Bay and 20 per cent Marlborough grapes. It's a no-fuss, full-bodied wine with crisp lemon/herbal flavours. Ready.

RONGOPAI TE KAUWHATA SAUVIGNON BLANC

DRY $15 AV

(☆☆☆)

The golden '95 is a lesser vintage, with crisp, distinctly honied flavours. The '96 (***1/2) lacks the pungency of more southern styles, but is still a very decent mouthful. Light straw in hue, it is mouthfilling and ripely flavoured, fleshy, figgy and rounded.

RONGOPAI WINEMAKER'S SELECTION OAK AGED SAUVIGNON BLANC

DRY $19 AV

☆☆☆☆

The 1993 and 1994 vintages are lush, rich-flavoured Te Kauwhata wines of impressive quality. Lovely now, the '96 (****) was French oak-aged for six months. Light gold, it's a very distinctive wine, fat, with very ripe, rich, lush tropical fruit flavours and a soft finish.

ROSEBANK SAUVIGNON BLANC

VINTAGE	95
WR	6
DRINK	97-9

DRY $15 AV

(☆☆☆)

This Canterbury winery's 1995 vintage (***) was grown in Marlborough's Omaka Valley, although the label doesn't say so. Pale and limey, with some passionfruit-like characters, it's an attractively full, crisp and lively wine.

ST JEROME HAWKE'S BAY SAUVIGNON BLANC

DRY $16 AV

☆☆☆

The 1995 vintage (***) is still fresh, with good body and depth of melon and green capsicum-like flavours. Drink now.

SAC. HILL RESE. BAR. FERM. SAUV. BLANC

VINTAGE	96
WR	6
DRINK	97-9

DRY $20 AV

☆☆☆☆

The quality of this oak-matured Dartmoor Valley wine has oscillated over the years, but the 1996 vintage (****1/2) is the finest yet. Fifty per cent of the final blend was fermented and lees-aged in American oak casks. Tightly structured and subtle, with concentrated, very ripe, non-herbaceous fruit flavours, oak/lees-aging richness, balanced acidity and a long, rich finish, it's an impressive and stylish wine, built to last.

SACRED	VINTAGE	94	**DRY $28 -V**
HILL	WR	6	
SAUVAGE	DRINK	97-01	(☆☆☆☆)

In his bid to produce "a unique style of New Zealand Sauvignon Blanc", Hawke's Bay winemaker Mark Mason uses natural, "wild" yeasts to ferment his hand-harvested, whole bunch-pressed, Puketapu fruit in brand-new French oak barrels. The 1994 vintage (****), oak-aged on its yeast lees for a year, is a powerful wine, weighty and ripe, with rich fig/quince flavours, bold oak influence and a satisfyingly long, well-rounded finish. An intriguing wine, but don't expect a typical, garden-fresh, herbaceous Sauvignon Blanc.

SACRED HILL   **DRY $13 V+**
WHITECLIFF
SAUVIGNON BLANC   ☆☆☆☆

The junior partner in the winery's trio of Hawke's Bay Sauvignons, this is a fruit-driven style. The 1996 vintage is a ripe, lively, tangy wine with very good freshness and zest and incisive melon/capsicum flavours. The '97 (****) is the best yet and top value. Ripely scented, it is a deliciously full, fresh wine with strong, ripe, tropical fruit flavours and a rich, zingy finish.

SAINT CLAIR	VINTAGE	96	95	94	**M/DRY $15 V+**
MARLBOROUGH	WR	7	6	7	
SAUV. BLANC	DRINK	97-8	P	P	(☆☆☆☆☆)

The very ripe, lush, deliciously intense 1994 vintage was a top-flight debut, and the fresh, strong-flavoured and zippy '95 enhanced Saint Clair's reputation. Grown by Neal Ibbotson in the Wairau and Awatere valleys and made by Kym Crawford at Rapaura Vintners, the 1996 vintage is another impressive wine. Tropical-fruit characters abound in a fragrant, concentrated style which displays lush, ripe fruit and a rich, well-rounded finish. Tasted in its infancy, the '97 (****) is typically impressive with very good depth of melon/capsicum flavour and appetising acidity. At $15, this is a "steal".

SAINT CLAIR SIN.	VINTAGE	96	**DRY $18 AV**
VINE. AWA. VAL.	WR	7	
SAUV. BLANC	DRINK	97-00	(☆☆☆☆)

Obvious oak gives a Chardonnay-like character to the first 1996 vintage (****) of this Marlborough wine. Half the wine was handled in stainless steel; the other half was fermented and matured for 10 months in oak casks. The bouquet is strongly wooded; the palate high-flavoured, with toasty oak, some complexity and very ripe, non-herbaceous fruit flavours.

SAINTS MARL.	VINTAGE	96	**DRY $17 V+**
SAUVIGNON	WR	7	
BLANC	DRINK	97-00	(☆☆☆☆☆)

The 1996 vintage (*****) is a delicious young Sauvignon displaying power and subtlety. Grown in Montana's Brancott Valley vineyards, 10 per cent of the wine was fermented in new American oak barriques. It's a notably intense and vigorous style with mouthfilling body, good acid spine, a touch of complexity and a very rich and persistent finish. Super value.

SCHNAPPER ROCK
MARLBOROUGH
SAUVIGNON BLANC

DRY $? V?

(☆☆☆☆☆)

Produced by Corbans exclusively for restaurant listings, the debut 1996 vintage (****) is a distinctive wine with a fresh, ripe, verdant bouquet. It's a mouthfilling, very crisp wine with strong, piercing green capsicum/melon flavours in a high impact style with a slightly creamy finish.

SEIBEL LIMITED EDITION
MARLBOROUGH
SAUVIGNON BLANC

DRY $15 -V

(☆☆☆)

The 1996 vintage (**¹/₂) was half tank-fermented, with the rest fermented and aged for eight months in old oak casks. It's a flinty, limey wine with a subdued bouquet, crisp and tangy but restrained for a '96 Marlborough.

SEIBEL LONG
RIVER
SAUVIGNON BLANC

DRY $9 V+

(☆☆☆)

The 1996 vintage (**¹/₂) is a decent all-purpose dry white, priced right. A marriage of 76 per cent Sauvignon Blanc, 16 per cent Chenin Blanc and 8 per cent Sémillon, predominantly from Hawke's Bay, with a "little bit" of oak, it offers fullness of body and plenty of crisp, grassy, lemony flavour.

SEIFRIED NEL.
SAUVIGNON
BLANC

VINTAGE	96	95	94	93	92	91	90
WR	5	5	6	6	6	5	5
DRINK	97-8	P	P	P	P	P	P

DRY $16 V+

☆☆☆☆

Regularly one of the country's best-value Sauvignons. The '95, reflecting the vintage, is slightly austere and unripe. The lifted, herbal fragrance of the 1996 vintage leads into a weighty, ripe, richly flavoured palate with firm acid backbone. A powerful wine, it offers excellent drinking right now. The '97 (****) looked excellent in its youth, with ripe tropical fruit flavours and a sliver of sweetness in a very punchy, zingy style.

SELAKS DRYLANDS
SAUVIGNON BLANC/
SÉMILLON

DRY $20 AV

(☆☆☆☆☆)

The new, 1996 vintage (****¹/₂), single-vineyard model of Selaks' famous Marlborough blend (see below) is an oak-matured style to which the 40 per cent Sémillon contributes "fatness and longevity", says Michael Selak. It's a herbaceous, nutty wine on the nose and palate, with impressive weighty, ripeness and complexity.

SELAKS FOUNDERS RESERVE
MATADOR ESTATE MARL.
SAUVIGNON BLANC

DRY $22 -V

(☆☆☆☆☆)

The 1996 vintage (****) of Selaks' flagship Sauvignon, fermented in new French oak barriques, reveals a highly appealing balance of fresh, rich, ripe, melon/capsicum flavours and subtle, nutty wood characters. Delicious in its youth, it's likely to be at its best around late 1997.

SELAKS	VINTAGE	97	96	95	94	93	92			**M/DRY $11 V+**
GISBORNE	WR	6	7	7	6	5	5			
FUMÉ	DRINK	97-9	97-8	P	P	P	P			(☆ ☆☆)

Past vintages of this medium-dry wine were nondescript, but the 1996 (****) is by far the best yet. It's a 50/50 blend of Sauvignon Blanc and Sémillon, matured in new and one-year-old oak casks. The bouquet displays ripe fruit and oak aromas; the palate is fresh, limey, zippy and flavoursome, with a well-balanced, surprisingly persistent finish. A great bargain!

SELAKS MARL.	VINTAGE	97	96	95	94	93	92	91	90	**DRY $14 V+**
SAUVIGNON	WR	7	6	6	7	5	5	7	6	
BLANC	DRINK	97-9	97-8	P	P	P	P	P	P	☆☆☆⅟

The "commercial" Sauvignon Blanc from Selaks, fermented in stainless steel and bottled early with an almost imperceptible sliver of sweetness. The 1996 vintage is an instantly likeable wine. Light lemon/green, with a fresh, limey fragrance, it's delicate and ripely flavoured, with excellent depth and a zesty finish. A full, tangy, incisive wine, very easy drinking in style. The '97 (****) is full and ripe-tasting with good weight and excellent depth of crisp, lively melon/lime flavours.

SELAKS MARL.	VINTAGE	96	95	94	93	92	91	90	**M/DRY $17 V+**
SAUV. BLANC/	WR	7	6	7	6	5	7	7	
SÉMILLON	DRINK	97-9	97-8	97-8	P	P	P	P	☆☆☆☆

At its best, this is a thrilling oak-matured wine, crammed with delicious fruit flavour and spine-tingling acidity. The 1994 vintage was champion white at the 1995 Sydney International Wine Competition. The '95 lacks the exceptional impact of a top vintage, but is still highly satisfying. A blend of 70 per cent Sauvignon Blanc and 30 per cent Sémillon, it was fermented in new and one-year-old French and American oak, with a total barrel time of four months. Light yellow, with a slightly toasty fragrance, it's a complex, herbal, high-flavoured, very persistent wine with a taut, trailing finish. The 1996 vintage (****) is a slightly more herbaceous style than the new Drylands Sauvignon Blanc/Sémillon (above). It doesn't match the arresting '94, but still delivers excellent depth of melon and green capsicum flavours, penetrating and zesty.

SELWYN RIVER		**DRY $10 V+**
SAUVIGNON		
BLANC		(☆☆☆)

Grown in Marlborough and produced by Giesen (although the label doesn't tell you either of those facts), the 1996 vintage (***) is a characterful wine, full and crisp. It's a penetrating, tangy wine with good flavour depth. Plenty of flavour for your dollar at $9.95.

SERESIN EST.	VINTAGE	97	96
MARL. SAUV.	WR	6	6
BLANC	DRINK	98-00	97-9

DRY $19 V+

(☆☆☆☆☆)

The very classy and rich debut 1996 vintage (*****) is that rare sort of Sauvignon that draws you back for a second glass, and a third ... Its touch of complexity, unusual in Sauvignon Blanc, comes from blending with 10 per cent Sémillon, some use of natural yeasts, 10 per cent fermentation in new French oak barriques, and some lees-aging. It's a distinctive and immaculate wine with ripe, piercing fruit flavours underpinned by lively acidity, excellent weight and a trailing finish. Lovely stuff!

SHINGLE PEAK	VINTAGE	96
MARL. SAUV.	WR	5
BLANC	DRINK	97-8

DRY $15 V+

☆☆☆☆

The Shingle Peak label is reserved for Matua Valley's Marlborough wines. The '95 is more satisfying than many other wines of the vintage, crisp and green-edged, with good length of lime and green capsicum-like flavours. The 1996 vintage is one of the finest yet. It's a mouthfilling, beautifully persistent wine, ripely scented, with pure, well-concentrated, fractionally off-dry melon/capsicum flavours and a crisp, lively finish. The '97 (****) is a punchy, well-balanced wine with strong passionfruit/lime flavours and a long lively finish.

SOLJANS	VINTAGE	96	95
HAWKE'S BAY	WR	6	4
SAUV. BLANC	DRINK	97-8	P

DRY $12 AV

☆☆☆

The '95 is full-bodied, with moderate depth of gooseberry and fresh-cut grass flavour, offering well-rounded, easy-drinking. A small portion (12 per cent) of the 1996 vintage (***) was fermented and lees-aged for four months in new French oak barriques, and given a softening malolactic fermentation. It's a pale straw wine, fleshy, nutty, ripe and rounded in an easy-drinking style with a touch of complexity. (The Marlborough Sauvignon Blanc 1997 (***1/2) is a very good effort – weighty, with strong, lively, ripely herbaceous flavours.)

SOLWAY
SAUVIGNON
BLANC

DRY $16 -V

(☆☆☆)

Past vintages of Masterton winemaker David Bloomfield's wine have been mouthfilling and tangy, but the fruit flavours have been restrained. The pale 1996 vintage (**1/2) lacks real ripeness and richness, but offers reasonable depth of green-edged, slightly sharp flavour.

STONE CREEK	VINTAGE	96	95	94
MARLBOROUGH	WR	6	4	5
SAUV. BLANC	DRINK	97-9	P	P

M/DRY $16 AV

(☆☆☆)

Stone Creek, Morton Estate's Marlborough label, is currently being phased out. Maturing better than most wines of the vintage, the '95 is light yellow, with a scented, gooseberryish fragance. It's a full, vibrantly fruity wine with pleasing flavour depth. The 1996 vintage (***) is a fresh and frisky wine with good depth of limey, capsicum-like flavour.

STONECROFT SAUVIGNON BLANC	VINTAGE	96	95	94	93	92	91	90	DRY $17 AV
	WR		6	6	5	6	5	5	5	☆☆☆☆
	DRINK		97-8	P	P	P	P	P	P	

At its best, this is a powerful, extremely satisfying Hawke's Bay Sauvignon. The '95, 10 per cent barrel-fermented, is a lively, mouthfilling wine with good depth of ripe tropical-fruit flavours, showing no sign of an adverse vintage. The 1996 vintage (****¹/₂) is a lush, soft style, not matured in wood. It's a fully dry wine, but its very ripe and rich, figgy, sweet fruit flavours give it great drinkability.

STONE. VINE. MARLBOROUGH SAUV. BLANC	VINTAGE	96	95	94	93	92	91	90	M/DRY $15 V+
	WR		7	6	7	6	7	7	6	☆☆☆☆
	DRINK		97-00	97-9	97-8	P	P	P	P	

Fresh-cut grass aromas abound in this piquant Marlborough wine. The Stoneleigh style is intensely herbaceous, with forthright, non-wooded flavour and bracing acidity. The 1996 vintage (****) is a typical Stoneleigh – fresh, zingy and full of appley, limey, herbaceous flavour. It lacks the sheer concentration of a five-star wine, but is a slightly more elegant and riper-tasting style than usual, with hints of tropical fruit characters, reflecting the favourable vintage.

TASMAN BAY RESERVE FUMÉ
DRY $19 AV
(☆☆☆☆)

Hugely drinkable, the 1996 vintage (****) is a blend of 63 per cent Sauvignon Blanc and 37 per cent Sémillon, grown mainly in Nelson and Gisborne, and fermented and lees-aged for seven months in French and American oak barriques. Oak and malolactic fermentation have added a soft, butterscotch-like richness without subjugating the fresh, ripe, tropical fruit, slightly herbaceous flavours. It's a distinctive style, flavourful, non-aggressive, and very seductive in its youth.

TE AWA FARM LONGLANDS SAUV. BLANC	VINTAGE	97	96	DRY $15 V+
	WR		6	7	(☆☆☆☆)
	DRINK		97-9	97-9	

The fragrant, incisively flavoured 1996 vintage was grown in the Gimblett Road/Roy's Hill district of Hawke's Bay. It's very well balanced, with good weight (13.5 per cent alcohol) and depth of fresh, ripe fruit flavours, delicacy and a crisp, lively finish. The '97 (***) is a solid, full-bodied wine with lemon/grass aromas and flavours, but lacks the richness of the '96.

TE KAIRANGA GISB./MARTIN. SAUV. BLANC	VINTAGE	96	95	DRY $14 -V
	WR		6	5	(☆☆)
	DRINK		97-9	97-8	

The price indicates that the winery rates its Martinborough wine higher than this regional blend – and so do I. The '95 is a pale, plain wine. The 1996 vintage (**¹/₂), based on 90 per cent Gisborne fruit, is fresh and clearly varietal, with moderate depth of crisp, appley, limey flavour. It's a solid but uninspiring wine, lacking richness.

TE KAIRANGA MARTIN. SAUV. BLANC	VINTAGE	96	95					DRY $17 AV
	WR	7	6					
	DRINK	97-00	97-8					(☆☆☆⯪)

The unwooded '95 is a vivacious Martinborough wine with the aromas of new-mown grass and a crisp, lively, dry finish – a real Marlborough look-alike. The attractive 1996 vintage (****) was half tank-fermented; the other half was fermented and matured for six months in seasoned oak barrels. The lifted, ripe aromas lead into a weighty palate (13 per cent alcohol) with well-ripened tropical fruit characters, a touch of oak/lees complexity and a crisp, long finish.

TE MANIA EST. NELSON SAUV. BLANC	VINTAGE	96	95					M/DRY $16 AV
	WR	5	4					
	DRINK	97-9	97-8					(☆ ☆☆)

The '95 vintage is crisp and clean, with cutting, green capsicum-like flavours in an enjoyably fresh and tangy style. Jon and Cheryl Harrey, grape-growers on the Waimea Plains, had the full-flavoured, very vigorous 1996 (***1/2) produced on their behalf at a local winery. A well-ripened style with zesty gooseberry and green capsicum-like flavours, it is the second satisfying Sauvignon in a row under this label.

TE MATA CAPE CREST SAUV. BLANC	VINTAGE	96	95	94	93	92	91	90	DRY $21 AV
	WR	6	7	7	6	6	7	5	
	DRINK	97-00	97-8	P	P	P	P	P	☆☆☆☆☆

This single-vineyard Hawke's Bay label is impressive not for the rapier-like herbaceousness that is the hallmark of Marlborough wines, but for its mouthfilling body and ripely herbal, sustained flavours. Since the 1991 vintage, oak-aging has added depth and clearly differentiated the wine from its non-wooded Castle Hill stablemate (below). The '95, half barrel-fermented (20 per cent new) is noticeably fuller and richer than the '95 Castle Hill, vigorous and limey, with the biscuity wood influence adding complexity and richness. The 1996 vintage (*****) was entirely barrel-fermented (15 per cent new oak) and matured on its yeast lees for four months. It's a notably full-bodied, firm and complex wine with rich, ripe, melon/lime characters, smoky wood adding subtlety and richness and a crisp, lingering finish.

TE MATA CASTLE HILL SAUV. BLANC	VINTAGE	97	96	95	94	93	92	91	90	DRY $16 AV
	WR		6	6	5	6	6	7	7	5	
	DRINK	97-8	97-8	P	P	P	P	P	P	☆☆☆☆

In most vintages this non-wooded wine is slightly less powerful and deep-flavoured than its stablemate, Cape Crest. Yet this is still a classic Hawke's Bay Sauvignon Blanc, dry, robust and flinty, with more weight and character than most. The '96 (****) is a generous, mouthfilling wine with crisp acidity underpinning its strong, ripe, sweet-fruit flavours.

TERRACE ROAD SAUVIGNON BLANC	VINTAGE	96	95					DRY $15 -V
	WR	4	3					
	DRINK	P	P					(☆☆⯪)

Cellier Le Brun's first stab at a Marlborough Sauvignon Blanc coincided with the poor 1995 vintage, yielding an austere, tart, grassy wine. The 1996 (**¹/₂) is more ripely attractive. Ten per cent barrel-fermented, it's a smooth, gentle wine with ripe fruit aromas in a rounded, easy-drinking style, but lacks a bit of concentration and zing.

| TERRACE VIEW SAUVIGNON BLANC | DRY $14 -V (☆☆⟆) |

Cool-fermented in stainless steel for early consumption, the 1996 vintage (**¹/₂) of Kemblefield's lower-tier Hawke's Bay wine is a full, weighty wine, ripely flavoured, but slightly lacks freshness, delicacy and zing.

TORLESSE MARL. SAUVIGNON BLANC	VINTAGE	96	95	94			DRY $15 V+
	WR		6	6			(☆☆☆☆)
	DRINK	97-8	P	P			

The '94 and '95 vintages are both punchy, intense wines in the classic Marlborough mould. Immense drinkability is what the stylish 1996 is all about. The bouquet is fragrant, fresh and ripely fruity; the palate full and lively but not aggressive, with real basket-of-fruit flavours, strong and lingering. The '97 (****¹/₂) is arguably the best yet, with a rich, ripe fragrance and lovely depth of passionfruit and lime-evoking, well-spined flavour. Excellent wine, sharply priced.

TRINITY HILL SHEPH. CROFT SAUV. BLANC	VINTAGE	97	96	M/DRY $18 -V
	WR	5	6	(☆☆☆)
	DRINK	97-8	97-8	

John Hancock's first Hawke's Bay Sauvignon Blanc under the Trinity Hill label, made in the 1996 vintage, was grown in the Ngatarawa district. It's a ripe, very fresh wine with lively acidity and a sliver of sweetness filling out its pleasing depth of melon/lime flavours. The '97 (**¹/₂) is less rewarding, with reasonable depth of fresh, moderately ripe melon/lime flavours.

TWIN IS. NEW ZEALAND SAUV. BLANC	VINTAGE	97	96	95	94	93	92	DRY $12 V+
	WR	5	5	3	7	4	4	(☆☆☆)
	DRINK	97-8	P	P	P	P	P	

Negociants' blend of Marlborough and Hawke's Bay fruit offers fine value. The 1996 vintage has a grassy bouquet and full palate, with fresh acidity and plenty of clearly varietal, green-edged flavour. Here's North Island drinkability coupled with South Island incisiveness – all for only $12! The '97 (***), already drinking well, reveals fresh, lifted, ripely herbaceous scents, good body, and plenty of smooth, crisp, gooseberryish flavour in a very easy-drinking style.

VAVASOUR AWATERE VAL. SAUV. BLANC	VINTAGE	96	DRY $21 AV
	WR	7	(☆☆☆☆☆
	DRINK	97-9	

The first 1996 vintage (*****) is a striking, delicious mouthful of piercing, ripely herbaceous flavour, high alcohol (13.5 per cent) and tangy acidity. Grown in two Awatere Valley vineyards, it was predominantly tank-fermented, but 5 per cent was barrel-fermented and matured on its light yeast lees. Pale and pungently aromatic, it is a very high impact style, yet refined, with the subtle oak adding richness and a long, intense finish.

VAVAS. SIN. VINE.	VINTAGE	96	95	94	93	92	91	90	DRY $27 -V
AWATERE VAL.	WR	7	NM	7	5	5	7	5	
SAUV. BLANC	DRINK	97-00	NM	97-8	P	P	P	P	☆☆☆☆☆

This wine has recently replaced the former Vavasour Reserve label, launched in 1989. The 1994 vintage (labelled Single Vineyard Marlborough and available in 1997) is striking stuff! Based on the ripest, hand-picked bunches in Vavasour's estate vineyard in the Awatere Valley, it was entirely barrel-fermented and given lengthy bottle maturation prior to release. Light yellow-hued and richly fragrant, it's a voluptuous wine with impressive weight and complexity, overflowing with rich, ripe fruit flavours fleshed out with subtle oak/lees characters. There is no '95. The 1996 (*****) was grown in a low-cropping block in the Awatere Valley vineyard, and half the wine was barrel-fermented and given a softening malolactic fermentation. It's a mouthfilling style (13.5 per cent alcohol) with penetrating, ripely herbaceous flavours, oak/lees-aging richness, complexity and a long, rounded finish. (Note: the 1990 to 1993 vintage ratings apply to Vavasour Reserve Sauvignon Blanc.)

VIDAL EAST	VINTAGE	96	95	94	93	92	91	90	DRY $12 V+
COAST	WR	6	6	6	7	6	6	6	
FUMÉ BLANC	DRINK	97-9	97-8	P	P	P	P	P	☆☆☆½

This typically full, ripe-flavoured marriage of Hawke's Bay and Gisborne fruit is bargain-priced. The stylish '96 is an 80 per cent Sauvignon Blanc, 20 per cent Sémillon blend, 30 per cent oak-aged. It's a ripely scented wine with fullness of body, excellent depth of fresh, lively tropical fruit characters and a well-rounded finish. The 1997 vintage (***1/2), labelled Lightly Oaked Sauvignon Blanc, is very fresh and fragrant, with attractively ripe and lively passionfruit/lime flavours.

VIDAL	VINTAGE	96	95	94	93	DRY $13 AV
EAST COAST	WR	6	5	6	6	
SAUV. BLANC	DRINK	97-8	P	P	P	(☆ ☆☆☆)

Don't confuse this unwooded wine with its oak-influenced stablemate, the Fumé Blanc (above). The 1995 vintage, a blend of Hawke's Bay (principally) and Gisborne fruit, is fresh, limey and soft. The '96 (***) is ripely aromatic, its lively, clearly varietal, tropical-fruit flavours and well-balanced, rounded finish adding up to a very easy-drinking package.

VIDAL	DRY $13 AV
HAWKE'S BAY	
SAUVIGNON BLANC	(☆☆☆)

The 1996 vintage (***) is an unwooded style with enticing, fresh, ripe fruit aromas. It's a full-bodied wine with attractive melon/pineapple flavours and a smooth, fractionally off-dry finish.

VILLA MARIA	VINTAGE	97	96	95	94	93	92	91	DRY $17 V+
CELLAR SEL.	WR	7	7	6	7	6	6	6	
SAUV. BLANC	DRINK	97-9	97-8	97-8	P	P	P	P	☆☆☆☆½

A fruit-uppermost style, with a hint of oak adding depth, but essentially a showcase for the intense gooseberry and capsicum-like flavours of Marlborough grapes. The intensely fragrant, very ripe and punchy 1996 vintage is a blend of Rapaura and Awatere Valley fruit, with a "small proportion" of oak aging. It's a lovely, rich wine, deep, powerful (13.5 per cent alcohol), zingy and explosively flavoured, with tropical fruit and herbaceous characters, great body and concentration. The '97 (*****¹/₂) is also highly impressive, with fresh, intense, limey aromas, mouthfilling body, lively, ripe melon/capsicum flavours and a powerful finish. Exceptional value.

	VINTAGE	97	96	95	94	93	92	91	M/DRY $13 V+
VILLA MARIA									
PRIVATE BIN	WR		6	6	6	7	5	5	7
SAUV. BLANC	DRINK	97-9	97-8	P	P	P	P	P	☆☆☆☆☆

For this modestly priced label, Villa Maria targets a "herbaceous, light and racy" style. The extremely approachable 1996 vintage is a three-way regional blend of Marlborough, Waikato and Hawke's Bay fruit. Highly fragrant and flavoursome, it's an attractively fresh, ripe and zingy wine, penetrating yet immensely drinkable, coupling green capsicum-like and riper, tropical fruit characters. The '97 (****) is sourced from the same three regions. Ripely aromatic, with fresh, pure tropical/herbal flavours, it promises to match the '96.

	VINTAGE	97	96	DRY $19 V+
VILLA MARIA				
RES. CLIF. BAY	WR	7	7	
SAUV. BLANC	DRINK	98-00	97-9	(☆☆☆☆☆)

Villa Maria's first Awatere Valley-grown wine from the 1996 vintage (*****) is stunning, with the leap-out-of-the-glass fragrance and zingy, explosive flavour of Marlborough Sauvignon Blanc at its inimitable best. It was made from fruit picked at a very ripe 24° brix from Seddon Vineyards' young vines. The palate is notably concentrated and succulent, with fullness of body and mouth-encircling, zesty gooseberry/capsicum flavours. Exciting stuff.

	VINTAGE	97	96	95	94	93	92	DRY $19 V+
VILLA MARIA RES.								
WAIRAU VAL.	WR		7	7	NM	7	NM	6
SAUV. BLANC	DRINK	98-00	97-9	NM	P	NM	P	☆☆☆☆☆

The powerful and punchy 1996 vintage was grown in three Marlborough vineyards and fermented in a mix of stainless steel tanks and French and German oak barriques. It's a truly exciting wine, explosively flavoured. The bouquet is very rich and pure; the palate weighty, with a splendid concentration of gooseberry/capsicum flavours and beautifully balanced acidity. It's high-priced, but worth every cent. The '97 (*****) is another arresting wine, with a voluminous bouquet and exciting depth of flavour, fresh, vibrant, rich and cutting. (Note: the 1992 to 1994 vintage ratings apply to Villa Maria Reserve Sauvignon Blanc, as the wine was formerly labelled.)

	VINTAGE	97	96	95	94	93	DRY $16 AV
VOSS EST.							
SAUVIGNON	WR		4	6	3	5	5
BLANC	DRINK	97-8	97-8	P	P	P	(☆☆☆)

This tiny Martinborough winery's 1996 vintage (***) is a fleshy, lightly aromatic wine with good depth of ripe, melon/capsicum flavours. It's a decent wine, but doesn't shine like the winery's top Chardonnay.

WAIPARA	VINTAGE	96	95
SPRINGS	WR	5	5
SAUV. BLANC	DRINK	98-00	97-8

DRY $15 AV

(☆☆☆)

The 1995 vintage, the first to be estate-grown, is an impressively rich, ripe wine with lively redcurrant and green capsicum flavours, deliciously intermingled. The more austere '96 (***½) is fresh, clean, crisp and herbaceous in a very cool-climate, tangy, limey style, but lacks the ripeness and intensity of the '95.

WAIPARA WEST	VINTAGE	96
SAUVIGNON	WR	5
BLANC	DRINK	97-8

DRY $18 -V

(☆☆☆)

The 1996 vintage (***) is a full-bodied North Canterbury wine (13.5 per cent alcohol), with lively acidity in a grassy, cool-climate style. It lacks a bit of ripeness and lushness, but the flavours are quite searching.

WAIRAU RIVER
RESERVE
SAUVIGNON BLANC

DRY $23 AV

(☆☆☆☆☆)

The first 1996 vintage (*****) is a gorgeous wine in an ultra-ripe style. Based on hand-picked fruit from very low-cropping Marlborough vines, partly matured in seasoned oak casks, it's a wonderfully scented wine without obvious herbaceous characters. The palate is very substantial, with great weight and depth of ripe pineapple and passionfruit-evoking flavours, balanced acidity and a very rich, trailing finish. Drink now onwards.

WAIRAU RIVER
RICHMOND RIDGE
SAUVIGNON BLANC

DRY $13 V+

(☆☆☆)

The 1996 vintage (***) of this Marlborough winery's lower-tier Sauvignon Blanc is a pungent style, fresh and lively, with nettley, strongly herbaceous flavour, appetising acidity and good length. Fine value.

WAIRAU RIVER
MARLBOROUGH
SAUVIGNON BLANC

 DRY $18 V+

☆☆☆☆☆

Proprietors Phil and Chris Rose produce an eye-catchingly weighty style of Sauvignon Blanc in which rich, lush flavours are coupled with rapier-like nettley characters and bracing acidity. The '95 is a very decent effort for the vintage, with good depth of crisp, ripe fruit characters, a herbal undercurrent and quite powerful finish. The back label of the 1996 vintage (*****) promises "elegance and power" – and delivers the goods. Mouthfilling and lively, with an exciting rush of fresh, pure flavour, it couples lush, rich fruit with piercing, grassy characters, leading to a flinty, superbly sustained finish.

WALNUT RIDGE	VINTAGE	97	**DRY $16 V+**
SAUVIGNON	WR	6	(☆☆☆☆☆)
BLANC	DRINK	97-9	

Bill Brink's first 1997 vintage (****¹/₂) Martinborough Sauvignon Blanc is an impressive debut. It's a succulent, basket-of-fruit style with very fresh, ripe scents and intense, non-herbaceous, sweet-fruit flavours, redolent of melons and passionfruit. Crisp, lively, immaculate.

WEST BROOK BLUE   **DRY $16 V+**
RIDGE MARLBOROUGH
SAUVIGNON BLANC   (☆☆☆☆)

The 1996 vintage is one of this small Henderson winery's best Sauvignons yet. Pale, fresh and frisky, it exhibits strong herbaceous aromas and incisive melon/capsicum flavours, lively and lingering. The '97 (***¹/₂) is slightly less intense, but still offers good depth of fresh, ripe passionfruit/lime flavours, lively and crisp.

WEST BROOK   **DRY $14 AV**
HAWKE'S BAY
SAUVIGNON BLANC   ☆☆☆

The 1996 vintage (***¹/₂) is a very attractive wine with scented, ripe fruit aromas. Still very fresh, it's full-bodied and crisp, with very good depth of melon/lime flavours. The '97, tasted from the tank, looked promising, with excellent flavour ripeness and weight.

WHITEHAVEN	VINTAGE	95	**M/DRY $20 AV**
BARREL FERM.	WR	5	(☆ ☆☆☆☆)
SAUV. BLANC	DRINK	97-8	

The '95 is a classy debut. Based on fruit hand-picked from young vines in the Le Grys vineyard, Marlborough, whole bunch-pressed, fermented and lees-aged for nine months in French and American oak barriques, it's a finely balanced wine, complex yet clearly varietal. The bouquet is fresh, nettley and nutty; the palate full-flavoured, grassy and lemony, with spicy oak and lots of vigour. The 1996 vintage (****) is also very characterful, with a complex, "malo"-influenced bouquet and a broad, soft palate with rich, nutty, ripely herbal flavour.

WHITEHAVEN   **M/DRY $16 V+**
MARLBOROUGH
SAUVIGNON BLANC   (☆☆☆☆)

Simon Waghorn, formerly chief winemaker at Corbans' Gisborne winery, produces consistently impressive wines under the Whitehaven label, priced right. Based on grapes harvested from two vineyards on five picking dates, and matured on its yeast lees to add a touch of complexity, the 1996 vintage is a deliciously full, subtle yet penetrating wine, finely balanced, with excellent depth of ripe, gently herbaceous flavour, fresh acidity and a dryish, long finish. The '97 (****) is also impressive, with fullness of body and excellent depth of ripe melon/capsicum flavours, fresh, tangy and lingering.

WINSLOW MARL. SAUVIGNON BLANC

DRY $15 AV

(☆☆☆)

The 1995 vintage (***) from this Martinborough winery is maturing well, with a gooseberryish, slightly honied fragrance, fullness of body and a dry, crisp finish. There is no '96.

WITHER HILLS MARLBOROUGH SAUV. BLANC

VINTAGE	97	96	95	94
WR	7	7	5	6
DRINK	97-00	97-9	P	P

DRY $18 V+

(☆☆☆☆☆)

The outstanding 1996 vintage fulfils the promise evident in the lush, first 1994 vintage of (Delegat's winemaker) Brent Marris's Marlborough wine. Barrel-fermented and matured in French oak barriques, the '96 has a voluminous bouquet, with intense, ripe fruit aromas and very subtle wood. A mouthfilling wine with a delicious wealth of sweet, ripe fruit, it is packed with flavour – fresh, ultra-ripe, subtle and long. Hugely drinkable, it is a more complex style than most, but still a celebration of Marlborough fruit flavours. In its youth, the '97 (****¹/₂) is full of promise, with powerful body and strong, lively, clearly herbaceous flavours building across the palate to a long, rich finish.

Sémillon

Sémillon is New Zealand's fifth most widely planted white wine variety, yet you'd never guess it from the small batch of Sémillons on the market.

The few New Zealand winemakers who a decade ago played around with Sémillon could hardly give it away, so aggressively stemmy and spiky was its flavour. Now, there are a few riper, richer, rounder Sémillons emerging – and they are ten times more enjoyable to drink.

The Sémillon variety is beset by a similar problem to Chenin Blanc. Despite being the foundation of truly great white wines in Bordeaux and the Hunter Valley of New South Wales, Sémillon is out of fashion in the rest of the world, and in New Zealand its potential is still largely untapped.

Sémillon is highly prized in Bordeaux, where as one of the two key varieties both in dry wines, most notably white Graves, and the inimitable sweet Sauternes, its high levels of alcohol and extract are perfect foils for Sauvignon Blanc's verdant aroma and tartness. With its propensity to rot "nobly", Sémillon forms about 80 per cent of a classic Sauternes.

Cooler climates like those of New Zealand, Tasmania and Washington state, however, bring out a grassy-green character in Sémillon which, coupled with its higher acidity in these regions, can give the variety strikingly Sauvignon-like characteristics. Widespread virus infection of the vines has also retarded grape ripeness and contributed to unattractive, unripe, green characters.

Grown predominantly in Marlborough (where over half the vines are concentrated), Gisborne and Hawke's Bay, Sémillon is commonly used in New Zealand as a minor (and anonymous) partner in wines labelled Sauvignon Blanc, contributing complexity and aging potential. By curbing the variety's natural tendency to grow vigorously and crop bountifully, several winemakers are now starting to overcome the aggressive cut-grass characters that in the past plagued the majority of New Zealand's unblended Sémillons. The recent arrival of clones capable of giving riper fruit characters (notably BVRC-14 from the Barossa Valley) is also contributing to quality advances. You'll hear a lot more about this grape in the future.

ASKERNE VINEYARD SÉMILLON/SAUVIGNON BLANC

DRY $16 AV

(☆☆☆)

Produced by John Loughlin (whose father, John, owns Waimarama Estate), the debut 1996 vintage (***) is a pale Hawke's Bay wine with a grassy bouquet. It's a clearly but not aggressively herbaceous wine, fresh and crisp, with good weight and depth of citrus/herbal flavours.

COLLARDS BARRIQUE FERM. SÉMILLON

VINTAGE	97	96	95	94	93	92	91
WR	NM	7	6	7	7	6	6
DRINK	NM	97-9	97-8	97-8	P	P	P

DRY $15 V+

☆☆☆☆

Estate-grown Henderson fruit, fermented in French oak barriques, yields this complex dry white. The '95 is a satisfyingly weighty wine with plenty of ripe, melon-like, slightly grassy flavour, fleshed out with restrained wood. The impressive 1996 vintage (****) is a beautifully balanced wine with rich, ripe melon/capsicum flavours, oak complexity and a crisp, long finish. It's drinking well now, but also a strong candidate for cellaring.

DE REDCLIFFE RESERVE SÉMILLON

DRY $17 AV

(☆☆☆☆)

The highly approachable, partly (15 per cent) barrel-fermented 1996 vintage (****) is a blend of 85 per cent Mangere and 15 per cent estate-grown Mangatawhiri fruit. Light yellow/green, it is fresh and attractive, with a touch of complexity and good depth of ripe, delicate melon/capsicum flavours. Youthful, well balanced wine for now to 99.

DE REDCLIFFE SÉMILLON

DRY $14 V+

(☆☆☆☆⟆)

The flinty, ripely herbal 1996 vintage (***½) of De Redcliffe's first 100 per cent Sémillon offers great value. A non-wooded blend of grapes grown at Mangere and Mangatawhiri, it is an attractive wine with satisfying depth of well-ripened, melon/capsicum flavours, clearcut varietal characters and a crisp, dry finish. Drink now or cellar.

DE REDCLIFFE SÉMILLON/ CHARDONNAY

DRY $13 AV

☆☆☆

Typically a medium-bodied wine with crisp, refreshing lemon/herbal flavours. The 1994 vintage, briefly oak-aged (for the first time), offers pleasant, ripe flavours with a slight herbal edge. The '95 deftly balances lively, lemony, slightly grassy flavours with a well-integrated touch of toasty oak. Good, flavoursome, well-priced drinking. The '96 (**½) lacks the richness of its Sémillon-based stablemates (above), but offers pleasant, smooth, gently herbal flavours.

FORREST	VINTAGE	97	96	95	94	93	92	91	DRY $15 V+
ESTATE	WR	5	4	NM	5	4	NM	3	
SÉMILLON	DRINK	98+	97+	NM	97-8	P	NM	P	☆☆☆⯪

Past vintages of John Forrest's Marlborough wine, labelled Barrel-Fermented Sémillon, were packed with zingy, herbaceous aromas and flavour. The 1994 vintage, which includes 15 per cent Sauvignon Blanc, is a subtle, but weighty and potentially quite complex wine, toasty, citrusy and herbal, with a long, rounded finish. The '97 (****) is a mouthfilling wine, vibrantly fruity with excellent depth of crisp, appley, grassy flavour.

HUNTAWAY RES.	VINTAGE	96	95	DRY $16 V+
GISBORNE	WR	7	7	
SÉMILLON	DRINK	97-02	97-00	(☆☆☆☆)

The debut 1995 vintage of Corbans' barrel-fermented, lees-aged wine promises "exotic fruit and smoky oak" – and delivers the goods. It's a very easy-drinking wine, light yellow, with ripe-tasting, lemony, grassy flavours, crisp and rich, and loads of character. The '96 (****) is again bursting with flavour. The grassy/oaky fragrance leads into a mouthfilling wine with rich, tropical fruit and herbal flavours, enriched with oak, and a crisp, sustained finish.

JACKMAN RIDGE	M/DRY $11 AV
SÉMILLON/SAUVIGNON	
BLANC	(☆☆⯪)

Pale, with fresh, stemmy aromas, the 1995 vintage is a well-made quaffer from Montana, with cutting, new-mown grass flavours and a fractionally sweet, mouth-wateringly crisp finish. The '96 (**¹/₂), grown in Gisborne, reveals a forthrightly grassy bouquet and reasonable depth of lemony, herbaceous , off-dry flavour.

KERR	VINTAGE	96	DRY $16 AV
FARM	WR	5	
SÉMILLON	DRINK	97-00	(☆ ☆☆)

The '96 (***) was grown at Kumeu and given some barrel fermentation, lees-aging and malolactic fermentation. It's a full, fresh wine, slightly grassy and nutty, with a touch of complexity and quite good flavour depth.

	VINTAGE	97	96	DRY $19 AV
KIM CRAWFORD	WR	5	6	
HAWKE'S BAY	DRINK	98-9	97-8	(☆☆☆☆)
SÉMILLON				

Promoted as "a wine of interest to anyone tiring of Chardonnay and Sauvignon Blanc", the debut 1996 vintage (****) was grown in the Scotland vineyard, tank-fermented, given a softening malolactic fermentation and then barrel-aged for six months. Based on the new to New Zealand, less herbaceous BVRC-14 clone, it's a ripely herbal, rather Chardonnay-like wine, strongly oak-influenced, buttery and complex, with very satisfying body and flavour richness.

KUMEU RIVER SÉMILLON

DRY $20 -V

(☆☆☆)

"Sémillon cries out for oysters," says winemaker Michael Brajkovich, an unabashed fan of the variety. The '95 (**½), fully fermented in seasoned oak barrels, is a sharp wine with austere, stemmy and flinty flavours that lack the ripeness and richness of the '93.

MERLEN SÉMILLON

DRY $15 V+

(☆☆☆☆)

Maturing splendidly, the 1994 vintage (****) was tank-fermented but oak-aged for 18 months. Pale straw, it's soft and weighty, with rich, ripe, persistent flavours, complexity, and a seductively creamy texture. Ready.

MISSION SÉMILLON/SAUV. BLANC

VINTAGE	94	93	92	91	90
WR	6	4	6	5	7
DRINK	97-00	P	P	P	P

DRY $11 V+

☆☆☆

Ideal for current consumption, the 1994 vintage (***) of this dry wine is a blend of 85 per cent Hawke's Bay Sémillon and 15 per cent Sauvignon Blanc. Lemon-green in hue, with a mildly herbaceous bouquet, it's an ideal seafood wine, with good weight and plenty of citrusy, slightly grassy, well-rounded flavour.

NEUDORF MOUTERE SÉMILLON

VINTAGE	96	95	94	93	92	91	90
WR	6	4	6	NM	6	6	5
DRINK	97-00	97-9	97-00	NM	97-8	P	P

DRY $17 AV

☆☆☆☆

At it's best, this is a mouth-watering, flavour-packed, full-bodied wine with strong, steely, searching flavours, lemony and gently herbaceous. Pale straw, the 1996 vintage (**½) was estate-grown, barrel-fermented and blended with 10 per cent Sauvignon Blanc. It's a flavoursome, high-acid wine with grassy aromas and flavours and some complexity, but lacks the ripeness and power of the label at its best.

OMAKA SPRINGS MARLBOROUGH SÉMILLON

DRY $12 -V

(☆☆)

The pale, very plain 1996 vintage (**) is a curiously restrained wine for Sémillon, with light, lemony, appley flavours and firm acidity, but an overall lack of character and depth.

PLEA. VAL. SIGN. SELE. GISBORNE SÉMILLON

VINTAGE	95
WR	6
DRINK	97-8

M/DRY $14 V+

(☆☆☆☆)

Crisp and verdant in its youth, the lightly oaked 1995 vintage (****) is maturing well, gaining complexity and richness. Bright, light yellow, it is ripe-tasting, with subtle toasty characters, power through the palate and good acid spine.

Sweet White Wines

The ravishing beauty of New Zealand's top sweet whites is starting to win acclaim overseas. At the 1996 Sydney International Wine Competition (often called the "Top 100"), the trophy for the champion dessert wine (unfortified) went to Highfield Estate Noble Late Harvest Riesling 1994, from Marlborough. A year earlier, at the same show, the same trophy was awarded to another Marlborough beauty: Corbans Cottage Block Noble Riesling 1991.

Stuart Pigott, a British author who lives at Bernkastel, on the Mosel, has written in his 1991 book, *Riesling*: "The most impressive [Rieslings] currently being made in New Zealand are the dessert wines produced by a handful of growers from *Botrytis*-affected grapes. If not quite in the same class as the finest wines made in this style in Germany and Alsace, they are nonetheless far more exciting than the majority of dessert Rieslings from Australia or North America."

New Zealand's most luscious, concentrated and honeyish sweet whites are made from grapes which have been shrivelled and dehydrated on the vines by "noble rot", the dry form of the *Botrytis cinerea* mould. Misty mornings, followed by clear, fine days with light winds and low humidity, are ideal conditions for the spread of noble rot, but in New Zealand this favourable interplay of weather factors occurs irregularly.

Marlborough has so far yielded a majority of the finest sweet whites. Most of the other wine regions, however – except Auckland (too wet) and Central Otago (too dry and cool) – can also point to the successful production of botrytised sweet whites in favourable vintages.

Riesling has been the foundation of the majority of New Zealand's most opulent sweet whites, but Müller-Thurgau, Sauvignon Blanc, Sémillon, Gewürztraminer, Pinot Gris, Reichensteiner, Chenin Blanc and Chardonnay have all yielded fine dessert styles; the Rongopai winery even conjured up a sticky from Pinot Noir. With their high levels of extract and firm acidity, most of these wines richly repay cellaring.

ALLAN SCOTT AUTUMN RIESLING	VINTAGE	95	SW $15 (375ML) V+
	WR	7	
	DRINK	P	(☆☆☆☆)

The 1993 vintage of this Marlborough wine displays enjoyable, but not intense, lemony, sweet, *Botrytis*-affected flavour. The amber-hued '95 (*****) is much richer, with rampantly botrytised, apricot/honey characters on the nose and palate. A striking wine: weighty, oily, treacly and soft.

CHIFNEY NOBLE CHENIN

SW $20 (375ML) AV

(☆☆☆☆⯪)

Chifney's Martinborough wines are going from strength to strength. The ravishing 1996 vintage (*****) is only 10 per cent alcohol, but very weighty. Fresh, honey/pear aromas lead into a lovely, richly concentrated palate with an exquisite balance of fruit, sweetness and acidity and a long, rich, lively finish. Packed with aging potential.

CHURCH ROAD NOBLE SÉMILLON

SW $?? (375ML) V?

(☆☆☆☆☆)

The debut 1994 vintage (*****) is Montana's first dessert wine made with input from the Bordeaux house of Cordier, owner of the great *premier cru* Sauternes, Chateau Lafaurie-Peyraguey. Harvested in Hawke's Bay at 38˚ to 42˚ brix, and fermented and matured in a high percentage of new French oak casks, it's a golden wine with a wonderfully rich, honeyish, intensely botrytised bouquet. The palate is very weighty, sweet, oily and concentrated. It's less complex than a top Sauternes, but superb by New Zealand standards. (In its infancy, the '96 looks even better. I tasted it this year, on 9 June, while the 1997 crop was still on the vines.)

COOPERS CREEK LATE HARVEST RIESLING

VINTAGE	97	96	95	94	93	92	91	90
WR		5	7	4	7	NM	NM	5	7
DRINK		97-8	98-00	P	97-8	NM	NM	P	P

SW $16 (375ML) V+

☆☆☆☆⯪

This Hawke's Bay beauty features late-harvested, ripe, freeze-concentrated fruit flavours rather than *Botrytis*. A perfect aperitif, sweet but not extremely sweet (50 grams/litre residual sugar), and bargain-priced. The 1995 vintage is less intense than usual, but still attractively perfumed and delicately flavoured. The '96 (****½) is very typical: stylish with strong lemon/lime flavours and a lovely balance of fresh, lively acidity and sweetness.

COOPERS GOLD

VINTAGE	96	95	94
WR	5	NM	7
DRINK	98-00	NM	00-10

SW $28 (375ML) AV

(☆☆☆☆☆)

Still ascending, the first 1994 vintage (*****) of this exceptional wine is a botrytised Hawke's Bay Chardonnay, oak-aged for 18 months. Golden, with an enticingly rich, treacly bouquet, it is a Sauternes-style wine with great weight and depth of honeyish, complex flavour and exciting power right through the palate. Superb now, but a prime candidate for cellaring.

COR. COT. BLOCK MARL. NOBLE RHINE RIESLING

VINTAGE	95	94	93	92	91
WR	7	NM	NM	NM	7
DRINK	05	NM	NM	NM	02

SW $23 (375ML) AV

(☆☆☆☆☆)

With Corbans' distinguished track record of glorious Marlborough sweet whites, it's no surprise the first 1991 vintage Cottage Block sticky is a winner – ravishingly perfumed, honey-sweet, soft and oily, with an apricot-like intensity. The '95 (*****) is a stunning wine, much sweeter and more powerful than its Private Bin stablemate (below). Based on individually selected berries, it is deep amber, with rich, apricot-like aromas and a mouthfilling, oily, well-spined palate awash with nectareous, rampantly botrytised flavour.

CORBANS EST. GISBORNE MUSCAT

VINTAGE	96	95
WR	7	6
DRINK	97-02	97-00

SW $10 (375ML) V+

(☆ ☆☆)

The 1996 vintage (***) is a delicious although uncomplicated wine, well-priced. Made from early-harvested, freeze-concentrated grapes, it is scented and musky, with light body (10 per cent alcohol) and very fresh, delicate, lemon/grapefruit flavours, sweet and crisp.

CORBANS PRIVATE BIN MARLBOROUGH NOBLE RHINE RIESLING

SW $12 (375ML) V+

(☆☆☆)

Some great wines appeared under this label in the past, but are now marketed under Corbans' top Cottage Block label (above). The modestly priced 1995 vintage (***) is light yellow, with a slightly piquant bouquet. The flavour is strong, citrusy and slightly honeyish, with a crisp, moderately sweet finish. It's a light, gentle wine; I'd drink it sooner rather than later.

COUNTRY SAUTERNES

SW $15 (3L) AV

(☆☆)

Not all sweet whites come in pricey half-bottles! Packaged in casks by Montana under its bottom-tier Woodhill's brand, Country Sauternes is a blend of local and imported wine. Pale and scented, fruity and soft, with reasonable fruit character and a grapey-sweet finish, it's ideal if you want a plain, unabashedly sweet quaffer.

CROSS ROADS LATE HARVEST RIESLING

SW $12 (375ML) V+

(☆☆☆)

Pale, with a light, ripely fruity bouquet, the 1996 vintage (***) is a sweet but not super-sweet Hawke's Bay wine, not lush but lively and well-balanced, with lemony, limey, slightly honeyed and zesty flavours.

DRY RIVER CHARDONNAY BOTRYTIS BERRY SELECTION

SW $26 (375ML) AV

(☆☆☆☆☆)

(The Classic designation applies to Dry River's range of sweet whites from different varieties.) The lush, decadent 1995 vintage (*****) was grown in the Straitsgaarde vineyard in Marlborough, picked on 19 May at 46° brix with advanced *Botrytis*-induced shrivelling, and "pressed and clarified with the greatest of difficulty," reports winemaker Neil McCallum. At a massive 270 grams/litre of sugar, it's the equivalent of a German *trockenbeerenauslesen*. Deep amber, it's a strikingly rich and oily wine with highly concentrated, apricot-like flavours, its advanced sweetness balanced by crisp acidity and great weight. It should cellar well, but why wait when it's so delicious now?

DRY RIVER PINOT GRIS SELECTION

SW $23 (375ML) AV

(☆☆☆☆☆)

The sweet but not super-sweet 1996 vintage (*****) was estate-grown in Martinborough and late-harvested in early May at 29° brix with natural berry shrivelling and some *Botrytis*. Fermented to over 13 per cent alcohol, yet still harbouring a residual sugar of 65 grams/litre, it's equivalent in style to an Alsace *vendange tardive*. A weighty, intensely varietal wine, it possesses notably rich, concentrated peachy/spicy/earthy flavours and great power through the palate. Still very youthful, it's worth cellaring to at least 1999.

DRY RIVER RIESLING BOT. BUNCH SEL.

VINTAGE	96	95
WR	7	7
DRINK	00-07	97-06

SW $23 (375ML) AV

(☆☆☆☆☆)

The '95 vintage is a slender, beautifully poised Martinborough wine with pure, richly scented lemon/honey aromas and delicate, piercing, appetisingly crisp flavours. The '96 (*****) is another aristocratic wine. Harvested at 34° brix with all bunches showing advanced *Botrytis* shrivelling, and at a residual sugar level of 170 grams/litre, it is equivalent in style to a German *beerenauslesen*. Ravishingly perfumed pear/honey aromas lead into an intense, very harmonious palate, low in alcohol (9 per cent), but with concentrated, delicate, honied, crisp flavours, delectably rich and lingering.

FORREST EST. LATE HARVEST RIESLING

VINTAGE	96
WR	4
DRINK	97+

SW $22 -V

(☆☆☆☆)

The first 1996 vintage (****) of this Marlborough wine is a weighty yet gentle wine. Light yellow, it reveals a delicate, citrusy, honied fragrance and excellent depth of poised, lemony, honeyish flavour.

FORREST EST. LATE HAR. SAUV. BLANC/SÉMILLON

VINTAGE	96
WR	6
DRINK	97+

SW $24 (375ML) -V

(☆☆☆☆)

Harvested in Marlborough at 38° brix and fermented in new oak barriques, the 1996 vintage (****) is a weighty Sauternes-style, slightly herbal and limey, but impressively oily, complex, sweet and rich.

FRAMINGHAM RESERVE LATE HARVEST RIESLING

SW $29 (375ML) AV

(☆☆☆☆☆)

Framingham Rieslings are always impressive, and the 1996 vintage of this Marlborough dessert wine (*****) is one of the greatest yet. Grown at Renwick, it was harvested right at the end of May at 35° brix, and harbours a residual sugar level of 130 grams/litre. It's a sweet, clearly but not rampantly botrytised style with a light gold hue, lovely fragrance of citrus fruits and honey and intense, delicate flavours, rich and harmonious. Now to 2000.

GIESEN	VINTAGE	95	94	93	92	91	90	
BOTRYTISED	WR	5	NM	NM	NM	7	5	SW $20 (375ML) V+
RIESLING	DRINK	97-05	NM	NM	NM	97-9	P	☆☆☆☆☆

The 1989, '90 and '91 vintages of this Canterbury wine were all brilliant: right in the vanguard of New Zealand's sweet whites. None was produced in the 1992–94 vintages. The '95 (*****) is another magnificent dessert style, with deep, golden colour and a voluminous fragrance. The palate is rich and succulent, with an arresting intensity of honey-sweet flavour, threaded with lively acidity. Superb value.

GIESEN NOBLE SCHOOL ROAD LATE HARVEST

SW $20 (375ML) AV

(☆☆☆☆)

The '95, labelled Botrytised Late Harvest Riesling, is a light, gentle, delicate wine with lemon, pear and honey flavours, soft and forward. Ensconced in a soaring blue bottle, the superior 1996 vintage (****¹/₂) is a Canterbury-grown blend of 60 per cent Riesling and 40 per cent Müller-Thurgau. Golden, with a marmalade-rich, honeyish fragrance, it is full-bodied despite its 9 per cent alcohol, with concentrated, sweet, *Botrytis*-enriched flavours threaded with lively acidity.

GLOVER'S RICHMOND RIESLING LATE HARVEST

SW $17 AV

(☆☆☆)

The pale, delicate 1996 vintage (***) of this Nelson wine harbours 50 grams/litre of residual sugar, which just qualifies it for the sweet wine section of this guide. It's a light-bodied wine (9 per cent alcohol), with citrusy, appley aromas and flavours and a Mosel-like raciness and delicacy.

HIGHFIELD NOB.	VINTAGE	96	95	94	93	92	91	90	
LATE HARVEST	WR	4	5	6	4	NM	NM	6	SW $17 (375ML) AV
RIESLING	DRINK	P	P	00+	P	NM	NM	97-00	(☆☆☆)

The 1994 vintage is a memorable Marlborough "sticky" – golden, with a heady, treacly fragrance and great power through the palate. The very weighty and oily, apricot and honey-flavoured '96 (**) was also slightly dull, sharp and piquant, and has peaked early. (The golden, barrel-fermented, very Sauternes-like Elstree Botrytised Sémillon/Sauvignon Blanc 1995 (****¹/₂) is far superior, with mouthfilling body and rich, honied, multi-faceted flavour.)

JACKSON EST.	VINTAGE	95	
BOTRYTIS	WR	5	SW $25 (375ML) AV
CHARDONNAY	DRINK	97-05	(☆☆☆☆☆)

Wow! The 1995 vintage (*****) of this hand-picked, super-ripe (52° brix), oak-aged Marlborough sticky is gorgeous. The colour is deep amber; the soaring bouquet is deliciously treacly, with an apricot-like richness; the palate is enormously concentrated and luscious, oily and honey-sweet. Treat yourself.

LINCOLN	VINTAGE	96					SW $16 (500ML) V+
ICE	WR	5					
WINE	DRINK	97-03					(☆ ☆☆)

The '95 is pale gold, with a perfumed, peppery bouquet and enjoyably spicy, smooth flavour. The 1996 vintage (***) is a freeze-concentrated Gisborne Gewürztraminer. Light (9.5 per cent alcohol), it's sweet and spicy in a forward style with moderate acidity. Sharply priced – note the bottle size.

LINTZ EST.	VINTAGE	96	95	94	93	92	91	SW $50 (375ML) -V
OPTIMA NOBLE	WR	7	7	7	7	6	6	
SELECTION	DRINK	00-06	02-05	00-10	01-10	00-10	98-05	(☆☆☆☆☆)

An ultra-sweet Martinborough wine based on the rare Optima variety, an extremely early-ripening, *Botrytis*-prone cross of Müller-Thurgau with another crossing of Riesling and Sylvaner. The 1994 is less ravishingly perfumed than Riesling, but the palate is huge, with a tidal wave of honeyish, oily, rampantly botrytised, super-sweet flavour. The deep amber '95 (*****) is the best yet (don't confuse it with the '95 Optima Late Harvest, a rich but slightly lighter and crisper wine, $35 per 500 ml). A gorgeously concentrated wine, intensely honeyish, it displays a lovely sugar/acid balance and greater fragrance, delicacy and style than in the past.

LINTZ EST.				SW $25 (375ML) AV
SPICY TRAMINER				
LATE HARVEST				(☆☆☆☆⯪)

The strapping 1996 vintage (****¹/₂) is based on Martinborough grapes, late-picked with 50 per cent *Botrytis* infection. It's a very mouthfilling style (14 per cent alcohol), light gold, with a perfumed, spicy, honeyish fragrance. Produced along the lines of an Alsace *vendange tardive*, it is very powerful, with a ripe, peppery, sweetish rather than super-sweet palate and long, well-spiced finish.

MARTINBOROUGH	VINTAGE	95	SW $20 (375ML) AV
VINEY. CHARD.	WR	6	
LATE HARVEST	DRINK	00	(☆ ☆☆☆)

The luscious 1995 vintage (****) was made from botrytised fruit picked at an average of 35˚ brix, fermented to a residual sugar level of 170 grams/litre and barrel-aged for a year. It's a full-bodied wine with intense peach/pineapple flavours, oak complexity and a marmalade-like, *Botrytis*-derived richness.

MARTIN. VINEY.	VINTAGE	96	95	SW $25 (375ML) AV
GEWÜRZTRAM.	WR	7	7	
LATE HARVEST	DRINK	00+	00+	(☆☆☆☆☆)

The 1995 vintage is very perfumed, weighty and peppery, with great power through the palate and a superb concentration of orange, spice and honey flavours. The '96 (*****) is unfortunately the last of the line; the vines have been uprooted. Botrytised fruit harvested at 33.5˚ brix (German *beerenauslesen* quality) was fermented to 11 per cent alcohol, leaving 160 grams/litre of residual sugar. It's a golden, vibrantly fruity wine with intense pepper and lychees flavours, *Botrytis*-derived honied richness and firm acidity. A beautifully balanced wine, already delicious.

MARTINBOROUGH	VINTAGE	96	SW $25 (375ML) AV
VINE. RIESLING	WR	7	
LATE HARVEST	DRINK	05+	(☆☆☆☆☆)

The brilliant 1996 vintage (*****) was made from grapes of the quality "most winemakers see but once in their careers," reports Larry McKenna. Botrytised fruit was harvested over 10 days at an average 39° brix (equal to German *trockenbeerenauslesen* quality) and slow-fermented to a very sweet style, retaining 195 grams/litre of sugar. It's a classic sweet Riesling, light gold, with a ravishingly rich, honied fragrance. The palate is equally exquisite, with concentrated citrus/honey flavours, firm acid spine and superb delicacy and length.

MATUA LATE	VINTAGE	96	SW $12 (375ML) V+
HARVEST	WR	7	
MUSCAT	DRINK	00+	☆☆☆

The heady perfume is a highlight of this bargain-priced dessert wine. The 1996 vintage (***) was made from Muscat Dr Hogg grapes grown in Hawke's Bay, freeze-concentrated, and then barrel-aged for four months. This is a mouthfilling, fruity, sweet and smooth white with clearcut citrus/orange varietal characters in an enjoyable although not luscious or complex style.

MILLTON VINE.,	VINTAGE	94	SW $39 (375ML) -V
THE, TÊTE DU	WR	6	
CUVÉE CHEN. BLANC	DRINK	98-08	(☆☆☆☆☆)

Rampantly botrytised Gisborne Chenin Blanc, 80 per cent barrel-fermented, in 1994 (*****) yielded a stunning, deep-amber beauty with intense, sweet, apricot-like aromas and flavours. The striking depth of honey-sweet flavour is interwoven with steely, authoritative acidity. An expensive but classy wine, with a long life ahead.

MISSION			SW $14 (375ML) AV
ICE			
WINE			(☆☆☆)

The 1996 vintage (***) is a freeze-concentrated wine based on ripe Müller-Thurgau grown at Greenmeadows. Light yellow, it's a mouthfilling wine (13 per cent alcohol), crisp, lemony and sweet, with plenty of flavour and drink-young appeal. Open 1998.

MISSION JEWEL	VINTAGE	96	SW $17 (375ML) AV
BOTRYTISED	WR	6	
RIESLING	DRINK	97-05	(☆☆☆☆)

The fairly rich 1996 vintage (****) of this Hawke's Bay wine is yellow-hued, with enticing lemon, pear and honey aromas. It's a very charming and harmonious wine, weighty, with succulent, sweet (but at 90 grams/litre of residual sugar, not super-sweet), citrusy flavours, crisp acidity and a distinct touch of *Botrytis*-derived honeyishness.

MISSION	VINTAGE	96	SW $27 (375ML) AV
JEWEL NOB.	WR	7	
RIESLING	DRINK	97-10	(☆ ☆☆☆☆☆)

The 1996 vintage (*****) has the inimitable beauty of classic sweet Riesling – intense citrusy fruit and rich, *Botrytis*-derived honey/marmalade characters, interwoven with steely acidity. Light gold, with a ravishing perfume, it is a weighty, very rich, beautifully poised wine, already delicious but sure to flourish well into next century.

MONTANA LATE	VINTAGE	95	SW $12 (375ML) AV
HARVEST	WR	5	
SELECTION	DRINK	97-00	(☆ ☆☆)

The golden 1994 vintage (**¹/₂) of this modestly priced, sweet Marlborough wine (originally labelled Late Harvest Müller-Thurgau) is a weighty style for that variety (12 per cent alcohol), with straightforward, lemon and pear-like flavours in a soft, gentle, slightly honeyed style. Ready.

| **MONTEL** | SW $6 AV |
| **SAUTERNES** | (☆☆) |

Montel, one of Corbans' oldest brands, reached the summit of its popularity in the days when sweetness, rather than quality, was most in demand by New Zealand wine drinkers. However, when wine arrived on supermarket shelves in 1990, sales surged again. It's a light, essentially nondescript wine, juicy, lemony, mild, smooth, sweet and soft.

MORTON ESTATE WHITE	SW $12 (375ML) V+
LABEL LATE HARVEST	
MARLBOROUGH RIESLING	(☆☆☆☆)

The bargain-priced 1996 vintage (****) is already delicious. Harvested at 32° brix, it was fermented and lees-aged for eight months in French oak barriques. It's a very ripe and flavourful wine, yellow hued, with attractive, ripe grapefruit/honey aromas. The palate is sweet and full, with citrusy, *Botrytis*-enriched flavours and fresh, firm acidity. Drink anytime from now onwards. An outstanding buy.

NGATARAWA ALWYN	SW $60 (375ML) -V
NOBLE	
HARVEST	(☆☆☆☆☆)

Alwyn Corban is extremely proud of this wine, so he put his name on it. And why not? The first 1994 vintage (*****) is a beauty. Estate-grown in Hawke's Bay, it was made from 100 per cent *Botrytis*-infected Riesling berries, harvested at 42° brix (compared to 35° brix for the same year's Glazebrook Noble Harvest). Looking for "an extra dimension and complexity", Corban then fermented and matured the wine in oak for 18 months. It's a powerful yet graceful wine, light gold, with a ravishing fragrance. A bolder, more succulent style than the Glazebrook, with oak adding richness without dominating, it displays great weight through the palate, yet retains Riesling's finesse; it is not a Sauternes-style. Drink now to 2000+.

NGATARAWA GLAZE. NOBLE HARVEST	VINTAGE	96	95	94	93	92	91		SW $30 (375ML) AV
	WR	7	NM	6	NM	6	5		(☆☆☆☆☆)
	DRINK	97-07	NM	97-05	NM	97-00	97-00		

This classic Hawke's Bay wine matures well for a decade; even longer. The '94 is ravishingly perfumed, with a beautifully poised and searching palate: citrusy, honeyish, crisp, very elegant and lingering. The 1996 vintage (*****) is also a beauty. Made from estate-grown Riesling harvested at 38° brix, it is already irresistible, with a light-gold hue, heady perfume and very concentrated, very sweet palate, honeyed, weighty and treacly.

NGATARAWA STABLES LATE HARVEST	VINTAGE	96	95	94	93	92	91	90	SW $12 (375ML) V+
	WR	4	NM	5	NM	7	6	5	☆☆☆
	DRINK	P	NM	P	NM	P	P	P	

This wine is called "a fruit style" by Hawke's Bay winemaker Alwyn Corban, meaning it doesn't possess the qualities of a fully botrytised wine. The 1994 has a floral, citrusy bouquet and fresh, delicate, lemony, slightly honeyish flavours. There is no '95. The 1996 vintage (**½) is a moderately sweet wine (50 grams/litre residual sugar) based entirely on Riesling. It's full-bodied and crisp, lemony and limey, but shy on the nose and lacking its customary depth and charm.

OKAHU ESTATE DESSERTÉ	VINTAGE	95	SW $19 (375ML) -V
	WR	5	(☆☆☆)
	DRINK	97-01	

Packaged in a distinctively tall and slender, see-through bottle, the '95 vintage (***) is made from botrytised Northland Chardonnay, oak-aged. Light lemon-green, with a restrained bouquet, it's a mouthfilling, broad, soft wine with a gentle *Botrytis* influence and sweet, smooth, fairly concentrated lemon/honey flavours.

PALLISER ESTATE BOTRYTIS RIESLING	SW $22 (375ML) AV
	(☆☆☆☆✩)

The 1995 vintage (****) of this Martinborough wine is deep amber, with tense acidity threading through its rich, sweet, honeyish flavour. It's a very good wine, quite forward in its appeal, but lacks the intensity and arresting beauty of the '92.

PEGASUS BAY NOBLE SÉMILLON/ SAUVIGNON	VINTAGE	95	SW $20 (375ML) AV
	WR	5	(☆☆☆☆)
	DRINK	97-02	

Intended by the makers for serving with cheese, nuts and dried fruits, but not dessert, the barrique-aged 1995 vintage (****) is a gently sweet Waipara wine, deep amber, with rich, *Botrytis*/apricot aromas. It's a full-bodied, honied, moderately complex wine with a strong *Botrytis* influence, oily, weighty, rich and rounded.

PHOENIX DESSERT GEWÜRZTRAMINER

SW $17 (375ML) -V

(✩✩✩)

The golden 1994 vintage has some lush, apricot-like characters, with an underlay of spice, but it lacks a bit of freshness and vivacity, with a very sweet, soft finish. The pleasant although not striking '95 (***) is a freeze-concentrated Gisborne wine. Golden, with a restrained bouquet, it's a very crisp wine with plenty of sweet, gingery flavour.

RONGOPAI RES. BOTRYTISED RIESLING

	VINTAGE	93	92	91
	WR	7	NM	6
	DRINK	01	NM	P

SW $28 (375ML) AV

(✩✩✩✩✩)

A label descended from the Riesling Auslese, which in the mid-80s earned Rongopai fame for its rampantly botrytised Te Kauwhata sweet whites. The '93 vintage (*****) is an alluring beauty, gloriously scented. There have been no releases from the 1994–96 vintages, but 1996 produced three other dessert wines; see below.

RONGOPAI BOTRYTISED SELECTION

SW $19 (375ML) AV

(✩✩✩✩)

The golden 1996 vintage (****) is a Gisborne-grown blend of Müller-Thurgau and Riesling. It isn't intensely perfumed, but oily, honeyish and well-structured, with ample sweetness threaded with firm acidity. It should mature well; open 1998 onwards.

RONGOPAI WINEMAKERS SELECTION BOTRYTIS RESERVE

SW $32 (375ML) -V

(✩✩✩✩✩)

Grown in Gisborne and Te Kauwhata, the 1996 vintage (*****½) is a blend of unspecified grape varieties. Dark gold, it is an opulent wine, heavily botrytised and richly honied, with plentiful sweetness and balanced acidity, but fractionally less perfumed and classy than Rongopai's top dessert wines of the past.

RONGOPAI WINEMAKERS SELECTION TE KAUWHATA BOTRYTISED PINOT NOIR

SW $25 (375ML) -V

(✩✩✩)

A sweet Pinot Noir? Rongopai's 1996 vintage (***) is New Zealand's first dessert wine made from the great red grape of Burgundy. Still very youthful, it's not especially concentrated or lush, but has the strawberry/earthy flavours of Pinot Noir, overlaid with *Botrytis*-derived apricot/honey characters. Open 1998 onwards.

SACRED HILL XS NOBLE SELECTION

	VINTAGE	96
	WR	7
	DRINK	97-02

SW $18 (375ML) AV

(✩✩✩✩✩)

"XS" is a fun name, but the 1996 vintage (*****) is a serious Hawke's Bay sticky. A 2:1 blend of Riesling and Müller-Thurgau, it was bunch-selected in the Ohiti Valley at an average of over 33˚ brix. A golden, weighty (yet only 10 per cent alcohol) beauty with mouth-encircling, lemony, honeyish, botrytised-enriched flavour, it has balanced acidity and a long, succulent finish. Drink now onwards.

SAINTS MARL. *NOBLE* *RIESLING*								SW $18 (375ML) AV
VINTAGE	96							(☆ ☆☆☆)
WR	7							
DRINK	97-02							

The classy 1996 vintage (****) is slightly less treacly and *Botrytis*-affected than the '91, with stronger fruit flavours. Light gold, with a richly scented bouquet of lemons, apricots and honey, it is a bold, mouthfilling sweet wine with lively acidity and lush, clearly varietal, grapefruit/honey flavours.

SEIFRIED *ICE* *WINE*								SW $16 (375ML) V+
VINTAGE	96	95	94	93	92	91	90	☆☆☆↳
WR	5	4	7	6	6	6	7	
DRINK	97-01	97-00	97-02	97-00	P	P	P	

The winery's ripest grapes are hand-picked into trays, frozen, and then loaded into the press. When the berries thaw, the sweetest juice runs off first – like sucking an ice-block. The '96 (***1/2) is restrained on the nose, but this Nelson blend of Riesling and Gewürztraminer is mouthfilling and lush, with rich, citrusy, spicy, sweet flavours and good acid structure.

SELAKS *ICE* *WINE*								SW $11 (375ML) V+
VINTAGE	96	95	94	93	92	91	90	☆☆☆
WR	7	7	7	6	7	6	6	
DRINK	97-9	97-8	P	P	P	P	P	

"We sell a power of this wine," reports Michael Selak. The fresh, light and lively 1996 vintage (***1/2) is a Marlborough blend of Riesling (which comes through with time) and Gewürztraminer (which dominates in the wine's youth). Light gold, with strong, citrusy, spicy aromas and flavours, it's a steal at $11.

SOLJANS *AUCKLAND* *MUSCAT*	SW $15 (375ML) AV
	(☆☆☆)

An easy-drinking, drink-young style, the first 1996 vintage (***) is based on July Muscat grapes grown in West Auckland. The fresh, ripe, orange/musk fragrance leads into a full, sweet (72 grams/litre) wine with soft, delicate but not concentrated flavours.

STONECROFT *GEWÜRZTRAMINER* *LATE HARVEST*	SW $18 (375ML) V+
	(☆☆☆☆↳)

The 1994 vintage of this Hawke's Bay wine is lovely, with a soaring bouquet of pepper and honey and a rich, concentrated, lusciously fruity palate, chockful of flavour. The '95 is less intense, but still attractive. The 1996 vintage (*****) is clearly one of the best yet. Harvested at 30˚ brix and fermented in new French oak casks, it's an impressively weighty wine with a voluminous, spicy, earthy, rather Alsace-like fragrance. The palate is rich and subtle, with sweet, concentrated , complex, lingering flavours.

TE WHARE RA BOTRYTIS BERRY SELECTION CHARDONNAY/SÉMILLON

SW $21 (375ML) -V

(☆☆☆☆☆)

The '95 Botrytis Berry Selection Chardonnay is a rich, nectareous Marlborough wine with good acid spine, an oily texture and a long, succulent finish. The '96 blend (****¹/₂) evolved from the fact that winemaker Allen Hogan had insufficient Sémillon to keep as a separate sweet wine. It's a rare wine; only 55 cases were produced. Yellow/green in hue, it's moderately rich, with very ripe, non-herbaceous fruit flavours, fresh, lively acidity and some *Botrytis*-derived honey characters.

TE WHARE RA BOTRYTIS BUNCH/BERRY SELECTION RIESLING

SW $21 (375ML) AV

☆☆☆☆☆

"Bunch selection" refers to sweet wines based on grapes with less than 60 per cent *Botrytis* infection, "berry selection" to those with over 60 per cent. The 1991 vintage Berry Selection unfurled a ravishing spread of intense, citrusy, crisp, richly honeyed flavours. The 1995 Berry Selection (****¹/₂) is slightly less intense. Light gold, with a scented, honied bouquet, it is beautifully flavoursome and oily, crisp and sweet and full of character. (The '96 is a Gewürztraminer/Riesling blend.)

VIDAL RES. NOBLE SÉMILLON

VINTAGE	96	95	94
WR	7	NM	6
DRINK	98+	NM	97-8

SW $39 (375ML) -V

(☆☆☆☆☆⯪)

Vidal's first dessert wine is a botrytised, partly barrel-fermented 1994 Gisborne Sémillon, based on a new, non-virused clone which gives non-herbaceous fruit characters. It's a lovely, ripe wine, light (10.5 per cent alcohol), soft and gentle on the palate, with rich, honey-sweet flavours. The even better '96 (*****) is based on botrytised Bridge Pa, Hawke's Bay fruit, harvested at 42° brix and wood-aged for six months. The bouquet is very stylish and intriguing – honied, slightly oaky, complex and rich. Light gold, it's a weighty, oily, subtle wine with luscious lemon/honey flavours and a Sauternes-like concentration and structure.

VILLA MARIA RES. NOBLE RIESLING

VINTAGE	96	95	94	93	92	91
WR	7	NM	7	7	6	6
DRINK	97-05	NM	97-00	97-9	97-9	97-00

SW $31 (375ML) AV

☆☆☆☆☆

New Zealand's top sweet wine on the show circuit. The 1994 vintage, grown in Hawke's Bay, is exceptional, with a ravishing outpouring of citrusy, honeyish aromas and an oily, succulent palate with lemon, pear and honey-like flavours, sweet, taut and superbly sustained. The '96 (*****) was harvested in late May in three Marlborough vineyards at 35° to 42° brix. Ensconced in a soaring, see-through bottle, it is light gold, with a stunningly rich, honied perfume. Already very expressive and hard to resist, it's a superbly weighty, oily wine with intense, very sweet honey/citrus flavours and a steely, lush, long finish.

WAIRAU RIVER RESERVE BOTRYTISED RIESLING

SW $30 (375ML) AV

(☆☆☆☆☆)

Don't miss this! The gorgeous, partly oak-aged 1996 vintage (*****) was made from hand-selected, nobly rotten berries, harvested in Marlborough in late May at 43° brix. Light gold, it's a robust, treacly, rampantly botrytised wine with a ravishing fragrance of pears and honey. Weighty, with strikingly rich citrus/honey flavours and steely acidity, it should live for ages but is already hard to resist.

WALNUT RIDGE BOTRYTISED SAUV. BLANC

VINTAGE	96
WR	6
DRINK	97-05

SW $24 (375ML) -V

(☆☆☆☆)

Launched from the 1996 vintage (***1/2), this Martinborough wine is light yellow, with ripe, non-herbaceous fruit characters. It's a full-bodied wine, not oak-aged but with plenty of sweet, crisp and lively, honied flavour.

Sparkling Wines

"How good are the sparkling wines from overseas?" asked the German publication, *Der Feinschmecker*, in April 1997. When 35 bubblies from outside Europe – California, South Africa, South America, New Zealand and Australia – were compared in price and quality, "New Zealand came up the best". Nautilus Cuvée Marlborough was praised as "by far the best", followed immediately by Morton Brut, and Lindauer Brut also placed in the top ten.

Fizz, sparkling wine, bubbly – whatever name you call it by (the word Champagne is reserved for the wines of that most famous of all wine regions), wine with bubbles in it is universally adored.

New Zealand's sparkling wines can be divided into two key classes. The bottom end of the market is dominated by extremely sweet wines, three or four times sweeter than the average Müller-Thurgau. These are typically "carbonated" wines, which acquire their bubbles by being pumped through a carbonator, a long cylinder in which the wine and carbon-dioxide are mixed counter-currently. Other cheap sparkling wines build up their carbon-dioxide pressure by undergoing a secondary fermentation in a tank whose relief valve is kept tightly closed.

At the middle and top end of the market are the much drier, bottle-fermented, "méthode traditionnelle" (formerly "méthode champenoise", until the French got upset) labels of Montana, Cellier Le Brun, Corbans, Morton Estate, Selaks and others, in which the wine undergoes its secondary, bubble-creating fermentation not in a tank but in the bottle, as in Champagne itself. Ultimately, the quality of any fine sparkling wine is a reflection both of the standard of its base wine, and of its later period of maturation in the bottle in contact with its yeast lees. Only bottle-fermented sparkling wines possess the additional flavour richness and complexity derived from extended lees-aging.

Pinot Noir and Chardonnay, both varieties of pivotal importance in Champagne, are also the foundation of New Zealand's top sparkling wines (although Meunier, the least prestigious but most extensively planted grape in Champagne, is still rare here). Marlborough has emerged as the country's premier region for bottle-fermented sparkling wines (although Corbans has also achieved glowing success with Amadeus and Verde in Hawke's Bay). The piercing flavours and tense acidity of Marlborough fruit have attracted not only local producers, but such illustrious Champagne houses as Deutz (in an eye-catchingly successful joint venture with Montana) and Möet & Chandon (through its Australian subsidiary, Domaine Chandon).

The vast majority of sparkling wines are ready to drink when marketed, and need no extra maturation. A short spell in the cellar, however, can benefit the very best bottle-fermented sparklings.

AQUILA

M/SW $8 V+

(☆☆☆)

Corbans' fresh and lively bubbly is a medium-sweet style, blended from Muscat and Müller-Thurgau. Ensconced in an eye-catching frosted bottle, it's a crisp and fruity sparkling in a light, simple but charming style that offers very easy-drinking.

BERNADINO SPUMANTE

SW $7 V+

☆☆☆

What irresistible value! Montana's hugely popular Asti-style bubbly is based on 80 per cent Dr Hogg Muscat and 20 per cent Early White Muscat, grown in Gisborne . At 9.5 per cent, it's a higher alcohol style than most true Asti Spumantes (which average around 7.5 per cent) and less perfumed. It's a highly enjoyable, uncomplicated wine with a light, grapey, well-balanced palate, fruity, sweet and rounded.

CHARDON

SW $6 V+

☆☆☆

Montana's popular bubbly (a runaway success for Penfolds NZ in its heyday 15 years ago) is based on Müller-Thurgau and other grapes grown in New Zealand, blended with Australian wine. Backblended with unfermented Muscat Dr Hogg grapejuice to add sweetness and fragrance, it is a fruity, frothy, simple but pleasant mouthful.

CHIFNEY CHIFFONNAY

M/DRY $20 -V

(☆☆☆)

The first release of this bottle-fermented Martinborough bubbly was based on 1994 Chenin Blanc (predominantly) with Sauvignon Blanc and Muscat. Floral and straightforward on the nose, this is a fresh, crisp, fruity but simple wine that lacks complexity and richness. The latest release, from 1995 (but like its predecessor, not vintage-dated) is entirely Chenin Blanc. It's a light wine (10.5 per cent alcohol) with fruity lemon/apple flavours, fresh, crisp and pleasantly balanced, but simple, lacking yeast-derived complexity.

COOPERS CREEK FIRST EDITION

VINTAGE	94	93	92
WR	5	5	6
DRINK	P	P	P

M/DRY $22 -V

(☆☆☆☆)

"I'm not after a clean, lean style like Deutz Marlborough Cuvée – I prefer Pelorus," says winemaker Kim Crawford. The '93 is toasty, yeasty and citrusy in a very high-flavoured style. Obvious oak characters on the nose and palate detract from the otherwise stylish and intensely flavoured '94 (***¹/₂). A 50/50 blend of Chardonnay and Pinot Noir, grown in

Hawke's Bay (predominantly) and Marlborough, it was fermented and lees-aged in seasoned oak barrels prior to its secondary fermentation in the bottle. Light straw in hue, it is rich, toasty and buttery in a full-flavoured, moderately yeasty, fairly soft style.

CORBANS AMADEUS CLASSIC RES.

VINTAGE	93	92	91	90
WR	6	6	6	7
DRINK	97-02	97-00	97-8	P

M/DRY $17 V+

☆☆☆☆⯪

Why pay around $28 – the standard price for a top New Zealand bubbly – when this Hawke's Bay wine is just as good? The 1990 and 1991 vintages won gold medals at the Air New Zealand Wine Awards. The '92 (winner of last year's Best Buy of the Year award) is a stylish and subtle wine with a persistent "bead", crisp, vigorous, delicate fruit, strong, nutty yeast autolysis characters and a long, complex, slightly creamy finish. The '93 (****) is a Pinot Noir-dominant style, with just 3 per cent Chardonnay. Matured on its yeast lees for three years before disgorging, it is a pale straw wine with quite rich, toasty flavour, rounded and slightly creamy. As good as the striking '92? Not quite, but at around $17, it's still an irresistible bargain.

CORBANS DIVA MARLBOROUGH CUVÉE

MED $11 AV

(☆☆☆)

A distinctive wine, sweeter than the dry, bottle-fermented styles at the top end of the market, but markedly drier than the sweet wines at the bottom. A tank-fermented (charmat method) blend of Marlborough Riesling and Muscat, it is light and pale, with a floral, citrusy fragrance and lots of appley, lemony flavour, crisp and slightly sweet.

CORBANS VERDE

M/DRY $15 V+

(☆☆☆☆⯪)

Watch out Lindauer... here comes Verde! Launched last year, this vivacious $15 bubbly sensationally scooped the trophy for overall champion wine of the 1996 Air New Zealand Wine Awards. Verde builds on Corbans' tradition of irresistibly well-priced bottle-fermented Hawke's Bay sparklings, established by Amadeus. Made from Pinot Noir and Chardonnay, it displays an enticingly yeasty, nutty fragrance. The palate is very crisp and lively, with a delicious balance and depth of citrusy, appley, yeasty flavours, subtle and slightly creamy. A magnificent buy.

DANIEL LE BRUN BLANC DE BLANCS

M/DRY $35 AV

☆☆☆☆☆

Despite the absence of Pinot Noir and Meunier, this very classy, all-Chardonnay Marlborough wine is still a mouthfilling style. The 1991 vintage is very distinctive: bold, upfront, with a voluminous fragrance and extremely high flavour; rich, citrusy and toasty on the nose; vigorous, yeasty, toasty and dry on the palate, with taut acidity and great intensity. This is an exciting and delicious mouthful. The '92 (****1/2) is a typically powerful wine with pale gold colour, a rich bouquet, substantial body and a strong surge of buttery, yeasty, toasty flavour. (To remove the wine from direct competition with the cheaper, sub-$50 Champagnes, its price was lowered this year from $45 to $35.)

DANIEL LE BRUN BRUT TACHÉ

M/DRY $27 AV

(☆☆☆☆)

This weighty, full-flavoured, non-vintage Marlborough wine is taché (stained) with the colour of Pinot Noir grapes, on which it is wholly based. Onion skin in hue, it's impressively full and yeasty, with strong raspberryish, earthy flavours in a complex, lively, creamy-soft style.

DANIEL LE BRUN CUVÉE ADELE

M/DRY $35 AV

(☆☆☆☆☆)

Dedicated by Daniel Le Brun (who left Cellier Le Brun in mid 1996) to his wife, Adele, this is a Chardonnay-predominant blend, lees-aged for several years. At a mid-1997 tasting of the Le Brun range of sparklings, the very refined, rich 1990 Cuvée Adele was the highlight. Golden, with a highly toasty bouquet, the 1990 vintage (*****) is a high impact wine, generously flavoured, crisp, yeasty and complex, with a rich finish. Both the '89 and '90 flourished with cellaring.

DANIEL LE BRUN MÉTHODE TRADITIONNELLE BRUT NV

M/DRY $28 V+

☆☆☆☆☆

Daniel Le Brun (who resigned from Cellier Le Brun last year) prefers "gutsy" sparkling wines and it shows in this typically rich-flavoured, toasty, characterful bubbly. For this big-selling, non-vintage label, Le Brun used 60 per cent Marlborough Pinot Noir, blended with 30 per cent Chardonnay and 10 per cent Meunier. Matured for two years on its yeast lees, in the past it was an exciting mouthful: light gold, with a persistent "bead" and layers of rich, nutty, meaty, yeasty flavour. Its quality slipped during 1996, but is now back on form. The wine I tasted in mid-1997 was made by Daniel Le Brun, but disgorged and liqueured by Allan McWilliams, the new winemaker. Impressively lively, crisp, yeasty and full-flavoured, it's lighter in colour and fresher, less oxidative in style than in the past, with a steady "bead" and fragrant, strawberryish aromas. A good buy.

DANIEL LE BRUN VINTAGE MÉTHODE TRADITIONNELLE BRUT

M/DRY $35 AV

☆☆☆☆☆

His vintage wines were Daniel Le Brun's own favourites. The Vintage Brut, blended from Pinot Noir and Chardonnay, is matured on its yeast lees longer than the non-vintage Méthode Champenoise Brut. This is a richer, deeper-flavoured, more complex wine than the non-vintage label. The explosively flavoured 1990 is one of the greatest bubblies ever produced in New Zealand. Slightly less intense than the exciting '90, the '91 is still impressively rich and smooth, full and broad, with earthy, strawberryish flavour and very good complexity and length. The '92 (****1/2) tasted soon after disgorging, is an excellent wine, but again slightly less powerful than the '90, reflecting the cool vintage. Light straw, with a rich, yeasty fragrance, it's a fresh, lively wine with strawberryish, appley, subtle flavours.

DEUTZ MARLBOROUGH CUVÉE BLANC DE BLANCS

M/DRY $35 -V

(☆☆☆☆⯪)

The 1990 was the first batch of this Chardonnay-dominated wine (5 per cent Pinot Noir) to be vintage-dated. Matured for several years on its yeast lees, it is an elegant cool-climate style with delicate, piercing, lemon/apple flavours, well-integrated yeastiness and a slightly creamy finish. The 1991 vintage (*****) is currently at the height of its powers, with superbly rich flavour. The '94 (the first release since the '91) was tasted soon after disgorging. A pale, scented wine with lively lemon/lime flavours and delicate yeast autolysis, it clearly needs time; open mid 1998 onwards. (Don't miss the salmon-pink, excitingly rich Deutz Marlborough Cuvée Blanc de Noirs, a Pinot Noir-based bubbly to be launched from the 1994 vintage.)

DEUTZ MARLBOROUGH CUVÉE

M/DRY $28 V+

☆☆☆☆☆

The marriage of Montana's fruit at Marlborough with the Champagne house of Deutz's 150 years of experience created an instant winner. Bottled-fermented and matured on its yeast lees for two and a half years, this non-vintage wine is evolving towards a less overtly fruity, more delicate and flinty style. Production is running at around 40,000 cases per year, yet finesse is its key achievement. The current release, a marriage of 60 per cent Pinot Noir and 40 per cent Chardonnay, is stylish and searching on the nose, with intense, delicate, vigorous, nutty, yeasty flavours and a long, fractionally sweet finish. A classic cool-climate style, beautifully balanced, penetratingly flavoured and lingering.

DOM. CHANDON MARLBOROUGH BRUT

VINTAGE	94	93
WR	7	6
DRINK	97-00	97-8

M/DRY $33 V+

(☆☆☆☆☆)

After the impressive 1990 debut, the next two vintages of this Marlborough sparkling from Möet & Chandon's Australian subsidiary, Domaine Chandon, showed significant improvement. The 1993 (*****) consolidates the great reputation of the '92, and these vintages are the finest sparkling wines ever made in New Zealand. A marriage of 54 per cent Pinot Noir, 32 per cent Chardonnay and 14 per cent Meunier, the '93 is excitingly concentrated and rich. The bouquet is beguilingly scented; the palate stylish and extremely intense, with layers of intricate, yeasty flavour, very subtle, smooth and sustained. A wonderfully classy and "complete" wine. Don't miss it.

MED $10 V+

☆☆☆⯪

FRICANTE

An easy-drinking, slightly sweet bubbly from Montana which (surprisingly, given its simple style and low price) has been bottle-fermented. A Gisborne-grown blend of 50 per cent Early White Muscat and 50 per cent Dr Hogg Muscat, it reveals a scented, floral bouquet and charmingly fresh, fruity, delicate, crisp flavours, harbouring a distinct splash of sweetness. It tastes like an upmarket, markedly drier version of Bernadino Spumante.

GIESEN VOYAGE

M/DRY $22 -V

(☆☆☆☆⯪)

Giesen's new bottle-fermented sparkling (***¹/₂) is a non-vintage, Pinot Noir-dominated (only 3 per cent Chardonnay) blend of 70 per cent Marlborough and 30 per cent Canterbury fruit, lees-aged for two years. "We want a broad style, for drinking with food," says winemaker Marcel Giesen. Pale straw, it's a fruity, buttery wine with a lively "bead" and a touch of yeast-derived richness, but not highly complex.

GILLAN BRUT RESERVE

M/DRY $26 AV

(☆☆☆☆)

The 1992 vintage was an auspicious debut – a stylish wine with searching, citrusy, yeasty, nutty flavours and a long, crisp, rich finish. The '93 (****) is a 70/30 blend of Marlborough Chardonnay and Pinot Noir, lees-aged for two years. Light gold, it is an easy-drinking style, full and lively, with excellent depth of buttery, citrusy, moderately yeasty flavour and a fractionally sweet and creamy finish.

HIGHFIELD ELSTREE CUVÉE

VINTAGE	93
WR	6
DRINK	97-00

M/DRY $35 -V

(☆☆☆☆)

The Champagne house of Drappier had a technical input into this Marlborough winery's first 1993 vintage bubbly (****). A very fresh and lively blend of 55 per cent Pinot Noir and 45 per cent Chardonnay, it is an elegant wine with delicate, green apple-like aromas and flavours, a creamy texture, moderate complexity and a slightly sweet, appetisingly crisp finish. With age, it is developing greater subtlety and richness.

HUNTER'S BRUT

VINTAGE	93	92	91	90
WR	6	6	5	6
DRINK	98	P	P	P

M/DRY $30 AV

☆☆☆☆

Hunter's best-kept secret, this consistently classy Marlborough wine is bottle-fermented and aged on its yeast lees for two and a half years. The 1992 vintage, half Chardonnay, half Pinot Noir and Meunier, is full and vigorous, with loads of citrusy, yeasty, nutty flavour and a slightly creamy, long finish. The '94 (****¹/₂) is pale straw, with a toasty, yeasty fragrance and broad, generous palate with rich, buttery, yeasty, lingering flavour.

HYLAND MÉTHODE TRADITIONNELLE BRUT

M/DRY $9 V+

(☆☆☆)

At its low price, this is a bargain. Produced by Montana, it is a bottle-fermented sparkling based on white grape varieties (no Pinot Noir) including Chasselas, and matured on its yeast lees for a year. Tasted in mid-1997, it's a decent but uncomplicated bubbly, light and delicate, with a touch of yeastiness and crisp, lively, slightly sweet finish.

ITALIANO
SPUMANTE

SW $6 V+

☆☆☆

"The fun starts here!" – with Corbans' Asti-Spumante look-alike. Based on Gisborne-grown Muscat, it is a light bubbly (8.5 per cent alcohol) with a grapey, musky perfume, gentle stream of bubbles and fresh, soft, grapey-sweet flavours.

	VINTAGE	92
JACKSON | WR | 5 |
VINTAGE | DRINK | 97-00 |

M/DRY $37 AV

(☆☆☆☆☆)

The first 1992 vintage (*****) of this Marlborough wine – still on the market – is a triumph. Estate-grown, it is a blend of 60 per cent Chardonnay and 40 per cent Pinot Noir, hand-harvested, whole bunch-pressed and matured on its yeast lees for two and a half years. It is very perfumed and stylish on the nose, with a lively, tight-knit palate and concentrated, flinty, complex flavours, impressively delicate, subtle and persistent.

	VINTAGE	92	91
JOHAN. CELLARS | | | |
EMMI MÉTHODE | WR | 5 | 4 |
CHAMPEN. BRUT | DRINK | 97-00 | 97-00 |

M/DRY $32 -V

(☆☆☆)

The scented, steely 1992 vintage (***) from this tiny Koromiko (Marlborough) winery is a blend of 60 per cent Chardonnay and 40 per cent Pinot Noir, matured on its lees for three years. The bouquet is strong, appley and nutty; the palate penetrating, limey and green-edged, with moderate yeast autolysis and a freshly acidic finish in a distinctly cool-climate style.

LIMEBURNERS
BAY THE
GOVERNOR

DRY $20 AV

(☆☆☆☆)

Named after William Hobson, the first governor of New Zealand, the 1993 vintage (***1/2) of this bottle-fermented bubbly is a good effort. A West Auckland blend of 80 per cent Pinot Noir and 20 per cent Chardonnay, it has a steady bead and a strong-flavoured, bone-dry palate, well-balanced and lively.

LINDAUER
BRUT

M/DRY $11 V+

☆☆☆☆

A three star-plus wine at a two-star price is a bargain in anyone's language. Montana's recipe for this hugely popular (in New Zealand and the UK) bottle-fermented bubbly is 50 per cent Pinot Noir, 25 per cent Chardonnay and 25 per cent Chenin Blanc, grown in Marlborough, Hawke's Bay and Gisborne, and matured on its yeast lees for 18 months. It's deliciously light and delicate, with a yeasty, strawberryish, slightly flinty flavour and mouth-wateringly crisp, impressively long and subtle finish. Amazing quality for $11.

LINDAUER ROSÉ

M/DRY $11 V+

(☆☆☆)

Montana's sparkling rosé, which gains its colour from brief skin contact with Pinot Noir grapes, is grown in Marlborough and Gisborne and bottle-fermented and lees-matured for at least 18 months. The colour is a youthful, bright pink; the palate light and fresh, with a touch of yeastiness in its raspberryish, appetisingly crisp flavour.

LINDAUER SEC

MED $11 V+

(☆☆☆)

The "Sec" version of Lindauer, a small production run for those with a sweeter tooth, is made from the same blend of grapes and vinified the same way as the Brut model (above). Harbouring about the same level of sugar as an average Müller-Thurgau, this is an elegant, light, lemony, delicate wine with a distinct touch of sweetness.

LINDAUER SPECIAL RESERVE

M/DRY $16 V+

(☆☆☆☆)

Packaged in a bulbous Italian bottle, Montana's hugely drinkable non-vintage wine is a blend of 70 per cent Pinot Noir and 30 per cent Chardonnay, grown in Hawke's Bay and Marlborough, given a full malolactic fermentation and matured *en tirage* (on its yeast lees) for two years. Pale pink, it is a distinctly Pinot Noir-dominant style with strong, strawberryish, slightly earthy flavours, delicate, yeasty, lively and smooth. A delicious mouthful and bargain-priced.

LINTZ EST. RIESLING BRUT

DRY $35 -V

(☆☆☆⚡)

Chris Lintz uses Riesling, rather than the customary Pinot Noir/Chardonnay combination, for his bottle-fermented Martinborough bubbly in order to achieve "a more exciting, appetising start to a meal, rather than the more mealy, fatter Champagne styles". The 1994 vintage (***¹/₂) is a mouth-wateringly crisp and high-flavoured wine with a very attractive, fragrant, slightly yeasty Riesling bouquet. The palate shows penetrating lemon/lime characters, light yeast autolysis and a slightly sweet finish. An excellent aperitif.

MARQUE VUE

SW $6 V+

☆☆⚡

A famous old McWilliam's brand now kept alive by Corbans, designed for consumers who want "a non-intimidating wine with no complexity or variation". Re-tasted in 1997, it is a trans-Tasman blend with strong, sweet, lemon/lime flavours and a slightly toasty character that reminded me of Spanish *cava*. Better than expected.

MARQUE VUE PINK

`SW $6 AV`

☆☆

This long-established label is a trans-Tasman blend marketed by the Corbans subsidiary, International Cellars. Deep pink in colour, it has a lifted, fresh, floral bouquet and a light, frothy, sweet, raspberryish palate, simple but pleasant.

MATUA NINETEEN NINETY-TWO BRUT

`M/DRY $25 AV`

☆☆☆☆

A golden, rich, smooth wine grown in Marlborough (predominantly) and Auckland. A 70/30 blend of Pinot Noir and Chardonnay, it was matured on its yeast lees for three years. Bold in style, it is fragrant, toasty and soft, with generous, yeasty, slightly buttery flavours and impressive complexity and length.

MILLS REEF

VINTAGE	94	93	92	91	90
WR	7	NM	7	6	6
DRINK	97-01	NM	97-00	97-8	97-8

`M/DRY $30 AV`

☆☆☆☆½

Simply labelled "Mills Reef", past vintages of this barrel and then bottle-fermented Hawke's Bay sparkling were a strikingly rich and creamy celebration of Chardonnay fruit flavours, overlaid with nutty oak and yeast-derived complexity. The '92 is a more elegant wine, with greater delicacy and finesse. Pale gold, with a scented, citrusy, nutty fragrance, it is a bold, highly characterful wine with searching, biscuity flavour, impressive yeast-derived complexity and a long, rich finish. The 1994 vintage (*****) is outstanding, with a very yeasty fragrance and searching, complex, tight-knit, dry flavour in a very Champagne-like style.

MILLS REEF CHARISMA

`M/DRY $20 V+`

(☆☆☆☆)

Here's a great buy! This classy non-vintage wine is a barrel and bottle-fermented blend of Hawke's Bay Pinot Noir (60 per cent) and Chardonnay, given a full malolactic fermentation and disgorged from its yeast lees after 12 to 18 months. Pale and delicate, it's a subtle, tight-knit, intensely flavoured wine with flinty, appley, biscuity flavours and a fractionally sweet, lingering finish.

MONT ROYAL MEDIUM

`SW $6 AV`

(☆☆)

A cheap sparkling made by "the Mont Royal Wine Co" (a subsidiary of Montana) for those with a sweet tooth. A mix of New Zealand and imported wine with very low (5.8 per cent) alcohol, it offers a gentle stream of bubbles, a shy bouquet and a light, very grapey and sweet, soft palate.

MONT ROYAL PINK

`SW $6 AV`

(☆☆)

Montana's pink-red bubbly is a low-alcohol (5.8 per cent) blend of local and imported wine. Boldly coloured, it is frothy, grapey and sweet, clean and fresh, raspberryish and soft.

MORTON BRUT

`M/DRY $19 V+`

(☆☆☆⟆)

Registering very highly on the drinkability scale, Morton Estate's lower-tier bottle-fermented sparkling is a non-vintage blend of 33 per cent Chardonnay and 20 per cent Meunier, grown in Hawke's Bay, with 47 per cent Marlborough Pinot Noir. Lees-aged for a year, it is fresh and lively, crisp and well-balanced, with a delicate yeastiness, good depth of strawberryish, slightly earthy flavours and a firm, flinty finish. A delicious aperitif.

MORTON EST. BL. LAB. MÉTHODE CHAMPENOISE

VINTAGE	91
WR	6
DRINK	98-9

`M/DRY $35 -V`

(☆☆☆⟆)

Morton's first Black Label sparkling, from the 1991 vintage (***½), is an easy-drinking style with a touch of complexity. The base wine – 65 per cent Bay of Plenty Pinot Noir, 30 per cent Hawke's Bay Chardonnay and 5 per cent Meunier – was French oak-matured for nine months, then bottle-fermented and lees-aged for 2½ years. It's a good wine – light and elegant, appley and slightly nutty, with a fractionally sweet, crisp finish – but a bit disappointing, given its high price and black label status.

MORTON EST. VINTA. METH. CHAMPENOISE

VINTAGE	96	95	94	93	92	91	90
WR	5	4	NM	NM	6	4	5
DRINK	00-03	99-01	NM	NM	97-8	P	P

`M/DRY $26 -V`

☆☆☆☆⟆

Typically a classy wine, its delicate fruit intermeshed with mature yeast autolysis characters. The 1991 vintage (***) is a blend of 70 per cent Pinot Noir and 30 per cent Chardonnay, grown in Hawke's Bay and the Bay of Plenty and lees-aged for three and a half years. Light yellow in hue, this is a brisk wine, less memorable than some earlier vintages, with strong, citrusy, slightly limey flavours, moderate yeastiness and an invigoratingly crisp finish.

NAUTILUS CUVÉE MARLBOROUGH

`M/DRY $28 AV`

☆☆☆☆☆

With this outstanding, non-vintage bottle-fermented sparkling, Nautilus want "an aperitif style rather than a food wine, elegance rather than richness, creaminess rather than steeliness". The batch on the market during most of 1997, based on 75 per cent Pinot Noir and 25 per cent Chardonnay, is probably the finest yet – very refined and fragrant, with rich citrus/yeast flavours, very crisp, firm and sustained. The batch being released in late 1997 was produced principally from 1995 base wine. Tasted soon after disgorging, it's a tightly structured wine with lively acidity, impressive delicacy of flavour and lovely yeast-derived bready characters, continuing the label's evolution to greater intensity.

PARKER
CLASSICAL
BRUT

DRY $28 -V

☆☆☆⛬

This rare, Gisborne bottle-fermented wine is blended from Pinot Noir and Chardonnay, with some primary (alcoholic) fermentation in seasoned oak barrels. Matured for a long period on its yeast lees before disgorging, it is typically several years old when released, yet still very fresh, lively and crisp, with appley, biscuity, strongly yeasty flavours in a bone-dry, slightly austere style.

PARKER
DRY
FLINT

DRY $18 AV

☆☆☆

This non-vintage, bottle-fermented Gisborne wine is 50 per cent Sémillon and 50 per cent Chenin Blanc – a rare blend on which to base a bubbly. It's a slightly austere style with herbal, tangy, yeasty, bone-dry flavours.

	VINTAGE	93	92	91	90
	WR	5	5	6	6
PELORUS	DRINK	98	P	P	P

M/DRY $40 AV

☆☆☆☆☆

Cloudy Bay's bottle-fermented sparkling is typically a very powerful wine, creamy, nutty and excitingly full-flavoured. The '91 is broad and seamless on the palate, intense and complex, with great finesse and a long, powerful finish. The robust, equally refined 1992 vintage (*****) was given its primary alcoholic fermentation in a mixture of stainless steel tanks, large oak vats and oak barrels, followed by spontaneous, complete malolactic fermentation and a nine-month period of aging on yeast lees prior to blending. After the final *assemblage* of 58 per cent Pinot Noir and 42 per cent Chardonnay, the wine was bottle-aged for three years on its yeast lees. The '92 continues the evolution to a less lush, buttery and toasty, more complex and taut style seen in the '91. A mouthfilling, bold, masculine style with superbly rich, intricate flavours, strong yeast characters, firm acidity and a slightly creamy texture, it rivals the '91 as the finest Pelorus yet.

PLEASANT VALLEY
SIGNATURE SELECTION
BRUT

M/DRY $22 AV

(☆☆☆⛬)

The smooth Brut '94 is Pleasant Valley's first bottle-fermented sparkling. A blend of Hawke's Bay Pinot Noir and Chardonnay, aged on its yeast lees for 18 months, it is scented, although not highly complex, on the nose, with a delicate, slightly sweet, crisp and lively palate showing a touch of yeast-derived subtlety. The '95 (****) is attractively lively and crisp, with smooth, delicate, yeasty, lingering flavour.

	VINTAGE	96
ROB. & BUT.	WR	7
CHARD. MARL.	DRINK	97-9
CUVÉE		

MED $10 AV

(☆☆⛬)

The debut 1996 vintage (**½) is a real style departure. Produced by the "charmat" (enclosed tank fermentation) method, it is a pale wine with fresh, green-edged aromas. The palate is very fresh and youthful, with crisp, green apple-evoking flavours in a simple and slightly sweet style.

SEIFRIED SEKT

MED $9 V+

☆☆⛢

An easy-drinking, medium-sweet bubbly, based on Riesling (a rare practice in New Zealand, but entirely successful here), blended with Sylvaner and Sémillon. Grown in Nelson and Marlborough, it's scented, light, crisp and vibrantly fruity: a delicious middle-of-the-road style.

SELAKS MATE I SELAK BLANC DE BLANCS

M/DRY $29 AV

☆☆☆☆

This label is a tribute to Mate Selak, a tenacious pioneer of New Zealand bottle-fermented sparkling wines. The fragrant, stylish, intensely flavoured 1990 vintage (****) is based wholly on Auckland Chardonnay, briefly oak-aged, bottle-fermented and then matured for four years on its yeast lees. A bold style, it is maturing well, with strong, crisp, lemony, lively flavours, well-developed yeastiness and a firm, lingering finish. A characterful wine, now at its peak.

SELAKS MÉTHODE TRADITIONNELLE BRUT

M/DRY $22 AV

☆☆☆☆

This impressively full-flavoured, non-vintage bubbly is a Marlborough blend of 55 per cent Chardonnay and 45 per cent Pinot Noir, lees-aged for over two years. Rich, toasty and earthy on the nose, it is full, complex and yeasty on the palate, with appetising acidity and a long, satisfying finish.

SOLJANS MOMENTO

SW $10 V+

(☆☆☆☆)

In the past labelled as Vivace, this very refreshing and more-ish Asti-style sparkling is based entirely on Dr Hogg Muscat grapes grown in Hawke's Bay. The richly scented bouquet leads into a delicious, vibrantly fruity palate, sweet and crisp, with strong, ripe Muscat flavours and loads of varietal character.

SOLJANS LEGACY

DRY $18 AV

(☆☆☆)

This small Henderson producer's debut bottle-fermented sparkling from the 1994 vintage is an easy-drinking style based on 70 per cent Pinot Noir and 30 per cent Chardonnay, grown in Hawke's Bay and given a full, softening malolactic fermentation. Straw/pink in hue, it is a fruity, soft-structured wine, moderately yeasty, with pleasing depth of lemony, buttery, toasty flavour. The '95 (**1/2) is pale, light, appley and crisp in a very delicate style that lacks flavour richness.

TWIN ISLANDS MARLBOROUGH BRUT

M/DRY $17 V+

☆☆☆⯪

The latest release (****) is a markedly better bottle-fermented sparkling than previous batches under this label. Negociants' mid-priced blend of 50 per cent Chardonnay, 30 per cent Pinot Noir and 20 per cent Chenin Blanc (principally from the 1995 vintage) is pale pink, with a strongly yeasty, delicately fruity, tight-knit and smooth palate. A real touch of finesse.

TWIN RIVERS

M/DRY $18 AV

☆☆☆

Delicate, dryish and invigoratingly crisp, this non-vintage, bottle-fermented bubbly is grown in Montana's Twin Rivers vineyard and made at The McDonald Winery in Hawke's Bay. A Chardonnay/Pinot Noir blend, lees-aged for two years, it's an elegant wine, not intense, but offering quite good depth of lemony, appley, moderately yeasty flavours.

VIDAL BLANC DE BLANCS

M/DRY $27 -V

(☆☆☆⯪)

All Chardonnay-based, the 1990 vintage (***) of this Hawke's Bay wine is still fresh, with delicate, lemony, appley flavours in a moderately yeasty, fairly straightforward style that lacks great complexity.

VIDAL BLANC DE NOIRS

M/DRY $27 -V

(☆☆☆⯪)

The smooth, subtle 1990 vintage (***½) is based exclusively on Hawke's Bay Pinot Noir. Pink-hued, with strawberryish aromas, it is slightly earthy, delicately flavoured and crisp, with "bready" yeast characters and good length.

VIDAL BRUT

VINTAGE	91	90
WR	6	6
DRINK	97-8	97-8

M/DRY $28 -V

(☆ ☆☆☆)

The delicious, beautifully balanced and harmonious 1990 vintage is a Hawke's Bay sparkling based on 64 per cent Chardonnay and 36 per cent Pinot Noir. Pale, full and soft, with a slightly creamy texture, it is a complex and delicately flavoured wine with fractional sweetness and a long, rich finish. The '96 (****) is also stylish, fresh and lively, with a richly yeasty fragrance and delicate, citrusy, nutty flavours of impressive depth.

Sherries

The word "sherry" is starting to disappear from the labels of local fortified wines, as the result of New Zealand's (still uncompleted) negotiations with the EC to protect regional wine names. True sherry comes from the searingly hot Jerez de la Frontera and Sanlucar de Barrameda regions on the Mediterranean south coast of Spain.

New Zealand "sherry", a fortified wine style with an average of 18 per cent alcohol, in the past enjoyed huge popularity. But our climate lacks the heat necessary to produce great fortified wines. Winemakers here have sought to compensate for their grapes' relative lack of natural lusciousness and sweetness by making heavy additions of sugar; hence most New Zealand sherries lack fruit character and merely taste like rather neutral fortified wines.

Many sherries are still produced by small, low-profile wineries with a strictly local clientele. The wines below all rank among the finer quality labels.

CELLARMANS EXTRA SPECIAL SHERRY

SW $9 V+

☆☆☆

Corbans are currently sourcing some of their leading fortified wines from Australia, but this is their top New Zealand sherry. The pale brown, seven-year-old Extra Special is a sweet style with a very smooth, creamy, slightly nutty palate.

MONTANA FLOR FINO

DRY $9 AV

☆☆☆

A pungently yeasty dry sherry produced by the "submerged flor" technique, whereby the wine doesn't acquire its distinctive flor character in the traditional way of being covered by a film of flor yeast, but by having flor yeast and oxygen pumped into it under pressure. It is important to avoid old stocks which have lost their fresh piquancy.

NGATARAWA OLD SADDLERS SHERRY

MED $12 V+

☆☆☆☆

Ngatarawa is one of the very few Hawke's Bay wineries to produce fortified wines. This light gold sherry is in the amontillado style. The blend now on the market is a very full-flavoured, medium-sweet wine with impressive mellowness and complexity derived from barrel-aging for over 10 years. Well worth buying.

OKAHU ESTATE DON DE MONTE OLOROSO SHERRY

SW $19 AV

(☆☆☆☆½)

The only sherry to win a medal (bronze) at the 1996 Air New Zealand Wine Awards, this Northland wine has been oak-aged for seven years. Amber-green, with fragrant "rancio" characters, it's rich and raisiny, sweet and complex in a very warm and satisfying style. One of the finest New Zealand sherries for a long time.

PLEASANT VALLEY AMONTILLADO SHERRY

M/DRY $10 V+

☆☆☆☆

When "Steppie" Yelas took over the reins of this old Henderson winery in 1984, following the death of his father, Moscow, he inherited hundreds of barrels of well-aged sherries and ports. Mature yellow-brown in hue, this is a nutty, dryish style with aged, "rancio" complexity and a rich and persistent flavour.

PLEASANT VALLEY AMOROSO SHERRY

MED $10 V+

☆☆☆☆

An amber-hued, medium-sweet style which displays the aged character typical of all Pleasant Valley's fortifieds, with plenty of "rancio" complexity and a rich, creamy-smooth flavour.

PLEASANT VALLEY OLOROSO SHERRY

SW $10 V+

☆☆☆☆

A great buy. Described by owner "Steppie" Yelas as "the nearest thing to Harvey's Bristol Cream", it has all the signs of lengthy cask-aging: a tawny hue and a raisiny-sweet, creamy, mellow, lingering palate, rich and mature.

SOLJANS PERGOLA SHERRY

SW $18 AV

☆☆☆☆

This raisiny-rich sweet sherry, produced from Palomino and Black Hamburg (normally eating) grapes grown in Soljans' estate vineyard at Henderson, is matured for between 10 and 15 years in old brandy barrels. After such patient aging, it emerges very tawny in colour, with a luscious mellowness and much more "rancio" complexity than most New Zealand sherries.

SOLJANS RESERVE SHERRY

SW $10 V+

☆☆☆

Junior to the Pergola Sherry (above), this Reserve label is matured for an average of eight years in native totara casks. Light tawny in hue, it has acquired less rancio complexity than the older Pergola Sherry, but is appealingly creamy-sweet.

Rosé and Blush Wines

Pink wines don't attract much attention in New Zealand, from the winemakers or wine drinkers. Only 17 rosés and blush wines were entered in last year's Air New Zealand Wine Awards and they collected just four medals – including a gold for Esk Valley Merlot Rosé 1996.

Don't blush if you can't tell the difference between a rosé and a blush wine. There is a style divergence, but in the glass it can be fun and games trying to tell them apart.

In Europe many pink or copper-coloured wines (like the rosés of Provence, Anjou and Tavel) are produced from red-wine varieties. Dark-skinned grapes are even used to make white wines: Champagne, heavily based on Meunier and Pinot Noir, is a classic case.

To make a rosé, after the grapes are crushed, the time the juice spends in contact with its skins is crucial; the longer the contact, the greater the diffusion of colour and other extractives from the skins into the juice. A rosé is typically held longer on the skins than a blush wine, picking up more colour, tannin and flavour. (The organisers of the Liquorland Royal Easter Wine Show stipulate that blush wines ought to be "made in the white wine style from varieties with some red pigmentation", whereas rosés should exhibit "red varietal character, and not just be coloured versions of white wine, e.g. blush".)

Cabernet Sauvignon, Cabernet Franc, Pinot Noir and (more and more) Merlot are the grape varieties most commonly used in New Zealand to produce rosé and blush wines. These are typically charming, "now-or-never" wines, peaking in their first 18 months with seductive strawberry/raspberry-like fruit flavours and crisp, appetising acidity. Freshness is the essence of the wines' appeal.

ALPHA DOMUS ROSÉ	VINTAGE	97	96			DRY $14 AV
	WR	6	6			(☆☆☆☆☆)
	DRINK	97-9	97-8			

The mouthfilling first 1996 vintage (***1/2) of this Hawke's Bay rosé is a blend of Merlot, Malbec and Cabernet Franc, briefly fermented on its skins. Bright raspberry/pink, it is fresh and weighty, with strong, raspberryish flavours, noticeable alcohol and a rounded, dry finish. Good drinking now to 1997.

ATA RANGI SUMMER ROSÉ	VINTAGE	97	96	95	94	M/DRY $16 AV
	WR	6	6	6	6	(☆☆☆☆☆)
	DRINK	97-8	P	P	P	

This delightful Martinborough wine is based on Cabernet Sauvignon, Merlot and a bit of Syrah: "A petit Célèbre, I suppose," says proprietor Phyll Pattie. At its best it is pink-hued, full, fresh and vivacious, with just a sliver of sweetness amid its rich yet delicate, strawberryish flavours. The '96 (****1/2) is a tyically lovely wine with a bright pink hue, good weight and soft, ripe raspberry/strawberry flavours.

CHARD FARM
PINOT
ROSÉ

M/DRY $13 AV

(☆☆☆)

The Hay brothers' 1996 Central Otago rosé (***) is a blend of 85 per cent Pinot Noir with 15 per cent Cabernet Sauvignon, Merlot and Cabernet Franc (for "weight and backbone"). Bright pink-red, it's an attractive, buoyant wine with slight sweetness and lively acidity amid its fresh, strong berryish flavours.

CHASSEUR
ROSÉ

MED $15 (3L) AV

(☆☆☆)

In a tasting of cask wines, this bright, pretty pink rosé from Corbans performed strongly. Crisp and lively, it more closely approaches a white than red-wine style with its fresh, floral scents and pleasant, light, slightly sweet, strawberryish flavours.

CLEARVIEW
ESTATE
BLUSH

VINTAGE	96	95
WR	6	5
DRINK	97-8	P

DRY $12 V+

(☆☆☆☆)

The 1996 vintage (***1/2) is based on Chambourcin, a superior French hybrid. A buoyant Hawke's Bay wine with light, pink/orange colour, it is quite weighty and generous, with fresh, strong flavour, balanced acid and a dryish finish.

ESK VALLEY
MERLOT
ROSÉ

VINTAGE	97	96	95	94	93	92	91
WR	6	7	7	6	5	5	7
DRINK	97-8	97-8	P	P	P	P	P

DRY $12 V+

(☆☆☆☆)

A "serious" Hawke's Bay rosé – but that doesn't prevent it being deliciously crisp and lively, with fragrant red berry-fruit aromas and an abundance of flavour. The 1996 vintage (****1/2) triumphed at last year's Air New Zealand Wine Awards – the first rosé to collect a gold since 1990. Strong, fresh raspberryish scents lead into a full-bodied palate (harbouring 13.5 per cent alcohol) with rich, smooth berry-fruit flavours and a fractionally off-dry, well-rounded finish.

FORREST EST.
MARLBOROUGH
ROSÉ

VINTAGE	96
WR	6
DRINK	97-8

M/DRY $14 V+

☆☆☆☆☆

At its best, this is a bright pink, enticingly fragrant Marlborough rosé, very fresh and charming. "I aim it to be perfect on New Year's Day [after the vintage]," says John Forrest. Based on Cabernet Sauvignon, Merlot and Cabernet Franc, the 1997 vintage (****) is typically fresh and lively, with ripe, raspberryish scents and flavours in a deliciously crisp, buoyant style.

HAU
ARIKI
ROSÉ

M/DRY $16 -V

(☆☆☆)

The Hau Ariki marae in Martinborough bases its slightly sweet rosé on the Champagne variety, Meunier. The '95 is full, with a rather red-winey colour and flavour. The 1996 vintage (**¹/₂) sports a full, bright pink colour, with reasonable depth of raspberryish, crisp flavour.

HUTHLEE EST. CABERNET FRANC ROSÉ

M/DRY $12 AV

(☆☆☆)

The 1996 vintage (***¹/₂) of this Hawke's Bay rosé is one of the best yet. Bright pink/red, it is vibrantly fruity, crisp and flavourful in a very fresh and summery style. Drink ASAP.

KAWARAU ESTATE ROSÉ

M/DRY $16 -V

(☆☆☆☆)

The delicious 1996 vintage (***¹/₂) is based on Pinot Noir, grown at the Morven Hill vineyard at Lake Hayes in Central Otago. It's a fresh and lively wine with a bright, pink-red colour and buoyantly fruity palate with dryish, raspberryish flavours enlivened by racy acidity.

LINTZ ESTATE ROSÉ

VINTAGE	97	96	95	94	93
WR	7	6	6	6	5
DRINK	97-8	P	P	P	P

M/DRY $16 -V

(☆☆☆☆)

Meunier, rare here but the most widely planted grape in Champagne, is the foundation of Chris Lintz's strong, rich-flavoured Martinborough rosé. The '96 (***¹/₂) has lots of character. Bright pink/red, with fresh raspberryish aromas, it's a very attractive wine with ripe, delicate, dryish flavours, fresh, crisp and berryish.

MELNESS ROSÉ

VINTAGE	94
WR	6
DRINK	97-8

M/DRY $12 -V

(☆☆☆)

Holding well but best drunk now, the 1994 vintage (**¹/₂) of this Canterbury wine is deep pink, with grassy, berryish flavours, still reasonably fresh and lively, and a slightly sweet, softening finish.

MILLS REEF MERE ROAD PINOT BLUSH

M/DRY $11 AV

(☆☆☆)

The pink, slightly copper-coloured 1995 vintage (***) of this Hawke's Bay wine is deliciously refreshing and zesty. Light and crisp, with slightly sweet, strawberryish, well-balanced flavour, it is a delicate, lively wine for drinking ASAP.

MILLTON VINEYARD, THE, CABERNET ROSÉ

DRY $13 V+

(☆☆☆☆)

The '95 vintage was about as good as rosé gets, with a delicious depth of delicate, strawberryish, fractionally sweet flavour, crisp, lively and lingering. The salmon-pink '96 (***¹/₂), blended from

Gisborne Cabernet Sauvignon, Malbec and Cabernet Franc, is a full-bodied dry style, very fresh and crisp, but not quite as richly flavoured and seductive as the '95.

MISSION ROSÉ

M/DRY $11 V+

(☆☆☆☆⯨)

This new, non-vintage rosé replaces Mission's spritzig (faintly bubbly) Crackling Rosé. A blend of Hawke's Bay Cabernet Sauvignon and Merlot, it's a very attractive wine, deep pink, with good body, a sliver of sweetness and fresh, smooth, finely balanced raspberry/strawberry flavours.

OKAHU EST. BEVERLEY'S BLUSH

M/DRY $14 -V

(☆☆☆⯨)

Named in honour of proprietor Monty Knight's wife, this very easy-drinking Hawke's Bay wine was launched from the 1996 vintage (**¹/₂). It's a pink, fresh, raspberryish wine, crisp, slightly sweet and smooth. Ready.

PALLISER ROSÉ OF PINOT

DRY $17 -V

(☆☆☆☆⯨)

The 1994 vintage was delightful, with a real touch of class. The '95 (***), made from a small proportion of juice drained off Martinborough Pinot Noir after 24 hours skin contact, sports an inviting salmon-pink hue. Dryish, with lightly tannic, raspberry/strawberry flavours, it's a "serious" style of rosé, but less delicate, intense and charming than the '94.

PROVIDENCE ROSÉ

DRY $30 -V

(☆☆☆☆)

Anjou was the model for Matakana winemaker James Vuletic when he made his first rosé in 1993 (****). Based on 80 per cent Cabernet Franc and 20 per cent Merlot, fermented and matured for six months in oak, it's an onion skin-hued wine, not overtly fruity, with very satisfying weight and deep, dry flavour. A "serious" style, it is reminiscent of the famous rosé of the Rhone: Tavel.

REDMETAL VINEYARDS ROSÉ

DRY $21 -V

(☆☆☆☆)

The debut 1997 vintage (****) is a barrel-fermented Hawke's Bay blend of Merlot and Cabernet Sauvignon, designed "more in the style of a Mediterranean light red wine than a typical rosé". Bright, raspberry/pink in hue, with deliciously fresh, floral, berryish scents, it's a vibrantly fruity, full-bodied, soft wine, very forward in its appeal, with a sustained, dry finish. Drink this summer.

RIPPON VINEYARD
GAMAY
ROSÉ

M/DRY $15 AV

(☆☆☆)

Is this Lake Wanaka wine made from the famous Gamay grape of Beaujolais, or a clone of Pinot Noir? Who really cares? The '95 is fresh, light, buoyant and full of raspberryish, slightly earthy and sweet flavour. The pink-red 1996 vintage (**¹/₂) lacks a bit of its usual ripeness and charm, with very crisp, frisky, green-edged flavours, fractionally sweet and raspberryish.

RIVERSIDE
ROSÉ

M/DRY $10 AV

(☆☆☆)

The 1995 vintage of this Dartmoor Valley wine is an easy-drinking style with berryish, slightly grassy flavours and an off-dry, smooth finish. The solid, bright pink/red '96 (**¹/₂) repeats the formula, with a fresh bouquet, crisp, berryish, green-edged flavours and a slightly sweet finish.

ROSÉBANK
ESTATE
ROSÉ

VINTAGE	94	93
WR	6	6
DRINK	P	P

M/DRY $12 AV

(☆☆☆)

Described by the winery as "more of a blush style", the 1994 vintage (**¹/₂) is a Marlborough blend of Müller-Thurgau (principally) and Cabernet Sauvignon. The colour is pretty pink; the bouquet berryish and fresh; the palate soft and slightly sweet in a very undemanding style.

TE KAIRANGA
CASTLEPOINT
CABERNET ROSÉ

M/DRY $13 -V

(☆☆☆)

The 1996 vintage (**¹/₂) of this Martinborough wine is light and fresh, with zesty, slightly sweet and grassy flavours.

TE MATA
ESTATE
ROSÉ

DRY $13 AV

☆☆☆

Designed as "a verandah wine for alfresco dining", this dry Hawke's Bay rosé is only available directly from the winery. A bright pink blend of Cabernet Sauvignon and Merlot, fermented on their skins for about 36 hours, it is typically an attractive wine with strawberryish, sometimes slightly green-edged flavours of good depth, freshness and liveliness.

VIDAL	VINTAGE	96	95		**M/DRY $11 V+**
MERLOT	WR	NM	6		
ROSÉ	DRINK	NM	P		(☆ ☆☆☆)

The 1994 vintage of this Hawke's Bay rosé was very seductive. The bright pink-hued '95 (***¹/₂) is a slightly "serious", yet delicious, wine with strong, strawberryish, cherryish flavours and a rounded, off-dry finish.

WAIPARA SPRINGS
CABERNET
BLUSH

M/DRY $12 -V

(☆☆☆)

Made from estate-grown Cabernet Sauvignon, the salmon-pink 1995 vintage (**¹/₂) is a light and lively wine with berryish, slightly grassy aromas and flavours and a fractionally sweet, freshly acidic finish.

WAITAKERE ROAD
VINEYARD CABERNET
FRANC ROSÉ

DRY $13 AV

(☆☆☆)

Kumeu-grown, the 1995 vintage (**¹/₂) is a weighty style with a deep pink/onion skin colour. It lacks a bit of freshness and charm, but is a decent food wine with plenty of berryish, slightly earthy flavour and a lightly tannic, dry finish.

WINSLOW	VINTAGE	97	96	**MED $25 -V**
ROSÉTTA	WR	6	7	
ROSÉ	DRINK	97-8	P	(☆☆☆☆☆)

In its youth, the 1996 vintage of this Martinborough wine was gorgeous. A medium style with an enticing, bright pink hue, it was made from very ripe Cabernet Sauvignon, fermented on its skins for 24 hours. Deliciously fresh, mouthfilling yet delicate, with a lovely surge of raspberry/strawberry flavours, a splash of sweetness and perfect sugar/acid balance, it was sheer delight. The '97 (****¹/₂) is also a superior rosé, although slightly less striking than the '96. With its bright pink hue and fresh, rich berryish flavours, slightly sweet and crisp, it is a vivacious wine for immediate consumption.

Red Wines

Cabernet Franc

Cabernet Franc is New Zealand's fourth most common red-wine variety, although its plantings are much smaller than those of the big three: Pinot Noir, Cabernet Sauvignon and Merlot. Cabernet Franc is probably a mutation of Cabernet Sauvignon, the higher profile variety with which it is so often blended. Jancis Robinson's phrase, "a sort of claret Beaujolais", aptly sums up the nature of this versatile and underrated red-wine grape.

As a minority ingredient in the recipe of many of New Zealand's top reds, Cabernet Franc lends a delicious softness and concentrated fruitiness to its blends with Cabernet Sauvignon and Merlot. Kumeu River, under its Brajkovich label, was the first to demonstrate what admirers of Château Cheval Blanc, the illustrious St Émilion (which is two-thirds planted in Cabernet Franc) have long appreciated: Cabernet Franc need not always be Cabernet Sauvignon's bridesmaid, but can yield fine red wines in its own right. The supple, fruity wines of Chinon and Bourgueil, in the Loire Valley, have also proved Cabernet Franc's ability to produce highly attractive, soft light reds.

The 1996 national vineyard survey predicted the bearing area of Cabernet Franc will rise from 73 to 96 hectares between 1996 and 1999. Over three-quarters of the vines are in the North Island, and over half in Hawke's Bay. As a varietal red, Cabernet Franc is lower in tannin and acid than Cabernet Sauvignon; or as Michael Brajkovich of Kumeu River puts it: "more approachable and easy".

ALEX. DUSTY ROAD CABERNET FRANC	VINTAGE	96	M/DRY $17 V+
	WR	6	(☆☆☆☆☆)
	DRINK	97+	

Recommended to be served slightly chilled, the 1996 vintage (****) from this tiny Martinborough winery is an exuberantly fruity red made from Marlborough grapes. Essentially a Beaujolais style, it is a slightly off-dry, uncomplicated red, not oak-aged, with deliciously strong, vibrantly fruity, raspberryish flavours, sappy and supple, with loads of drink-young charm.

BABICH CABERNET FRANC

DRY $13 V+

(☆☆☆⟨)

The first 1996 vintage (***¹/₂) is a fragrant, medium-bodied Gisborne wine with a highly attractive combination of ripe, berryish fruit and lively acidity. Not wood-aged, it is a refreshing wine in a vibrantly fruity and supple Beaujolais style, for drinking in its youth, rather than cellaring.

BRAJKOVICH CABERNET FRANC

DRY $15 V+

☆☆☆⟨

Judged as a fruity, supple, easy-drinking red, this can be hard to beat. Made from Kumeu fruit and not matured in oak, it is a full, soft red with more stuffing than you'd expect from its typically fairly light ruby-red hue. The 1996 vintage (****) is one of the best yet. Rich raspberry/floral aromas lead into a full-bodied red with excellent depth of ripe, sweet-tasting, berryish flavours and moderately firm tannin. The Brajkovich family drink it with "lamb, poultry, even fish".

HARRIER RISE CABERNET FRANC

VINTAGE	96
WR	7
DRINK	97-8

DRY $19 V+

(⟨☆☆☆☆⟨)

Less overtly fruity than most New Zealand reds, the '96 (****¹/₂) is a highly satisfying, complex Kumeu wine, based entirely on Cabernet Franc and matured for eight months in French oak casks (10 per cent new). Weighty, with floral, red berry aromas and an excellent concentration of slightly earthy, spicy flavour, it is a savoury, tight-knit red with power through the palate and distinct overtones of Bordeaux. Good, firm food wine.

MISSION JEWEL FRANC/ CABERNET

VINTAGE	95
WR	5
DRINK	97-03

DRY $20 AV

(⟨☆☆☆☆)

The concentrated 1995 vintage (****) of this Hawke's Bay red is a blend of 72 per cent Cabernet Franc and 28 per cent Cabernet Sauvignon, grown in the Ohiti Road and Moteo districts and matured for 18 months in French oak barriques (half new). The colour is deep; the bouquet minty and toasty; the palate fresh, with ripe, elegant fruit characters and strong, dark plum/spice flavours, chewy and tannic. A serious yet charming red, already deliciously drinkable, but worth cellaring.

Cabernet Sauvignon and Cabernet-predominant Blends

Cabernet Sauvignon is proving a tough nut to crack in New Zealand, as overseas wine writers don't hesitate to point out. A Canadian journalist reported having tasted 275 wines during 1995. "By far the worst was a bottle of Marlborough Cabernet Sauvignon 1992 ... vile tasting plonk."

"The best vintages from the best producers in Hawke's Bay are of international standard," Australian wine writer and author, James Halliday, acknowledged recently in *Cuisine* magazine, "but these are exceptions to the rule of wines which are too herbaceous and/or minty, too lacking in flesh, structure and tannins to travel successfully outside New Zealand."

Cabernet Sauvignon was first planted here last century. By the 1890s, this most famous variety of red Bordeaux was cultivated in W. Heathcote Jackman's vineyard on an arm of the Kaipara and Bernard Chambers' Te Mata vineyard in Hawke's Bay, and was well-respected throughout the colony. Romeo Bragato, the government viticulturist, in 1906 praised Cabernet Sauvignon as "one of the best varieties grown here ... the wine produced is of an excellent quality."

The modern resurgence of interest in Cabernet's potential in New Zealand was led by Tom McDonald, the legendary Hawke's Bay winemaker. In 1964 McDonald served Andre Simon, the great Paris-born wine writer, a 1949 McDonald "Cabernet" cheek-by-jowl with a 1949 Château Margaux. Simon later recorded: "The Margaux had a sweeter finish and a more welcoming bouquet, greater breed, but it did not shame the New Zealand cousin of the same vintage."

The string of elegant (though, by today's standards, light) Cabernet Sauvignons McDonald later fashioned under the McWilliam's label, from the much-acclaimed 1965 vintage to the gold-medal winning 1975, proved beyond all doubt that fine quality red wines could be produced in New Zealand, and set the scene for today's snowballing interest in red-winemaking.

Montana showed in the early 1970s that it had absorbed McDonald's lesson, although it was to Gisborne, and then Marlborough, that the company turned for the volume of fruit it needed to produce New Zealand's first "commercial" quality red. Nick Nobilo at Huapai, too, created a surge of excitement in the 1970s with his eye-catchingly rich and powerfully oaked Cabernet Sauvignons.

The Te Mata winery, with John Buck freshly at the helm, then swung the spotlight back to Hawke's Bay when its 1980 and 1981 Cabernet Sauvignons both carried off the trophy for champion red wine at the

National Wine Competition. With the growing selection of fine claret-style reds that has emerged from the region in the past decade, Hawke's Bay has established itself as the country's top source of Cabernet-based reds, their quality rivalled only by the relatively tiny volumes of splendid reds from the Auckland region, notably Waiheke Island.

Cabernet Sauvignon is New Zealand's second most widely planted red-wine grape (behind Pinot Noir, principally used in sparkling wine production), and the fourth most common variety overall. Over half of all the vines are concentrated in Hawke's Bay, but in the coolness of Marlborough, where in most vintages growers have struggled to fully ripen their fruit, plantings of this late-ripening variety are gradually declining.

What is the flavour of Cabernet wine? When newly fermented a greenish, herbal character is common, intertwined with blackcurrant-like fruit aromas. New oak flavours, firm acidity and mouth-puckeringly astringent tannins are other hallmarks of young, fine Cabernet Sauvignon. With maturity the flavour loses its aggression and the wine develops roundness and complexity, with assorted cigar-box, minty and floral scents emerging. It is infanticide to broach a Cabernet-based red with any pretensions to quality at less than three years old; at about five years old the rewards of cellaring start to flow.

Kym Milne, former chief winemaker for the Villa Maria/Vidal/Esk Valley stable (the source of a major share of New Zealand's foremost reds) has summarised the key factors behind the rising standard of our Cabernet-based reds. "Each year fewer of the green, vegetative style of Cabernet are being produced. This is because more virus-free clones are coming into bearing, vines are reaching maturity, vines are being planted on less fertile soils, canopy management is improving and more oak is being used."

Nevertheless, herbaceous, leafy-green characters still mar the quality of many of New Zealand's Cabernet-based reds, especially those from the cooler South Island. In the North Island, in vineyards planted in heavy soils, the late season Cabernet Sauvignon often fails to achieve full ripeness. Current planting trends suggest that the earlier-ripening Merlot will eventually overhaul Cabernet Sauvignon as New Zealand's principal red-wine variety.

AKARANGI CABERNET/ MERLOT

DRY $18 -V

(☆☆)

The 1995 vintage (**¹/₂) is a decent Hawke's Bay quaffer, blended from 45 per cent each of Cabernet Sauvignon and Cabernet Franc, with 10 per cent Merlot. Ruby-hued, with a slightly brown tint, it is a forward style with quite good weight and depth of blackcurrant/plum flavours, slightly grassy and rustic, and a well-rounded finish. Drink now.

VINTAGE	96	95	94
WR	6	5	4
DRINK	98-05	97-02	97-00

ALEXANDER

DRY $28 -V

(☆☆☆☆)

Kingsley and Deborah Alexander's 1994 red, a blend of 85 per cent Cabernet Sauvignon and 15 per cent Cabernet Franc, was an exciting debut: vibrantly fruity, with delicious blackcurrant and plum flavours to the fore, oak complexity and a supple finish. The '95 is even better, with the freshness typical of Martinborough reds, deep colour, mouthfilling body and strong, ripe, slightly minty flavours, braced by firm tannins. The 1996 vintage (****) is again classy. Matured for a year in new and seasoned French oak casks, it is a very elegant wine with sweet-fruit characters, strong, ripe cassis, plum and spice flavours and oak richness in a fresh and supple style, capable of maturing well.

ALPHA DOMUS
AD CABERNET/
MERLOT/MALBEC

VINTAGE	96
WR	6
DRINK	99-06

DRY $34 AV

(☆☆☆☆☆)

It's a tentative assessment only, but when tasted as an unfined, unfiltered barrel sample in mid 1997, the first 1996 vintage (*****) of this Hawke's Bay red was exciting. A blend of 50 per cent Cabernet Sauvignon, 30 per cent Merlot and 20 per cent Malbec, matured for 15 months in new oak casks, it reveals very dark, almost impenetrable, purple-black colour. It's a strapping, bold wine with supple tannins, crammed with lush, sweet-tasting, blackcurrant and dark plum flavours.

ALPHA DOMUS
CABERNET
SAUV./MERLOT

VINTAGE	95
WR	6
DRINK	97-9

DRY $18 AV

(☆☆☆☆)

Sturdy and supple, the debut 1995 vintage (***1/2) of this Hawke's Bay red was made by Grant Edmonds, formerly chief winemaker for the Villa Maria empire. Matured for a year in French and American oak casks, it's an attractive, forward, easy-drinking wine with good colour depth, generous, ripe, blackcurrant/plum flavours, oak richness and rounded tannins.

AZURE BAY
CABERNET
SAUVIGNON

DRY $10 V+

(☆☆☆)

Montana's trans-Pacific blend of Chilean and New Zealand wine delivers great value. The '95, French and American oak-aged for a year, is a chewy, satisfying wine with good depth of warm, ripe, spicy flavour and some richness in a clearly cool-climate style with a touch of complexity and positive tannins. The 1996 vintage (***) is a full-bodied, lightly oaked red, fruity and smooth, with plenty of ripe cassis/plum flavour. A bargain.

BABICH HB CABERNET/ MERLOT

VINTAGE	96	95	94	93	92	91	90
WR		6	6	7	5	4	6	6
DRINK		97-00	97-00	97-9	97-8	P	97-8	P

DRY $14 AV

☆☆☆

Typically a decent red, not concentrated but well balanced and highly drinkable. The 1995 vintage is an appealing wine with buoyant, ripe, plum/spice flavours and a touch of oak complexity. The '96 (***1/2) is a 3:1 blend of the two Bordeaux grapes, French oak-aged for a year. Ruby-hued, it is berryish, light and smooth, offering pleasant, undemanding drinking, but is clearly a lesser vintage, lacking a bit of stuffing and richness.

BABICH IRON. CABERNET/ MERLOT

VINTAGE	95	94	93	92	91	90
WR	6	7	NM	7	7	7
DRINK	98-04	97-00	NM	97-00	97-00	97-00

DRY $26 V+

☆☆☆☆☆

Grown in the stony Irongate vineyard in Gimblett Road, Hawke's Bay (where the red-wine plantings are 75 per cent Cabernet Sauvignon, 17 per cent Merlot and 8 per cent Cabernet Franc) and matured for over a year in Nevers oak barriques, this is a deep-coloured red with rich, concentrated cassis and strong oak flavours, underpinned by taut tannins. It matures well; the '89 is currently drinking superbly. The '94 is a beautifully crafted wine with a fragrant, spicy, cedary bouquet and a palate revealing great finesse, although (as with other top '94s) a trace of herbaceousness is emerging with age. Finesse is a key attribute of the classy 1995 vintage (*****). The colour is deep and youthful; the flavours are fresh and strong, with a lovely balance of warm, cassis and plum-like flavours and quality oak. It's already approachable, but sure to mature well past 2000.

BABICH MARA ESTATE CAB. SAUVIGNON

VINTAGE	96	95	94	93	92
WR	7	7	7	NM	6
DRINK	98-04	97-00	97-00	NM	97-9

DRY $17 V+

(☆☆☆☆)

Still fresh, the 1995 vintage (****) of this unblended Hawke's Bay red was grown in Gimblett Road and matured for a year in French and American oak barrels. It's a full-bodied, firmly structured wine, still purple-flushed, with strong, plummy, slightly minty flavours, needing a bit more time to soften and show at its best. The '96, tasted as a barrel sample, showed quite good concentration of ripe plum/spice flavours, firm tannins and more stuffing than its Merlot stablemate of the same vintage.

BABICH THE PATRIARCH CAB. SAUVIGNON

VINTAGE	95
WR	7
DRINK	00-07

DRY $30 AV

(☆☆☆☆☆)

Babich's flagship red. The debut 1994 vintage is a very complete wine with an enticing perfume, full, vibrant colour, lovely, sweet fruit and very intense, persistent flavour. The '95 (*****) is an unblended Cabernet Sauvignon, grown in Gimblett Road, Hawke's Bay, and matured for 20 months in half French, half American oak casks. The aromas of blackcurrants and sweet, perfumed oak lead into a seductively warm, ripe and complex palate with very rich yet delicate, spicy, sweet-fruit flavours and quality oak. This is a notably classy red with drink-young charm yet the power and structure to mature well.

	VINTAGE	95	94	93	92	91	90		DRY $35 -V
BENFIELD	WR	6	5	NM	NM	5	6		
AND	DRINK	97-10	97-10+	NM		NM	97-05	97-05	☆☆☆☆⯪
DELAMARE									

Bill Benfield and Sue Delamare specialise in claret-style reds at their tiny Martinborough winery. A top-flight wine with vibrant fruit and strong oak, Benfield and Delamare is typically slightly leaner than the leading Hawke's Bay reds, yet intensely flavoured and taut. The richly coloured 1995 vintage possesses a fragrant bouquet of blackcurrants and cedar, leading into a ripe, concentrated palate with quality oak and firm tannins. It's a serious red for cellaring. The '96 (****¹/₂), blended from Cabernet Sauvignon, Merlot and Cabernet Franc, is as usual an elegant rather than blockbuster red with full colour, ripe tannins and intense flavours of cassis, plums and oak, complex and long.

BENFIELD & DELAMARE A SONG FOR OSIRIS

DRY $24 AV

(☆☆☆☆)

Dedicated to Osiris, an ancient patron of the grape and wine, compared to its big brother (above) this red is designed as "a lively, more fruit-driven style, more suitable for early drinking". The '95, a Martinborough blend of Cabernet Sauvignon, Merlot and Cabernet Franc, is a very rewarding wine with an intensely spicy fragrance and excellent depth of flavour, firmly structured but already approachable and enjoyable. A vibrantly fruity, Bordeaux-like red with oak complexity and impressive concentration, it is full of character and quality. The 1996 vintage (***¹/₂) is a slightly lighter, ruby-hued wine with fragrant, berryish aromas, attractively ripe, berryish, slightly nutty flavours and firm tannins. It's a characterful red with some richness and complexity.

BIRCHWOOD CABERNET/ MERLOT

DRY $11 AV

(☆☆⯪)

A Hawke's Bay red, produced by Selaks exclusively for Foodtown. The 1995 vintage (**¹/₂) is a solid, easy-drinking wine with moderate depth of berryish, slightly herbaceous, firm flavour. Priced right.

BLACK GECKO CABERNET/ MERLOT

DRY $9 V+

(☆☆⯪)

If you like to "consummate, stimulate, stay up late...", this trans-Tasman blend could be the wine for you. Montana's non-vintage red is a mix of Hawke's Bay, Marlborough and South Australian wine. It's a decent quaffer with pleasant, reasonably ripe, red berry and spice flavours and a rounded finish. Priced right.

	VINTAGE	95		DRY $18 -V
BLACK RIDGE	WR	5		
CABERNET	DRINK	97-00		(☆☆⯪)
SAUVIGNON				

It slightly lacks warmth and complexity, but for a Cabernet Sauvignon grown so far south, the 1995 vintage (**¹/₂) of this Alexandra red is a good effort. It's a deeply coloured wine, still purple-flushed, with fresh, red berry/herbal aromas. The palate is chunky and vibrantly fruity, with strong, fresh, crisp, berryish flavours and restrained French oak.

| *BLOOMFIELD CABERNET SAUVIGNON/MERLOT/ CABERNET FRANC* | DRY $26 -V ☆☆☆☆ |

David Bloomfield's generous 1994 vintage (****) Masterton red is distinctly classy. Blended from 75 per cent Cabernet Sauvignon, 15 per cent Merlot and 10 per cent Cabernet Franc, it's a classic claret-style red with deep colour, blackcurrant/spice aromas, mouthfilling body and impressive depth of ripe, spicy, oaky flavour. Open 1998 onwards.

BROOKFIELDS CAB/MER. (GOLD LABEL)	VINTAGE	95	94	93	92	91	90	DRY $46 -V
	WR	7	7	NM	NM	7	6	☆☆☆☆☆
	DRINK	05	99+	NM	NM	97-01	97-00	

At its best, Peter Robertson's Hawke's Bay red is of thrilling quality. Opened in the past year, the 1990 vintage is very elegant and Bordeaux-like, ripe and cedary; the '91 is still developing, with intense colour and flavour. The 1994 vintage, a blend of 65 per cent Cabernet Sauvignon, 30 per cent Merlot (more than usual) and 5 per cent Cabernet Franc, is amazingly harmonious, complex and approachable for so young a wine. Slightly lighter and softer than usual, with a hint of greenness on the nose but deep, supple flavour, it's a more forward style than its predecessors. Still a baby, but packed with potential, the '95 (*****) is a blend of 85 per cent Cabernet Sauvignon, 10 per cent Merlot and 5 per cent Cabernet Franc, matured for 18 months in new French oak barriques. It's an exceptionally intense wine with bold, purple-flushed colour, dense to the rim. Crammed with ripe, very rich cassis, plum and mint flavours, it is concentrated, complex and tannic, with a powerful finish.

BROOKFIELDS ESTATE CABERNET	VINTAGE	95	94	DRY $17 AV
	WR	6	6	☆☆☆
	DRINK	98	97+	

Brookfields' lower-tier Hawke's Bay red is typically medium to full-bodied, with its accent on fresh cassis and red berry-fruit flavours and a moderately tannic finish. Not highly concentrated but flavoursome, the 1995 vintage (***) is an unblended Haumoana Cabernet Sauvignon, matured for a year in two and three-year-old French oak barriques. Ruby-hued, fruity and firm, with berryish, plummy flavours, it is an unpretentious but satisfying food wine, capable of short-term aging.

BROOKFIELDS RESERVE CAB. SAUV.	VINTAGE	95	94	93	92	91	90	DRY $34 AV
	WR	7	NM	NM	NM	7	6	☆☆☆☆☆
	DRINK	02	NM	NM	NM	97-01	97-00	

Typically a strapping, dark-hued Hawke's Bay wine; proof of the variety's ability to produce superb unblended reds. Slightly more austere than the Cabernet/Merlot, with a rush of blackcurrant-evoking, spicy flavours and a tautly tannic structure, it needs several years' cellaring to unfold its full splendour. The 1995 vintage (*****) is a very serious claret-style red. Matured for 18 months in Nevers oak barriques (90 per cent new), it sports a rich, bright colour and a bouquet of toasty, nutty oak. It's a bold wine with a powerful surge of very ripe blackcurrant/plum flavours, wrapped in quality oak, and a tannic, sustained finish.

CANADORO CABERNET SAUVIGNON	VINTAGE	96	95	94	93		DRY $25 AV
	WR	7	6	7	5		
	DRINK	99-05	98-02	98-02	97-8		(☆☆☆☆)

The 1994 vintage is an impressively gutsy and ripe-flavoured Martinborough red, with spicy, blackcurrant-like, chocolate-rich flavour. There's a slight lack of warmth in the crisp, fresh '95, but it's still a satisfyingly full-bodied wine with plenty of firm, spicy flavour. The 1996 vintage (****) is full of character. The colour is bold; the palate generous and rich, with mouthfilling body, balanced tannins and excellent depth of nutty, complex flavour. A powerful wine for the long haul.

CHANCELLOR MT CASS RD CABERNET	VINTAGE	96	DRY $19 AV
	WR	6	
	DRINK	98+	(☆☆☆☆)

Needing time, the 1996 vintage (***1/2) of this Waipara, North Canterbury red is a flavourful, chewy wine, matured for a year in French and American oak casks. The colour is purplish and deep; the flavour lively, plummy, slightly herbal and impressively concentrated, with oak complexity and a moderately firm finish.

CHIFNEY CABERNET SAUVIGNON	VINTAGE	96	95	DRY $25 AV
	WR	5	6	
	DRINK	99-00	98-00	☆☆☆☆

His Cabernet Sauvignon was Martinborough winemaker Stan Chifney's "favourite" wine. The 1994 vintage is a strong-flavoured, fresh, slightly spicy red. The colour is bright and deep; the bouquet fresh, green-edged and berryish. Medium-bodied, it is a vibrantly fruity style with crisp, berryish flavours. Still youthful, the '95 (****) is richly coloured, mouthfilling and chewy, with a tauter tannin structure than is typical of most New Zealand reds, but impressive concentrated and complexity. The '96, tasted as a barrel sample, looked very promising: deep-coloured, fleshy, brambly, ripe and rich-flavoured.

CHIFNEY ENIGMA CAB/MER.	VINTAGE	96	95	DRY $18 AV
	WR	5	4	
	DRINK	98-00	98-00	(☆☆☆)

The first 1995 vintage (which superseded the Garden of Eden label in the Chifney range) is a full-bodied, crisp, spicy and flavoursome wine in a no-fuss, drink-young style. The '96 (***1/2), grown in Martinborough and aged for a year in predominantly French oak, is a warm and characterful wine with fullness of body, good depth of ripe blackcurrant/plum flavour, well-integrated wood and balanced tannins. Enjoyable now, it can also be cellared for a couple of years.

CHURCH ROAD CABERNET SAUV./MER.	VINTAGE	95	94	93	92	91	90	DRY $23 V+
	WR	7	6	4	5	6	5	
	DRINK	98-00+	97-00+	97-9	97-9	97-9+	P	☆☆☆☆⯪

Who said you had to pay a fortune for a top class New Zealand red? For sheer finesse and drinkability, Montana's high profile Hawke's Bay wine, produced at The McDonald Winery with technical input from the Bordeaux house of Cordier, is hard to beat. The 1993 is less ripe and concentrated than the '91 or '92, with plenty of berryish, slightly leafy flavour, restrained oak and supple tannins. The '94 vintage is a rich, nutty, warm and complex wine, distinctly Bordeaux-like in structure, with many years of fine drinking ahead of it. Still in its infancy, the '95 (****½) is a top vintage. A classic, concentrated claret style red with ripe, brambly, spicy, chocolatey, cedary flavours framed by taut tannins, it's well worth cellaring for a couple of years or longer.

CHURCH ROAD RES. CABERNET SAUV./MER.	VINTAGE	95	94					DRY $35 AV
	WR	7	6					
	DRINK	98-00+	97-9					(☆☆☆☆☆)

The first 1994 vintage reserve red under Montana's Church Road label is a cracker. The back label recommends cellaring it for "up to 10 years'" but it's already hard to resist. Grown in the Esk Valley and at Fernhill and matured in French oak at The McDonald Winery, it's a warm and supple, flavour-packed wine with full, maturing colour and a highly perfumed, nutty fragrance. Robust, with rich, complex, brambly flavours and very well-rounded tannins, it combines power and charm and is arguably Montana's greatest red yet (at least until the '95!) The 1995 (*****), a bigger wine than the '94, is a very bold, generous red with great depth of lovely, superbly ripe and concentrated blackcurrant/plum flavours wrapped in quality oak (all French, 60 per cent new). A notably substantial, warm, spicy and complex red, it looks likely to out-perform the '94 in the cellar.

C.J. PASK CABERNET SAUVIGNON	VINTAGE	96	95	94	93	92	91	90	DRY $20 AV
	WR	6	7	6	5	4	6	6	
	DRINK	00	00	00	98	P	P	P	☆☆☆☆

A trump card for the C.J. Pask winery is its vineyards in Gimblett Road, Hawke's Bay, an area renowned for reds. Matured in French and American oak casks for just over a year, the 1994 vintage is a gutsy, perfumed red with lots of character. It is richly coloured, with pleasing depth of brambly, spicy flavour, warm oak characters and well balanced tannins. The pleasant, ripely flavoured '95 (***) is a fruity, although not complex, wine with good depth of plum/berry flavours and a smooth finish.

C.J. PASK CABERNET/ MERLOT	VINTAGE	96	95	94	93	92	91	90	DRY $20 -V
	WR	6	7	6	5	5	6	6	
	DRINK	00	00	00	98	P	P	P	☆☆☆

Past vintages of this Hawke's Bay red have been deliciously robust, plummy, fragrant and soft. However, some recent releases (1993 and 1994) have been distinctly leafy-green on the nose and palate. Flavourful but again green-edged, the '95 (***½) is a 50/50 blend of Cabernet Sauvignon and Merlot. Matured for over a year in French and American oak casks, it is full and rounded, with a slightly herbal bouquet and fruity, supple palate with some complexity.

C.J. PASK RESERVE CAB. SAUV.	VINTAGE	95	94	DRY $29 AV
	WR	7	7	
	DRINK	04	01	(☆☆☆☆½)

The gold medal-winning 1994 vintage (a Cabernet/Merlot/Malbec) is an elegant, rather than blockbuster, Hawke's Bay red, matured for 17 months in new oak casks. There are distinct herbal touches on the nose and palate, but the flavours are seductively rich, plummy and lingering. The highly enjoyable '95 (****½) was grown in Gimblett Road and matured for almost two years in new American oak casks. There's strong, sweet oak on the nose and warm, ripe blackcurrant/mint flavours on the palate, leading to a rich, firm finish.

CLEARVIEW ESTATE CAPE KIDNAP. CAB.	VINTAGE	96	95				DRY $29 AV
	WR	5	6				
	DRINK	98-9	98-9				(☆☆☆☆☆)

Still developing, the 1995 vintage (****) of this Te Awanga, Hawke's Bay red is deep garnet, with mouthfilling body and rich, ripe, dark chocolate and herb aromas and flavours, braced by strong but fine tannins. Very characterful and bargain-priced.

CLEARVIEW EST. RES. OLD OLIVE BLOCK	VINTAGE	96	95	94			DRY $30 -V
	WR	NM	6	6			
	DRINK	NM	99-03	97-03			(☆☆☆☆☆)

Launched from 1994, this Te Awanga red is made only in "exceptional" vintages. It is grown in the small estate vineyard, which has a 60-year-old olive tree in the centre. The '94 is an impressively bold red with dark colour and an enticingly rich fragrance. Bursting with lush blackcurrant, spice, plum and sweet oak flavours, braced by fine, silky tannins, this is a powerful, complex and yet sensuous red. The delicious 1995 vintage (****1/2) is a blend of 80 per cent Cabernet Sauvignon, 15 per cent Merlot and 5 per cent Cabernet Franc. It's a dark-hued, fragrant, full and generous red with lots of warm, chocolate/plum/spice flavour and a rounded, very persistent finish.

CLOUDY BAY CABERNET/ MERLOT	VINTAGE	94	93	92	91	90	DRY $26 -V
	WR	6	NM	NM	6	5	
	DRINK	99	NM	NM	P	P	(☆☆☆☆☆)

Weighty and firm, with plummy, spicy, complex flavours, this Marlborough wine typically lacks the power and richness of the greatest North Island reds, but is still classy. The 1994 vintage (****) is one of the best yet. Elegant, with good depth of delicate, blackcurrant, plum and spice flavours, French oak complexity and balanced tannins, it's a classic claret-style red, not a blockbuster but stylish, and very more-ish.

COLLARDS CABERNET/ MERLOT	VINTAGE	96	95	94	93	92	91	90	DRY $13 AV
	WR	6	6	6	6	6	6	7	
	DRINK	98-9	97-8	97-8	P	P	P	P	☆☆☆

Generally a smooth, light, gently oaked, easy-drinking quaffer. The 1994 vintage is pleasantly ripe and berryish. The '95 (**1/2) grown in Auckland, Te Kauwhata and Hawke's Bay, is ruby hued, with fresh, leafy, red-berry aromas and a light, fruity, supple, green-edged palate.

COLLARDS ROTH. VINE. CAB. SAUV.	VINTAGE	96	95	94	93	92	91	90	DRY $18 AV
	WR	7	6	7	7	6	6	6	
	DRINK	97-02	97-00	97-00	97-9	P	P	P	☆☆☆☆

The launch of the 1990 Cabernet from Collards' Rothesay vineyard at Waimauku plugged a major gap in the winery's range: the lack of a premium red. Reflecting the great Auckland vintage, the 1993 is full and deep-coloured, with plenty of blackcurrant and spice flavour, oak complexity and a lingering finish. The equally good '94 is a mouthfilling wine with enticingly dark colour, a rich, toasty fragrance and deep, spicy flavours. The 1995 vintage (***) is less warm and rich than its predecessors. It is fairly light in colour and leafy on the nose, but still reveals some complexity and plenty of berry, spicy flavour.

COOKS WINEMAKERS RES. CAB. SAUV.

VINTAGE	95	94	93	92	91	90
WR	7	NM	NM	NM	NM	7
DRINK	98-05	NM	NM	NM	NM	97-00

DRY $23 V+

(☆☆☆☆⯪)

The 1995 vintage (*****) is the first release under this label since 1990. An impressively fragrant and flavour-packed Hawke's Bay red, it's a blend of 77 per cent Cabernet Sauvignon, 12 per cent Cabernet Franc and 11 per cent Merlot, picked from Corbans' Tukituki vineyard and matured for 18 months in French and American oak barriques. Deep garnet, with the cedary, toasty perfume of new oak, it is a robust, rich wine, already drinking well, with loads of ripe, brambly fruit in a deeply flavoured, concentrated, firmly structured style that should reward cellaring for several years.

COOPERS CREEK HB CABERNET SAUVIGNON

VINTAGE	96	95	94
WR	5	5	6
DRINK	97-9	97-8	97-8

DRY $16 AV

(☆☆☆)

With its fresh, brambly flavours, not concentrated but ripe, and touch of sweet-tasting oak, the 1994 vintage is drinking well now. The '95, oak-aged for six months, is very better, with rich colour, concentrated, ripe, spicy flavour and a supple finish. However, the 1996 vintage (**½) is on a lower plane. American oak-aged for six months, it is a pleasant, reasonably flavoursome, slightly herbaceous red, plummy and smooth but lacking the richness of the '95.

COOPERS CREEK HUAPAI CAB./ MERLOT

VINTAGE	96
WR	5
DRINK	97-8

DRY $20 AV

(☆☆☆⯪)

The 1996 vintage (***½) is from a year which did not yield the Reserve Huapai red (below). A 3:1 blend of Cabernet Sauvignon and Merlot, oak-aged for a year, it displays deep, bright colour and an appealing, minty fragrance. Still youthful, it's a chunky wine with strong plum/mint flavours wrapped in sweet, toasty oak and a moderately firm finish.

COOPERS CREEK RESERVE HB CAB. SAUV.

VINTAGE	96	95	94
WR	NM	7	6
DRINK	NM	97-02	97-00

DRY $22 AV

(☆☆☆☆)

The 1994 vintage is deeply coloured, with a rich fragance of blackcurrants and spicy wood. Generous, ripe, cassis/plum flavours are wrapped in sweet-tasting oak, creating a complex yet instantly attractive wine for drinking anytime from now onwards. The '95 (*****½) is very similar. Matured for almost a year in American oak casks, it is a powerful, chewy red with dark, still purple-flushed colour, sweet, toasty oak on the nose and palate and concentrated cassis, mint, plum and spice flavours.

**COOPERS CREEK
RESERVE HUAPAI
CAB./MER.**

VINTAGE	95	94	93	92	91	90
WR	6	7	7	6	5	4
DRINK	99-02	98-01	97-00	P	P	P

DRY $28 AV

☆☆☆☆☆

This Huapai red has soared in quality since the deliciously flavour-packed 1992 vintage. The 1993, tasted last year, was impressively rich, though slightly green. The 1994 is highly concentrated, with fresh, strong, vibrant blackcurrant, plum and mint flavours and lovely overall balance. The powerful, complex '95 vintage (*****) is a blend of 60 per cent Cabernet Sauvignon and 40 per cent Merlot, American oak-aged for a year. The richly oaked bouquet leads into a robust, warm, tight-knit, concentrated palate with searching blackcurrant and spice, slightly earthy flavours, chewy tannins and a sustained finish. (Note: the 1996 Huapai Cabernet/Merlot is not under a Reserve label.)

**CORBANS COT.
BLOCK HB
CAB. SAUV./FRANC**

VINTAGE	94	93	92
WR	7	NM	6
DRINK	10	NM	05

DRY $35 -V

(☆☆☆☆☆)

The debut 1992 vintage (a Cabernet/Merlot) of Corbans' top Hawke's Bay red lacked the concentration expected of a $30-plus red, but the '94 (*****) is a big step up. American oak-aged for 14 months, this distinguished wine is delicious now, but will live for ages. The colour is full and deep; the bouquet rich, spicy and cedary; the palate mouthfilling, with an arresting intensity of ripe, complex, blackcurrant-and-cedar flavour, with the Cabernet Franc contributing a seductive fruitiness and suppleness. A classy wine, still developing, it's one of the top Hawke's Bay reds of the vintage.

**CORBANS PRI.
BIN HB CAB.
SAUV./MERLOT**

VINTAGE	95	94	93
WR	7	7	6
DRINK	99-05	98-05	97-00

DRY $22 AV

(☆☆☆☆)

Corbans' second-tier claret-style red from Hawke's Bay, positioned below the Cottage Block red (above). The richly coloured '94 (labelled as a straight Cabernet Sauvignon) was matured for 14 months in new French and American oak barriques. It's a full-bodied, strongly wood-influenced wine with ripe, moderately intense, blackcurrant and plum-like flavours, buttressed by firm tannins. The impressive 1995 vintage (****½) is a blend of 70 per cent Cabernet Sauvignon, 20 per cent Merlot and 10 per cent Cabernet Franc, matured for over a year in French and American oak casks. A fragrant, full-bodied, intense red with bold, bright colour and ripe, sweet-fruit flavours, it is warm, spicy, chewy and complex, and well worth cellaring.

**CORBANS WHITE
LABEL CABERNET
SAUVIGNON**

DRY $9 V+

(☆☆☆)

The 1995 vintage (***½) is a trans-Tasman blend of Marlborough, Hawke's Bay and Australian grapes (including 15 per cent Shiraz), oak-aged for six months. It's a solid quaffer with fairly light colour, a green-edged bouquet and berryish, slightly herbal, smooth flavour. It lacks richness and ripeness, but the price is right.

CORNERSTONE VINEYARD CAB./MERLOT	VINTAGE	95	94					DRY $28 -V
	WR	6	5					(☆ ☆☆☆)
	DRINK	00+	98+					

Marlborough winemaker John Forrest and Bob Newton, an Australian viticulturist, are partners in the Newton/Forrest vineyard in Gimblett Road, Hawke's Bay. The debut 1994 vintage is a lovely, fragrant, elegant wine with rich, vivid colour and very good depth of spicy, plummy flavour. The big, generous '95 (****¹/₂) was matured in 70 per cent French and 30 per cent American oak casks. Still in its infancy, it's richly coloured, with an instantly inviting, perfumed bouquet and bold palate revealing excellent depth of rich, ripe, spicy, cedary flavour supported by fine tannins.

CROSS ROADS CABERNET/ MERLOT	VINTAGE	95	94	93	92			DRY $18 AV
	WR	5	6	6	7			(☆ ☆☆)
	DRINK	97-9	97-9	P	97-00			

Labelled "Cabernet" in 1992, "Cabernet Sauvignon" in 1993 and "Cabernet/Merlot" from 1994, this is typically a decent, very enjoyable Hawke's Bay red. The gutsy, full-coloured 1994 vintage is a 90/10 blend, grown at Fernhill and in the Dartmoor Valley, and matured for a year in predominantly French oak. It's a generous wine, full of berryish, spicy, slightly minty fruit in a smooth-flowing style. The '95 (* – ***) has shown some bottle variation, with one batch distinctly flawed. However, the batch I tasted most recently was fresh and attractive, with good colour depth and strong, ripe blackcurrant flavours, well-balanced for current consumption.

CROSS ROADS RESERVE CAB./MERLOT	VINTAGE	95	94					DRY $24 AV
	WR	6	6					(☆ ☆☆☆)
	DRINK	97-00	97-00					

The 1994 vintage is a robust Hawke's Bay blend of 90 per cent Cabernet Sauvignon and 10 per cent Merlot. Fleshy, with lots of blackcurrant, plum and oak flavour, it's a soft, generous wine for drinking now. Also delicious now, with warm, ripe, supple flavours, the '95 (****) is a powerful red, oak-aged for two years. It's a full-coloured wine, big and chewy, with excellent depth of soft, nutty, complex, lingering flavours.

DASHWOOD MARLBOROUGH CAB. SAUV.	VINTAGE	96	95	94	93	92	91	DRY $19 AV
	WR	7	NM	6	NM	4	7	☆☆☆☆½
	DRINK	97-00	NM	97-8	NM	P	97-8	

The dark, chunky 1996 vintage (***¹/₂) of this Awatere Valley red is a blend of Cabernet Sauvignon with 8 per cent Malbec and 7 per cent Syrah, matured for a year in French and American oak. The minty, leafy bouquet leads into a mouthfilling (13.5 per cent alcohol) palate with moderate tannins and impressive depth of blackcurrant, spice and mint flavour. Drink 1998.

DELEGAT'S HB CABERNET/ MERLOT	VINTAGE	96	95	94	93	92	91	90	DRY $14 AV
	WR	5	5	6	4	6	5	5	☆☆½
	DRINK	97-8	P	P	P	P	P	P	

Delegat's lower-tier red, a blend of Hawke's Bay fruit matured for a year in older oak barrels, is typically fresh and plummy, crisp and straightforward in flavour. The 1995 vintage is a better wine than the '94. The bouquet is berryish and slightly herbal; the palate medium-full in body, warm, spicy and smooth, with a touch of complexity and moderate tannins. The '96 (**¹/₂), matured for six months in seasoned French and American oak casks, is an easy-drinking red with reasonable depth of blackcurrant/plum flavour, fresh and crisp.

DELEGAT'S PROP. RESERVE CAB. SAUV.

VINTAGE	95	94	93	92	91	90
WR	5	6	NM	5	7	6
DRINK	97-9	97-9	NM	97-8	P	P

DRY $25 AV

☆☆☆☆

Strong, spicy Cabernet Sauvignon flavours typify this Hawke's Bay wine. The ripe, moderately intense '94 was blended with 15 per cent Merlot and French oak-aged for a year. It's a full-flavoured, peppery wine with toasty oak aromas, an appealing nutty complexity and well balanced tannins. The 1995 vintage (****) is deeply coloured, with generous body and excellent depth of ripe blackcurrant, spice and cedary oak flavours, braced by firm tannins. This is a weighty, taut (only 5 per cent Merlot), complex wine for cellaring to at least 1998. Tasted from the barrel, the 1996 and 1997 vintages look likely to be the best yet – very dark, powerful and richly flavoured.

DE REDCLIFFE CABERNET SAUV./MERLOT

VINTAGE	96	95
WR	6	6
DRINK	97-8	P

DRY $16 AV

(☆☆☆)

The fruity, smooth 1994 vintage is a fresh, berryish red with leafy, herbal touches in the bouquet and a supple, lightly oaked palate with moderately ripe, blackcurrant and raspberry-evoking flavours. The '95 (***¹/₂) is one of the best De Redcliffe reds yet. A Hawke's Bay blend of 80 per cent Cabernet Sauvignon and 20 per cent Merlot, matured for a year in new and seasoned French oak casks, it is ruby-hued, full and firm, with good depth of warm, ripe cassis/plum flavours, some complexity and positive tannins.

DUNLEAVY CABERNET/ MERLOT

VINTAGE	96
WR	6
DRINK	97-00

DRY $19 AV

(☆☆☆⛧)

The second-tier red from Waiheke Vineyards, best known for its outstanding Te Motu Cabernet/Merlot. A drink-young style, the 1996 vintage (***¹/₂) is fresh and smooth, with a full, bright purple-red hue and ripe berry fruit aromas. Supple and flavoursome, although not complex, it offers sweet, ripe blackcurrant/plum flavours, lightly oaked and well tuned for current consumption, but with enough depth to develop into 1998.

ESKDALE CABERNET SAUVIGNON

DRY $25 AV

☆☆☆☆

Kim Salonius matures his Esk Valley-grown red in French oak barrels for up to three years, longer than any other winemaker in the country. It typically emerges full of character, with rich, spicy, herbal, chocolatey, impressively complex flavours and well-rounded tannins. The 1994 (***¹/₂) is a solid but not memorable vintage, with firm, moderately rich berry/spice flavours.

	VINTAGE	96		
	WR	7		**DRY $45 AV**
FENTON	DRINK	98-02		(☆ ☆☆☆☆☆)

A consistently beautiful Waiheke Island red, grown by Barry Fenton at the Twin Bays Vineyard at Oneroa and produced at the Coopers Creek winery. The 1994 vintage, blended from Cabernet Sauvignon, Merlot and Cabernet Franc (and the same wine that won a gold medal and trophy under the Stonyridge Airfield label) is dark, with a voluptuous, very ripe fragrance and splendidly rich, supple flavour. The 1993 vintage debut was equally top-flight. The '96 (*****) is again highly seductive, with deep, bright, purple-red colour and a minty, sweet-oak fragrance. It's a fleshy, generous wine with a wealth of blackcurrant, plum and spice flavour, soft, ripe tannins and a supple, very sustained finish. Drink 1998 onwards.

	VINTAGE	96	
FENTON			
THE	WR	5	**DRY $24 -V**
RED	DRINK	97-8	(☆☆☆☆)

This Cabernet/Merlot blend is the second-tier red from the Twin Bays vineyard on Waiheke Island, better known for its top Fenton label (above). The 1996 vintage (***1/2) was produced at the Coopers Creek winery. It wasn't oak-aged, but it's still a satisfying wine, with bright, full colour and an invitingly fragrant, ripe and spicy bouquet. Vibrantly fruity, with very good depth of ripe fruit flavours and moderate tannins, it offers very enjoyable drinking through 1998.

	VINTAGE	96	95	94	
FORREST GIB.					
CREEK CAB./	WR	4	NM	5	**DRY $15 AV**
FRANC/MER.	DRINK	97+	NM	P	☆☆☆

Marlborough winemaker John Forrest aims for "a softer [red wine] style than most with ripe berry flavours integrated with subtle oak characters". The sturdy, full-flavoured 1996 vintage (***) possesses a bright, full ruby hue and scented, minty/herbal bouquet. It's a characterful red with lots of blackcurrant and spice, slightly green-edged flavour, moderate tannins and strong drink-young appeal.

GATEHOUSE	**DRY $12 AV**
CAB./MER./	
MALBEC	(☆☆☆)

West Melton is not an easy place to succeed with Cabernet Sauvignon. You can taste that in the 1995 vintage (**1/2) of this pleasant, ruby-hued red. It's a distinctly cool-climate style, crisp and green-edged, but fresh and reasonably flavoursome.

GLADSTONE	**DRY $15 -V**
CAB./MER.	
"RED LABEL"	(☆☆☆)

Not to be confused with the top Cabernet/Merlot (below), this is the Wairarapa winery's `house red'. The wine on the market in 1997 is a medium-bodied style with light, maturing colour. Soft and forward, with pleasant, ripe, plummy flavour, it's a decent quaffer for drinking now.

GLADSTONE CAB. SAUV./ MERLOT	VINTAGE	95	94	93	92	91	90	DRY $22 AV
	WR	6	6	NM	NM	6	5	☆☆☆☆
	DRINK	97-00	97-00	NM	NM	P	P	

A typically flavour-packed Wairarapa red, grown at Gladstone on old alluvial terraces of the Ruamahanga River. The '94 is right on form, with rich colour and bold, ripe, very generous and lush, silky-smooth flavours. The charming 1995 vintage (****) is a fresh, strong red with a minty fragrance and deep, bright colour. A buoyantly fruity wine, it reveals moderately complex, blackcurrant and raspberry-evoking flavours in a fresh, crisp yet ripe and supple, distinctly cool-climate style.

GLOVER'S MT LODESTONE CABERNET

DRY $16 -V

(☆☆☆)

The 1996 vintage (**1/2) is Dave Glover's only Cabernet Sauvignon from a year when he didn't make the top Moutere label (there was no '95 either). Matured in seasoned oak casks, it lacks a bit of ripeness, but offers quite good depth of fresh, berryish, crisp flavour. Drink 1997–98.

GOLDWATER CAB./MER./ FRANC	VINTAGE	97	96	95	94	93	92	91	90	DRY $47 -V
	WR	7	7	6	7	7	5	6	7	☆☆☆☆☆
	DRINK	02-15	00-15	00-10	02-20	15	98	05	05	

Kim and Jeanette Goldwater's stunning Waiheke Island wine is one of New Zealand's greatest reds. With its flashing purple-red hues, minty and oaky bouquet, wealth of blackcurrant-like fruit flavours and strong tannin grip, this is a superb claret-style red. Tasted this year, the '92 is a lesser vintage, aging well but lacking a bit of its customary warmth and intensity; the '91 is deliciously complex, soft and rich. The '94 is exciting stuff. Matured for 14 months in half-new French oak barriques, it has the beguiling fragrance of cassis and new oak and exceptionally concentrated, spicy, firm flavour, finely balanced and long. The 1995 (*****) is from a relatively wet vintage, but the Goldwaters have come up with another classy wine. Deeply coloured, it's a very elegant and rich red, slightly lighter, softer and more forward than the top vintages, but still concentrated and chewy, with spicy, chocolatey, firm, complex flavour. Drink it before the more powerful and tautly structured '93 and '94.

HAU ARIKI CABERNET SAUVIGNON

DRY $28 -V

(☆☆☆)

There's plenty of body and flavour in the 1995 vintage (**1/2) of this French oak-aged Martinborough red, but it lacks real warmth and ripeness. The colour is bold and bright; the bouquet berryish and minty; the flavour very fruity and fresh, with noticeably high acidity and a chewy, green-edged finish.

HERON'S FLIGHT	VINTAGE	96	95	94	93	92	91
CABERNET	WR		NM	NM	7	6	5	7
SAUV./MERLOT	DRINK		NM	NM	97-00	97-9	97-8	97-00

DRY $27 AV

☆☆☆☆⯪

The 1994 vintage (*****) of David Hoskins and Mary Evans' Matakana red is clearly the best since the richly perfumed, mouthfilling, exceptionally full-flavoured '91. It possesses a warmth and depth of flavour that makes it very attractive already, yet it also has enough power to age well. Deep purple-red, it has a lifted, spicy, oaky bouquet and a big, generous palate, ripe, slightly earthy and supple, with a rich, persistent finish. There is no '95 or '96 ("too wet," says Hoskins) but the 1997 vintage will probably yield a 50/50 blend of Cabernet Sauvignon and Montepulciano.

HUTHLEE EST. CABERNET/ MERLOT

DRY $23 -V

(☆ ☆☆⯪)

The sturdy, softening 1994 vintage (***1/2) is a Hawke's Bay blend of 60 per cent Cabernet Sauvignon and 40 per cent Merlot, matured for over a year in French and American oak casks. It's a smooth wine with ripe, sweet-fruit flavours and some complexity, offering satisfying drinking 1997–98.

HUTHLEE EST. CABERNET SAUVIGNON

DRY $21 -V

(☆ ☆☆⯪)

The 1995 vintage (***1/2) of this Hawke's Bay red is an unblended Cabernet Sauvignon, French oak-aged for just over a year. The bouquet of fresh, ripe, red berry aromas leads into an attractively buoyant palate with fresh berry/mint flavours of good depth, light oak influence and a well-rounded finish. It's still youthful; drink 1998.

JACKMAN RIDGE	VINTAGE	95	94	93	92	91
CABERNET	WR	6	6	5	5	4
SAUVIGNON	DRINK	97-00	97-9	97-8	P	P

DRY $11 V+

(☆ ☆☆)

The 1994 vintage of Montana's budget-priced red is a chocolatey, spicy, full-flavoured wine, competitive with cheap Aussie reds. The 1995 (***) is a blend of Chilean and New Zealand wine, French and American oak-aged. Like the '94, it's a characterful red, chunky, with full colour and good depth of warm, well-ripened blackcurrant/plum flavours, a touch of spice and rounded tannins. Good value.

JOHN MELLARS	VINTAGE	95	94	93
GREAT BARRIER	WR	6	5	6
CABERNET	DRINK	98-05	97-02	97-03

DRY $40 -V

(☆–☆☆☆ ☆)

The 1996 vintage (****) of John Mellars' Great Barrier Island red is an elegant style, rather than a blockbuster, and by far the best since the hearty, richly flavoured debut '93. It was matured for up to 20 months in French oak barriques (one-third new). The bouquet is fragrant, with the aromas of ripe berry fruits, spice and cedary oak; the palate full-bodied and quite forward in its appeal, with very good depth of blackcurrant, spice and plum flavours, oak richness and firm but balanced tannins. It's a delicately flavoured, complex red, amazingly enjoyable already, yet sure to age well.

KANUKA FOR.	VINTAGE	94	93	DRY $18 -V
CAB. SAUV./	WR	6	5	
MERLOT	DRINK	97-8	P	(☆ ☆☆)

Grown on the coast at Thornton, near Whakatane, the 1993 vintage is a middle-weight red, with moderate depth of cassis, red berry and wood flavours and firm tannins. It's not flash, but still a decent debut. The '94 (**1/2) is very similar. Ruby-hued, with a slightly herbaceous, oaky bouquet, it's not concentrated but offers quite good depth of moderately ripe, woody flavour and balanced tannins.

KEMBLEFIELD	VINTAGE	94	93	DRY $19 -V
CAB. SAUV./	WR	6	4	
MERLOT	DRINK	97-9	P	(☆ ☆☆)

The debut 1993 vintage of this Hawke's Bay red is pale, with a green-leafy bouquet and soft, herbaceous palate. The '94 (**1/2) a blend of 50 per cent Cabernet Sauvignon, 40 per cent Merlot and 10 per cent Cabernet Franc, French oak-matured for 17 months, is distinctly better, but still a bit pricey. A solid red with fairly light colour and a fresh, green-tinged bouquet, it's crisp and berryish, with reasonable flavour depth, a touch of wood complexity and a moderate tannin grip.

KERR FARM	VINTAGE	96	95	DRY $19 -V
CABERNET	WR	6	5	
SAUVIGNON	DRINK	97-01	97-00	(☆ ☆☆)

The decent 1995 vintage reveals a medium-full ruby hue, good body and plenty of ripe, berryish, spicy, moderately tannic flavour. The '96 (***), estate-grown at Kumeu and matured in French and American oak casks, possesses good colour and a ripe, raspberryish fragrance. It's not intense, but offers pleasing depth of fresh, buoyant, ripe blackcurrant, red berry and spice flavours in a lightly wooded style for drinking now onwards.

LAKE CHALICE	VINTAGE	96	95	DRY $17 -V
CABERNET/	WR	5	4	
MER./FRANC	DRINK	97-00	97-8	(☆ ☆☆)

Appealing as a drink-young proposition, the 1995 vintage (**1/2) of this Marlborough red is a blend of 50 per cent Cabernet Sauvignon, 36 per cent Merlot and 14 per cent Cabernet Franc, matured for eight months in French and American oak barriques. It's full, fresh and spicy, with a supple, peppery, slightly short finish.

LANDMARK EST.		DRY $20 -V
HB CABERNET		
SAUVIGNON		(☆ ☆☆)

Landmark is the Vitasovich family's long-established Henderson winery, formerly known as Public Vineyards. Matured for two years in French oak barriques, the 1994 vintage (**1/2) has a full, brick-red colour, plenty of body, good depth of spicy, slightly pruney flavour and moderate tannins. It lacks delicacy and class, but is certainly a characterful quaffer.

LIMEBURNERS BAY CABERNET SAUVIGNON

`DRY $25 AV`

☆☆☆☆

This Hobsonville, estate-grown red is typically dark, chunky and rich-flavoured. The 1993 vintage (****) is a bold, spicy wine, deeply coloured and hearty. Just starting to soften, it's a very satisfying wine with excellent concentration of brambly, slightly earthy flavour, oak complexity and a long finish. In lesser years like 1995, the lower-priced Cabernet/Merlot (below) is released.

LIMEBURNERS BAY CABERNET/ MERLOT

`DRY $15 AV`

(☆☆☆)

A second-tier red produced in years when the top label (above) does not appear, this West Auckland wine still offers very enjoyable drinking. The '95 (***) is a smooth, warm, berryish red, not concentrated but with a touch of savoury complexity. It slips down very easily. Drink 1997–98.

LINCOLN HB CABERNET SAUVIGNON

VINTAGE	96
WR	5
DRINK	97-9

`DRY $14 -V`

(☆☆☆)

Forward in its appeal, the 1995 vintage is a warm, flavoursome red. The colour is full; the palate chunky and supple, with a touch of complexity and good depth of spicy, slightly chocolatey, blackcurrant-like flavours. The less impressive '96 (***½) includes 15 per cent Merlot and was matured for eight months in French and American oak barriques. The colour is light; the flavour fruity and lightly spicy, with gentle tannins. It's a pleasant wine, but lacks any real depth.

LINCOLN THE HOME VINEYARD CABERNET/ MERLOT

`DRY $17 AV`

☆☆☆

Typically a fragrant, chunky, full-flavoured red, grown predominantly in the large Henderson "home vineyard". The 1993 shows reasonable depth of green-edged flavour, but lacks the quality of past vintages. There is no '94. The characterful 1995 vintage (****½) is a 70/30 blend, matured for a year in seasoned, predominantly American oak casks. The colour is full; the flavours are minty and chewy, with some complexity and very good depth through the palate.

LINCOLN VINT. SEL. CAB./ MERLOT

VINTAGE	95	94	93	92	91
WR	5	NM	7	NM	7
DRINK	97-03	NM	99	NM	98

`DRY $25 AV`

(☆☆☆☆☆)

The 1993 vintage of Lincoln's top-tier red, grown in Kumeu and Henderson, marks the winery's finest red-wine hour. Richly coloured, with minty, oaky aromas, it is generous and dense-packed, with an impressive depth of cassis and toasty wood flavours, ripe and sustained. The '95 (****), grown in Hawke's Bay, is a blend of 60 per cent Cabernet Sauvignon and 40 per cent Merlot, matured for a year in American oak casks (two-thirds new). Maturing well, it is a full-bodied, generous and complex red with excellent depth of ripe, spicy flavour.

LINDEN EST.	VINTAGE	95	94	93	92	DRY $18 AV
CABERNET/	WR	7	6	3	5	
MERLOT	DRINK	97-01	97-00	P	97-9	(☆ ☆☆)

Full and ripe, the 1994 vintage has plenty of blackcurrant and plum-like, earthy flavour in a slightly rustic style. The '95 (****) is a much more charming red. An Esk Valley blend of 60 per cent Cabernet Sauvignon and 40 per cent Merlot, matured for two years in American oak casks (25 per cent new), it is highly fragrant, with perfumed, sweet oak. The flavours are spicy and plummy, with very good depth, complexity and a backbone of ripe, supple tannins.

LINDEN EST.	VINTAGE	94	DRY $32 -V
RESERVE	WR	6	
CAB./MER.	DRINK	00	(☆ ☆☆☆)

The chunky, full-flavoured, debut 1994 vintage (****) of this Esk Valley red is a 60/40 blend, French oak-aged for 18 months. The full, bright colour leads into a mouth-filling palate with good depth of ripe, blackcurrant/plum flavours and a firm, persistent finish. Good now, but also worth cellaring.

LINTZ EST.	VINTAGE	96	95	DRY $15 V+
CAB. EST.	WR	6	6	
CUVEE	DRINK	97-9	97-8	(☆ ☆☆)

The 1995 vintage (***) of this Martinborough red is a blend of 50 per cent Cabernet Sauvignon, 35 per cent Cabernet Franc and 15 per cent Merlot, wood-aged for 10 months. It's a mouthfilling (13.5 per cent alcohol) wine with light colour but plenty of berryish flavour, moderate tannins and a touch of oak complexity. With maturity, a slight leafiness is emerging.

LINTZ ESTATE	VINTAGE	96	95	94	93	92	91	DRY $25 AV
CABERNET/	WR	6	6	7	7	4	5	
MERLOT	DRINK	00-03	99-02	98-00	97-9	P	P	☆☆☆☆

Chris Lintz makes notably burly and flavour-crammed Martinborough reds. The '94 is dark, with a slightly green-edged bouquet wrapped in sweet oak and a mouthfilling (13.5 per cent alcohol), generous palate packed with rich, slightly pruney, persistent flavour. The '95 (***1/2) is deeply coloured, with a fragrant bouquet of berries, herbs and oak. It's a weighty, generous red with fresh, concentrated blackcurrant/herbal flavours and firm tannins, already drinking well.

LINTZ EST.	VINTAGE	95	94	93	92	91	DRY $28 -V
VITESSE	WR	7	7	6	NM	6	
CAB. SAUV.	DRINK	00-08	02-10	98-01	NM	97-9	(☆ ☆☆☆)

Winemaker Chris Lintz doesn't pull his punches: "This wine proudly lays claim to being Martinborough's most powerful red wine." The strapping '91 is rich, concentrated, complex and tautly structured, and the '93 is pretty successful too – chunky, minty and tannic. The 1994 vintage (*****1/2), grown in the Vitesse vineyard, is a muscular red (13.5 per cent alcohol) with bold, purple-black colour. It's a very concentrated, tannic wine with intense blackcurrant/dark plum flavours, crying out for cellaring.

LONGRIDGE OF HB CAB. SAUV./MER.

	VINTAGE	96	95	94	93	92	91	90
	WR	7	7	7	5	5	6	6
	DRINK	98-03	97-02	97-00	97-8	97-8	97-8	P

DRY $16 AV

☆☆☆

A very solid Hawke's Bay red from Corbans that is matured in French and American oak casks, the American wood giving a noticeably sweet, aromatic perfume to the bouquet. The 1994 vintage, a 60/40 blend, oak-aged for 10 months, is a medium to full-bodied wine with lightish colour, a green-edged bouquet and pleasant, firm, gently oaked, red berry-fruit flavours. The fragrant, mouthfilling '95 (***¹/₂) is the best Longridge red yet. Oak-matured for a year, with 45 per cent Merlot, it reveals medium-full colour depth, sturdy body and lots of firm, plummy, spicy flavour, fleshed out with toasty wood. A tannic wine with good length, it's still developing and worth cellaring for a year or two.

LONGVIEW EST. SCARECROW CAB. SAUV.

	VINTAGE	96	95	94
	WR	6	NM	5
	DRINK	00-02	NM	98-9

DRY $24 AV

(☆ ☆☆☆)

From a small, terraced vineyard south of Whangarei flows this richly coloured, perfumed red crammed with ripe, brambly, spicy flavours. The '94 is powerful and persistent, with sweet, concentrated fruit, well-integrated oak and soft fruit tannins. The 1996 vintage (***¹/₂) is still a baby. Matured for over a year in French (two-thirds) and American oak casks, it has good, bright colour and a minty bouquet. The palate offers strong, still very youthful blackcurrant/mint flavours wrapped in oak, with an underlay of firm, balanced tannins.

MATAWHERO CAB. SAUV./ MERLOT

	VINTAGE	92	91	90
	WR	6	NM	5
	DRINK	97-03	NM	97-00

DRY $30 -V

☆☆☆☆

One of Matawhero's flagships, and in quality terms it has consistently been at the forefront of Gisborne's reds. The 1990 vintage is brambly and spicy, robust and tannic in a very rich, gutsy, characterful and satisfying style. The '92 (****) is again a very powerful (over 14 per cent alcohol) and chewy red with deep colour and impressively concentrated, brambly, complex, tannic flavour.

MATAWHERO ESTATE CABERNET

DRY $18 AV

(☆☆☆)

The characterful 1993 vintage (***) of this Gisborne red reveals maturing colour of medium depth, positive tannins, and good depth of chocolatey, earthy, spicy flavour, with some complexity.

MATUA SMITH-DARTMOOR EST. CAB. SAUV.

	VINTAGE	95	94	93	92	91	90
	WR	6	6	NM	5	6	4
	DRINK	00+	00+	NM	97-9	97-8	P

DRY $21 AV

☆☆☆☆

At its best, a seductively rich and smooth Dartmoor Valley, Hawke's Bay red. Deep-coloured and weighty, and distinctly voluptuous in its youth, it's always highly enjoyable, but in the past exhibited a leafy greenness that slightly detracted from its quality (although the '87, opened on its 10th birthday, had lasted the distance well, with leathery, herbal, spicy, complex flavours). The 1994 vintage is a classy wine with great drinkability. The blackcurrant-like, peppery fruit flavours are sweet and ripe, with an underlay of supple tannins. The '95 (****) is already delicious. Matured for 17 months in French oak casks (new and one-year-old), it's a quite powerful and complex wine, full and well-rounded, with ripe, sustained cassis/plum flavours.

MATUA SMITH- DARTMOOR CAB. SAUV./MER.	VINTAGE	95	94	93	92	91	DRY $14 V+
	WR		6	5	6	6	5	
	DRINK		98-00	97-9	97-8	97-8	P	(☆☆☆)

An easy-drinking, flavoursome, mid-priced red. The '94 is chunky and supple with sweet oak and reasonably ripe plum/spice flavours. The 1995 vintage (***) offers typically good value. A blend of 70 per cent Cabernet Sauvignon and 30 per cent Merlot, grown in the Dartmoor Valley and matured for 10 months in one and two-year-old casks, it displays good colour depth and a chunky, supple palate with sweet oak and moderately ripe plum/spice flavours. A decent although not distinguished red.

MELNESS CABERNET SAUVIGNON	VINTAGE	94	DRY $17 AV
	WR	5	
	DRINK	97-00	(☆☆☆☆)

The attractive 1994 vintage (***1/2) from this tiny Canterbury winery was made from Marlborough grapes and oak-matured for nine months. The colour is good and bright; the palate well-balanced and free of undue herbaceousness, with plenty of blackcurrant and spice flavour and moderately firm tannins. Maturing well, it offers satisfying, although not highly complex, drinking.

MIDDLETON CABERNET SAUVIGNON	VINTAGE	95	DRY $12 -V
	WR	4	
	DRINK	97-8	(☆☆)

Produced by the Melness winery in Canterbury, the 1995 vintage (**) is a briefly oak-aged Marlborough red. Light, crisp and green-edged, it's a simple, berryish wine, lacking ripeness and depth, but OK as a drink-young quaffer. Drink up.

MILL ROAD CABERNET/ MERLOT	VINTAGE	96	95	DRY $13 AV
	WR	6	5	
	DRINK	98-02	97-9	(☆☆☆)

There's no mention or sign of oak, but the 1995 vintage is a pleasant Beaujolais-style red from Morton Estate: ruby-hued, with fresh, smooth, plummy flavours. The '96 (***1/2) is a Hawke's Bay blend of 69 per cent Cabernet Sauvignon, 26 per cent Merlot and 5 per cent Cabernet Franc, French oak-aged for just six weeks. It's a solid, fairly simple red, ruby-hued, with moderately ripe, berryish, spicy flavours and a light tannin grip.

MILLS REEF ELSPETH CAB./MER.	VINTAGE	95	94	DRY $29 AV
	WR	7	7	
	DRINK	02	00	(☆☆☆☆☆)

The powerful 1994 vintage is Mills Reef's first under its flagship Elspeth label. Bold and brambly, with a flashing, purple-red hue and toasty oak aromas, it is a deep-flavoured wine with ripe fruit, oak richness and a tight tannin grip. The impressively dark, fragrant and mouthfilling '95 (****¹/₂) is a 70/30 blend of Hawke's Bay fruit, French oak-aged for 14 months. The rich, minty, toasty bouquet leads into a very chewy and tightly structured palate with intense cassis/plum flavours. A powerful, complex wine for the long haul.

MILLS REEF MOFFAT ROAD CAB. SAUV.	VINTAGE	96	95	94	DRY $13 AV
	WR		6	5	6
	DRINK	01	00	98	(☆☆☆)

The 1995 vintage (labelled Mere Road) is a very easy-drinking Hawke's Bay red with sweet oak aromas and a medium-bodied, smoothly fruity, ripe-tasting palate. It lacks concentration, but is an appealing drink-young style. The ruby hued '96 (**¹/₂) includes 10 per cent Merlot, and was matured for six months in one and two-year-old French oak casks. Designed as a drink-young style, it has floral, raspberryish aromas, medium-full body and pleasant, smooth berry/spice flavours.

MILLTON VINEYARD, THE, TE ARAI RIVER CABERNET SAUVIGNON/MERLOT

DRY $23 -V

(☆☆☆☆)

Fined [clarified] with "fresh free-range egg whites", the characterful 1994 vintage (***¹/₂) is a Gisborne blend of 40 per cent Cabernet Sauvignon, 40 per cent Merlot, 11 per cent Malbec and 9 per cent Cabernet Franc, fermented with natural yeasts and matured in French and American oak barriques. It's an attractive, ripely fruity wine with medium-full colour, good depth of berryish, spicy flavours, some complexity and a well-balanced, rounded finish.

MISSION HB CABERNET SAUVIGNON	VINTAGE	96	95	94	93	92	91	DRY $14 V+
	WR		5	5	6	3	4	5
	DRINK	97-00	97-8	P	P	P	P	☆☆☆

In favourable vintages, this reasonably priced Hawke's Bay red offers very appealing value. The '95 is a fragrant, gutsy, moderately ripe wine with good colour depth, rich, spicy, plummy flavour and some complexity. The '96 (***¹/₂) shows the label in top form. A blend of 75 per cent Cabernet Sauvignon, 20 per cent Merlot and 5 per cent Cabernet Franc, matured in French and American oak barriques (25 per cent new), it is toasty and minty on the nose, with a full, characterful palate. Warm and spicy, with satisfying flavour depth, it can be enjoyed anytime from now onwards.

MISSION HB CAB. SAUV./ MERLOT	VINTAGE	96	95	94	93	92	91	DRY $14 AV
	WR		5	6	7	4	5	6
	DRINK	97-00	97-00	97-9	P	P	P	☆☆☆

An easy-drinking Hawke's Bay red. Its quality usually mirrors the vintage; in warmer years like 1994 and '95, it is ripe and soft, with medium-full body and light, pleasant but not intense blackcurrant flavours; cooler years like '92 and '93 yield a fresh, simple, green-leafy red. The 1996 (**¹/₂), grown at Fernhill and oak-aged for six months, is a lighter wine than its Cabernet Sauvignon stablemate (above) of the same vintage. It's a gentle red with reasonable depth of berryish, plummy flavour and soft tannins in an easy-drinking style.

MONTANA CAB. SAUVIGNON/ MERLOT

VINTAGE	96	95	94	93	92	91	90
WR	6	5	6	6	5	6	6
DRINK	97-00	97-00+	97-00+	97-9+	97-8+	97+	P

DRY $13 V+

☆☆☆½

The addition since the 1994 vintage of Merlot and Hawke's Bay fruit to Montana's former Marlborough Cabernet Sauvignon has transformed the old warhorse – it's much richer and riper. The 1995 vintage preserves the quality improvement seen in the '94. Full and fruity, with perfumed American oak, it is smooth and supple, with plenty of ripe berry/plum flavour. The 1996 vintage (***) is based on 60 per cent Marlborough and 40 per cent Hawke's Bay fruit, with most of the Merlot originating from Hawke's Bay. Matured in French and American oak casks, it is a full-bodied, ruby-hued red with good depth of blackcurrant/plum flavours and an engagingly smooth finish. This astute marriage of Marlborough's fresh, minty flavours and the warmth and power of Hawke's Bay fruit works well.

MONTANA FAIRHALL EST. CAB. SAUV.

VINTAGE	96	95	94	93	92	91	90
WR	7	NM	6	NM	NM	NM	NM
DRINK	98-03	NM	97-02+	NM	NM	NM	NM

DRY $30 -V

(☆☆☆☆½)

Here's proof of Marlborough's ability to yield top-flight claret-style reds. The first 1989 vintage of this premium label is a lovely, supple, delicate wine awash with chocolate and plum-like, complex, firm flavours. The label disappeared from 1990 to 1993, but the fresh, vibrantly fruity 1994 vintage (****) is fragrant, berryish and plummy, with peppery, minty nuances and a ripe, supple finish. The '96, tasted prior to bottling, looked full of promise – a powerful, concentrated wine with rich, plummy fruit characters and chewy tannins.

MORTON EST. WHITE LABEL HB CAB./MER.

VINTAGE	96	95	94	93	92	91	90
WR	5	6	6	4	4	6	4
DRINK	97-9	97-00	97-8	P	P	97-8	P

DRY $17 AV

☆☆☆

The full-bodied and flavourful 1995 vintage (***) is a blend of 72 per cent Cabernet Sauvignon and 28 per cent Merlot, French oak-aged for nine months. It's a very solid, spicy, tannic wine, still youthful, with good depth of slightly herbaceous, cassis and plum-like flavours.

MOUNT RILEY CABERNET/ MERLOT

DRY $15 AV

(☆☆☆)

Produced by Allan Scott, the 1996 vintage (***) is a rare marriage of Waipara, North Canterbury Cabernet Sauvignon and Marlborough Merlot. It's a straightforward red, ruby-hued and berryish, with a cool-climate freshness, crispness and mintiness that makes it an attractive drink-young style for 1997–98.

MOUTERE HILLS NELSON CAB./ MERLOT

DRY $18 -V

(☆☆½)

A pleasant quaffer for 1998, the '96 vintage (**½) is a 2:1 blend of Cabernet Sauvignon and Merlot, half estate-grown at Upper Moutere, with the rest from Richmond. Oak-aged for 10 months, it has light colour and a strongly herbaceous bouquet. On the palate, it lacks ripeness, richness and complexity, but offers reasonable depth of fresh, crisp, berryish flavour in a drink-young style.

NAUTILUS CAB. SAUV./MER./ CAB. FRANC

VINTAGE	96	95	94	93	92	91	90
WR	5	4	5	4	4	5	4
DRINK	98-00	97-9	97-9	P	P	P	P

DRY $22 -V

(☆☆☆⚟)

Autumn dryness drew Nautilus to Marlborough rather than Hawke's Bay for this premium red. Merlot "gives flesh and modifies the herbaceousness", and aging in American oak "adds a sweet, cedary character", says winemaker Alan Hoey. From the poor 1995 vintage in Marlborough, Nautilus produced a very respectable red (****1/2), still developing. An American oak-aged blend of Cabernet Sauvignon (55 per cent), Merlot (23 per cent) and Cabernet Franc (22 per cent), it is slightly leafy on the nose, but the palate is full, fruity and flavoursome, with a firm, persistent finish.

NGATARAWA CLASSIC CAB./ MERLOT

DRY $13 AV

(☆☆☆)

The first 1996 vintage (***) of Ngatarawa's lower-tier label is a decent, no-fuss Hawke's Bay red, blended from 60 per cent Cabernet Sauvignon and 40 per cent Merlot, and oak-aged for nine months. The berryish, slightly leafy bouquet leads into a full-bodied wine with quite good depth of moderately ripe berry/spice flavours and gentle tannins. A smooth red for 1997–98.

NGATARAWA GLAZEBROOK CAB./MERLOT

VINTAGE	95	94	93	92	91	90
WR	7	6	5	5	6	6
DRINK	00-05	99-04	97-8	P	97-9	P

DRY $26 AV

☆☆☆☆⚟

The company's flagship red is typically a concentrated Hawke's Bay wine, displaying intense, spicy and cassis-like flavours. The latest vintages are more fragrant and welcoming than the slightly austere reds of several years ago. The '94 has an enticing perfume, rich yet delicate blackcurrant, spice and oak flavours and a supple, complex finish. The stylish 1995 vintage (****1/2) is an estate-grown blend of 75 per cent Cabernet Sauvignon and 25 per cent Merlot, matured for a year in new French oak barriques. Richly coloured, it possesses excellent weight and depth of warm, ripe cassis, plum and spice flavours, complex and sustained, braced by firm tannins.

NGATARAWA STABLES CAB./MER.

VINTAGE	96	95	94	93	92
WR	7	6	5	5	5
DRINK	97-8	97-8	P	P	P

DRY $16 AV

☆☆☆

A chunky Hawke's Bay red with an easy-drinking appeal and lots of flavour. The 1995 vintage (***) is a blend of 75 per cent Cabernet Sauvignon and 25 per cent Merlot, matured for a year in seasoned French and American oak casks. It's not concentrated, but fresh, smooth and ripe-tasting, with enough weight and depth of blackcurrant and plum flavours to be enjoyable.

NOBILO FALL	VINTAGE	95		M/DRY $10 AV
HARVEST	WR	5		(☆ ☆☆)
CAB. SAUV.	DRINK	97-8		

The first 1995 vintage (**¹/₂) is a flange-topped, synthetic-stoppered, smartly packaged Marlborough red. A ruby-hued wine with leafy aromas, it offers pleasing depth of smooth, berryish flavour. Oak-matured for five months, it's an easy-drinking style, lacking complexity, with a sliver of sweetness to broaden the appeal for those new to reds.

NOBILO HB	VINTAGE	94	93	92	DRY $19 -V
CABERNET	WR	6	NM	5	(☆ ☆☆)
SAUVIGNON	DRINK	P	NM	P	

Past vintages of this red have offered plenty of berryish but green-edged flavour. The '94 (**¹/₂) is a smooth, easy-drinking wine, matured in French oak for 18 months. Ruby-hued, with a slightly grassy bouquet, it offers moderate depth of berryish, plummy, herbaceous flavour. An over-priced quaffer.

NOBILO MARL.		DRY $18 AV
CABERNET		(☆☆☆)
SAUVIGNON		

With its accent on fresh, buoyant fruit flavours, this can be a very easy-drinking wine: fragrant, plummy and vibrantly fruity. Still buoyant, the American and French oak-aged 1994 vintage (***) is full and berryish, with some fruit sweetness and a well-rounded finish. It lacks any great warmth and richness, but offers very pleasant drinking right now.

ODYSSEY	VINTAGE	96	95	94	DRY $16 AV
CABERNET	WR	6	5	5	(☆☆☆)
SAUVIGNON	DRINK	97-02	97-9	97-9	

Rebecca Salmond, winemaker at Pleasant Valley, makes consistently attractive wines under her own Odyssey label. Grown at Kumeu, one-half of the 1996 vintage (***¹/₂) was handled in tanks; the other half was matured for 10 months in one and two-year-old French and American oak barriques. It's an elegant wine, medium to full-bodied, with good depth of blackcurrant and spice, slightly earthy flavours, a touch of complexity and integrated tannins.

OMAKA SPRINGS		DRY $14 AV
MARLBOROUGH		(☆☆☆)
CABERNET/MERLOT		

One-half of the 1996 vintage (***) was handled in oak, but its chief appeal lies in its fresh, vibrant fruit characters. Bright pink-red in hue, with floral, raspberryish aromas, it is full-bodied, slightly minty and supple, offering good, no-fuss drinking through 1998.

ONEROA BAY CABERNET SAUVIGNON/MERLOT

DRY $25 -V

(☆☆☆⛧)

This sturdy Waiheke Island red is Peninsula Estate's second-tier label. The '94 is a robust and chewy style, with slightly hard tannins amid its enjoyably rich, blackcurrant, spice and plum-like flavours. An 80/20 blend, matured in American oak casks, the 1995 vintage (****¹/₂) is slightly green-edged, full-bodied and tannic, with plenty of chewy, nutty, spicy flavour.

PEGASUS BAY CABERNET/ MERLOT

VINTAGE	96	95	94	93	92
WR	7	6	6	5	4
DRINK		97-10	97-01	97-00	97-8	97-8

DRY $22 AV

☆☆☆☆

Grown at Waipara, this is one of the best claret-style reds to flow from Canterbury. The 1994 vintage (labelled Cabernet Sauvignon/Cabernet Franc/Merlot) has lots of appeal, with a berryish, leafy fragrance, good weight and satisfying depth of vibrantly fruity, complex, moderately tannic flavour. The '95 (****) is fresh, dark and chunky, with intense, blackcurrant, spice and mint flavours, complex and firm. A generous and characterful red.

PENINSULA ESTATE CABERNET SAUVIGNON/MERLOT

DRY $35 -V

☆☆☆☆⛧

This small Waiheke Island winery produces strapping, tautly structured reds that cry out for cellaring. The dark, muscular, flavour-packed and tannic 1993 vintage proved the potential. The '94 (****¹/₂) possesses a deep, bright colour and very tight-knit palate – gutsy, with an impressive concentration of ripe blackcurrant/spice flavours, strong oak influence and grippy tannins. A huge wine with masses of fruit; open 1998 onwards.

PHOENIX CABERNET SAUVIGNON

DRY $14 -V

☆☆⛧

This quaffing red is grown in heavy soils in the Henderson estate vineyard behind the Pacific winery. The 1994 vintage (**¹/₂), matured for 20 months in French and American oak casks (half new), is a dark wine with a shy bouquet. It's a chunky, leafy red with moderately ripe flavour and slightly hard, green tannins.

PLEASANT VAL./ SIG. SEL. AUCK. CAB./MER.

VINTAGE	95
WR	6
DRINK	97-9

DRY $18 AV

(☆☆☆☆)

Estate-grown in the Henderson Valley, the 1994 vintage is a classic young claret-style red, intense and tautly structured, with excellent aging potential. The '95 (***¹/₂) is softer and attractive already. A blend of 80 per cent Cabernet Sauvignon and 20 per cent Merlot, oak-matured for a year, it is slightly leafy on the nose, but full-bodied and supple, with good depth of cassis/plum flavours.

PLEASANT VAL.	VINTAGE	95					
SIG. SEL. AUCK.	WR	5					
CAB. SAUV.	DRINK	97-8					

DRY $16 V+

(☆ ☆☆☆☆)

This old Henderson Valley winery makes rich claret-style reds at bargain prices. French oak-matured, the 1995 vintage (****) is a weighty, firm, serious wine with loads of strongly spicy, complex flavour and a powerful finish.

QUARRY ROAD	VINTAGE	95
CABERNET	WR	5
SAUVIGNON	DRINK	00

DRY $15 V+

(☆ ☆☆☆)

The 1995 vintage (****) of this Te Kauwhata red, from the winery once called Aspen Ridge, offers great value. French oak-aged for a year, it reveals deep, still purple-flushed colour. It's a big, chewy, generous wine with excellent concentration of fresh, plummy, spicy flavour, braced by firm tannins.

RIVERSIDE	VINTAGE	96	95	94	93	92	91	90
CABERNET/	WR	5	4	4	4	3	5	4
MERLOT	DRINK	98-00	97-00	97-8	P	P	P	P

DRY $15 -V

(☆☆)

Grown in the Dartmoor Valley, this has typically been a plain, light and leafy red. The '94 and '95 vintages (**) both lacked ripeness and staying power. The 1996, tasted as a barrel sample, looked likely to be a big step up, with full, bright colour and quite good depth of ripe, smooth flavour.

ROCKWOOD
CABERNET
SAUVIGNON

DRY $13 AV

(☆☆☆⟩)

The '96 (**1/2) is a solid quaffer, but nothing more. Grown in Hawke's Bay, with some maturation in French and American oak casks, it's a fruity, smooth but slightly unripe-tasting red with berryish, grassy aromas and flavours in a simple, drink-young style.

ROSÉBANK EST.	VINTAGE	94	93
CABERNET/	WR	7	6
SHIRAZ	DRINK	97-9	97-8

DRY $20 -V

(☆ ☆☆)

An odd but workable marriage, the 1994 vintage (***) of this Canterbury-based label is a 70/30 blend of Marlborough Cabernet Sauvignon and Barossa Valley Shiraz. It's a robust (13.5 per cent alcohol), soft red with dark colour, restrained oak influence and loads of spicy, herbal, blackcurrant-like, well-rounded flavour. The Shiraz makes a powerful impact, creating a markedly bolder wine than most local reds.

RUBY BAY
CABERNET
SAUVIGNON/MERLOT

DRY $20 -V

(☆☆☆)

Past vintages of this Nelson wine have been impressive, but the 1995 (**1/2) lacks its customary richness. It's a fruity but simple wine, green-edged and lacking warmth and depth.

St Jerome Cabernet Sauvignon

VINTAGE	95
WR	7
DRINK	97-9

DRY $20 -V

(☆☆☆½)

Past vintages have been light and plain, but the 1995 (***) is the most characterful red yet under St Jerome's second-tier label. Grown in West Auckland and Hawke's Bay and matured for a year in French oak casks, it's a forward wine with a hint of maturity in its medium-full colour, leathery, pruney, spicy flavours and firm but balanced tannins.

St Jerome Cabernet Sauv./Mer.

VINTAGE	94	93	92	91	90
WR	6	6	NM	6	6
DRINK	00-06	99-05	NM	97-04	98-06

DRY $40 -V

☆☆☆☆½

A strapping Henderson red that is Davorin and Miro Ozich's "pride and joy". A densely coloured, powerful wine which makes no concessions to early-drinking appeal, the 1993 vintage is a 60/40 blend of estate-grown fruit, matured in French oak for the unusually long period of three years. The bouquet is still a bit closed, but it's a strapping wine with concentrated flavours of cassis, spice and oak and a taut finish. The 1994 (****½) is the second best vintage yet, trailing only the '91. As always it is serious stuff, designed for the long haul, but slightly more supple and approachable than the '93. Robust and tannic, with excellent concentration of sweet-tasting fruit and nutty oak, it is a complex, taut wine, best cellared for another couple of years.

St Nesbit

VINTAGE	92	91	90
WR	NM	7	7
DRINK	NM	97-10	97-00

DRY $48 -V

☆☆☆☆☆

This high-flying South Auckland red exhibits very impressive complexity. The 1989 vintage (60 per cent Merlot, 30 per cent Cabernet Sauvignon and 10 per cent Cabernet Franc) is exceptional. Dark, with a stunning surge of spicy, chocolate-rich flavour, it is complex and supple, with a voluptuous richness rare in New Zealand reds. The 1990, almost as good as the '89, is based on 70 per cent Cabernet Sauvignon and equal parts of Cabernet Franc and Merlot, barrique-aged for three years. Cedary and subtle, it is again very reminiscent of true claret, with impressively complex, chocolatey, spicy, leathery flavours. It's now at its peak. The more youthful '91 (*****) reveals a rich, brambly bouquet, full colour with a hint of maturity, and a mouthfilling palate with rich, concentrated, spicy, slightly earthy flavours, braced by firm tannins. Due to vineyard replanting, the release of the 1991 vintage in 1997 was the last release of St Nesbit until 2001 or 2002.

Sacred Hill Basket Press Cab. Sauv.

VINTAGE	95
WR	6
DRINK	97-00

DRY $20 V+

(☆☆☆☆½)

Sacred Hill wines are going from strength to strength. French and American oak-aged, the 1995 vintage (****½) is a stylish, unblended Hawke's Bay Cabernet Sauvignon, full-bodied and fruity, with an abundance of warm, plummy, spicy flavour, firm yet supple, and lovely overall balance.

SAINTS HB CABERNET/ MERLOT

VINTAGE	96	95	94
WR	6	7	6
DRINK	97-00	97-02	97-00

DRY $17 V+

(☆ ☆☆☆)

New Zealand makes very few reds of this quality at this price. Produced by Montana, the '95 shows rich, ripe fruit on the nose and palate, with balanced oak adding complexity, good weight, fine tannins and a long, rounded finish. A good drink-now or cellaring proposition, the 1996 vintage (***¹/₂) is well-coloured, smooth and moderately ripe-tasting, with berryish, very slightly herbaceous aromas, oak richness and good depth of supple, plum/spice flavour.

SEIBEL HB CABERNET/ MERLOT

DRY $15 -V

(☆ ☆☆)

The light 1994 vintage (**¹/₂) is a 60/40 blend, matured for two years in old oak casks. It's a mellow, slightly grassy red with crisp, berryish flavours, lacking weight and richness, but with a touch of mushroomy, earthy complexity. Ready.

SEIBEL LONG RIVER CABERNET SAUVIGNON/PINOTAGE

DRY $10 V+

(☆ ☆☆)

Here's a bargain! The 1996 vintage (**¹/₂) is a blend of Hawke's Bay Cabernet Sauvignon and Auckland Pinotage, matured for 10 months in seasoned oak barrels. Ruby-hued, with very restrained wood influence, it's a simple but enjoyable red, buoyant, ripe, berryish and smooth. Drink now.

SEIFRIED NEL CABERNET/ MERLOT

VINTAGE	96
WR	5
DRINK	97-04

DRY $16 -V

(☆ ☆☆)

The solid but undistinguished 1996 vintage (**¹/₂) is a 60/40 blend, matured for 10 months in two and three-year-old French oak barriques. It's a drink-young style, lacking warmth and concentration, with fresh, berryish, slightly herbaceous flavours and very light oak influence.

SEIFRIED NEL CABERNET SAUVIGNON

VINTAGE	96	95	94	93	92	91	90
WR	5	NM	7	6	6	6	6
DRINK	97-04	NM	97-02	97-00	97-9	P	P

DRY $16 -V

☆☆☆

Light and leafy in cool years, this wine is more satisfyingly robust and ripe in warmer vintages. Enjoyable already, the '96 (***) is an unblended Cabernet Sauvignon, matured for eight months in one to three-year-old French oak barriques. Ruby-hued, it is flavoursome and balanced, with reasonably ripe-tasting, slightly crisp blackcurrant/plum characters, restrained wood influence and rounded tannins.

SELAKS	VINTAGE	96	95					DRY $13 AV
CABERNET	WR	6	6					
SAUVIGNON	DRINK	97-9	97-8					☆☆☆

The standard of this modestly priced red has climbed steadily in recent vintages. The 1995 is a pleasant, berryish red offering fresh, smooth, no-fuss drinking. The '96 (***) is the best yet. A blend of 85 per cent Hawke's Bay Cabernet Sauvignon and 15 per cent Marlborough Merlot, French oak-aged, it is an enjoyable although not complex wine with medium-full colour and ripe, berryish flavours, fresh and supple.

SETTLER	DRY $14 AV
CABERNET/	
MERLOT	(☆☆☆)

Evert Nijzink's 1995 Hawke's Bay red (***) is based on bought-in grapes, grown at Te Awanga and in the Dartmoor Valley. It's a lightly coloured, medium weight red, not herbaceous, with pleasant plum/spice flavours and a touch of oak complexity.

SHALIMAR	DRY $14 AV
CABERNET/	
MERLOT	(☆☆☆)

Ready now, the 1995 vintage of this ruby-hued Gisborne red (**½) offers pleasant but not concentrated plummy flavours in a very forward style. The '96, tasted as a barrel sample, looked better, with plenty of ripe, berryish, moderately firm flavour.

SOLJANS BAR.	VINTAGE	96	95	94	93	92	91	DRY $16 AV
SELECTION	WR	6	NM	6	6	NM	3	
CAB./MER.	DRINK	98-02	NM	97-9	P	NM	P	☆☆☆☆

The 1994 vintage is a seductive, very smooth-flowing wine, estate-grown at Henderson and matured for a year in seasoned French oak casks. The '96 (***) is already enjoyable, with ripe berry/plum flavours and gentle oak influence in a supple forward style.

SOLWAY CAB.	DRY $16 -V
SAUV./MERLOT/	
CAB. FRANC	☆☆☆

Solway is the second-tier label of the Bloomfield winery at Masterton. The characterful, slightly rustic 1994 vintage is fresh, fruity and leafy, offering flavoursome, no-fuss drinking. The '95 (**½) is a decent quaffer with fresh berry/spice flavours, light oak and moderate tannins, drinking well now.

STONELEIGH	VINTAGE	96	95	94	93	92	91	90	DRY $16 -V
VINE. MARL.	WR	6	NM	7	6	7	7	5	
CAB. SAUV.	DRINK	98-00	NM	97-00	97-8	97-8	97-9	P	☆☆☆

Typically a smooth, slightly herbaceous wine, mingling fresh cassis, herbal and restrained oak flavours. The 1994 vintage is Stoneleigh at its best: ripe and free of green-leafy characters, fresh and flavoursome, with plummy, slightly peppery fruit characters, gentle tannins and good drinkability. The '96 (***¹/₂) doesn't offer good value at over $15. Matured for a year in French and American oak casks, and including 10 per cent Merlot, it is light in colour and lacks any real concentration. That said, it's still a pleasant, smooth red with plum/spice, slightly leafy flavours.

STONYRIDGE AIRFIELD CABERNETS	VINTAGE	95	94	93	92			DRY $25 AV
	WR	6	6	6	6			
	DRINK	97-9	97-01	97-00	97-8			☆☆☆☆

Despite its junior status, Stonyridge's second-tier Waiheke Island red is still classy. The 1994 vintage, grown in the Fenton vineyard, is a lovely wine: fragrant, richly coloured and oozing ripe, velvety fruit. The 1995 (****), based on young vines in the Stonyridge vineyard, is less intense than its predecessor, but very approachable, with bright, deep colour and sweet-tasting, berry/mint flavours, supple and smooth.

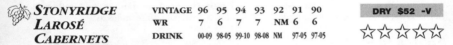

STONYRIDGE LAROSÉ CABERNETS	VINTAGE	96	95	94	93	92	91	90	DRY $52 -V
	WR		7	6	7	7	NM	6	6	
	DRINK	00-09	98-05	99-10	98-08	NM	97-05	97-05	☆☆☆☆☆

A stunning Waiheke Island wine, packed with rich, spicy, minty fruit flavours and powerful oak. It is sold largely on an "en primeur" basis, whereby the customers, in return for paying for their wine about nine months in advance of its delivery, secure a substantial price reduction. Nevertheless, the price has doubled between the 1990 (released at $26) and the 1996 vintage ($52), reflecting the wine's quality and scarcity, and strong demand. Tasted in the past year, the '89 is majestic, showing great intensity and structure; the '91 is still developing, but less intense and complex than the '89. The magical 1993 bursts with sweet-tasting, blackcurrant and plum-evoking flavours, with a suppleness of tannins that gives it amazing drinkability. The '94, from a lower-cropping vintage, is a massive, tannic, very serious and powerful red, for drinking beyond 2000. The '95, from a wet vintage, is a lighter and, in its youth, more approachable wine than the magnificent '94, but still classy, with rich colour and concentrated, ripe blackcurrant/plum flavours wrapped in quality oak, finishing long and firm. The 1996 vintage (*****) is a blend of 56 per cent Cabernet Sauvignon, 19 per cent Merlot, 12 per cent each of Malbec and Cabernet Franc, and a splash of Petit Verdot. Tighter than the '93, a bit lighter than the '94, it boasts a deep, inky colour, fragrant bouquet bursting with berry and mint aromas, and an exuberantly fruity palate that needs several years' cellaring to reveal its full power and richness.

TE AWA FARM LONG. CAB./MER.	VINTAGE	96	95	94	DRY $18 AV
	WR	6	6	5	
	DRINK	98-01	97-00	P	(☆☆☆☆)

From the Lawson family's vineyard near Gimblett Road in Hawke's Bay, the instantly appealing '95 is full and smooth, with a ripe, plummy, spicy fragrance, good weight and lots of warm, well-rounded flavour. The '96 (***¹/₂), matured for a year in French and American oak barriques, shows the "vibrant fruit characters" promised on the label. Ruby-hued, it's a full-bodied red with subtle wood influence, placing its accent on fresh, ripe, plummy fruit flavours, with a finely balanced, moderately tannic finish. Not highly complex, but well made and satisfying.

TE AWANGA VINEYARDS CABERNET/MERLOT

DRY $19 -V

(☆☆☆⯪)

The solid, supple 1995 vintage (**½) is a Hawke's Bay blend of 50 per cent Cabernet Sauvignon, 35 per cent Merlot and 15 per cent Cabernet Franc, French oak-aged for 15 months. It's an easy-drinking red, fresh, plummy and smooth, but just lacks the flavour depth to justify a higher rating. Drink 1997–98.

TORLESSE RES. WAIPARA CAB. SAUV.

VINTAGE	95
WR	6
DRINK	98-00

DRY $25 AV

(☆☆☆☆)

One of the most convincing Canterbury Cabernet Sauvignons yet, the 1995 vintage (****) was grown in winemaker Kym Rayner's vineyard and oak-aged for 15 months. Deep ruby, with an attractive fragrance of berries and mint, it's a firmly structured, vibrant, complex and subtle red with berry/spice flavours, strong, sweet oak, and very satisfying depth and weight.

TE KAIRANGA CABERNET SAUVIGNON

VINTAGE	95	94
WR	5	5
DRINK	98-00	98-02

DRY $21 -V

☆☆☆

"Cabernet's an easy variety to grow, but [in Martinborough] not an easy variety to get ripe," admits Glenys Hansen, Te Kairanga's viticulturist. The 1994 vintage is one of the best so far – vibrantly fruity, plummy and raspberryish, with a restrained wood influence and smooth tannins. The easy-drinking '95 (***), matured for a year in French and American oak barriques, has light colour, smooth tannins and good depth of firm, plummy, youthful flavour wrapped in sweet oak. Much riper and more enjoyable than the reds of the early '90s.

TE KAIRANGA CABERNET SAUV./MER.

VINTAGE	95	94
WR	5	5
DRINK	98-00	98-02

DRY $24 -V

(☆☆☆)

The 1994 vintage is one of the best claret-style reds yet from this Martinborough winery. It is a distinctly cool-climate style, fresh, vibrantly fruity and crisp, with ripe plum/red berry flavours in an appealingly smooth style. The '95 (***) is another good vintage, but a bit pricey for what it offers. French oak-aged for a year, with 15 per cent Merlot, it is full-bodied, berryish and firm, with toasty oak adding richness. It lacks real intensity, but is still a decent red, with some depth.

TE KAIRANGA CASTLEPOINT CABERNET SAUVIGNON/MERLOT

DRY $15 -V

(☆☆)

The '93 vintage of this Martinborough red is very leafy and unripe, and the 1995 (**) is again short of colour and flavour. A blend of 70 per cent Martinborough and 30 per cent Hawke's Bay fruit, with 30 per cent Merlot, it was French oak-aged for a year. It's a plain quaffer, simple and herbaceous, lacking ripeness and richness.

TE MATA EST. AWATEA CAB./MER.	VINTAGE	96	95	94	93	92	91	90
	WR	6	6	6	6	5	7	6
	DRINK	99-05	99-05	98-05	98-04	97-00	97-99	97-99

DRY $27 AV

☆☆☆☆☆

From the 1982 to 1988 vintages, Awatea was an extraordinarily good single-vineyard Hawke's Bay red. Since the 1989 vintage, however, Awatea has evolved into "a blend of wines from Te Mata's spectrum of vineyard sites", positioned slightly below its Coleraine stablemate. Compared to Coleraine, in its youth Awatea is more seductive, more perfumed, and tastes more of sweet, ripe fruit, but is more forward and slightly less concentrated. The '94 is a classic Awatea: richly fragrant, boldly coloured and very fleshy and lush, with strong, ripe, blackcurrant and plum-like flavours, oak complexity and and a long, supple finish. The 1995 vintage (*****) is a blend of 55 per cent Cabernet Sauvignon, 35 per cent Merlot and 10 per cent Cabernet Franc, matured for 18 months in new and used oak. Already very approachable, it possesses rich colour and a very forthcoming, classy, claret-like bouquet of spice, blackcurrants and cedarwood. A mouthfilling, vibrantly fruity red, it has a lovely suppleness of texture and an abundance of rich, ripe, distinctly minty flavour, finishing long and soft.

TE MATA EST. CABERNET/ MERLOT	VINTAGE	96	95	94	93	92	91	90
	WR	6	6	6	6	5	6	6
	DRINK		98-00	97-01	97-00	P	P	P	P

DRY $17 V+

☆☆☆☆

Not to be confused with its Coleraine and Awatea big brothers, this lower-priced Hawke's Bay red is still an impressive mouthful. In top years, it is a generous, ripe-tasting, exuberantly fruity red. The 1994 vintage is fleshy and packed with ripe, blackcurrant and plum-evoking flavours, with a rich, well-rounded finish. Cabernet Franc (37 per cent) and Merlot (35 per cent) dominate the '95 vintage (****), with 28 per cent Cabernet Sauvignon. Matured for a year in new and seasoned oak barriques (including some American), it's a rich red with generous colour, loads of red berry and cassis flavour with a slight herbal influence, and a well-rounded, long finish. Already very satisfying.

TE MATA EST. COLERAINE CAB./MER.	VINTAGE	96	95	94	93	92	91	90
	WR		6	6	7	NM	NM	7	6
	DRINK		00-08	02-10	99-10	NM	NM	97-99	+99+

DRY $36 AV

☆☆☆☆☆

Breed, rather than brute power, is the hallmark of Coleraine, which since its first vintage in 1982 has carved out a reputation second-to-none among New Zealand's reds. A single-vineyard Hawke's Bay wine from 1982 to 1988, since 1989 Coleraine is no longer exclusively based on the Coleraine vineyard, but has become part of a tiered group of labels, blended from several vineyards, with Coleraine at the top. Compared with its Awatea stablemate (above), Coleraine is more strongly influenced by new oak, more concentrated and more slowly evolving. Tasted in the past year, the '85 is a wine of some elegance, but not exciting, with highish acidity and some herbal characters; the '87 is savoury and persistent; the '89 very fragrant and Bordeaux-like. The exceptionally intense and stylish 1991 vintage is arguably the greatest Coleraine yet, and currently in devastating form. The 1995 vintage (*****) is a marriage of 59 per cent Cabernet Sauvignon, 34 per cent Merlot and 7 per cent Cabernet Franc, oak-aged for 19 months. The colour is vibrant and deep; the bouquet still fairly closed. Chunky, with rich, brambly, tautly tannic flavour, it is a big wine – one of the boldest Coleraines yet – but still very youthful.

TE MOTU CABERNET/ MERLOT

VINTAGE	95	94	93
WR	5	6	5
DRINK	97-02	98-10	97-00

DRY $40 -V

(☆ ☆☆☆☆ ☆)

Waiheke Vineyards' top red. The debut 1993 vintage is notably fragrant, dark and concentrated. Mouthfilling and taut, with very intense blackcurrant and spice flavours in a rich, tannic, complex style, the '94 confirmed the label as a Waiheke heavyweight. The stylish but lighter '95 (****½), from a wet vintage on the island, was matured in one and two-year-old barrels (40 per cent American). Already very approachable, it is fragrant, with medium-full colour (lighter than usual), warm, ripe blackcurrant/spice flavours wrapped in quality oak and smooth tannins. It lacks the intensity of the '93 and '94, but is still a very harmonious, supple and satisfying red, for drinking now onwards.

TERRACE VIEW CABERNET/ MERLOT

VINTAGE	94
WR	5
DRINK	P

DRY $15 -V

(☆ ☆☆ ☆)

The 1994 vintage (***½) is strictly a quaffer. Produced by Kemblefield from Hawke's Bay grapes, and French oak-aged for 16 months, it lacks colour depth and the bouquet is leafy. It's a simple, light red.

TE WHARE RA SARAH JENNINGS CABERNET SAUVIGNON/ MERLOT/CABERNET FRANC

DRY $25 -V

(☆ ☆☆☆ ☆)

Consistently one of Marlborough's best claret-style reds. The 1994 vintage (***) is an exuberant, deliciously fruity wine with bright, full, purple-red colour and a berryish, leafy fragrance. Fresh and vibrant on the palate, berryish and smooth, it offers highly enjoyable drinking.

TIMARA CABERNET SAUVIGNON/MERLOT

DRY $9 V+

☆☆☆

The non-vintage red currently on sale is a blend of Hawke's Bay, Marlborough, Chilean and Australian wine, American oak-aged for nine months. For under $10, Montana's wine offers great value. Tasted in late 1997, it reveals full, youthful purple-red colour and a light but ripe bouquet. It's a very decent red, not complex but satisfying, with plenty of ripe, cassis/plum flavour and smooth tannins.

VIDAL CAB. SAUVIGNON/ MERLOT	VINTAGE	96	95	94	93	92	91	90	DRY $15 V+
	WR	6	6	6	5	6	5	6	☆☆☆☆
	DRINK	97-00	97-00	97-98	P	P	P	P	

The Hawke's Bay winery's second-tier red-wine label, but in most vintages it is very satisfying. Drinking extremely well right now, the '95 is a finely balanced wine with good colour depth, sweet-tasting fruit characters and impressive depth of smooth, fruity, ripe cassis/plum flavours, supple and persistent. The '96 (****½), oak-aged for a year, is satisfyingly full in colour and body, with bouyant, ripe blackcurrant/plum flavours, oak richness (it saw more new oak than the '96 Villa Maria Private Bin), moderate tannins and good length. Worth cellaring until mid-98.

VIDAL RES. CABERNET SAUVIGNON	VINTAGE	95	94	93	92	91	90	DRY $30 AV
	WR	6	6	NM	NM	6	7	☆☆☆☆☆
	DRINK	98+	97+	NM	NM	97+	97+	

Ranked among Hawke's Bay's most distinguished reds, this is a slightly more austere style than its voluptuous stablemate, the Reserve Cabernet Sauvignon/Merlot (not produced since 1992). The '94 vintage has an abundance of ripe, blackcurrant and plum-evoking flavours and a complex, tight, very persistent finish. The '95 (*****) is a generous, youthful red, grown in Villa Maria's Ngakirikiri vineyard, near Gimblett Road, and French oak-aged for 20 months. Mouthfilling, with deep, purple-flushed colour and a powerful surge of ripe, plummy, strongly spiced flavour, it is still vibrantly fruity, with an underlay of firm, supple tannins and a rich, trailing finish.

VILLA MARIA PRIV. BIN CAB. SAUV./MER.	VINTAGE	96	95	94	93	92	91	90	DRY $14 V+
	WR	6	6	6	5	5	5	5	☆☆☆
	DRINK	98-00	97-99	97-99	P	P	P	P	

Top vintages of this typically chunky, flavour-packed red are a good buy. The '95 is supple, buoyantly fruity and flavoursome, with strong drink-young appeal. The very solid 1996 vintage (***) is a blend of Te Kauwhata and Hawke's Bay grapes (25 per cent Merlot) matured for a year in seasoned oak casks. With its moderate tannins, touch of wood complexity and good depth of plum, berry and spice flavours, it's an ideal all-purpose red for drinking from now onwards.

VILLA MARIA RES. CAB. SAUV./MER.	VINTAGE	95	94	93	92	91	90	DRY $30 AV
	WR	NM	6	NM	6	7	6	☆☆☆☆☆
	DRINK	NM	98-00	NM	97-99	97-00	97-99	

This much-acclaimed red is typically dark and mouth-filling, with great depth of blackcurrant, capsicum and plummy flavours, and the tightness of structure to mature well over the long haul. In a vertical tasting in 1995 of the 1986 to 1991 vintages, the '87 was powerful, exuberantly fruity and still ascending; the '89 distinctly herbaceous; the '90 and '91 both very approachable, but with enough stuffing and vigour to warrant further cellaring. The still youthful, purple-flushed 1994 vintage (****½) is a 60/40 blend of Hawke's Bay fruit, matured for 20 months in new French and American oak barriques. It's fragrant and ripe, mouthfilling and firmly structured, with an array of penetrating, blackcurrant, plum, mint and spice flavours, wrapped in quality oak, and a crisp, lingering finish that slightly lacks warmth and roundness. It needs time: open 1998 onwards. (There is no '95; see Villa Maria Reserve Merlot/Cabernet Sauvignon.)

VOSS WAIHENGA CAB./MER.	VINTAGE	95	94	93		DRY $21 AV
	WR	4	6	3		
	DRINK	97-00	97-01	P		(☆ ☆☆☆⯨)

Estate-grown in Martinborough (Waihenga) this is Voss's top claret-style red. The 1994 vintage is a very satisfying red with strong, red berry-fruit and mint flavours and taut tannins. The '95 (***), from a year when the Merlot was "not up to scratch", is 90 per cent Cabernet Sauvignon. Oak-aged for 14 months, it slightly lacks ripeness and warmth, but is vibrantly fruity, with good depth of fresh, crisp, berryish, spicy, firm flavour.

WAIMARAMA ESTATE CAB./MER.	VINTAGE	95	94	93	92	91		DRY $26 AV
	WR	7	6	NM	5	7		
	DRINK	99-08	97-06	NM	97-00	97-00		(☆ ☆☆☆☆)

Both the 1991 and 1992 vintages are classy, concentrated and complex Havelock North reds. The '94 lacks the fragrance of its predecessors, but is still fleshy, with a quite rich array of berryish, plummy, slightly herbal flavours, oak complexity and a supple finish. The 1995 vintage (****¹/₂) is a 70/30 blend, French oak-aged for 14 months. It's a complex, fine, Bordeaux-like red with very elegant and persistent, plummy, minty, nutty flavours and a firm finish, approachable now but well worth cellaring.

WAIMARAMA ESTATE CAB. SAUV.	VINTAGE	95	94	93	92	91		DRY $27 AV
	WR	7	6	5	5	7		
	DRINK	99-08	98-04	P	97-00	97-00		(☆ ☆☆☆☆)

Like its Cabernet/Merlot stablemate (above), this is a highly concentrated Hawke's Bay red, packed with flavour. The debut 1991 vintage, tasted in 1997, was lovely: powerful, ripe, supple and rich-flavoured. The '94, French oak-aged for a year, is restrained in bouquet but possesses good depth of ripe, blackcurrant/plum flavours, fresh and strong, with supple tannins. The 1995 vintage (****¹/₂) is the finest since '91, and bolder, more tautly structured than its '95 Cabernet/Merlot stablemate (above). French oak-aged for 14 months, it's a mouthfilling red with rich, well-ripened blackcurrant and cedarwood flavours and firm, chewy tannins.

WAIPARA DOWNS CAB. SAUV.	VINTAGE	96		M/DRY $16 -V
	WR	5		
	DRINK	97+		(☆ ☆☆)

A typically flavoursome but distinctly green-edged North Canterbury wine. The '94, aged in American and French oak casks, is distinctly grassy but chunky, with plenty of smooth, berryish, plummy, herbal flavour. The 1996 vintage (**) is an unblended Cabernet Sauvignon, matured in half American, half French oak casks. Made to drink early, it's an unusual wine with vivid, purplish colour, a distinct touch of sweetness and strong, minty, plummy flavours. It's a very juicy red, but lacks warmth and vinosity.

WAIPARA	VINTAGE	95	94			DRY $18 -V
SPRINGS	WR	5	5			
CAB. SAUV.	DRINK	97-99	97-98			(☆ ☆☆⅃)

The enjoyable 1994 vintage (a Cabernet Sauvignon/Franc/Merlot) is a fruity, easy-drinking style with good weight and plenty of crisp, buoyant, berryish, slightly herbal flavour. The '95 (***½) was matured for a year in French oak barriques (30 per cent new). Grown in the Cemetery vineyard at Waipara, it's a solid red, ruby-hued, fresh, plummy and green-edged, but lacks real warmth and depth.

WALNUT	VINTAGE	96	95			DRY $20 -V
RIDGE	WR	5	4			
CAB. SAUV.	DRINK	97-00	97-98			(☆ ☆☆☆)

The first 1994 and 1995 vintages of Bill Brink's Martinborough red are flavoursome, but herbaceous and bitingly crisp, with a lack of full ripeness and warmth. The '96 (****½) is much more attractive. Matured in French oak casks (40 per cent new), it's a markedly riper, vibrantly fruity and supple wine with bright, full colour, very good depth of fresh, berryish, minty flavour, some spicy, oaky complexity and a positive underlay of tannins.

WEST BROOK	VINTAGE	95	94	93	92	DRY $18 -V
BLUE RIDGE	WR	6	6	7	5	
CAB./MER.	DRINK	98-05	97-04	97-03	97-99	(☆ ☆☆⅃)

The Blue Ridge label is reserved for the top wines from the small West Brook winery in Henderson. The dark, tannic 1994 vintage is an estate-grown blend of 85 per cent Cabernet Sauvignon and 15 per cent Merlot, French oak-aged for 15 months. It's a rather hard, extractive style, but also displays ripe fruit characters with some intensity. The '95 (***) includes 15 per cent Merlot and was matured in seasoned French oak barrels for 15 months. It's a middleweight style, not highly complex but aging gracefully, with satisfying depth of red berry/plum flavours and a slightly peppery, firm finish.

WINSLOW	VINTAGE	96	95	94		DRY $28 -V
PETRA	WR	7	6	6		
CAB. SAUV.	DRINK	00-07	99-10	98-05		(☆ ☆☆☆⅃)

Winslow's 100 per cent Cabernet Sauvignon is a less "complete" Martinborough wine than its blended stablemate (below), but is still a delicious mouthful. The bold, generous 1994 vintage is fragrant and deep-coloured, with ripe tannins and lots of lush, blackcurrant-like, spicy, slightly herbal flavour. The '95 (***½) matured for a year in American (predominantly) and French oak barriques, is another very good effort, with lots of colour, body and fresh, blackcurrant and mint flavour. (The '96, tested as a barrel sample, is impressively concentrated, with rich berry/mint flavours wrapped in sweet oak.)

WINSLOW	VINTAGE	96	95	94	93	92	91	DRY $35 -V
TURAKIRAE	WR	7	6	6	4	NM	6	
RESERVE	DRINK	99-06	98-05	97-04	97-00	NM	97-00	(☆ ☆☆☆☆⅃)

The lush, concentrated 1991 vintage of this Martinborough blend (then labelled Reserve Cabernet Sauvignon/Cabernet Franc), announced the arrival of Winslow as an accomplished red-wine producer. Typically riper and more complex than its Petra stablemate (above), it's boldly coloured and beautifully floral, with deep, vibrant, blackcurrant-like flavours and silky tannins. The 1995 vintage is a 3:1 blend of Cabernet Sauvignon and Cabernet Franc, matured for a year in French oak casks (half new). It's an impressively dark, mouthfilling and supple wine with rich, ripe, complex flavours wrapped in quality oak and a superbly sustained finish. The '96 (****¹/₂) was picked at 24° brix (the ripest yet) and matured in French oak casks (80 per cent new). Densely packed and tightly structured, it is a concentrated, nutty, complex, tannic red, ideal for cellaring.

Generic and Branded Reds

If you come across a wine labelled Joe Bloggs's Dry Red, its station in life isn't too high. "Dry reds" and other non-varietal wines are typically, but not always, the sort of low-priced reds you quaff rather than ponder over.

Before the New World fashion for "varietal" labelling swept the country in the 1970s, most New Zealand table wines were given "generic" names, like "Burgundy" and "Mosel", which aped those of classic European wine regions. The link between, for example, a deep-scented and supple Pinot Noir grown in the Cote d'Or of Burgundy, and a red labelled "Burgundy" which was produced from hybrid grapes in the North Island, was always far-fetched. In theory the New Zealand wine was similar in style to the famous overseas wine whose name it had copied. Essentially, however, it was a marketing ploy to give New Zealand wines (then hard to sell) the benefit of association with more familiar and prestigious overseas names. The long defunct Bordeaux Wines of Henderson once marketed a "Claret" and "Burgundy" – the sole difference being that one was oak-aged, the other was not.

Today the names Burgundy and Claret have vanished from New Zealand wine labels and lower-priced reds are commonly called "Dry Red". A "Dry Red" is a quaffing wine with no particular style model.

Branded reds range in quality from light, sweet quaffers like Velluto Rosso to expensive labels like Ata Rangi Célèbre, Pegasus Bay Maestro and Stonecroft Ruhanui.

	VINTAGE	97	96	95	94	93	92	91	90	DRY $28 -V
ATA *RANGI* *CÉLÈBRE*	WR	6	7	6	6	5	4	7	6	☆☆☆☆
	DRINK	99-01	98-00	97-00	97-98	P	P	97-99	P	

A distinctive Martinborough red which blends Syrah and Merlot with the predominant Cabernet Sauvignon. Robust and vibrantly fruity, it's typically tinged with the leafy character that cool-climate conditions accentuate in Cabernet-based reds, but also displays impressive extract, flavour and complexity. The '95 was blended from 55 per cent Cabernet Sauvignon, 30 per cent Merlot and 15 per cent Syrah. Fragrant, with plum/herbal/spice flavours wrapped in quality oak, it's a rich and complex red with firm tannins, loads of flavour and an impressively long finish. The '96 (****) is richly coloured, with loads of firm, minty flavour and the depth and structure to age well.

DRY $7 V+

BAKANO *CLARET*

☆☆☆

This low-priced red, in the '60s and '70s a hugely popular McWilliam's (NZ) label, was resurrected by Corbans in the late 1980s and is now based wholly or partly on Australian fruit. It's a decent quaffer: youthful, with ample body and strong berry-fruit flavours, dry and firm.

BLUE **ROCK** **MAGENTA**	VINTAGE	95	94	93	92	91	DRY $20 -V
	WR		5	5	5	NM 7	(☆ ☆☆)
	DRINK		97+	P	P	NM	P

Cabernet Sauvignon, Cabernet Franc, Pinot Noir, Meunier, Syrah ... it's hard to think of a grape missing from this Martinborough blend. Matured for a year in seasoned oak barrels, it is typically crisp and fresh, lacking the warmth and roundness of fully ripe fruit, but offering good depth of berryish, minty, distinctly herbal flavour.

C.J. PASK **ROY'S HILL** **RED**	VINTAGE	96	95	94	93	92	91	DRY $14 AV
	WR		7	6	7	5	5	6	☆☆☆
	DRINK		98-00	P	P	P	P	P

A "fruity, soft, easy-drinking" style is winemaker Kate Radburnd's goal with this Hawke's Bay red. Matured briefly in older oak casks ("for softening rather than wood flavour"), the 1995 vintage is a blend of 50 per cent Cabernet Sauvignon, 30 per cent Cabernet Franc and 20 per cent Merlot. It's a drink-young style with fresh, plum/herbal aromas and berryish, slightly minty, well-rounded flavour. The riper-tasting '96 (***) is again fresh and flavourful, with medium body and crisp, berryish flavours in an attractively buoyant and supple style.

CROSS ROADS **THE** **TALISMAN**	VINTAGE	95	94	DRY $35 -V
	WR	7	7	(☆☆☆☆☆☆)
	DRINK	99-04	00-06

"The Talisman is different to any other New Zealand wine," says winemaker Malcolm Reeves. The first 1994 vintage, from a blend of unspecified varieties estate-grown at Fernhill, was matured for two years in all-new French oak barriques. It's a voluptuous wine with bold colour, a highly fragrant bouquet and mouthfilling palate, bursting with ripe plum, spice and wood flavours. The '95 (****¹/₂), not quite as memorable but still classy, is a rich wine with concentrated plummy flavours, sweet oak complexity and a positively tannic, persistent finish.

COUNTRY **SOFT** **RED**		M/DRY $15 (3L) AV
		(☆☆)

This gutsy, semi-dry cask red is a blend of imported and New Zealand wine, marketed under Montana's bottom-tier Woodhill's brand. It's a chunky and tannic red with full colour and strong blackcurrant-like flavours in a generous, slightly rough, slightly sweet and characterful style.

ESK VALLEY **THE** **TERRACES**	VINTAGE	95	94	93	92	91	DRY $59 -V
	WR		7	7	NM	7	7	☆☆☆☆☆
	DRINK		00-10	97-05	NM	97-00	97-05

Grown on the steep terraced hillside flanking the winery at Bay View, Hawke's Bay, this is the richest and most concentrated of all New Zealand reds. The debut 1991 vintage is a monumental, yet fragrant and supple wine, purple-black, with a rich, spicy, complex bouquet, great weight and marvellous intensity of spicy, crushed red berries, minty, tannic flavour. The 1992 is not as massive, but shows a weight and warmth rare in the '92s. There is no '93. The '94 is an excitingly concentrated wine, very powerful, with a rush of plummy, spicy, complex flavour, braced by firm yet supple tannins. The 1995 vintage (*****) is the most striking since the '91. Based on ultra low-cropping vines (under one tonne/acre), it's a blend of 40 per cent Merlot, 40 per cent Malbec and 20 per cent Cabernet Franc, matured in new French oak barriques for almost two years. The colour is huge – an impenetrable purple-black. It's a statusesque red with a tidal wave of splendidly ripe blackcurrant, plum and spice flavours and very supple tannins. It looks capable of enormous complexity; bury it until 1999 and beyond.

FAIRHALL RIVER CLARET

DRY $8 V+

☆☆⛧

Here's a two-and-a-half-star quaffer at a one-star price! Montana's ruby-hued, non-vintage red is a blend of Pinot Noir and Pinotage grown in Marlborough and Hawke's Bay. It's fresh, fruity and supple, with plenty of body and berryish, dry, gently tannic flavour.

FROMM LA STRADA VINO ROSSO

DRY $17 AV

(☆☆☆)

Predominantly Pinot Noir, the 1994 vintage of this Marlborough red is fragrant, fresh, vibrantly fruity and supple – a generous, full-flavoured wine, richer and more satisfying than most of the region's reds. The lighter '95 (**¹/₂) offers strong raspberry and herbal flavours, slightly peppery, crisp and fresh. It's not complex, but still a very decent quaffer.

GLENMARK WAIPARA RED

DRY $15 -V

(☆☆⛧)

The 1991 vintage of this North Canterbury red, based on Cabernet Sauvignon, won a gold medal. The '95 (**) is again Cabernet-based, with some "very ripe" Merlot and Pinot Noir. It's very forward, with light, maturing colour and green-edged, rustic flavour.

GLOVER'S HOARY HEAD

DRY $15 -V

(☆☆⛧)

Named after a hill on the skyline west of Dave Glover's Upper Moutere winery, the 1995 vintage (**¹/₂) is a chunky quaffer blended from 60 per cent Hawke's Bay Cabernet Sauvignon and 40 per cent estate-grown Pinot Noir. Matured in oak for 18 months, it's a sturdy, berryish, firm-finishing red, quite flavoursome, with the Cabernet coming through strongly on the nose and palate. Drink now.

HERON'S FLIGHT LA CERISE

VINTAGE	95
WR	5
DRINK	97-8

DRY $18 AV

(☆ ☆☆)

The supple, light-bodied 1995 vintage (***) is a Matakana Merlot, oak-aged for 10 months.

Attractively packaged in a clear glass bottle with see-through label, it is a buoyant, easy-drinking style with moderate tannins, hints of tobacco and spice and a touch of savoury complexity. Satisfying drinking for right now.

HUNTER'S	VINTAGE	95	94	93	92	91	90	DRY $14 -V
ESTATE	WR	5	6	5	4	7	4	
RED	DRINK	98	P	P	P	P	P	☆☆⛧

A solid, although not complex, Marlborough red with strong, vibrant blackcurrant and herbal characters. Principally Cabernet Sauvignon and Merlot, it is blended with minor proportions of such varieties as Pinot Noir, Cabernet Franc and Syrah. Matured in seasoned French oak barriques, it's typically a ruby-hued wine with spicy, smooth flavour.

HUTHLEE	VINTAGE	95	94	93	DRY $13 -V
ESTATE	WR	5	5	5	
KAWEKA RED	DRINK	97-8	P	P	(☆☆⛧)

The 1993 vintage of this Hawke's Bay red is pretty good. An oak-aged blend of Merlot and Cabernet Franc, it's fresh, fragrant, buoyantly fruity and supple. The ruby hued '94 (**1/2) lacks richness but is chunky, with reasonable flavour depth – a solid quaffer for current drinking.

MATAWHERO
BRIDGE
ESTATE

DRY $28 -V

(☆☆☆☆)

This single-vineyard Gisborne red is dedicated to the memory of Matawhero's founder, Bill Irwin. The 1991 vintage is maturing well and full of character. A blend of 45 per cent Merlot, 20 per cent Malbec, 18 per cent Cabernet Sauvignon and 17 per cent Cabernet Franc, it is a powerful, complex wine with full colour, a spicy bouquet, chunky body and loads of ripe, rich, chocolatey, firm, well-sustained flavour. Open 1997–98. The '92 (****1/2) is almost equally bold and beefy.

MATUA
RED
JACKET

DRY $11 AV

(☆☆⛧)

Launched from the 1993 vintage, this budget-priced wine replaced Matua's Claret. The '95 (**1/2), grown in Auckland, Hawke's Bay and Marlborough, draws together Pinot Noir (55 per cent) and Cabernet Sauvignon (40 per cent) in the same bottle – a rare blend which would make Frenchmen throw up their wine goblets in horror. Pinotage makes up the balance. A quarter of the blend was oak-aged for six months. It's berryish, lively and smooth, but a bit green, lacking ripeness and depth.

DRY $8 V+

MISSION
MIRAGE

☆☆⛧

Mission's bottom-tier red is a simple Hawke's Bay quaffer. Cabernet Sauvignon-based, and matured for up to eight months in older oak casks, it's typically a decent, smooth red with plenty of plummy, spicy, slightly chocolatey flavour.

MOUTERE HILLS SUNRISE VALLEY RED

M/DRY $13 -V

(☆☆)

Sold as "a sort of Moutere Hills nouveau", the very pale 1996 vintage (**) is based on the first crop of Pinot Noir vines, oak-aged for three months. It's a light, cherryish, slightly herbaceous red, simple, fractionally sweet and crisp, lacking the enticing fragrance and fresh, vibrant fruit of a good "nouveau".

MUIRLEA RISE JUSTA RED

DRY $15 -V

(☆☆☆)

Willie Brown's Martinborough red is a non-vintage, oak-aged blend based principally on Pinot Noir. The characterful wine I tasted in late 1996 was ruby-hued and full-bodied, with savoury Pinot Noir aromas and strong, tannic but slightly hard flavour.

NEUDORF YOUNG NICK'S RED

DRY $14 V+

(☆☆☆☆)

A decade ago, this small Nelson winery produced a popular Beaujolais-style, Young Nick's Red, from its Pinot Noir vines – then decided to fashion a more serious, oak-aged Pinot Noir. The resurrected Young Nick's Red from 1996 (****) is a lovely, unwooded Pinot Noir, ruby-hued, attractively full and smooth, with sweet-fruit appeal, loads of berryish, supple flavour and a dry, persistent finish. Very yummy in its youth.

NOBILO'S CONCEPT

VINTAGE	86	85	84
WR	6	6	6
DRINK	P	P	P

DRY $28 -V

☆☆☆☆

The "concept" was to produce a distinctive Huapai red based principally on Pinotage, with smaller amounts of Cabernet Sauvignon and Merlot, matured for 21 months in French oak casks. Only three vintages have been marketed: 1984, 1985 and the currently available 1986 (***1/2). Concept Three is a characterful wine with a mature, browning colour and mushroomy, earthy, spicy bouquet. The flavour is complex, leathery, pruney and gamey, with firm tannins. It's starting to dry out; drink now.

OKAHU EST. NINETY MILE RED

VINTAGE	95	94	93	92	91
WR	5	5	6	5	5
DRINK	97-02	97-01	97-01	97-99	P

DRY $20 -V

☆☆☆

At its best, this is a very characterful Northland red: fleshy, with lots of savoury, spicy, blackcurrant-like flavour and a firm tannin grip. The '94 is warm, earthy, firm and spicy. The 1995 vintage (***) is a Kaitaia, estate-grown blend of Cabernet Sauvignon and Merlot, French oak-aged for 18 months. It's rustic on the nose – as was the '93 – but chunky and firm, with good depth of berryish, spicy, slightly earthy flavour in a fairly ripe style with some complexity.

OKAHU EST.	VINTAGE 95 94	**DRY $16 AV**
SHIPWRECK	WR 5 6	
BAY RED	DRINK 97-01 97-01	(☆ ☆☆)

The generous, robust, well-rounded style of this Northland red (especially the very good '94) has reminded me of a tyical southern Rhône. Named after a surfing bay at the foot of Ninety Mile Beach, the 1995 vintage (***) is a Kaitaia, estate-grown blend of 40 per cent Pinotage, 40 per cent Chambourcin (a highly regarded French hybrid), and 20 per cent Cabernet Sauvignon, matured in older American (60 per cent) and French oak casks. The bouquet is slightly rustic, but the palate is full and soft, with the ripeness and warmth typical of Okahu Estate's reds, plenty of plum/spice flavour and moderate tannins.

PARKER	**DRY $12 AV**
FIRST LIGHT	
RED	☆☆☆

Phil Parker's "nouveau" red is made by the whole-berry fermentation technique perfected in Beaujolais. Based on Pinot Noir or Pinotage grown in Gisborne, it is typically a light red, fragrant and supple, with fresh, soft, red berry flavours. Wine like this (a "now-or-never" style) should be drunk in its infancy.

PEGASUS	VINTAGE 94	**DRY $30 -V**
BAY	WR 6	
MAESTRO	DRINK 97-06	(☆ ☆☆☆☆)

This North Canterbury winery's slightly lower-priced Cabernet Sauvignon/Cabernet Franc/Merlot is impressive, but this reserve version is even finer. The 1994 vintage (****¹/₂) is based on a similar blend of grapes from older vines and matured in a higher percentage of new oak casks. Mouthfilling, it possesses very dark, purplish colour, intense blackcurrant, spice and mint flavours and a lovely suppleness of texture with ripe, rounded tannins. The best Cabernet-based red ever made in Canterbury.

	DRY $62 -V
PROVIDENCE	(☆☆☆☆☆)

James Vuletic, a former partner in The Antipodean, in 1995 launched New Zealand's priciest red: the 1993 vintage (*****) of Providence at $62 per bottle. The 2ha Providence vineyard at Matakana is planted in Merlot (70 per cent), Cabernet Franc (20 per cent), and Malbec vines. The wine is fermented with natural yeasts and matured for up to two years in all-new French oak barriques. With its beguiling fragrance, lush fruitiness and sweet, silky, sustained finish, the '93 stands up well against the other (and cheaper) top Auckland reds of the vintage, but does not overshadow them. A voluptuous red, hugely seductive in its youth due to its high Merlot content, it is clearly superior to The Antipodean. No stars for value, but five stars for quality.

RONGOPAI WAERENGA RED

DRY $14 -V

(☆☆☆)

The rustic 1995 vintage (**¹/₂) of this Waikato red is based on Cabernet Sauvignon (40 per cent) and Merlot (35 per cent), with smaller proportions of Pinot Noir and Malbec. French oak-aged, it lacks fragrance, but is full and rounded, with reasonable depth of blackcurrant/plum flavour.

ST HELENA PORT HILLS DRY RED

DRY $9 AV

(☆☆☆)

The non-vintage Canterbury wine currently on the market (**¹/₂) is an estate-grown Pinot Noir, given "no oak, no nothing", reports proprietor Robin Mundy. Aimed at a Beaujolais style, it's a supple, raspberryish red, crisp and simple, with reasonable flavour depth.

ST JEROME DRY RED

VINTAGE	95
WR	4
DRINK	97-98

DRY $11 -V

(☆☆)

The West Auckland winery's bottom-tier red from 1995 (**) is a light Hawke's Bay Cabernet Sauvignon, briefly oak-aged. It's a solid quaffer, berryish and slightly spicy, but as a "drink now" style could use greater freshness and liveliness.

SANDIHURST PATIO RED

DRY $9 AV

(☆☆☆)

Designed as a "luncheon red", this non-vintage wine is based predominantly on Pinot Noir, grown in Canterbury. It's fresh, raspberryish, cherryish and crisp, with a transparent ruby hue and firm, dry finish. I'd be tempted to serve it lightly chilled as a decent dry rosé.

SELAKS PRIVATE BIN RED

VINTAGE	96	95
WR	5	5
DRINK	97-98	P

DRY $12 -V

(☆☆)

For many years labelled as Private Bin Claret, this is Selaks' bottom-tier red. A North Island blend of Cabernet Sauvignon and Pinot Noir, matured in one and two-year-old French oak puncheons and barriques, it's typically solid but plain, with light, fresh, berryish flavours.

DRY $11 AV

SOLJANS EBONY

(☆☆☆)

For a pleasant quaffer, priced right, this non-vintage red (**¹/₂) launched in 1997 is worth trying. It's a 3:1 blend of West Auckland Cabernet Sauvignon and Pinotage, matured for nine months in seasoned French oak casks. Medium-bodied, it's reasonably ripe and warm, with berryish, spicy, earthy flavours and moderate tannins. Nothing flash, but satisfying.

STONECROFT CROFTER'S RED

DRY $18 -V

(☆☆☆⯨)

The Hawke's Bay winery's lower-priced red is made from fruit off young vines, together with wine which, at blending, winemaker Alan Limmer prefers to omit from his top Ruhanui and Syrah labels. Each release is numbered rather than vintage-dated; the debut Crofter's Red Number One (***1/2) is from 1995. Oak-matured for 18 months, it's a Cabernet Sauvignon-based red, with Merlot and Syrah. A fairly rich wine with full colour, a peppery bouquet and strong, moderately firm, berryish, herbal, plummy flavours, it offers very decent drinking from now onwards.

STONECROFT RUHANUI

VINTAGE	95	94
WR	5	6
DRINK	98+	98+

DRY $30 -V

(☆☆☆☆⯨)

The 1994 vintage replaced the Cabernet/Merlot in Alan Limmer's range. Past vintages have been dense-coloured, muscular, tannic Hawke's Bay reds with impressive fruit intensity and proven staying power. For his '94, Limmer added 15 per cent Syrah to the blend for the first time. It's a softly mouthfilling wine with a very spicy fragrance, deep colour, a seductive intensity of blackcurrant and pepper flavours (like many other top '94s, not entirely free of herbaceousness), and a rich, firm but supple finish. The 1995 vintage (****1/2) is very similar: dark and chewy, with rich spicy, plummy flavour and a firm, long finish.

VELLUTO ROSSO

MED $6 AV

☆⯨

This sweetish, low-priced wine from Corbans has introduced legions of medium white wine drinkers to the world of reds, although not dry reds. It's labelled as "a rich red wine, velvet smooth". I agree with the second part of that description, but certainly not the first. A trans-Tasman blend with a low (9.5 per cent) alcohol content, it's rosy-hued, light, sweet, raspberryish, inoffensive but bland.

VILLA MARIA PRIVATE BIN VINTAGE SELECTION RED

DRY $10 V+

(☆☆☆)

Here's a decent, drink-young red, sharply priced. The '96 (***) is a lightly oaked blend of Merlot and Cabernet Sauvignon, with quite good depth of purple-red colour. It's not complex but buoyantly fruity, with fresh raspberry/plum flavours, ripe and supple, in a forward style with enough body and flavour to be satisfying.

WALKER ESTATE NOTRE VIGNE

DRY $22 -V

(☆☆☆☆)

This Martinborough wine was previously labelled as Syrah, but the true identity of the Walkers' vines is unknown. The gutsy, French oak-aged 1995 vintage (****) is a notably warm and powerful red with rich, dark colour and a chunky palate offering loads of brambly, plummy flavour, very ripe and smooth.

WOHNSIEDLER CLASSIC RED

M/DRY $6 V+

(☆☆)

At $6, this is hard to beat, provided you don't mind a dollop of sweetness in your red! A blend of imported and New Zealand wine, it's ruby-hued and reasonably full-bodied, with a gentle tannin grip, a bit of character, and plenty of slightly sweet flavour.

WOODHILL'S VINEYARD SMOOTH RED

SW $13 (3L) AV

(☆☆)

If you're a dry red fan (at whom this "soft, velvety smooth medium red" cask is definitely not aimed), you'll find it a hair-raising experience. Blended by Montana from imported and New Zealand wine, it's only 5.8 per cent alcohol, which gets the excise tax (and retail price) down a couple of dollars. It's in a style all of its own, with a flavoursome, very sweet palate.

Merlot

Merlots are flooding onto the shelves – almost 40 new labels are featured in this edition. The 1995 vintage yielded a bumper Merlot crop, over double the previous record, and in 1997 the Merlot harvest was almost three-quarters that of the old stalwart, Cabernet Sauvignon.

Should Merlot replace Cabernet Sauvignon as our principal red-wine variety? Numerous winemakers believe that it should. Excitement is currently running high in New Zealand about this most extensively cultivated red-wine grape in Bordeaux.

Everywhere in Bordeaux – the world's greatest red-wine region – except in the Médoc and Graves districts, the internationally much-higher-profile Cabernet Sauvignon variety plays second fiddle to Merlot. The elegant, fleshy wines of Pomerol and St Émilion bear delicious testimony to Merlot's capacity to produce great, yet relatively early-maturing, reds.

In New Zealand, after decades of preoccupation with the more austere and slowly evolving Cabernet Sauvignon, the rich, persistent flavours and (more practically) earlier-ripening ability of Merlot are now stirring up intense interest. Poor fruit "set" can be a major drawback with the older clones, reducing yields, but Merlot ripens ahead of Cabernet Sauvignon, a major asset in cool-climate regions, especially in vineyards with colder clay soils. Merlot grapes are typically lower in tannin and higher in sugar than Cabernet Sauvignon's; its wines are thus silkier and a shade stronger in alcohol.

Hawke's Bay has over half of New Zealand's Merlot vines, but Marlborough, Auckland and Gisborne also have substantial areas. Merlot is now the country's sixth most widely planted grape variety, and between 1996 and 1999 the total area of bearing vines is expanding by over 50 per cent.

Until recently, Merlot's key role in New Zealand was that of a minority blending variety, bringing a soft, mouthfilling richness and floral, plummy fruitiness to its marriages with the predominant Cabernet Sauvignon. With the swelling stream of straight Merlots and Merlot-predominant blends, this aristocratic grape is now building a strong profile as a top varietal in its own right.

AKARANGI
MERLOT

`DRY $18 AV`

(☆☆☆)

The 1995 vintage (***) is the finest red I've tasted from this tiny Havelock North winery. Richly coloured, it is a big, fruity, although not complex style, resting its case on strong, blackcurrant and raspberry-like flavours, ripe, generous and supple. Drink now to 1998.

ALLAN SCOTT MERLOT	VINTAGE 95	DRY $21 -V
	WR 6	(☆)
	DRINK P	

Allan Scott's Marlborough wines are typically of high quality, but I can't find much to enjoy in the debut 1995 Merlot (*), which is very pongy. It's bright purple-red, fleshy, plummy and firm, but the bouquet is very off-putting.

ARAHURA CLEVEDON MERLOT	VINTAGE 94	DRY $28 AV
	WR 6	(☆☆☆☆☆)
	DRINK 97-00	

The 1994 vintage (****½) is the first wine to flow from the Clevedon area of South Auckland – and a very auspicious debut. Harvested at 23.5˚ brix, it was bottled unfiltered after maturing for 18 months in new French and American oak barriques. Just 40 cases were produced. It's a rich, generous red with medium-full colour and perfumed oak on the nose. With its excellent weight, concentrated, ripe, complex, slightly earthy flavour and strong but supple tannins, it's a powerful but very approachable red, maturing well.

BABICH MARA ESTATE MERLOT	VINTAGE 96 95 94	DRY $17 V+
	WR 6 7 7	(☆☆☆☆)
	DRINK 98-04 97-00 97-99	

Grown in Gimblett Road, Hawke's Bay, this is a consistently attractive red, sharply priced. The second 1995 vintage (****½) is the finest yet, with bold colour, a perfumed, spicy bouquet and seductively rich, firm, brambly, plummy flavours, complex and long. The '96, tasted as a barrel sample, lacked the notable power of the '95, but showed pleasantly ripe, non-herbaceous, berryish flavours.

BRADSHAW ESTATE MERLOT/ CABERNET SAUVIGNON		DRY $17 -V
		(☆☆☆)

The 1994 vintage, a straight Hawke's Bay Merlot, isn't rich but offers quite good depth of buoyant, raspberry/spice flavours and a firm finish. The 1995 (***½) is a 3:1 blend, matured for 10 months in older French oak casks. It's a medium to full-bodied, moderately flavoursome wine – fruity, plummy, supple and forward. Ready.

BRADSHAW ESTATE RESERVE MERLOT/ CABERNET SAUVIGNON		DRY $23 -V
		(☆☆☆)

The easy-drinking 1995 vintage (***) is a full, fresh, supple Hawke's Bay red with quite good depth of plummy fruit, toasty oak and moderate tannins. Ready.

BRAJKOVICH KUMEU MERLOT

DRY $16 V+

☆☆☆⯪

A deeper, more tannic Kumeu River wine than its Cabernet Franc stablemate: spicy, berryish and firm. The '95 is very typical: chunky, with good depth of red berry/plum/spice flavours and a positive tannin grip. The 1996 vintage (****) is probably the best yet. French oak-aged for a year, it's impressively concentrated, with ripe, plummy aromas and vivid colour. Weighty, with excellent depth of fresh, ripe plum/spice flavour, some savoury complexity and supple tannins, it's already highly enjoyable, but should also repay cellaring for a year or two.

CHURCH ROAD RESERVE MERLOT

VINTAGE	95	94
WR	7	7
DRINK	98-05	97-04

DRY $32 AV

(☆☆☆☆☆)

Finesse is the key quality of Montana's magnificent 1994 red, produced at The McDonald Winery in Hawke's Bay. It's a very subtle and complex wine with a scented, deep, brooding bouquet, hinting of great riches to unfold, and rich, ripe, very delicate dark plum and spice flavours, wrapped in quality oak, with warm, supple tannins. The '95 (*****) was grown in the Esk Valley and at Fernhill, and matured for 16 months in French oak barriques (60 per cent new). It's another splendid wine, deeply coloured, rich and soft, bursting with ripe, sweet-tasting, blackcurrant/plum flavour in a classy, complex style.

C.J. PASK MERLOT

VINTAGE	96	95
WR	6	7
DRINK	00	00

DRY $20 V+

(☆☆☆☆☆)

The 1995 vintage (*****) is a highly seductive Gimblett Road, Hawke's Bay red. The scented, cigar box bouquet leads into a supple, generous palate with lovely depth of sweet, ripe, berry/plum fruit and cedary oak adding complexity. An elegant, rich, well-crafted, top value wine, for drinking now onwards.

CLEARVIEW EST. RES. MERLOT

VINTAGE	96	95	94	93	92	91
WR	5	6	6	4	NM	6
DRINK	98-00	98-00	98-99	P	NM	P

DRY $30 AV

(☆☆☆☆⯪)

The '94 vintage of this Te Awanga red (the first labelled Reserve) is very weighty and concentrated, with dark colour and spicy, almost sweet-tasting fruit in a robust, complex style. Still in its infancy, the '95 (****¹/₂) sports a full, vivid colour and perfumed, toasty bouquet. It's a characterful, rich wine, packed with fruit in a very fragrant, fleshy and full-flavoured style that's bound to mature well.

COOPERS CREEK HB MERLOT

VINTAGE	96	95	94	93	92
WR	5	6	5	4	5
DRINK	97-99	98-99	P	P	P

DRY $16 V+

☆☆☆⯪

The '95 has deep colour, a perfumed bouquet and loads of berryish, minty, spicy, lush flavour. The 1996 vintage (***) is lighter than the '95. American oak-aged for six months, it's a forward wine, plummy and supple, not intense but enjoyably fresh and smooth.

COOPERS CREEK RES. MERLOT	VINTAGE	96	95				DRY $25 AV
	WR	NM	6				
	DRINK	NM	99-01				(☆☆☆☆)

The 1994 vintage of this Hawke's Bay red is richly coloured and perfumed, vibrantly fruity and strong-flavoured, with complexity and a firm finish. The '95 (****) is a fragrant marriage of sweet oak and plum/blackcurrant fruit, fresh, supple and flavourful, with lots of upfront appeal.

CORBANS COT. BLOCK MARL. MER./CAB. SAUV.	VINTAGE	94	93	92	DRY $28 -V
	WR	7	NM	6	
	DRINK	04	NM	00	(☆☆☆☆)

Soft, spicy, herbal and rich, the first, 1992 vintage of Corbans' premium Merlot (labelled as a straight Merlot, but including a splash of Cabernet Sauvignon and Cabernet Franc) is a stylish wine. The '94 Merlot/Cabernet Sauvignon (****) was hand-picked, foot-plunged and given "extended" aging in French oak barriques. It's a powerful, robust (13.5 per cent alcohol) wine with lush, ripe, densely packed blackcurrant and plum-like flavour, but currently very soft, and may lack the backbone for long-term cellaring.

CRAB FARM MERLOT		DRY $17 AV
		(☆☆☆)

The 1994 vintage (***) of this Hawke's Bay red is a generous, ripe, supple wine with rich colour. It reveals good depth of blackcurrant and plum-like, slightly leathery flavours. Ready.

DELEGAT'S PROP. RES. MERLOT	VINTAGE	95	94	93	92	91	90	DRY $25 AV
	WR	5	6	NM	5	7	5	
	DRINK	97-9	97-9	NM	P	P	P	☆☆☆☆½

A savoury, supple Hawke's Bay red of high quality. The 1994 vintage is fragrant and sturdy, with sweet, ripe fruit, cedary oak, nuances of chocolate, spice and tobacco and a firmly structured finish. The '95 (****½) is robust and warm, with loads of flavour – complex, savoury, leathery and supple. Tasted from the barrel, both the '96 and '97 looked potentially outstanding, with inky colour and strikingly rich, sweet fruit characters.

DE REDCLIFFE HB MERLOT/ CAB./FRANC	VINTAGE	96	95	DRY $15 -V
	WR	6	5	
	DRINK	97-8	P	(☆☆½)

The '95, a straight Merlot grown in Hawke's Bay and oak-aged for four months, is light in colour, body and flavour. The 1996 vintage (**½) is a blend of 67 per cent Merlot, 30 per cent Cabernet Sauvignon and 3 per cent Cabernet Franc, bottled without oak maturation. A fresh, medium-bodied red, crisp and berryish, it's a pleasant, simple style for early drinking.

ESK VALLEY MERLOT

VINTAGE	96	95	94
WR	6	7	6
DRINK	97-00	97-00+	97-98

DRY $20 AV

(☆ ☆☆☆ ☆)

I was impressed with the 1995 vintage of this Hawke's Bay red from the start. It's full-coloured, robust and supple, with a lovely depth of warm, spicy flavour. The '96 (****) is almost as good. Matured for a year in French and American oak barriques, it's a generous, weighty wine with full colour, excellent depth of ripe, plummy flavour and power right through the palate.

ESK VALLEY MERLOT/ CAB. SAUV.

VINTAGE	96	95	94	93	92	91	90
WR	6	7	6	5	6	6	6
DRINK	97-00	97-00	97-99	P	97-98	P	P

DRY $20 AV

☆ ☆ ☆ ☆

This Hawke's Bay winery is a specialist in Merlot-predominant reds. Maturing well, the 1995 vintage (****) is a blend of 54 per cent Merlot, 40 per cent Cabernet Sauvignon and a splash of Cabernet Franc, matured for a year in French and American oak casks. Full, lively and spicy, it's a very well balanced, tightly structured wine with ripe plum/red berry flavours, toasty oak and firm tannins.

ESK VAL. RES. MER./MALBEC/ CAB. SAUV.

VINTAGE	95	94	93	92	91	90
WR	7	7	NM	6	6	7
DRINK	98-05	97-02	NM	97-00	97-02	97-00

DRY $40 AV

☆ ☆ ☆ ☆ ☆

The name and varietal blend of this very classy Hawke's Bay red vary slightly from year to year. The arrestingly dark and power-packed 1995 vintage (*****) is blended from 65 per cent Merlot, 25 per cent Malbec and 10 per cent Cabernet Sauvignon, matured for 18 months in French oak barriques (70 per cent new). Still fresh and youthful, it's crammed with very rich, sweetish, dark plum/blackcurrant flavours, with quality oak, balanced tannins and a long, supple finish. A striking wine with tonnes of cellaring potential.

FROMM LA STRADA FROMM VINEYARD MERLOT/MALBEC/SYRAH

DRY $24 -V

(☆☆☆ ☆)

The full-flavoured 1995 vintage (***1/2) of this Marlborough red is a very good effort for a '95. Matured for 16 months in half new, half older casks, it's a characterful wine with full, bright colour and a minty, spicy fragrance. The crisp finish reflects a slight lack of ripeness and warmth, but there's plenty of fresh plum/herbal/spice flavour on offer, with some complexity. Drink 1998.

FROMM LA STRADA MARLBOROUGH MERLOT

DRY $19 -V

(☆☆ ☆)

The 1996 vintage (**1/2) lacks a bit of warmth and stuffing. Not oak-matured, it is ruby-hued, crisp and fresh, with raspberry/spice flavours, firm tannins and quite high acidity in a distinctly cool-climate style.

GIESEN
CANTERBURY
MERLOT

DRY $23 -V

(☆☆☆)

The 1995 vintage (***) of this North Canterbury red is an enjoyable, buoyantly fruity middleweight, with moderate depth of colour, pleasant but not concentrated plum/spice flavours, light oak influence and firm tannins.

GILLAN
MARLBOROUGH
MERLOT

VINTAGE	96	95	94
WR	5	NM	5
DRINK	98-01	NM	98-99

DRY $19 -V

(☆☆☆)

The debut 1994 vintage is a lightish (11.5 per cent alcohol), slightly herbaceous wine with pleasant plum/cherry flavours. The '96 (***1/2) is bigger and riper-tasting. Matured for 15 months in French oak casks, it's buoyant and supple, full-bodied and smooth, with warm, berryish flavours and savoury nuances of tobacco and leather adding complexity. Drink now or cellar.

GOLDWATER ESSLIN
WAIHEKE ISLAND
MERLOT

DRY $65 -V

(☆☆☆☆⟡)

More forward than the winery's famous Cabernet-based blend, the first 1996 vintage (*****1/2) is an impressive, very high-priced red. Boldly coloured, it is fresh and youthful, with very strong, vibrant plum/cassis flavours, toasty oak and firm but supple tannins. Open 1998–99.

GUNN EST.
MERLOT/
CAB. SAUV.

VINTAGE	96
WR	6
DRINK	97-00

DRY $16 AV

(☆☆☆)

The 1995 vintage, a Hawke's Bay blend of 60 per cent Merlot and 40 per cent Cabernet Sauvignon, is an attractive, ruby-hued wine, fresh and fruity, with ripe, spicy, raspberryish flavours in a soft, easy-drinking style. The weighty, buoyant and supple '96 (***1/2) is a 70/30 blend grown in Ohiti Road. Oak-aged for eight months, it's still youthful, with ripe, berryish, slightly earthy flavours and a touch of complexity.

GUNN ESTATE
RESERVE
MERLOT

VINTAGE	96
WR	6
DRINK	97-01

DRY $25 AV

(☆☆☆☆)

The 1996 vintage (****) is an instantly likeable Hawke's Bay red, oak-aged for 14 months. Buoyantly fruity and smooth, with very good depth of warm, ripe, plum/spice flavours, it's a full-bodied style, finely balanced, with a long finish. Drink now or cellar.

HARRIER RISE	VINTAGE	96							DRY $17 AV
MER./CABS.	WR	6							
FRANC & SAUV.	DRINK	97-98							(☆ ☆☆)

Reminiscent of a French country red, the 1996 vintage (***) of this Kumeu wine is a blend of Merlot, Cabernet Franc and Cabernet Sauvignon, matured for three months in French oak barriques (25 per cent new). It's a slightly rustic, earthy style with good mouthfeel and plenty of savoury, spicy, chewy flavour. Drink now to 98.

HARRIER RISE	VINTAGE	95	94	93	92	91		DRY $19 AV
UPPERCASE	WR	NM	6	6	4	5		
MERLOT	DRINK	NM	97-8	97-8	P	P		(☆☆☆☆⸽)

A consistently satisfying, full-flavoured, rich and earthy Kumeu wine. The powerful, meaty, supple '93 was impressive, and so is the 1994 vintage (***1/2). It's a deeply coloured, fleshy, very warm and harmonious red, with positive, well-integrated tannins. There is no '95.

HIGHFIELD	VINTAGE	96	95	94	93	92	91	90	DRY $19 -V
MARLBOROUGH	WR		5	4	5	4	NM	6	5	
MERLOT	DRINK	97-00+	97-00	97-00+	P	NM	97-00+	97-00+	☆☆☆

The 1994 vintage, French oak-aged for a year, is an easy-drinking style with charm, persistence and positive tannins. The '96 (**1/2), a medium-bodied wine with fairly light colour and a raspberryish fragrance, is a straightforward, buoyantly fruity style with cool-climate crispness and freshness.

HUNTAWAY RES.	VINTAGE	95	94				DRY $25 AV
GIS. MATAWHERO	WR	7	7				
MERLOT	DRINK	97-05	97-04				(☆☆☆☆⸽)

The first 1994 vintage is seductively fruity and smooth, its plummy, spicy flavours revealing great depth. The '95 (****) is less memorably lush and silky, but still very rewarding, with excellent depth of rich, plummy, supple flavour, a distinct touch of herbaceousness and soft, fine tannins.

HUTHLEE			DRY $21 -V
ESTATE			
MERLOT			(☆☆☆)

Estate-grown in the Ngatarawa district of Hawke's Bay, the 1995 vintage (***) reveals good, bright colour and a chunky, well-concentrated, tautly structured palate in a quite bold style. It lacks a bit of sweet-fruit charm, but is fresh and firm, with definite cellaring potential.

KUMEU RIV.	VINTAGE	96	95	94	93	92	91	90	DRY $25 -V
MERLOT/	WR	7	6	6	6	5	7	6	
CABERNET	DRINK	99-03	97-00	97-00	97-99	P	P	P	☆☆☆⸽

Typically a full-bodied red, firm and savoury, its high percentage of Merlot giving attractive tobacco and leathery touches. Still youthful, the 1995 vintage (****) is 90 per cent Merlot, with the rest Cabernet Franc and Malbec; there is no Cabernet Sauvignon in the blend. Matured for a year in French oak casks (20 per cent new), it offers a fragrant bouquet of plums and cedar, with ripe, non-herbaceous, complex flavour of good depth. A barrel sample of the '96 looked excellent, with scented, sweet-tasting, well-concentrated berry/plum fruit.

LINCOLN GISBORNE MERLOT	VINTAGE	96		DRY $12 AV
	WR	5		(☆ ☆☆)
	DRINK	97-99		

The '95 vintage, matured in seasoned French and American oak casks, is a forward, fruity, raspberryish, soft red, offering moderately flavoursome, no-fuss drinking. The '96 (**), briefly oak-aged, is light in colour and flavour. It's OK as a slightly rustic quaffer, but lacks freshness and vibrant fruit characters.

LINDEN ESTATE MERLOT	VINTAGE	95	94	93	DRY $18 AV
	WR	5	6	4	(☆☆☆)
	DRINK	97-98	97-99	P	

The 1994 vintage is a chunky, full-flavoured quaffer, but fragrance and finesse are lacking. The '95 (****1/2) is one of the most appealing reds I've tasted from this Esk Valley winery. Ruby-hued, fragrant and supple, with good depth of delicate, plummy, slightly peppery flavour and oak richness, it is stylish and firm, offering excellent drinking from now onwards.

LOMBARDI MERLOT/ CABERNET		DRY $15 -V
		(☆☆☆)

A drink-young style, the 1996 vintage (**1/2) of this Hawke's Bay red was aged for 10 months in French and American oak casks. It's ruby-hued, with fresh berry/herbal aromas and flavours, lightly wooded. A pleasant but simple wine, fruity and supple.

LONGBUSH GISBORNE MERLOT		DRY $19 -V
		(☆☆☆)

The 1994 vintage is rich, with supple tannins underpinning concentrated blackcurrant and red berry flavours, ripe and lingering. The 1995 (**1/2), matured for 10 months in half new, half year-old American oak casks, is on a much lower plane: light in colour and very forward, lacking the power, richness and distinction of its predecessor.

LONGVIEW EST. MARIO'S MERLOT	VINTAGE	96	95	94	DRY $24 AV
	WR	6	NM 5		(☆☆☆☆)
	DRINK	00	NM	98-99	

Mario Vuletich's reds are doing a great deal to boost Northland's hitherto modest wine reputation. With its rich, vibrant colour, perfumed, spicy bouquet and ripe, raspberry and plum-evoking flavours, underpinned by firm tannins, the 1994 vintage is an impressively chewy, flavour-packed red. The '96 (***1/2) is slightly lighter, but offers a noseful of sweet oak and ripe berry fruit aromas. The palate is full, with strong, sweet oak influence and plenty of plummy, spicy flavour, with a solid underlay of tannins.

MANUKA HILL *MERLOT/* *CABERNET*

DRY $11 -V

(☆☆)

Lincoln's 1995 (**) red is a rustic blend of two-thirds Gisborne Merlot and one-third Hawke's Bay Cabernet Sauvignon, matured for three months in seasoned American oak barriques. It's strictly a quaffer, with light colour, medium-full body and some savoury plum/leather characters. Drink up.

MATAWHERO *ESTATE* *MERLOT*

DRY $18 AV

(☆☆☆½)

Full of character, the enjoyable 1994 vintage (***½) of Denis Irwin's Gisborne red is rather Bordeaux-like. Ready now, it is a supple wine with strong, savoury, chocolatey, spicy flavour in a supple, forward style.

MATUA ARARIMU *MERLOT/CAB.* *FRANC/CAB.*

VINTAGE	94	93	92	91
WR	7	7	NM	7
DRINK	00+	00+	NM	98+

DRY $32 AV

☆☆☆☆☆

The 1993 and 1991 vintages of Matua's flagship red were Cabernet-predominant, but the 1994 is 60 per cent Merlot, with equal proportions of the two Cabernets: Sauvignon and Franc. The '91 has not aged as splendidly as I anticipated, but the '93 is of arresting quality, with dense, purple-black colour, a voluminous bouquet and an exciting concentration of brambly, spicy, tautly tannic flavour. The '94 (*****) is a blend of fruit grown in Matua Valley's home vineyard at Waimauku and in the Smith-Dartmoor vineyard in Hawke's Bay. Matured in new French oak barriques for 16 months, it is a voluptuous, exuberantly fruity red, packed with rich, very ripe, brambly, plummy fruit, with a long, lush, supple finish. Very classy.

MATUA SMITH- *DARTMOOR* *EST. MERLOT*

VINTAGE	95	94	93	92	91	90
WR	6	6	NM	6	6	NM
DRINK	00+	00+	NM	97-98 P	NM	

DRY $22 AV

(☆☆☆☆)

The 1994 vintage of this typically full-bodied, vivaciously fruity red offers loads of flavour. Grown in the Dartmoor Valley of Hawke's Bay, it is fresh and buoyant, plummy, berryish and spicy, with a long, well-rounded finish. The '95 (***½) is a gentle wine (only 11.5 per cent alcohol), not highly concentrated, but offers smooth, ripe, plummy, spicy flavour, already very enjoyable, with a moderate underlay of tannin.

MISSION JEWEL *MER./CAB.* *SAUVIGNON*

VINTAGE	95
WR	6
DRINK	98-05

DRY $30 AV

(☆☆☆☆☆)

Capable of great complexity, the 1995 vintage (*****) of this Hawke's Bay red is a 60/40 blend, matured for 20 months in French oak barriques (half new). It's a dark wine with concentrated, brambly fruit encased in sweet, toasty oak. Powerful, tight-knit and ripe, with densely packed flavours and firm underlying tannins, it's a serious style, well worth cellaring.

MONTANA RESERVE BARRIQUE MATURED MERLOT

DRY $18 V+

(☆☆☆☆⚬)

The lovely debut 1996 vintage (****¹/₂) looks like a signpost to the future for Marlborough reds. French oak-aged, with deep colour and a ripe, brambly fragrance, it's a very full, rich wine with ripe blackcurrant/plum flavours, nutty oak, complexity and a firm yet supple finish. A great buy.

MORTON EST. BLACK LABEL MERLOT

VINTAGE	95	94	93	92	91	90
WR	6	NM	NM	NM	7	6
DRINK	98-04	NM	NM	NM	97-98	P

DRY $29 -V

(☆☆☆☆)

The 1991 vintage is a delicious Hawke's Bay red packed with rich, plummy, berryish fruit. The label took a break during the 1992–94 vintages, but returned from 1995 (***¹/₂). Grown in the Riverview vineyard and French oak-aged for 15 months, it's a good but not great wine, lacking the warmth and concentration of the region's top reds from that year, but still offering good depth of firm, raspberry and plum-evoking flavours and some complexity.

MORTON ESTATE BLACK LABEL MERLOT/CABERNET SAUVIGNON

DRY $35 -V

(☆☆☆☆)

Grown in Hawke's Bay, the 1995 vintage (****) is a blend of 55 per cent Merlot and 45 per cent Cabernet Sauvignon, French oak-aged for 15 months. It's a fragrant, supple, generous red with full, bright colour and impressive depth of reasonably ripe, blackcurrant, plum and spice flavours. It just slightly lacks the warmth and intensity of the top '95 reds.

MORTON ESTATE WHITE LABEL HAWKE'S BAY MERLOT

DRY $18 AV

(☆☆☆)

Morton Estate is increasingly turning to Merlot, rather than Cabernet Sauvignon, for its Hawke's Bay reds. Oak-matured for a year, the debut 1996 vintage (***) is a vibrantly fruity, ruby-hued, moderately ripe-tasting wine with quite good depth of plum/spice flavours.

NGATARAWA GLAZEBROOK MERLOT

DRY $25 AV

(☆☆☆☆)

From a bountiful Merlot harvest in Hawke's Bay, the first Glazebrook Merlot from 1995 (****) is a substantial wine. To marry "sweet fruit and sweet oak", it was matured for 18 months in new American oak barriques. A serious, mouthfilling red with moderately firm tannins and excellent concentration, it's well worth cellaring to 1998–99.

OMAKA *SPRINGS* *MERLOT*	VINTAGE	96	DRY $14 AV
	WR	7	
	DRINK	97-01	(☆☆☆)

The 1995 vintage of this French oak-aged Marlborough red is a fresh, light style with pleasant, but not rich, flavour. The smooth '96 (***) displays full, bright colour and good depth of blackcurrant, plum and spice-like flavour. It's not a complex style but fresh, ripe, buoyant and sensibly priced.

PHOENIX *MERLOT*	DRY $14 AV
	(☆☆☆)

Estate-grown at Pacific's vineyard in Henderson, the debut 1994 vintage (**¹/₂) was matured for 22 months in French and American oak barriques (half new). It's a solid but slightly rustic red with quite good colour, a vegetative bouquet and plenty of firm, spicy, green-edged flavour, lacking full ripeness.

QUARRY *ROAD* *MERLOT*	VINTAGE	96	DRY $17 -V
	WR	5	
	DRINK	00	(☆☆)

The 1996 vintage (**) of this Te Kauwhata red doesn't have the richness of its Cabernet Sauvignon stablemate from 1995. French oak-matured for 14 months, it's light in colour and grassy on the nose, with fresh, crisp, simple flavours that lack ripeness, warmth and concentration. Drink young.

REDMETAL VINE. *BAS. PRESS* *MER./CAB.SAUV.*	VINTAGE	96	DRY $29 AV
	WR	5	
	DRINK	99-05	(☆☆☆☆☆)

The striking 1996 vintage (*****) is a superb debut for this Hawke's Bay red. Grown and made at Maraekakahoe by Grant Edmonds, it's a sophisticated, beautifully rich and supple wine with bright, vivid colour. Robust and bursting with ripe blackcurrant/plum flavours, underpinned by firm, balanced tannins, it's a supple, intense red with a powerful finish. It's already delicious, but too good not to keep for another couple of years.

REDMETAL *VINEYARDS* *MERLOT*	VINTAGE	96	DRY $22 V+
	WR	5	
	DRINK	97-00	(☆☆☆☆☆)

Amazingly attractive in its youth, the generous, warm and supple, debut 1996 vintage (****¹/₂) was grown and made at Maraekakahoe in Hawke's Bay by Grant Edmonds. Extremely good for a second label (see above), it's fleshy, rich and soft, with bold colour, mouthfilling body and intense, plummy, deftly oaked, well-rounded flavour. Delicious drinking now onwards.

	VINTAGE	96	95	94	DRY $12 AV
RIVERSIDE	WR	5	4	6	
MERLOT	DRINK	98-99	97-99	97-99	(☆☆)

The 1994 vintage of this Dartmoor Valley red is slightly unripe-tasting, with moderate depth of raspberry, plum and herbal flavours. Tasted from the barrel, the '96 (**) is very similar – ruby-hued, herbaceous and smooth, but lacking real ripeness and richness. Priced right.

ROCKWOOD MERLOT/
CABERNET
SAUVIGNON

DRY $16 AV

(☆☆☆⯪)

The '95 vintage (***½) is a very decent red. A 3:1 blend of Hawke's Bay grapes, it is full-bodied, with strong, plummy, spicy flavour, ripe and rounded. Still fresh, it is a characterful wine for drinking now or cellaring to 1998.

	VINTAGE	95	DRY $20 AV
SACRED HILL	WR	5	
BAS. PRESS	DRINK	97-98	(☆☆☆☆)
MER./CAB. SAUV.			

Hand-picked from low-yielding vines in the Dartmoor Valley, the generous 1995 vintage (****) is a substantial, rich-flavoured wine. Hugely drinkable, it possesses good weight (13 per cent alcohol), strong, plummy, slightly minty flavours, fleshed out with sweet-tasting oak, and a well-rounded finish.

	VINTAGE	95	DRY $35 AV
SACRED HILL	WR	7	
BROKENSTONE	DRINK	97-02	
MERLOT			(☆☆☆☆☆☆)

Matured in 100 per cent new French oak barriques, the debut 1995 vintage (*****) is a striking Hawke's Bay red with deep, bright colour and a rich, nutty fragrance. Packed with sweet-tasting fruit, it is still youthful, with a lovely concentration of flavour – warm, plummy, spicy, complex and persistent. It's a top-flight debut, and a worthy candidate for cellaring.

SACRED HILL
WHITECLIFF
MERLOT

DRY $15 AV

(☆☆☆)

The flavourful 1996 vintage (***) is an enjoyable, although not complex, Hawke's Bay red with medium-full colour and fresh, berry/spice aromas. It's a very lightly oaked wine with fairly ripe cassis/plum flavours and gentle tannins. A bouyant drink-young style for 1997–98.

	VINTAGE	96	DRY $17 V+
SAINT	WR	6	
CLAIR	DRINK	97-98	
MERLOT			(☆☆☆)

The buoyantly fruity 1996 (***) is an attractive drink-young style, released six months after the vintage. Ruby-hued, it is an unwooded Marlborough wine with pleasing depth of fresh, supple blackcurrant/plum flavours.

958585 5858 5858 5858 5858 5858 5858 5858 5858 5858585858585858

SAINT CLAIR SINGLE VINEY. MERLOT

VINTAGE	96
WR	7
DRINK	97-02

DRY $23 AV

(☆☆☆☆⋆)

With its dark purplish colour, lush ripe fruit and sweet oak, the first 1996 vintage (****) is a rather Aussie-style red. Grown in Rapaura Road, Marlborough, and matured in new oak barrels for 10 months, it has an upfront appeal, with mouthfilling body and impressively concentrated, brambly flavour, buoyant and supple.

SHINGLE PEAK MARLBOROUGH MER./CAB.

VINTAGE	95
WR	4
DRINK	97-00

DRY $15 AV

(☆☆☆)

Matua Valley's 1995 red clearly reflects the poor vintage in Marlborough. It's a simple, light, crisp wine with moderate colour depth and a fresh, berryish, herbal bouquet and flavour. The '96 (***) is much more attractive, with full ruby colour and fresh, plummy, smooth flavour.

SOLJANS BARR. RES. AUCKLAND MERLOT

VINTAGE	95
WR	6
DRINK	97-00

DRY $16 AV

(☆☆☆)

The 1995 vintage (***) is the first of this West Auckland red, matured for nine months in new and older French and American oak casks. It's a solid debut: plum-red in colour and chewy, with ripe tannins and enjoyable depth of berryish, spicy, slightly meaty and leathery flavour.

TASMAN BAY MERLOT/CAB./ FRANC

DRY $19 AV

(☆☆☆☆⋆)

The 1994 vintage is a chunky red with warm, rich, chocolate, spice and blackcurrant flavours. The pleasantly smooth and fruity '95 (***) is 50 per cent Merlot, blended with equal portions of Cabernet Sauvignon and Cabernet Franc, grown in the North Island and Upper Moutere. Oak-aged for eight months, it offers ripe plum/berry flavours and moderate tannins in an easy-drinking style.

TE AWA FARM BOUNDARY MERLOT

VINTAGE	95
WR	6
DRINK	97-02

DRY $27 AV

(☆☆☆☆☆⋆)

The highly attractive 1995 vintage (****½) of this Hawke's Bay red displays impressive concentration and complexity. Grown at Roy's Hill (and including 11 per cent Malbec and 4 per cent Cabernet Sauvignon), it is deeply coloured, mouthfilling and chewy, with ripe, plummy, spicy flavours and a long, rich, firm finish. Still youthful and fresh, this is a very stylish wine, enjoyable now but also an ideal candidate for cellaring.

TE AWA FARM
LONGLANDS
MERLOT

VINTAGE 96
WR   6
DRINK   97-01

DRY $19 AV

(☆ ☆☆☆)

The Lawson family set out to produce consistently fine Hawke's Bay reds – and they're succeeding. The first 1996 vintage (****) was estate-grown at Roy's Hill and matured for a year in French and American oak barriques. It's a well-coloured, full-bodied, complex wine with a subtle array of plum, spice and oak flavours and firm but balanced tannins, sure to age well.

TE AWANGA VINEYARDS
HAWKE'S BAY
MERLOT

DRY $18 AV

(☆☆☆)

Attractive already, the 1996 vintage (***) is a smooth-flowing red with 15 per cent Cabernet Franc and 5 per cent Cabernet Sauvignon, matured for 14 months in new and old French and American oak casks. Ruby-hued, with a perfumed bouquet, it's not concentrated but supple, with pleasant red berry and plum-evoking flavours fleshed out with sweet oak.

TWIN ISLANDS
MERLOT/CAB.
SAUVIGNON

VINTAGE 96 95
WR   6   4
DRINK   97-99 97-98

DRY $15 AV

(☆ ☆☆)

The 1995 vintage is a light style, not concentrated, but offering reasonable depth of fresh, berryish, slightly herbal, smooth flavour. The richer '96 (***), a blend of Marlborough and Hawke's Bay fruit, matured in American oak casks (30 per cent new), is a weighty red with medium-full colour and a slightly herbal bouquet with sweet oak aromas. Chunky, with Merlot richness and ripeness and Cabernet Sauvignon structure and density, it's a plummy, supple wine with good flavour depth.

VIDAL THE BAYS
MERLOT/CABERNET
SAUVIGNON

DRY $20 AV

(☆☆☆☆)

The first 1995 release (****) of this elegant, Hawke's Bay claret-style red is a blend of 55 per cent Merlot, 33 per cent Cabernet Sauvignon and 12 per cent Cabernet Franc, oak-aged for 18 months. The colour is deep; the palate ripe and firm, with good fruit/wood balance, pleasing depth of delicate, plum/spice flavours and fine, positive tannins. Open 1998.

VILLA MARIA CEL.
SEL. MERLOT/
CAB. SAUV.

VINTAGE 95 94
WR   6   6
DRINK   97-00+ 97-00+

DRY $20 AV

(☆ ☆☆☆)

The 1994 vintage, labelled Merlot/Cabernet Sauvignon/Cabernet Franc, is impressively fragrant, with lots of plummy, crisp, slightly herbal flavour and good aging potential. The '95 (****1/2) is a very stylish Hawke's Bay wine. A blend of 55 per cent Merlot and 45 per cent Cabernet Sauvignon, it has good colour depth and a ripe, welcoming fragrance. It's forward in its appeal, with strong, ripe, brambly, spicy fruit flavours wrapped in toasty oak and a lingering, well-rounded finish.

VILLA MARIA	VINTAGE	95				DRY $32 AV
RESERVE	WR	7				
MERLOT	DRINK	97-00+				(☆☆☆☆☆)

The first 1995 vintage (*****) is a very seductive Hawke's Bay red. Deep-coloured, with a floral, enticing bouquet, it is full and fleshy, with a lovely depth of warm, plum and blackcurrant-like flavours, sweet oak and a long, rich finish. A powerful, stylish red for now onwards.

VILLA MARIA	VINTAGE	95				DRY $32 AV
RES. MER./	WR	7				
CAB. SAUV.	DRINK	97-00+				(☆☆☆☆☆)

I've only tasted it once, when judging at a competition, but looking at my notes, the 1995 vintage of this Hawke's Bay red (*****) made a big impression: "Rich, bright colour. Mouthfilling, ripe, densely packed, tannic. Still very youthful and very stylish."

WAIMARAMA			DRY $26 AV
ESTATE			
MERLOT			(☆☆☆☆½)

The 1995 vintage (****½) of this Hawke's Bay red will appeal strongly to lovers of fine Bordeaux. French oak-aged, it's not a blockbuster red but very subtle and harmonious, with rich colour and excellent depth of soft, spicy, cedary, complex flavour. Already highly approachable.

WEST BROOK	VINTAGE	95	94	93	92	91	90	DRY $15 AV
HENDERSON	WR	5	6	7	4	7	6	
MERLOT	DRINK	97-00	97-02	97-00	97-8	P	P	☆☆☆

This estate-grown, West Auckland red is typically chunky and reasonably ripe with fruity, blackcurrant and plum-like flavours and a smooth finish. Drinkability is the key appeal of the 1995 vintage (***), which includes a minor proportion of Cabernet Sauvignon. It's a characterful, fresh red, lightly wooded, with quite good depth of plummy, spicy, earthy flavour. Open 1998.

Pinotage

Pinotage lives in the shadow of Pinot Noir, Cabernet Sauvignon and Merlot in New Zealand, but it is the country's fourth most extensively planted red-wine variety, level-pegging with Cabernet Franc.

Pinotage is a cross of the great Burgundian grape, Pinot Noir, and Cinsaut, a heavy-cropping variety popular in the south of France. Cinsaut's typically "meaty, chunky sort of flavour" (in Jancis Robinson's words) is also characteristic of Pinotage. Valued for its reasonably early-ripening and disease-resistant qualities, and good yields, Pinotage has long been a favourite of Auckland's winemakers. Today, plantings are concentrated in Marlborough (especially), Gisborne, Hawke's Bay and Auckland. Between 1996 and 1999, the area of bearing Pinotage vines is expanding from 76 hectares to 96 hectares.

A well-made Pinotage displays a slightly gamey bouquet, medium-full body and a soft, berryish, peppery palate reminiscent of the Rhône's warm reds. It matures swiftly and usually peaks two to three years after the vintage.

BABICH PINOTAGE/ CABERNET		DRY $11 V+ ☆☆☆

Over nearly three decades this soft, fruity, top value dry red has won a strong following. Estate-grown Henderson and Gisborne fruit (two-thirds Pinotage and one-third Cabernet Sauvignon) is matured for a year in seasoned French oak casks. The 1995 vintage (***) is savoury and forward, less fruity and berryish than usual. The light ruby colour has hints of approaching maturity; the palate is full, smooth and supple, with a touch of spicy complexity.

KERR FARM PINOTAGE	VINTAGE	96	95	DRY $15 -V
	WR	7	6	(☆☆☆)
	DRINK	97-00	97-98	

Vibrantly fruity and smooth, the 1995 vintage has strong drink-young appeal, with attractive raspberry/spice aromas and lots of flavour – crisp, persistent and very more-ish. The '96 (* – ****1/2), matured in French and American oak casks, has shown marked batch variation. The first two bottles I tasted were unpleasant, but the third was much more enjoyable, with full, bright colour, plenty of body and good depth of smooth, berryish flavour – a sort of Kumeu Beaujolais.

NOBILO HUAPAI VAL. PINOTAGE	VINTAGE	94	93	92	91	90	DRY $25 -V
	WR	6	7	NM	6	5	☆☆☆☆
	DRINK	98-00	97-00	NM	P	P	

Huapai-grown, and matured in oak casks for a year (previously 18 months), this is typically a strong-flavoured red, peppery and zesty. The 1993 vintage is a fresher, less wood-influenced style than in the past. The '94 (***¹/₂) is maturing well, with good weight and depth and a positive tannin grip. The bouquet is earthy, with a touch of gamey complexity; the palate warm, spicy and persistent, with restrained oak influence. It reminded me of a minor southern Rhône, but the '93 vintage was just as good and $10 cheaper.

NOBILO'S RES. PINO./CAB. SAUVIGNON	VINTAGE 87 WR 6 DRINK P	DRY $22 -V (☆☆☆)

Who else is selling ten-year-old red wine? Grown at Huapai in the "exceptional" 1987 vintage (***¹/₂), and matured for two years in new and one-year-old French oak puncheons, it's a pleasant, mellow, gamey, leathery but fairly light red, with leafy aromas and flavours, lacking the richness of the Concept series (see Generic and Branded Reds) it was presumably originally part of.

OHINEMURI ESTATE PINOTAGE	VINTAGE 96 95 WR 5 5 DRINK 97-98 P	M/DRY $15 AV ☆☆☆

One of the highlights of Horst Hillerich's range is his Gisborne-grown Pinotage "primeur". Some of the grapes are whole-bunch fermented, using the traditional Beaujolais technique. The 1996 vintage (***) was 35 per cent whole-bunch fermented and briefly oak-aged. It's a characterful wine, brick red in colour, with soft, berryish, fractionally sweet flavour and a touch of savoury, gamey complexity. Ready.

PLEASANT VAL. SIG. SEL. AUCK. PINOTAGE	VINTAGE 96 95 94 93 92 91 90 WR 6 6 7 NM 7 7 6 DRINK 97-98 P P NM P P P	DRY $14 V+ ☆☆☆☆

Hill-grown at Henderson and briefly aged in older oak barrels, this is consistently a deliciously fruity, savoury and supple red; a top-flight, drink-young style. The '95 offers ripe, sweet berry fruit flavours in a supple style with gentle tannins and good depth. With a Beaujolais-like immediacy of appeal, the '96 (****) is a deliciously buoyant and supple red. The floral/raspberryish aromas lead into a ripely fruity palate with strong red berry fruit flavours, fresh and soft.

SOLJANS AUCKLAND PINOTAGE	VINTAGE 96 95 94 93 92 WR 6 6 6 5 4 DRINK 97-00 97-99 98 P P	DRY $14 V+ ☆☆☆☆

Tony Soljan's favourite red is made from West Auckland fruit and matured in seasoned oak casks. A decent Beaujolais-style, the 1996 vintage (***¹/₂) is a quite deep-coloured, purple-tinged red with good depth of fresh, youthful, vibrant raspberry/plum flavours and a well-rounded finish.

| *VILLA MARIA* *PRI. BIN PINO./* *CAB. SAUV.* | VINTAGE 96 95 94 WR   5 5 5 DRINK   97-98 97-98 P | DRY $10 V+ (☆☆☆) |

As a $10, no-fuss, drink-young red, this works well. The 1995 vintage (***) is an equal blend of Pinotage and Cabernet Sauvignon, grown in Gisborne and Hawke's Bay, and matured for four months in seasoned French and German oak barrels. It is floral and raspberryish on the nose, with a buoyantly fruity, fresh, supple palate showing good flavour depth.

Pinot Noir

New Zealand's Pinot Noirs are enjoying rising international applause. "They sing. There is a natural balance to them, a wealth and a breadth of flavour which [New Zealand] producers always seem to struggle to bolt into Cabernet or Merlot," wrote Andrew Jefford last year in London's *Evening Standard*. When Martinborough Vineyard Reserve Pinot Noir 1994 won the trophy for champion Pinot Noir at the 1997 International Wine and Spirit Competition in London, the trophy went to New Zealand for the third year in a row.

If all the Pinot Noir grown in New Zealand was processed into red wine, we'd have more Pinot Noir than Cabernet Sauvignon to drink. The 1997 vintage yielded 3427 tonnes of Pinot Noir grapes, well ahead of Cabernet Sauvignon with 2824 tonnes.

Pinot Noir is the princely grape variety of red Burgundy. Cheaper wines typically display light, raspberry-evoking flavours which lack the velvety riches of classic Burgundy. Great red Burgundy has substance, suppleness and a gorgeous spread of flavours: cherries, fruit cake and coffee.

The Burgundian variety has now arrived as a serious New Zealand red-wine style. The vine is our most extensively planted red grape, and is our third most commonly planted variety overall, trailing only Chardonnay and Sauvignon Blanc. In Marlborough, however, where many of the vines are concentrated, the majority of the crop is reserved for bottle-fermented sparkling wine, in which Pinot Noir brings fullness and flavour richness to its blends with the scented, steely Chardonnay.

The variety is well established in Hawke's Bay, the Wairarapa, Nelson, Marlborough, Canterbury and Central Otago. It is a notoriously frustrating variety to grow. Because it buds early it is vulnerable to spring frosts; its compact bunches are also very prone to rot. One crucial advantage is that it ripens early, ahead of Cabernet Sauvignon. Low cropping and the selection of superior clones are essential aspects of the production of fine wine.

The Wairarapa is currently the capital of New Zealand Pinot Noir. South Island winemakers are also enjoying success, especially in Central Otago.

ATA RANGI	VINTAGE	96	95	94	93	92	91	90
PINOT	WR		7	6	7	7	7	6	6
NOIR	DRINK	98-02	97-00	97-00	97-99	97-98	P		P

DRY $30 AV

☆☆☆☆☆

This exceptional, multiple gold medal and trophy-winning Martinborough red is a winning marriage of perfumed, cherryish, seductively sweet-tasting fruit with astute oak handling. Recent vintages have been bolder and firmer than the floral, supple wines of the past. The '94 (likened by British wine writer Andrew Jefford to "Nuits-St-Georges or Gevrey") is more powerful than the '93, with deliciously intense ripe-fruit aromas and flavours, new-oak complexity and a taut, lingering finish. The '95 is another weighty, spicy wine with bold colour, concentrated, ripe cherryish flavours, smoky oak and positive tannins. The '96 (*****) is also very distinguished, with great elegance, rich, concentrated, supple flavour and power right through the palate.

BABICH				**DRY $12 AV**
PINOT				
NOIR				☆☆☆⟩

A pleasant, fruity, light-bodied red, designed for early drinking. Based on the Bachtobel clone grown in the Henderson Valley estate vineyard, it is matured for up to a year in seasoned oak barrels. The Beaujolais-like 1996 vintage (***1/2) is typically light and supple, and developing a touch of savoury complexity with bottle-age. Drink during 1998.

BAZZARD EST.	VINTAGE	96
RES. PINOT	WR	6
NOIR	DRINK	98-05

DRY $27 -V

(☆☆☆☆☆)

Is the 1996 vintage (the first to carry a reserve label) Charlie Bazzard's finest Huapai red yet? It was matured for 10 months in seasoned oak casks (two-thirds French, one-third American). A very substantial wine with strong, ripe fruit flavours in a complex style with a lovely suppleness of texture, it has enough power and tannin to age well and a rich, lingering finish.

BLACK	VINTAGE	96	95	94	93	92	91	90
RIDGE	WR	6	6	6	5	4	4	3
PINOT NOIR	DRINK	97-00	97-00	97-99	P	P	P	P

DRY $24 AV

☆☆☆☆☆

A chunky, vibrantly fruity Alexandra red, awash with plum, cherry and subtle oak flavours in a fleshy, forward style with gentle tannins. The 1996 vintage (***1/2), French oak-aged for six months, is a seductive, still purple-flushed wine, not highly complex but softly mouthfilling, with very good depth of sweet-tasting raspberry/plum flavour and a silky texture. (A worthy memorial to the talents of winemaker Mike Wolter, who died in mid 1997.)

BLOOMFIELD PINOT NOIR

DRY $32 -V

(☆☆☆)

The savoury, mellow 1995 vintage (***) of this Masterton red is nearing its peak. Ruby-hued, it is full-bodied and soft, with quite good depth of plum/cherry flavours. Drink now. Expensive but rare.

CHARD FARM BRAGATO RES. PINOT NOIR

VINTAGE	96	95	94	93
WR	5	6	NM	5
DRINK	98-99	97-98	NM	P

DRY $29 -V

(☆☆☆☆)

The 1993 vintage of the Hay brothers' flagship red is light but stylish; the '95 is a big step up, with mouthfilling body and a powerful surge of sweet, ripe fruit. The 1996 (****), matured for almost a year in all-new French oak barriques, is already highly attractive. It's a classy, rich Central Otago wine, full-bodied, with strong, sweet fruit flavours wrapped in spicy oak and a seductively silky texture.

CHARD FARM PINOT NOIR

DRY $22 AV

☆☆☆½

Rob and Greg Hay's "standard" Central Otago Pinot Noir typically displays strong, almost sweet raspberry and cherry flavours, fleshed out with restrained wood. The '95 is an immensely charming and satisfying, intensely varietal wine. The 1996 vintage (***1/2) lacks a bit of the power and richness of the '95, but is maturing well, with good depth of colour, fullness of body and cherryish, spicy, persistent flavour. Vibrantly fruity and supple, it offers attractive drinking from now onwards.

CLOUDY BAY PINOT NOIR

VINTAGE	95	94	93	92
WR	NM	5	NM	4
DRINK	NM	98	NM	P

DRY $26 AV

☆☆☆☆½

Pinot Noir isn't the first grape you associate with Cloudy Bay, but the 1989, '92 and '94 vintages are all rewarding. The highly impressive '94 (****1/2) was grown in the Wairau Valley, 25 per cent whole-bunch fermented and matured in French oak barriques (40 per cent new). Mouthfilling (13.5 per cent alcohol), it has an enticingly smoky bouquet and is generous, ripe and complex on the palate, with concentrated, dark cherry and spice flavours and a supple, long finish. There is no '95.

COLLARDS MARLBOROUGH PINOT NOIR

VINTAGE	96	95	94	93	92
WR	6	NM	7	7	7
DRINK	97-99	NM	97-98	97-98	P

DRY $23 AV

(☆☆☆☆)

This rich-flavoured wine is based on the highly rated Pommard clone, French oak-aged and produced with "minimal handling and filtration". The '94 is a lovely, fragrant, supple wine, weighty, with ripe, concentrated, cherryish flavours overlaid with smoky oak. The 1996 vintage (****) is slightly lighter than the '94 but still impressive, with strawberry/wood aromas, fresh, ripe, supple fruit flavours, oak complexity and a well-rounded finish.

COOKS WINE.	VINTAGE	95			DRY $23 -V
RESERVE	WR	6			
PINOT NOIR	DRINK	98-02			(☆☆☆☆⯪)

The first 1995 vintage (***¹/₂) of Corbans' Hawke's Bay red, grown near Taradale, is still youthful and taut, with a medium-full ruby hue, moderately ripe fruit wrapped in strong, toasty oak, some complexity developing and a slightly astringent finish. Open 1998 onwards.

COOPERS CREEK	VINTAGE	95		DRY $14 AV
HUAPAI	WR	4		
PINOT NOIR	DRINK	P		(☆☆⯪)

Designed as a drink-young style, the unwooded 1995 vintage is a lightish, ripe and supple wine with pleasant, crisp, raspberryish, slightly spicy flavours. The '96 (**) was based on the Bachtobel clone and handled entirely in stainless steel. Light in colour and body, with moderate depth of soft, strawberryish flavours, it's a clean, simple wine, best treated as a rosé and served chilled. (The winery's lower-tier Pinot Noir from 1997 is made from Hawke's Bay fruit.)

COOPERS CREEK	VINTAGE	96	95	DRY $25 AV
RES. HB	WR	6	6	
PINOT NOIR	DRINK	98-01	98-00	(☆☆☆☆☆⯪)

Amazingly enjoyable in its youth, the 1995 vintage (****¹/₂) was French oak-aged for 10 months. The bouquet is highly fragrant, with enticing nuances of spice, smoke and coffee. Impressively robust, rich and supple, it offers strong berryish fruit flavours, wrapped in charry oak, and a deliciously well-rounded finish.

CORBANS COT.	VINTAGE	94	93	92	DRY $35 -V
BLOCK MARL.	WR	7	6	7	
PINOT NOIR	DRINK	97-00	97-98	97-98	(☆☆☆☆⯪)

The 1992 vintage is New Zealand Pinot Noir at its mushroomy, multi-faceted best: robust, very rich and complex. It's drink-up time for the '93, a mouthfilling red with a slightly tawny colour and aged, leathery, slightly herbal flavours with some mushroomy richness. The 1994 (*****) is a distinguished wine, one of Marlborough's finest Pinot Noirs yet. Medium-full ruby, it is robust, with very rich flavours of plums and cherries, now developing a lot of savoury, subtle complexity. Finely balanced and long, it offers superb drinking now onwards.

COVELL	VINTAGE	92	91	DRY $25 -V
ESTATE	WR	6	5	
PINOT NOIR	DRINK	97-03	97-99	(☆☆⯪)

Bob and Des (Desarai) Covell produce a light but clearly varietal red at their tiny vineyard nestled against the flanks of the Ureweras at Galatea, near Murupara. The 1991 vintage has matured well, with an attractive, savoury, perfumed bouquet and subtle flavours. Still on sale (and "getting better all the time," reports Bob), the '92 (**¹/₂), one-third whole bunch-fermented and oak-matured for two years, is also at or near its peak but a bit lighter and less appealing than the '91.

CRAB FARM PINOT NOIR

DRY $20 -V

☆☆☆

The 1993 vintage of this Bay View, Hawke's Bay red has an earthy, mushroomy bouquet and satisfyingly rich, supple flavour. The 1994 (***) is a big wine with a rather earthy rusticity, but savoury and firm, with plenty of character.

CROSS ROADS PINOT NOIR

VINTAGE	96	95	94	93
WR	7	5	6	7
DRINK	98-01	97-99	97-99	97-99

DRY $19 AV

(☆☆☆☆½)

The enticingly fragrant, vibrantly fruity, rich and sustained 1994 vintage (the best yet) proved that fine quality Pinot Noir doesn't have to cost $30. Drinking well now, the 1995 vintage of this Hawke's Bay red is a soft and delicate style with attractive, ripe cherryish flavours, some complexity and a velvet-smooth finish. The fleshy, ripe '96 (***), French oak-aged for 10 months, is still purple-flushed, with floral/raspberry aromas and good depth of plummy, slightly spicy, supple flavour in an easy-drinking style.

DANIEL SCH. CANTERBURY PINOT NOIR

VINTAGE	97	96	95	94
WR	5	7	7	6
DRINK	98-99	97-98	97-99	97-98

DRY $20 -V

☆☆☆

Danny Schuster's regional blend, not his single-vineyard flagship (below). The 1994 vintage has more power and richness than its light colour suggests, with pleasing depth of savoury, cherryish flavour. The '95 has raspberryish, herbal flavours in a drink-young style. The graceful 1996 vintage (***½) is easily the finest yet. A blend of fruit grown in the Omihi Hills vineyard at Waipara and at Rakaia, south of Christchurch, it was partly whole berry-fermented and oak-matured for eight months. Designed for early consumption, it's a stylish, supple, fleshy wine with strong cherryish flavour and a rich finish. Highly enjoyable in late 1997, it should offer excellent drinking through 1998.

DANIEL SCH. OMIHI VINE. PINOT NOIR

VINTAGE	96	95	94	93	92
WR	7	7	NM	6	5
DRINK	00-05	00-05	NM	98-00	P

DRY $31 -V

(☆☆☆)

Schuster's pride and joy, in the past labelled Reserve Waipara, is produced from a "selection of the best fruit from the Omihi Vineyard, aged in a mixture of new and older Troncais oak." The '93 is light in colour, fragrant and savoury on the nose, with strong, supple beetroot/cherry flavours and mellow oak characters. The 1995 vintage (***½) was made from fruit off very low-cropping vines (below 4 tonnes per hectare) and matured in French oak casks (30 per cent new). A big wine, it lacks the warmth and richness of the country's finest Pinot Noirs, but offers good depth of crisp, cherryish flavour and firm tannins, with some savoury complexity.

DARJON PINOT NOIR

VINTAGE	96	95
WR	5	5
DRINK	99-00	98-99

DRY $22 -V

(☆☆½)

A solid first effort, the 1995 vintage (**½) was estate-grown at Swannanoa, in Canterbury, and gently oaked. It's a light style, strawberryish and slightly savoury, with a touch of complexity and a well-rounded finish.

DASHWOOD MARLBOROUGH PINOT NOIR

DRY $20 AV

(☆☆☆⅟)

The generous 1996 vintage (***¹/₂) was grown in Vavasour's vineyard in the Awatere Valley and French oak-aged for a year. It's a very forward style, already highly enjoyable, with rich colour, mouthfilling body (13.5 per cent alcohol), and very good depth of vibrant plum, cherry and smoky oak flavours, fresh and supple.

DE REDCLIFFE PINOT NOIR

VINTAGE	96
WR	7
DRINK	98

DRY $17 -V

☆☆⅟

A solid but unmemorable upper North Island red, lacking the satin-like texture and sheer intensity of varietal character found in more southern regions. The '94 (**¹/₂), grown at Te Kauwhata and matured for four months in new oak casks, has more body than its light colour suggests, with reasonable depth of raspberry/plum flavours and a slightly green finish. There is no 1995 vintage, but the label returns from 1996.

DRY RIVER PINOT NOIR

VINTAGE	96	95	94	93	92	91	90
WR		7	7	7	7	6	6	7
DRINK		97-03	97-00	97-05	97-01	P	P	P

DRY $36 AV

☆☆☆☆☆

Deliciously dark, concentrated and firm, the 1993 and subsequent vintages of Neil McCallum's Martinborough red have catapulted the label into the front rank of New Zealand's Pinot Noirs. The '95 is strapping (14 per cent alcohol), with very strong berry, plum and spice flavours, smoky oak and firm tannins. Described by McCallum as "not a wine for wimps", the 1996 vintage (*****) is exceptionally dark and muscular. Still a baby, its dense, purple-black colour would be deep even by Cabernet Sauvignon standards. It's an extraordinarily concentrated wine with enormous body, packed with rich, firm, plummy, spicy fruit, crying out for two or three years' cellaring.

FROMM LA STRADA PINOT NOIR

VINTAGE	96	95	94
WR	6	4	7
DRINK	97-00	97-00	97-98

DRY $24 AV

(☆☆☆☆)

For a non-wooded wine, the 1994 vintage of this Marlborough red is extremely good: generous, warm and ripe-tasting, with strong, supple cherry/plum flavours. (The La Strada Reserve Pinot Noir 1994 is even finer: dark, peppery, characterful.) The '95 vintage, matured for 10 months in French oak barriques (15 per cent new), is mouthfilling, with deliciously ripe, concentrated cherry/plum flavours, supple and long. In its youth, the 1996 vintage (***) surprisingly shows less richness and charm than the '95, but may take longer to unfold. Its colour is lighter than in past vintages, with quite good depth of raspberry and spice flavours and a crisp, firm finish.

GIBBSTON VAL.	VINTAGE	96	95	94	93	92	91	90	89	DRY $27 -V
CEN. OTAGO	WR	5	6	6	6	4	6	6	4	
PINOT NOIR	DRINK	97-00	97-00+	97-98	97-00	P		97-98	P	P	☆☆☆☆

A consistently satisfying red. Tasted in late 1996, the '93 is soft, savoury, a bit leafy and mature; the '94 is concentrated, vibrantly fruity and aging well; the '95 is mouthfilling and supple, with strong berry/plum flavours, some complexity and positive tannins. Already enjoyable, the French oak-aged '96 (***¹/₂) is ruby-hued, fresh, supple and lively, with ripe cherry/raspberry flavours, slightly less intense than the '95, a touch of oak complexity and a rounded finish.

GIBBSTON VALLEY
GOLD RIVER
PINOT NOIR

DRY $15 V+

(☆☆☆)

Unwooded, with a Beaujolais-like simplicity and charm, the thoroughly enjoyable 1996 vintage (***) was grown on the banks of the Kawarau River in Central Otago. Medium to full-bodied, it offers ripe, well-balanced, raspberryish flavours, fresh and supple.

GIBBSTON	VINTAGE	96	DRY $40 -V
VAL. RES.	WR	6	
PINOT NOIR	DRINK	98-05	(☆☆☆☆☆)

It's pricey, but the outstanding 1996 vintage (*****) of this Central Otago wine builds on the reputation established by the splendidly rich-flavoured '95. Grown on the banks of the Kawarau River and aged in all-new French oak casks, it has a full, purple-flushed ruby hue. Buoyant and fresh, with strong, ripe, sweet-tasting raspberry and spice characters, it is a mouthfilling style with depth right through the palate and a light tannin grip to add structure. Well worth keeping to 1999.

GIESEN
CANTERBURY
PINOT NOIR

DRY $25 -V

(☆☆☆)

The 1995 vintage is moderately ripe, with fresh, berryish fruit, charry oak and the potential to improve for a year or two, but in its youth lacked the beguiling fruit sweetness and overall richness of Giesen's Marlborough Pinot Noir from '94. (Marcel Giesen says to give it time: 2–3 years after bottling.) The '96 (***¹/₂), a blend of fruit from four vineyards near Christchurch, is an elegant wine with a spicy, toasty fragrance leading into a subtle palate with oak complexity and smooth, ripe cherry/raspberry flavours with quite good depth. Open 1998–99.

GLENMARK	VINTAGE	95	94	93	DRY $21 -V
PINOT	WR	7	NM	5	
NOIR	DRINK	97-00	NM	97-00	(☆☆☆)

Light and fragrant, the 1993 vintage of this Waipara red was a pleasant drink-young style, but it lacked weight and flavour depth. The '95 (**¹/₂), given some whole-berry fermentation and oak-aged, again lacks richness and warmth, but offers reasonable depth of crisp, berryish flavour.

GLOVER'S MOUTERE PINOT NOIR BACK BLOCK	VINTAGE	96	95	94
	WR	6	6	6
	DRINK	98-03	97-99	97-99

DRY $24 -V

(☆ ☆☆☆½)

Since 1994, Upper Moutere winemaker Dave Glover has kept to one side the grapes from the hot, north-facing slope behind the winery. The '94 is attractively perfumed, with good extract and strong, ripe, meaty, raspberryish flavours. The '95 is gutsy, firm and full-flavoured, with high acidity. Of Glover's four Pinot Noirs from 1996 (***½), this is my choice. The bouquet is peppery; the palate weighty and savoury, with firm but balanced tannins bracing strong, meaty, spicy, slightly green-edged flavours, characterful and complex.

GLOVER'S MOU. PINOT NOIR FRONT BLOCK	VINTAGE	96	95	94
	WR	6	6	6
	DRINK	98-03	97-99	97-99

DRY $24 -V

(☆ ☆☆☆½)

The 1994 vintage is a floral style with sweet fruit flavours, more approachable in its youth than its Back Block stablemate (above). The '95, matured for eight months in one-year-old barrels, is a mouthfilling, chewy, spicy wine with positive but not austere tannins and some complexity. The slightly more forward 1996 (***) is ruby-hued, with a green-edged bouquet, full body, firm tannins and quite good depth of savoury, herbal, spicy, crisp flavour.

GLOVER'S MOUTERE PINOT NOIR MICHAEL

DRY $27 -V

(☆☆☆)

A "oncer", the 1996 vintage (***) was produced by Dave Glover's son, Michael. It's an appealing wine, lightly wooded, with a bright ruby hue and floral, raspberryish aromas. Fresh, fruity and supple, it's a fairly simple but attractive wine with lots of youthful charm.

GLOVER'S NELSON PINOT NOIR CERISE

DRY $15 V+

(☆☆☆)

Offering fine value, Dave Glover's 1996 red (***) is designed as an easy-drinking style. Based on grapes grown at the Pomona vineyard at Ruby Bay and French oak-matured, it's a charmingly soft wine with smooth, ripe flavours and a touch of complexity. No sign of the famous Glover love affair with tannin in this red!

HAU ARIKI PINOT NOIR

DRY $30 -V

(☆☆☆)

Produced by Martinborough's Hau Ariki marae, the robust 1995 vintage (**½) lacks fragrance, delicacy and finesse, but offers moderate depth of firm, chewy flavour.

HUNTER'S PINOT NOIR

VINTAGE	95	94	93	92	91	90
WR	4	5	5	5	6	5
DRINK	98	P	98	P	P	P

DRY $21 -V

☆☆☆

The 1991 vintage was Hunter's first convincing Marlborough Pinot Noir: fragrant, full, vibrantly fruity and supple. The French oak-aged '94 (****¹/₂**) displays a maturing ruby colour and crisp, slightly green-edged flavours with some complexity.

JACKSON ESTATE MARLBOROUGH PINOT NOIR

VINTAGE	96
WR	4
DRINK	97-00

DRY $19 AV

(☆☆☆)

The 1995 vintage is a pale, light, drink-young style that lacks real concentration, but offers pleasant, strawberryish, sweet-fruit flavours well balanced with a touch of smoky oak. The '96 (***¹/₂) is markedly better. Harvested at 23˚ brix, it was given some whole-berry fermentation and matured in French oak barriques. Bigger, richer than its light colour suggests, it's like a superior Beaujolais – fresh and very supple, with sweet fruit characters and lots of flavour in a deliciously approachable style.

JOHANNESHOF CELLARS MAY. MARL PINOT NOIR

VINTAGE	96
WR	5
DRINK	97-01

DRY $23 -V

(☆☆☆)

French oak-aged for 16 months, the 1996 vintage (***) is a solid red, full-bodied and chewy, with strong, crisp, strawberryish flavour and some complexity. Open 1998 onwards.

KAITUNA VALLEY PINOT NOIR

VINTAGE	96	95	94	93
WR	6	NM	7	6
DRINK	98-02	NM	97-01	97-00

DRY $28 AV

(☆☆☆☆⯪)

When the 1993 collected a gold medal and trophy at the 1995 Liquorland Royal Easter Wine Show, it was the first time a Canterbury Pinot Noir had won gold since the St Helena '84. It is grown at a vineyard on Banks Peninsula planted in 1979 by Graeme Steans and recently purchased by winemaker Grant Whelan. The 1994 vintage, matured in French oak barriques, is an impressively mouthfilling and savoury wine with concentrated, cherryish, smoky flavour, complexity, and a seductive depth and richness. There is no '95. The '96 (****) has a lovely perfume of ripe raspberries and spice. Delicious in its youth, it's a stylish, harmonious wine with cool-climate freshness, oak complexity, suppleness and charm. A rare, skilfully made wine, worth getting to know.

LANGDALE ESTATE MELTON HILLS PINOT NOIR

DRY $20 -V

(☆☆☆)

A bigger, slightly darker wine than its stablemate (below), the 1996 vintage (***) of this West Melton red was made from the ripest fruit and matured in French and American oak barriques. It's a flavoursome although not intense wine, with sweet oak fleshing out its ripe, berryish, smooth flavours. Drink 1998.

LANGDALE ESTATE PINOT NOIR

DRY $16 -V

(☆☆⯪)

Estate-grown at West Melton, the 1996 vintage (**¹/₂) is a light, smooth Beaujolais style red. Light ruby-hued, it is pleasantly fresh and berryish, but simple and a bit short. Ready.

LARCOMB PINOT NOIR

DRY $16 -V

(☆☆)

Past vintages of this Canterbury red have been enjoyable (the deep-coloured, richly fruity '88 and lighter but elegant '91 opened well late last year), but the 1995 vintage (**) is disappointing, with an unattractive bouquet and crisp, simple, rustic flavours.

LAWSON'S DRY HILLS MARLBOROUGH PINOT NOIR

DRY $25 -V

(☆☆☆⯪)

The gutsy debut 1996 vintage (***¹/₂) was harvested at a ripe 23˚ brix and matured in a mix of new to four-year-old oak barriques. The colour is bright and bold; the palate full, with strong plummy flavours and chewy tannins. In its youth, it impresses more with power than complexity and finesse, but may well reward cellaring; open mid 1998 onwards.

LINTZ ESTATE PINOT NOIR

VINTAGE	96	95	94	93	92	91
WR	7	7	6	6	4	5
DRINK	97-03	99-02	98-99	97-98	P	P

DRY $25 -V

☆☆☆⯪

Chris Lintz produces a bold, weighty style of Martinborough Pinot. The 1994 vintage, a muscular wine with strong, tannic, raspberry and spice flavours, impresses more with power than charm and finesse. The '95 (****), the best yet, is more fragrant and softer than its predecessors. It's still a fleshy wine (14 per cent alcohol), with rich colour, strong, ripe cherry/spice flavours, savoury, complex characters and a rounded finish.

MARGRAIN PINOT NOIR

VINTAGE	96
WR	5
DRINK	98-00

DRY $28 -V

(☆☆☆⯪)

Launched from the 1996 vintage (***¹/₂), this Martinborough red is a fairly complex style that should age gracefully. Ruby-hued, with fragrant cherry/oak aromas, it is full-bodied, savoury and supple, with sweet cherryish fruit, smoky oak flavours and positive tannins. It needs time; open 1998 onwards.

MARK RATTRAY AQUILON WAIPARA PINOT NOIR

DRY $14 V+

(☆☆☆)

Expressly designed for early consumption, the 1996 vintage (***) is a reasonably full Canterbury red with pleasing depth of plummy, buoyant flavour, a touch of complexity from maturation in seasoned oak casks, and moderate tannins. It's enjoyable now, but also capable of short-term improvement.

MARK RATTRAY WAIPARA PINOT NOIR	VINTAGE	96	95	94	93	92	DRY $22 AV
	WR		6	6	5	7	6	
	DRINK	98-00	98-00	97-99	00	97-99	(☆☆☆☆⯪)

The 1992 to 1994 vintages established Mark Rattray as one of Canterbury's top Pinot producers. The '95 is an elegant middleweight, with fresh, ripe, raspberryish flavours wrapped in quality oak and firm tannins. Still youthful, the 1996 vintage (****¹/₂) is an attractive wine with quite good depth of raspberryish, slightly spicy flavour, sweet fruit characters and a supple mouthfeel. Harbouring high alcohol (13.5 per cent) and with reasonably firm tannins, it should age well.

MARTINBOROUGH VINEYARD PINOT NOIR	VINTAGE	96	95	94	93	92	91	90	DRY $30 AV
	WR	7	7	7	6	5	7	5	
	DRINK	00+	00+	99+	P	P	P	P	☆☆☆☆☆

The justly famous Pinot Noir is produced from a variety of clones – predominantly 10/5, which gives "good fruitiness", and Pommard, "full-bodied, structured and tannic" – and matured for a year in French oak barriques. It impresses with its fragrance and finesse rather than scale (British writer Andrew Jefford recently likened it to Volnay, a Cote de Beaune village famous for its silky but not heavy Pinot Noirs.) The 1995 vintage is a slightly bolder wine than the fragrant, supple, lingering '94. Packed with sweet-tasting fruit, it is enticingly scented and full, with spicy, savoury, very persistent flavours and positive tannins. The '96 (*****¹/₂) is still very youthful, with strawberry, smoky aromas and flavours in a very elegant style, lighter than the '96 Ata Rangi.

MARTINBOROUGH VINEYARD PINOT NOIR RES.	VINTAGE	95	94	93	92	91	DRY $45 AV
	WR	NM	7	NM	NM	7	
	DRINK	NM	00+	NM	NM	96+	(☆☆☆☆☆)

Winemaker Larry McKenna sees this as "a cut above the regular label – trophy-winning wine." The 1991 vintage was a striking debut with its intense, cherry, mushroom and smoky-oak aromas and complex, highly concentrated flavour. There was no '92 or '93. In his self-confessed bid to emulate Burgundy, McKenna says, "the '94 is as close to the truth as I've got." A magisterial wine, the 1994 vintage (*****) is even greater than the '91. Based on the company's oldest vines (10 to 15 years old), which yield grapes with greater ripeness and stuffing, it was matured in French oak barriques for 18 months. It's a deep-coloured wine with a very rich and complex fragrance, suggestive of sweet, very ripe fruit. The palate is mouthfilling and crammed with spicy, dark cherry flavours. A classic, it's still youthful and just needs time to mellow.

MATAWHERO PINOT NOIR	DRY $28 -V
	(☆☆☆☆)

Based predominantly on the powerful Pommard clone of Pinot Noir, this is typically a deeply coloured Gisborne wine with a concentrated, spicy/chocolatey flavour. The 1990 vintage is a beauty, with exceptional richness. The '92 (***¹/₂) is a big, mellow, complex, slightly rustic wine with light, mature colour and a rich, meaty, spicy, smoky fragrance. Cherryish, oaky and very soft, it's an intensely varietal wine. Ready.

MATUA	VINTAGE	96	95	94	93	92	91	DRY $14 V+
WAIMAUKU EST.	WR		5	5	6	6	6	5	
PINOT NOIR	DRINK		98-00	98	P	P	P	P	☆☆☆

In the past this was a light, pleasant Pinot, not the sort to ponder over but priced right, but the latest vintages are more characterful. The '95 is a clearly varietal, supple red with quite good weight and attractive, berryish, spicy flavours. The 1996 vintage (***) was crop-thinned to achieve greater richness and matured for a year in one and two year-old oak barriques. It's a lighter style of Pinot Noir, but still the real thing, with quite good depth of buoyant, ripe, strawberryish, slightly savoury and spicy flavour and smooth tannins.

MELNESS	VINTAGE	95	DRY $25 AV
PINOT	WR	7	
NOIR	DRINK	97-00	(☆☆☆☆)

The impressive 1995 vintage is a fleshy, richly flavoured Canterbury red. A concentrated wine, it has deep colour, strong plum/raspberry flavours encased in sweet oak and a spicy, crisp finish. The slightly lighter 1996 (***1/2) is a blend of Canterbury and Marlborough fruit, oak-aged for nine months and bottled without filtration. Still very fresh, it's a moderately complex wine with full colour, strong, spicy, berryish aromas and a generous, smooth palate with good depth of plummy, slightly peppery flavour. Open mid 1998 onwards.

MILL ROAD	DRY $13 V+
HAWKE'S BAY	
PINOT NOIR	(☆☆☆)

A good buy, Morton Estate's lower-tier Pinot Noir from 1996 (***) is based on ripe fruit (harvested at 24° brix), given "some" maturation in French oak. Light ruby-hued, it offers pleasant cherry/spice flavours in a supple style with some richness.

MILLS REEF	VINTAGE	95	94	DRY $20 AV
RESERVE	WR	6	6	
PINOT NOIR	DRINK	99	97-98	(☆☆☆☆)

Gutsy, warm and supple, the 1994 vintage of Paddy Preston's Hawke's Bay red was a very good debut. The 1995 vintage (****) is a characterful wine, still developing. Full, fleshy and supple, with sweet fruit and quality oak influence, it offers very good concentration of smoky, cherryish flavour.

MILLTON VINEYARD, THE,	DRY $25 -V
CLOS DE STE ANNE NABOTH'S	
VINEYARD PINOT NOIR	(☆☆☆)

Launched from the 1994 vintage (***), this single-vineyard Gisborne wine is a solid first effort. Ruby-hued, with ripe, strawberryish fruit, it's a flavoursome wine with some forest floor complexity but a hard, tannic finish that robs it of a bit of charm.

MONTANA RESERVE PINOT NOIR

DRY $18 V+

(☆☆☆☆)

Launched from the 1996 vintage (****), this Marlborough red is scarce – only 500 cases were made, compared to 3000 cases in 1997. Matured in French oak barriques (60 per cent new), it's a fairly complex style, full-bodied and savoury, with warm, ripe fruit flavours, strong oak influence and chewy tannins. Open 1998–99.

MORTON EST. WHITE LABEL HB PINOT NOIR

VINTAGE	96	95	94	93	92	91	90
WR	5	4	6	4	5	5	4
DRINK	97-03	P	97-9	P	P	P	P

DRY $18 V+

☆☆☆½

The 1994 vintage is one of the most delicious Pinots ever produced in Hawke's Bay. The '95 lacks the beguiling fragrance, intense varietal character and charm of the riper '94, but offers plenty of meaty, spicy flavour, braced by firm tannins, and some savoury complexity. The 1996 vintage (***) is an attractive although not concentrated wine, matured for nine months in French oak barriques (20 per cent new). It's a fragrant, delicately flavoured wine, crisp, strawberryish and moderately complex.

MORTON ESTATE WHITE LABEL MARLBOROUGH PINOT NOIR

DRY $18 AV

(☆☆☆)

The immediately appealing debut 1996 vintage (***) was grown in the company's Stone Creek Vineyard and matured for nine months in French oak barriques (20 per cent new). Ruby-hued, it's a savoury, supple wine with good depth of spicy, strawberryish flavour. Drink 1997–98.

MUIRLEA RISE PINOT NOIR

VINTAGE	95	94	93
WR	5	7	4
DRINK	97-99	97-00	97-98

DRY $25 -V

☆☆☆½

The charming 1993 vintage of this Martinborough red is a highly fragrant, light to medium-bodied, smooth wine with subtle, cherryish, mushroomy flavours, drinking well now. The '94 sports an exceptionally deep, purple-black colour and a mouthfilling, creamy-smooth palate packed with rich, soft, dark plum, slightly meaty flavour. The '95 (***½) is more akin to the '93: a lighter style, floral and supple, with drink-young appeal but sufficient backbone to cellar medium-term.

MURDOCH JAMES PINOT NOIR

DRY $32 AV

(☆☆☆☆☆)

This rare red is grown in the Martinborough vineyard of Roger Fraser, a Sydney-based Kiwi, and produced on his behalf by Ata Rangi. Both the 1993 and 1994 vintages have won gold medals. The '94 is a very impressive wine: full of ripe, plummy flavour, soft and lingering. The 1995 vintage (*****) is a fragrant, mouthfilling, very refined wine, richly flavoured and smooth, with sweet-tasting fruit, complexity and lovely harmony.

NEUDORF MOUTERE PINOT NOIR	VINTAGE	96	95	94	93	92	91	90
	WR	6	5	5	6	6	6	5
	DRINK	98-04	97-98	97-00	97-00+	97-00	97-98	P

DRY $28 AV

☆☆☆☆⯪

Typically a stylish Nelson red, packed with the ripe fruit flavours of raspberries and plums, finishing long and firm. The 1994 vintage is a classy wine, built to last. The soft, slightly green-edged '95, labelled "Village Pinot Noir", was reduced in price, reflecting the difficult vintage. The powerful, complex 1996 vintage (****¹/₂) boasts good, medium-full ruby colour, a rich, spicy fragrance and a weighty, supple palate with strong, youthful cherryish flavours wrapped in quality oak. It's an impressive wine, already approachable but sure to reward cellaring.

PALLISER
BAY
PINOT NOIR

DRY $18 AV

(☆☆☆)

A good entry-level Pinot Noir with character, the easy-drinking 1995 vintage (***) is based on fruit from the Martinborough winery's heavier-cropping vines, matured in older oak casks. The attractive, strawberryish, savoury aromas lead into a middle-weight palate with moderately ripe, clearly varietal, mushroomy flavours and a rounded finish.

PALLISER
ESTATE
PINOT NOIR

DRY $30 -V

☆☆☆☆

Martinborough winemaker Allan Johnson is searching for "rich Pinot Noir with the roast coffee aromas of ripe fruit and good structure". Although rewarding, the wine is typically slightly overshadowed by those of Ata Rangi, Martinborough Vineyard and Dry River. The 1994 vintage is a mouthfilling style, generous, meaty and complex, with (yes) nuances of coffee and spice and positive tannins. The 1995 (***¹/₂) lacks the concentration of the top '95s, but is full-flavoured and savoury, with ripe, berryish flavours and strong smoky oak in a firm, complex style.

PEGASUS BAY PINOT NOIR	VINTAGE	96	95	94	93	92	91
	WR	7	6	5	6	5	5
	DRINK	97-06	97-03	97-02	97-00	P	P

DRY $30 -V

☆☆☆☆

This characterful Waipara red is one of Canterbury's leading Pinot Noirs, typically rich in body and flavour. Opened late last year, the '93 is chunky and flavoursome but very herbaceous. The 1994 vintage is a bold, enticingly dark and scented wine with layers of cherry, plum and smoky oak flavours and a velvety finish. The 1995 vintage is a classy wine, rich and silky, but with a greenish thread not evident in the '94. The powerful, supple '96 (*****) is clearly superior to the '95, with rich, bold, purple-flushed colour and superbly concentrated, cherryish, complex flavour.

RIPPON VINE. SEL. PINOT NOIR

VINTAGE	95	94	93	92	91
WR	NM	NM	7	7	6
DRINK	NM	NM	10	00	98

DRY $43 -V

☆☆☆☆☆

The stunning quality of Rolfe and Lois Mills's perfumed, concentrated Lake Wanaka red established it as one of New Zealand's finest Pinot Noirs, and Central Otago's first classic wine. The 1991 vintage is superbly rich and complex, its strong wood flavours balanced by bold, savoury fruit. The '93, from a cool vintage, slightly lacks warmth and roundness, but is very fragrant, fresh and lively, with excellent depth of raspberryish, spicy, oaky flavour. The wine is typically alluring in its youth, yet retains its cool-climate freshness for a long time and is worth cellaring for five years; perhaps longer. There is no '94 or '95.

RIPPON VINEYARD PINOT NOIR

VINTAGE	96	95	94	93	92	91	90
WR	5	6	5	6	5	6	6
DRINK	99+	00+	P	98	P	P	P

DRY $31 -V

☆☆☆☆

A delicious, scented, vibrantly fruity Lake Wanaka red with plenty of body and ripe, berryish flavours, less oak-influenced than its Selection stablemate (above). The 1995 is a full, fairly rich-flavoured Central Otago red with a distinct herbal influence on the nose and palate, oak complexity and moderate tannins. The '96 (****) has slightly high acidity, but offers good colour, a fragrant bouquet and intense cherry/oak flavours, rich, buoyant and supple. It's delicious now, but worth keeping for another year or two.

ROSSENDALE BARREL SELECTION PINOT NOIR

DRY $25 -V

(☆☆☆)

Estate-grown at the base of the Port Hills, the 1995 vintage (***) of this Canterbury red is light ruby-hued, with a fragrant, cherryish, spicy nose and some savoury richness in an attractively light and supple style.

ROSSENDALE PINOT NOIR

DRY $14 V+

(☆☆☆)

Here's a bargain! The 1996 vintage (***1/2) of this Canterbury red is full-bodied and rich. One-half matured in new French oak casks for three months, it's a concentrated wine with smoky aromas and strong raspberry/cherry flavours. Open 1998.

ST HELENA PINOT NOIR

VINTAGE	96	95	94	93	92	91	90
WR	6	6	5	5	5	6	5
DRINK	97-00	97-8	P	P	P	P	P

DRY $18 AV

☆☆☆

A decade ago Robin Mundy's Belfast red set the Canterbury wine scene on fire with the 1982's gold medal success. Now it lacks its old notable power and flavour richness, but is still an attractive, highly varietal red, priced right. Still youthful, the 1996 vintage (***1/2) is an attractive middleweight. Ruby-hued, with fresh, lifted strawberryish aromas, it is buoyant and spicy, with a touch of toasty oak and well-rounded finish.

ST HELENA	VINTAGE	96	95
RESERVE	WR	NM	6
PINOT NOIR	DRINK	NM	97-9

DRY $25 AV

(☆☆☆☆)

The 1995 vintage (****) is St Helena's finest Pinot Noir of the 90s. A distinctly cool-climate style, it reveals a fragrant, raspberryish, slightly smoky bouquet. The palate is full and still youthful, with a crisp, buoyantly fruity and supple palate, persistent and potentially quite complex.

SANDIHURST	VINTAGE	95
PINOT	WR	3
NOIR	DRINK	P

DRY $13 AV

(☆☆☆)

Pinot Noir from this small West Melton vineyard shows promise, although the '93 and '94 lack full ripeness. I prefer the '95 (**¹/₂) produced in a Beaujolais style. Not oak-aged, it is light, buoyantly fruity and soft.

SANDIHURST	VINTAGE	95
RESERVE	WR	5
PINOT NOIR	DRINK	97-99

DRY $20 -V

(☆☆☆)

Fragrant, with cherryish, smoky aromas, the 1995 vintage (***) was estate-grown at West Melton and matured for 10 months in all-new French oak barriques. It slightly lacks warmth and richness, but still offers plenty of crisp, moderately ripe, savoury, spicy, subtle flavour and should respond well to cellaring.

SEIFRIED	VINTAGE	96	95	94	93	92	91	90
NELSON	WR	5	NM	6	6	5	5	5
PINOT NOIR	DRINK	97-01	NM	98-00	97-8	P	P	P

DRY $16 -V

☆☆☆

Fresh, berryish fruit flavours hold sway in this undemanding Nelson red, which typically has a Beaujolais-like fruitiness, softness and simplicity that makes it enjoyable in its youth. The 1996 vintage (**¹/₂), matured for 10 months in two and three-year-old French oak barriques, is a typically forward style with lightish colour and straightforward plum/berry flavours, fruity and crisp.

SHERWOOD ESTATE
CANTERBURY
PINOT NOIR

DRY $12 AV

☆☆☆

Dayne Sherwood sees this low-priced wine as offering "a glimpse of what Pinot Noir can be". Ensconced in a claret-shape bottle, the 1996 vintage (**) is a simple quaffer, based on heavier-cropping vines at West Melton. Forty per cent of the final blend was matured in seasoned oak casks. Light in colour, body and flavour, it offers fresh, simple, crisp, raspberryish flavours, lacking ripeness and richness.

SHERWOOD EST.	VINTAGE	95						DRY $27 -V
PINOT NOIR	WR	6						
RESERVE	DRINK	98-9						☆☆☆☆⟨

Dayne Sherwood's top red. The 1995 vintage (****) was grown in Canterbury and Marlborough, matured in new French oak barriques and bottled without filtering. It's an impressively scented wine, ruby-hued, with sweet fruit characters and excellent depth of ripe, spicy flavour, firm and complex.

TASMAN BAY			DRY $15 V+
MARLBOROUGH			
PINOT NOIR			(☆☆☆)

The light-bodied, not highly complex but pleasant 1996 vintage (***) contains a small amount of Merlot and Cabernet Franc; proprietor Phil Jones loves blending. Barrel-aged for seven months, it's a drink-young style with some sweet-fruit charm and a touch of flavour complexity. Open 1997–98.

TE KAIRANGA	VINTAGE	96	95	94	93	92	91	90	DRY $23 AV
PINOT	WR		7	6	7	5	5	6	5
NOIR	DRINK	00-04	98-01	97-00	97-9	97-8	P	P	☆☆☆☆

A consistently attractive Martinborough Pinot Noir. The perfumed 1994 vintage is a medium-weight style full of ripe, spicy, plummy, persistent flavour, with some complexity and a long, silky finish. Lovely now, the French oak-aged '95 (****) is a generous, full-bodied and supple wine with sweet, spicy fruit flavours, now developing some bottle-aged complexity.

TE KAIRANGA	VINTAGE	95	94	93	92	91	DRY $35 AV
RESERVE	WR		7	7	NM	NM	7
PINOT NOIR	DRINK	99-02	98-01	NM	NM	P	(☆ ☆☆☆☆☆

Bold, fleshy and packed with lush, sweet-tasting fruit, the 1991 vintage went from strength to strength in the bottle. The '94 is another voluptuous Martinborough red, oozing rich, very ripe fruit. Starting to unfold considerable complexity, the 1995 vintage (****1/2) was matured for 18 months in new French oak barriques. Powerful through the palate, it's mouthfilling, supple and savoury, with an excellent depth of sweet-tasting, plummy fruit and a lovely overall harmony.

TERRACE	VINTAGE	96	DRY $17 -V
ROAD	WR	4	
PINOT NOIR	DRINK	97-9	(☆ ☆☆⟨)

The 1996 vintage (**1/2) of Cellier Le Brun's Marlborough red was matured in a mix of one to two-year-old French oak barriques and large oak casks. Light ruby-hued, it is cherryish and spicy, but slightly lacks the warmth and roundness of fully ripe fruit. Still, it's more flavoursome, fresh and vibrantly fruity than previous Pinot Noirs from Le Brun.

TORLESSE SOUTH ISLAND PINOT NOIR

VINTAGE	95
WR	6
DRINK	97-00

DRY $22 -V

(☆☆☆)

"South Island", for the 1995 vintage (***) means a blend of 80 per cent Marlborough and 20 per cent Canterbury fruit, oak-aged for a year. Crisp and full-bodied, it slightly lacks warmth and roundness, but still offers good depth of fresh, raspberryish flavour and a touch of savoury complexity. A solid wine, approaching its peak.

TWIN ISLANDS PINOT NOIR

DRY $17 V+

(☆☆☆☆)

The first 1996 vintage (***½) of Negociants' Marlborough red offers good value. It was matured in French oak barriques (30 per cent new). Light to medium in colour, it is full and soft, with quite good depth of cherry/plum flavours and a well balanced, velvety finish. Drink 1997–98.

VIDAL PINOT NOIR

DRY $19 V+

(☆☆☆☆)

The excellent 1996 vintage (****) is the best wine yet under this label, and one of the best value Pinots on the market. Grown in Hawke's Bay and oak-aged for nine months, it is ruby-hued, with toasty oak on the nose and attractive fullness of body. It's quite a big wine for Pinot Noir, already approachable, with oak complexity and very good depth of supple, cherryish flavour. A good bet for 1998–99.

VILLA MARIA PRIVATE BIN PINOT NOIR

DRY $15 AV

(☆☆☆)

Don't expect the earth to move, but the 1995 vintage (***) is an enjoyable Hawke's Bay red, French and American oak-aged for four months. Ruby-hued, light, buoyant, raspberryish, slightly spicy and crisp, it is a drink-young style with a touch of complexity.

VOSS ESTATE PINOT NOIR

VINTAGE	96	95	94	93
WR	6	6	6	4
DRINK	98-04	98-02	97-01	P

DRY $25 AV

(☆☆☆☆)

Voss is a tiny Martinborough winery with a very big Pinot Noir. The '95 is slightly less intense than the '94, but still rewarding, with mouthfilling body and very good depth of ripe, slightly peppery, complex flavour. Quite full-coloured, with strapping body (14.5 per cent alcohol) and a raspberryish, spicy fragrance, the 1996 vintage (****) is a warm, generous red with strong, ripe flavour and firm tannins, offering good potential for cellaring.

WAIPARA DOWNS PINOT NOIR	VINTAGE	96			DRY $16 -V
	WR	5			(☆☆)
	DRINK	97+			

The Pinot Noir style is still evolving at Keith and Ruth Berry's North Canterbury winery. The 1994 vintage is herbaceous, with the sweet fragrance of American oak. The '96 (**), designed as a drink-young style, is a simple, crisp, raspberryish wine with a very smooth, fractionally sweet finish.

WALNUT RIDGE PINOT NOIR	VINTAGE	96	95	94	DRY $22 AV
	WR	6	5	6	(☆☆☆☆)
	DRINK	97-02	97-8	97-8	

Bill Brink's Martinborough red shows consistently impressive quality. Currently delicious, the bright ruby-hued, savoury 1995 vintage is a "serious" style, mouthfilling and firm, with strong oak influence and excellent depth of cherry, plum and spice flavours. The '96 (****) is another impressive wine. Matured in French oak casks (30 per cent new), it is a big wine with good colour depth and an abundance of warm, cherryish, smoky flavour, complex and firm. A concentrated, tannic style, it's built for cellaring.

Syrah

The "Syrah" of the Rhône, the "Shiraz" of the Barossa Valley, the "Hermitage" of the Hunter Valley – they're all the same grape variety. On the rocky, baking slopes of the upper Rhône Valley, and in several Australian states, this noble grape yields red wines renowned for their marvellous concentration of peppery, "smoke and tar" flavours. In New Zealand, although Syrah (as it is increasingly known) is still rare, interest in the classic variety is stirring.

Syrah was well known in New Zealand a century ago. Government viticulturist, S.F. Anderson, wrote in 1917 that Shiraz was being "grown in nearly all our vineyards [but] the trouble with this variety has been an unevenness in ripening its fruit". For today's winemakers, the problem has not changed: Syrah has never favoured a too-cool growing environment. Having said that, it thrives in poor soils, is easy to cultivate, and yields more generously than Cabernet Sauvignon.

The latest, 1996 vineyard survey showed the paucity of Syrah vines in New Zealand. Only 43 hectares will be bearing in 1999, which doubles the 22 hectares cropping in 1996. Half the vines are concentrated in Hawke's Bay, with smaller plantings in Marlborough and the Wairarapa. A small knot of enthusiasts are now eagerly unravelling Syrah's potential in this country's warmer vineyard sites.

BABICH MARA EST. SYRAH

VINTAGE	96	95	94
WR	6	7	7
DRINK	98-04	97-00	97-00

DRY $17 V+

(☆☆☆☆½)

Clearly New Zealand's best-value Syrah. The 1995 (*****) grown in Gimblett Road, Hawke's Bay, is a dark, very powerful wine, softer and rounder than the debut '94, with a fragrant, spicy bouquet and outstanding richness of brambly, peppery flavour. A very lush, complex and supple red with a tight, persistent finish, it's one of the finest Syrahs yet made in New Zealand. The '96, tasted as a barrel sample, is less ripe and concentrated, yet still impressive and highly varietal, with medium-full colour, black-pepper aromas and firm, strong, plummy, spicy flavours.

LINTZ ESTATE SHIRAZ

DRY $30 AV

(☆☆☆☆☆)

Syrah may well have a future in Martinborough, to judge from Chris Lintz's debut 1995 vintage (*****). It's a very classy wine, dark, with a spicy, complex, not too pungently peppery bouquet. On the palate, it's weighty and supple, with concentrated plum/pepper flavours, positive tannins and a rich, lingering finish.

MURDOCH JAMES SHIRAZ

DRY $24 AV

(☆☆☆☆)

Better known for its top-flight Pinot Noir, this tiny Martinborough producer released 50 cases of Syrah from 1995 (****). Pronounced black-pepper aromas lead into a mouthfilling, fleshy wine with medium-full colour, strong plum/spice flavours and firm tannins. A serious wine for cellaring; open 1998 onwards.

OKAHU ESTATE SHIRAZ

VINTAGE	95
WR	5
DRINK	98-01

DRY $25 AV

(☆☆☆☆)

The first 1994 vintage of Monty Knight's Kaitaia red (under the premium Kaz Shiraz label) scooped the first gold medal awarded to a New Zealand Syrah and the first gold for a Northland wine at the 1996 Liquorland Royal Easter Wine Show. It's a strapping, succulent, well-ripened, soft red with almost opaque colour and a bold, very rich and smooth palate packed with berryish, minty, peppery flavour. The '95 (****) is slightly lighter and more restrained (and therefore not labelled Kaz Shiraz), but still impressive, with quite full body, French oak complexity, pleasing depth of ripe, sweet, black-pepper flavours and moderate tannins – a clearly varietal, finely balanced and satisfying wine.

STONECROFT SYRAH

DRY $38 AV

☆☆☆☆☆

Alan Limmer was the first to prove that top-flight Syrah could be made in this country. The warm local climate and dry, deep gravels of his Hawke's Bay vineyard are tailor-made for Syrah, and the wine is astonishingly bold. This is typically a dark, almost opaque red, muscular, rich and smooth, with a wealth of peppery, dark chocolate flavours and a firm, lingering finish. The 1994 vintage, the best since the superb '91, is a generous wine with grippy tannins, loads of well-spiced, plummy flavour, an intense, peppery perfume and rich colour. The '95 (****½) was French oak-aged for 20 months. Slightly less ripe-tasting than past Syrahs from drier harvests, it's still very impressive, with a strongly peppery fragrance and rich, intense plum/spice flavours braced by firm tannins.

TE MATA BULLNOSE SYRAH

DRY $30 AV

(☆☆☆☆☆)

The 1995 vintage (*****) is clear evidence that Syrah can yield complex, structured reds in Hawke's Bay. Matured for 14 months in new and seasoned oak casks, it's a classy wine with cool-climate delicacy and intensity of varietal character. The flavour is impressively concentrated, raspberryish and peppery, finishing long and firm. It needs time; open 1998 onwards.

TRINITY HILL SHEP.	VINTAGE	97	96	DRY $23 V+
CROFT SYRAH/MER./	WR	6	5	
CABERNET FRANC	DRINK	99-02	98-01	(☆☆☆☆⚊)

Already delicious, the debut 1996 vintage (****½) of John Hancock's red was grown in the Ngatarawa district of Hawke's Bay and French oak-aged for 15 months. The colour is bright and bold; the palate flavour-packed and smooth, with plenty of pepperiness, power and warmth. This is a generous, meaty and supple red, very attractively priced.

VILLA MARIA	VINTAGE	94	DRY $24 AV
RESERVE	WR	6	
SYRAH	DRINK	98-00	(☆☆☆☆)

Villa's first "reserve" Syrah, from 1994 (****) was grown in Marlborough. It lacks the warmth and roundness of the top Hawke's Bay Syrahs, but is a powerful wine with rich, still purple-flushed colour, mouthfilling body and strong, youthful, spicy, raspberry/plum flavours, still fresh and crisp. Worth cellaring for a couple more years.

Ports

It's asking too much to expect New Zealand to make great Sauvignon Blanc and great "port". Port, strictly speaking, is the famous fortified red wine flowing from the hot, rugged vineyards of the upper Douro Valley in Portugal. "Port" (or rather an imitation of the classic dessert wine) is now made in most New World wine countries, and 30 years ago enjoyed lively demand in New Zealand. Today, with popular tastes swinging to table wines, its production has dwindled to a trickle, with the range of bulk port labels much diminished, and only a few finer quality ports enjoying climbing sales (boosted by the growing band of cigar smokers).

New Zealand's cool grape-growing climate is not naturally well-suited to port production, because the best fortified wines are produced from grapes with soaring sugar levels and luscious fruit flavours, qualities consistently achieved only in warmer regions. The basic port production process starts with the fermentation of red-wine varieties on the skins to extract their colour. The partially fermented, still sweet juice is then drained off its skins and fortified to about 18 per cent alcohol. The wine is then matured in small oak casks or, if it is to be a low-priced quaffing port, in bulk storage tanks.

Varietal characteristics are not sought after in port; its trademark flavours are developed by lengthy oxidative maturation. Nor are pronounced wood aromas and flavours desirable, so most ports are matured in seasoned oak barrels.

Ruby styles are bottled young, while still vibrantly fresh and fruity. Tawny port, a blend of different years, slumbers in barrels for several years, gradually fading in colour and developing a mellow, deep-scented "rancio" complexity. Vintage styles, produced from grapes of a single year, are matured only briefly in casks (or perhaps not at all), but are designed for lengthy cellaring.

BABICH RESERVE PORT

SW $23 AV

☆☆☆☆

This is a barrel-matured tawny style with a highly perfumed "rancio" complexity, less obvious sweetness than most New Zealand ports, and the seductive smoothness and mellowness of well-aged stocks.

CHIFNEY OLD STAN'S TAWNY

SW $20 -V

(☆☆☆)

In too-cool vintages, when Chifney's Cabernet Sauvignon grapes aren't up to scratch for the premium Martinborough red, they end up blended into an oak-aged port. The wine I tasted was more of a ruby style, sweet, but lacking the aged colour, maturity and mellowness of a tawny.

COLLARDS TAWNY PORT

SW $13 AV

(☆☆☆☆)

Amber-brown in hue, this smooth tawny is a blend of wines averaging 10 years old – originally Pinotage and Pinot Noir, more recently Cabernet Sauvignon. Rich, raisiny and nutty, it offers fine value for money.

CORBANS PRI. BIN CABERNET PORT

VINTAGE	91	90
WR	6	6
DRINK	05	05

SW $18 AV

☆☆☆☆

The oak-matured 1991 vintage (***) is weighty and flavoursome, with mature colour. Extremely pleasant, although not complex, it offers rich blackcurrant, liquorice and prune-like flavours, mellow spirit and a creamy-smooth finish. Ready.

DE REDCLIFFE DESSERT CABERNET SAUVIGNON

SW $17 (375 ML) -V

(☆☆☆☆)

"Most people who try this wine want a case lot – immediately," says winemaker Mark Compton. Grown in the Waikato, with just a small proportion of the final blend aged in seasoned oak, it's dark, purple-flushed, rich and smooth, with attractive, soft, sweet, pruney flavours.

DE REDCLIFFE TAWNY PORT

SW $17 (375 ML) -V

(☆☆☆✧)

This deliciously mellow tawny is based on Waikato and Hawke's Bay fruit, principally Cabernet Sauvignon, and oak-aged for an average of eight years. With its perfumed "rancio" complexity and raisiny, creamy-smooth palate, it is one of the better New Zealand ports on the market.

HUNTAWAY RESERVE TAWNY PORT

SW $17 (375 ML) -V

(☆☆☆☆)

Corbans' classy port is based principally on Cabernet Sauvignon, harvested in 1989 in Gisborne and matured for seven years in old French and American oak casks. Other, old and young material was added to the blend before bottling "to add complexity and freshness." It's a fragrant, mellow port, finely balanced, with an aged, tawny hue and rich, sweet, chocolatey, raisiny flavour.

LIMEBURNERS BAY DESSERT CABERNET SAUVIGNON

SW $13 (375 ML) AV

☆☆☆

A popular wine modelled on the fortified *vins doux naturel* (naturally sweet wines) of the south of France. Produced from the "pressings" of West Auckland grapes, fortified with whey alcohol and barrel-aged, it is a distinctive, although not complex wine – a sort of very full-bodied sweet, smooth red.

LINCOLN SIXTIETH ANNIVERSARY PORT

SW $50 -V

(☆☆☆☆✧)

In the past labelled as Anniversary Show Port, this old tawny won the Fellows Shield for the champion port at the 1991 Air New Zealand Wine Awards, a repeat of its 1988 triumph. Amber-green in hue, it is very rich, raisiny, creamy-smooth and lingering, and noticeably smoother and mellower than the Old Tawny (below). Proprietor Peter Fredatovich believes the average age of the material in the blend is 30 years.

LINCOLN OLD TAWNY PORT

SW $25 -V

(☆☆☆✧)

Amber-green, this 25-year-old West Auckland port is very characterful, with loads of nutty, sweet, raisiny flavour, but its slightly fiery spirit robs it of a mellow finish.

LOMBARDI DESSERT CABERNET

SW $9 (375 ML) AV

(☆☆☆⯪)

In the past this Hawke's Bay winery specialised in fortified wines, so it's no surprise this is a decent drop. Matured in oak barrels, it is densely coloured, with impressively intense blackcurrant-like flavours and a sweet, firm, tannic finish.

LONGVIEW GUMDIGGERS PORT

SW $18 -V

(☆☆☆)

Estate-grown just south of Whangarei, this characterful port is dark, not complex, but offering lots of youthful, chocolate-rich, sweet, smooth flavour.

MISSION FINE OLD PORT

SW $13 -V

(☆☆⯪)

This Hawke's Bay tawny is a blend of Cabernet Sauvignon and Pinot Noir. Predominantly based on two to three-year-old stocks, it includes some material up to 10 years old. Amber-hued, it is a solid wine with sweet, raisiny flavour and some mellowness.

MUIRLEA RISE APRÈS LIQUEUR WINE

SW $24 (500 ML) -V

(☆☆☆☆⯪)

Martinborough winemaker Willie Brown reports that his deliciously decadent fortified wine has become "a bit of a cult thing; people give it for 21sts and so on, and it goes all over the world with backpackers". It's basically a vintage-dated, briefly oak-aged ruby "port". Robust and purple-black, it has a powerful, creamy, harmonious palate bursting with blackcurrant and plum-like flavours, seductively sweet, smooth and rich. Drink it young, urges Willie, "with chocolate and stinky cheeses."

OKAHU ESTATE OLD BROTHER JOHN'S TAWNY PORT

SW $20 AV

(☆☆☆☆⯪)

Monty Knight's Northland port, estate-grown at Kaitaia and oak-aged for seven years, is one of the finest New Zealand ports on the market. Amber-green, it is raisiny and smooth, with a fragrance, intensity of fruit character, complexity and mellowness that takes it a lot closer to the traditional Portuguese style than most.

PACIFIC RESERVE PORT

SW $15 AV

(☆☆☆)

Each year at the Pacific winery in Henderson, three puncheons of Cabernet Sauvignon are put down to mature for this 10-year-old tawny. It's a fragrant, raisiny, sweet port with some rancio aged characters in a reasonably mellow style.

PLEASANT VALLEY AGED FOUNDER'S

SW $19 AV

(☆☆☆☆⚬)

When Moscow Yelas died in 1984, he bequeathed a treasure trove of old ports to his son, Stephan. This distinguished port, about 15 years old, grows "smoother, richer and sweeter [due to evaporation] with age," reports Yelas. This is a very raisiny, very smooth, very mellow port, clearly one of the most mature New Zealand ports available.

PLEASANT VALLEY OLD TAWNY

SW $10 V+

(☆☆☆)

This oak-aged Henderson Valley dessert wine is raisiny, sweet and smooth, mellower than most, and bargain-priced.

ST HELENA PEERS' PORT

SW $13 -V

(☆☆⚬)

Canterbury's cool climate isn't the obvious place to make fortified wines. Tasted recently, this is a full, fruity, raisiny-sweet port, but it lacks warmth and mellowness.

SOLJANS CABERNET PORT

SW $11 (375 ML) -V

(☆☆☆⚬)

Tony Soljan's port has a light, tawny hue, attractive perfume and good depth of sweet, mature, raisiny flavour.

WAIMARAMA DESSERT CABERNET

SW $18 (375 ML) -V

(☆☆☆⚬)

"This wine is approached with suspicion by many educated tasters who regard dessert and Cabernet Sauvignon as incompatible concepts," reports Hawke's Bay winemaker, John Loughlin. French oak-aged for a year, it is a mouthfilling, fortified sweet wine with opaque, purple-black colour and a spicy, herbal fragrance. The flavours are rich, raspberryish and chocolatey, though not complex. Serve with chocolates or chocolate dessert.

WAIPARA RIVER RUBY PORT

VINTAGE 95
WR   6
DRINK 97+

SW $12 AV

(☆☆☆)

The Waipara Downs winery in North Canterbury is an unlikely home for a solid ruby port, but the oak-aged 1995 vintage (***) is enjoyable. A 50/50 blend of estate-grown Cabernet Sauvignon and Pinot Noir, it lacks the richness and strength of a fine quality port, but is attractively fresh and buoyant and reasonably smooth.

WINSLOW WILLIAM ROSS CABERNET LIQUEUR

SW $18 (375 ML) -V

(☆☆☆☆)

Not intended as a port style (and certainly not mainstream Martinborough!) this very distinctive dessert wine is perfect on a cold night by the fireside. The addition of such spices as cinammon and cloves, and fortification with French brandy, has produced a tawny-hued wine with a richly spiced fragrance and deliciously sweet, spicy flavour, smooth and warming.

THE WINES AND VINEYARDS OF NEW ZEALAND

The Wines and Vineyards of New Zealand is a celebration, a book dedicated to the winemakers of New Zealand as they step onto the world stage.

With a meticulously researched and authoritative text by Michael Cooper, outstanding colour photographs by John McDermott, vineyard-location maps, and an extensive collection of labels, this is by far the most comprehensive and attractive work on the subject.

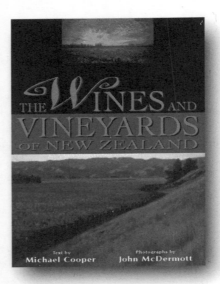

Winner of the 1997 Montana Leisure and Lifestyle Award

This is a superb gift or record of New Zealand's most dynamic industry. Available from all good bookshops.